BRITISH LAW AND LITERATURE IN THE LONG EIGHTEENTH CENTURY

The law underwent significant changes in eighteenth-century Britain as jurists and legislators adapted doctrines to fit the needs of an increasingly commercial, industrial, and imperial society. This volume reveals how legal developments of the period shaped and were shaped by imaginative writing. Reading canonical and lesser-known texts from the Restoration to the Romantic era, the chapters explore literary engagements with libel law, plague law, marriage law, naturalization law, the poor laws, the law of slavery and abolition, and the practice of common-law decision-making. The volume also considers the language and form of legal treatises and judicial decisions, as well as recent appropriations of the period's literature and legal norms by the Christian right. Through these varied case studies, the volume deepens our knowledge of law and literature's mutual entanglements in the long eighteenth century while shedding light on legal and ethical questions that remain of concern to this day.

MELISSA J. GANZ is Associate Professor of English at Marquette University. She is the author of *Public Vows: Fictions of Marriage in the English Enlightenment* (2019), winner of the Walker Cowen Memorial Prize. Her essays on legal and ethical dimensions of British fiction have appeared in journals including *Eighteenth-Century Studies*, *Eighteenth Century: Theory and Interpretation*, *Nineteenth-Century Literature*, *Review of English Studies*, and *ELH*, as well as in several edited collections. She holds a JD from the University of Pennsylvania Carey Law School and a PhD in English literature from Yale University.

BRITISH LAW AND LITERATURE IN THE LONG EIGHTEENTH CENTURY

EDITED BY

MELISSA J. GANZ

Marquette University

CAMBRIDGE
UNIVERSITY PRESS

CAMBRIDGE
UNIVERSITY PRESS

Shaftesbury Road, Cambridge CB2 8EA, United Kingdom

One Liberty Plaza, 20th Floor, New York, NY 10006, USA

477 Williamstown Road, Port Melbourne, VIC 3207, Australia

314–321, 3rd Floor, Plot 3, Splendor Forum, Jasola District Centre, New Delhi – 110025, India

103 Penang Road, #05-06/07, Visioncrest Commercial, Singapore 238467

Cambridge University Press is part of Cambridge University Press & Assessment, a department of the University of Cambridge.

We share the University's mission to contribute to society through the pursuit of education, learning and research at the highest international levels of excellence.

www.cambridge.org
Information on this title: www.cambridge.org/9781009224130

DOI: 10.1017/9781009224185

When citing this work, please include a reference to the DOI 10.1017/9781009224185

First published 2025

A catalogue record for this publication is available from the British Library

A Cataloging-in-Publication data record for this book is available from the Library of Congress

ISBN 978-1-009-22413-0 Hardback

Contents

Figures

Contributors

DAVID ALFF is Associate Professor of English at SUNY-Buffalo, where he works on eighteenth-century British literature and culture, with a special interest in infrastructure. He is the author of *The Wreckage of Intentions: Projects in British Culture 1660–1730* (2017) and *The Northeast Corridor: The Trains, the People, the History, the Region* (2024).

ANDREW BENJAMIN BRICKER is Associate Professor of English Literature in the Department of Literary Studies at Ghent University and a senior fellow at the Andrew W. Mellon Society of Fellows in Critical Bibliography at the Rare Book School at the University of Virginia. His research focuses on interdisciplinary approaches to early modern and eighteenth-century literature, satire, the law, laughter, and humor. His book *Libel and Lampoon: Satire in the Courts, 1670–1792* (2022) examines the development of defamation law in Britain in relation to both written and visual satire.

STEPHANIE DEGOOYER is Associate Professor of English at the University of North Carolina at Chapel Hill. She is the author of *Before Borders: A Legal and Literary History of Naturalization* (2022) and coauthor of *The Right to Have Rights* (2018). Her essays have appeared in *ELH*, *American Literary History*, and *Humanity*, as well as in several edited collections. She is working on a book about the history of asylum.

ANNE FREY is Associate Professor of English at Texas Christian University. She is the author of *British State Romanticism: Authorship, Agency, and Bureaucratic Nationalism* (2010) and has published articles on the Romantic national tale, Romantic poetry, and the politics of poetic form.

MELISSA J. GANZ is Associate Professor of English at Marquette University. She is the author of *Public Vows: Fictions of Marriage in the English Enlightenment* (2019), winner of the Walker Cowen Memorial

Prize. Her essays on legal and ethical dimensions of British fiction have appeared in journals including *Eighteenth-Century Studies*, *Eighteenth Century: Theory and Interpretation*, *Nineteenth-Century Literature*, *Review of English Studies*, and *ELH*, as well as in several edited collections. She holds a JD from the University of Pennsylvania Carey Law School and a PhD in English literature from Yale University.

SUZANNA GEISER is Assistant Legal Research and Writing Professor at Norman Adrian Wiggins School of Law, Campbell University. Her research focuses on law and literature, eighteenth- and nineteenth-century fiction, and narrative legal theory. Her article on William Godwin's *Caleb Williams* and penal reform appears in *The Age of Johnson* (2021), and she has several entries forthcoming in *The Cambridge Guide to the Eighteenth-Century Novel, 1660–1820*. She holds a JD from the University of Iowa and a PhD in English and comparative literature from the University of North Carolina at Chapel Hill.

MARK SCHOENFIELD is Professor of English and Robert Penn Warren Chair of the Humanities at Vanderbilt University. He is the author of *The Professional Wordsworth: Law, Labor, and the Poet's Contract* (1996) and *British Periodicals and Romantic Identity: "The Literary Lower Empire"*, co-winner of the 2009 Colby Prize. A former Guggenheim fellow, he writes about material culture within the context of institutions and the knowledge they produce, with particular attention to the interplay of law, literature, and periodicals and to scenes of litigation. He coedited John Galt's *The Entail* for Edinburgh University Press (2022).

SIMON STERN is Professor of Law and English at the University of Toronto. He is coeditor of *The Oxford Handbook of Law and Humanities* (2020) and *The Routledge Research Companion to Law and Humanities in Nineteenth-Century America* (2017), and editor of William Blackstone's *Commentaries on the Laws of England, Book II: Of the Rights of Things* (2016). He has published articles on copyright and authorship, obscenity, the law of search and seizure, legal aesthetics, and legal narrative. He is working on a study of the history and theory of legal fictions in the common law.

KATHRYN D. TEMPLE is Professor of Law and Humanities at Georgetown University. She is the author of *Loving Justice: Legal Emotions in William Blackstone's England* (2019) and *Scandal Nation: Law and Authorship in England* (2003). She has published widely on the history of legal emotions in journals such as *Eighteenth Century: Theory and Interpretation*, *Law and Literature*, and *Law, Culture and the Humanities*, and is coeditor of Edward Elgar's *Research Handbook on Law and Emotion* (2021). Her current book project focuses on ambivalence as a productive emotion in law and life.

SARAH WINTER is Professor of English and Comparative Literary and Cultural Studies at the University of Connecticut, Storrs, and Co-Director of the Research Program on Humanitarianism at the University of Connecticut's Gladstein Family Human Rights Institute. She is the author of *The Pleasures of Memory: Learning to Read with Charles Dickens* (2011) and *Freud and the Institution of Psychoanalytic Knowledge* (1999). She is completing a book on the human rights narratives that have emerged from activists' uses of habeas corpus to contest slavery and colonial violence in the British Empire.

NICOLE MANSFIELD WRIGHT is Associate Professor of English at the University of Colorado, Boulder. She is the author of *Defending Privilege: Rights, Status, and Legal Peril in the British Novel* (2020), which examines the weaponization of claims of victimhood by heirs, landowners, slaveholders, and other elites to advance reactionary legal and political objectives. Her essays have appeared in journals including *Eighteenth-Century Studies*, *Eighteenth-Century Fiction*, *Eighteenth-Century: Theory and Interpretation*, and *Toronto Quarterly*, as well as in *The Chronicle of Higher Education* and *Inside Higher Ed*.

Acknowledgments

It is a pleasure to thank the many people who helped make this volume possible. First and foremost, I want to thank Bethany Thomas, George Paul Laver, and the entire team at Cambridge University Press for their support of and assistance with this project. I am also grateful to Franklin Matthews Jebaraj for overseeing the volume's production and to Fiona Little for meticuluous copyediting. My sincere thanks go, as well, to the anonymous readers for their thoughtful feedback on the proposal and swift reading of the manuscript.

This volume emerged from and reflects the insights of a vibrant community of scholars working at the intersection of eighteenth-century studies and law and literature. I am grateful to all the contributors for their inspiring work in the field and their collaboration on this volume. Special thanks go to Simon Stern and Kathryn D. Temple for their comments on the Introduction and their long-standing friendship and support. I am grateful, as well, to Katherine Gilbert, Christine Holbo, Tal Kastner, Adam Kozaczka, Adam Schoene, Lisa Siraganian, and Jolene Zigarovich for ongoing discussions and collaborations around law and literature. In addition, I thank Sarah Ailwood, Michael Demson, James Engell, Kelly Fleming, Rachel Gevlin, Stephanie Hershinow, Regina Hewitt, Nancy E. Johnson, Susan S. Lanser, Jayne Lewis, Elizabeth Neiman, Sal Nicolazzo, Eric Oberle, Sarah Raff, Miriam Wallace, and Sharif Youssef for enriching conversations over the years.

A 2021–22 Laurance S. Rockefeller Visiting Faculty Fellowship at Princeton University's Center for Human Values supported work on the initial stage of this project and stimulated my thinking about legal and moral judgment. I am indebted to Melissa Lane, Kim Lane Scheppele, and Hendrik Hartog for welcoming me to Princeton and the UCHV community, and to all the fellows, especially Elizabeth Cohen, Luara Ferracioli, Alexandre Lefebvre, and Gavin Sullivan, for an exhilarating year.

I am grateful, as well, to my colleagues at Marquette University for supporting my work. I want to thank the Committee on Research, in particular, for awarding me a Way Klingler Fellowship and a Summer Faculty Fellowship. Over the past few years, I benefited from the encouragement of my chairs, Gerry Canavan and Leah Flack, and the good cheer of many colleagues in the English Department, including especially Amelia Zurcher and Jason Farr. I also benefited from Max Gray's unfailingly prompt assistance with my book requests and library queries. I am very grateful, too, for the friendship of Deirdre Dempsey and Corinne Bloch-Mullins. Special thanks go to Albert J. Rivero and Sarah Wadsworth for their advice and interest in this volume.

Last but not least, I thank my parents, Eli and Jerilyn Ganz, and my sister, Caryn Ganz, for their love and support.

Introduction

Melissa J. Ganz

The law underwent significant developments in eighteenth-century Britain as jurists and legislators adapted older doctrines to fit the needs of an increasingly commercial, industrial, and imperial society. These developments at once shaped and were shaped by the period's imaginative writing. In an era when disciplinary boundaries had not yet hardened, some men trained for the law or worked in the political arena before turning to literature; others continued to work as magistrates or MPs while pursuing careers as writers. As scholars have noted, the legal and political experiences of authors including Daniel Defoe, Samuel Richardson, Henry Fielding, and Sir Walter Scott played an important role in the development of prose fiction.[1] But legal questions also permeated the broader culture. Criminal biographies, execution broadsides, and trial narratives received wide dissemination, and parliamentary speeches – themselves highly rhetorical in nature – were routinely reported and discussed in the popular press. The growth of literacy and the expansion of the print public sphere contributed to the diffusion of legal concerns, enabling those without formal training or professional connections to weigh in on legal matters in novels, poems, plays, autobiographies, and essays throughout this period.[2]

[1] See Lance Bertelsen, *Henry Fielding at Work: Magistrate, Businessman, Writer* (New York: Palgrave, 2000); Kieran Dolin, *Fiction and the Law: Legal Discourse in Victorian and Modernist Literature* (Cambridge: Cambridge University Press, 1999), 45–70; Hal Gladfelder, *Criminality and Narrative in Eighteenth-Century England: Beyond the Law* (Baltimore: Johns Hopkins University Press, 2001); and Tom Keymer, *Richardson's "Clarissa" and the Eighteenth-Century Reader* (Cambridge: Cambridge University Press, 1992).

[2] See Lincoln B. Faller, *Turned to Account: The Forms and Functions of Criminal Biography in Late Seventeenth- and Early Eighteenth-Century England* (Cambridge: Cambridge University Press, 1987); David Lemmings, ed., *Crime, Courtrooms and the Public Sphere in Britain, 1700–1850* (Farnham: Ashgate, 2012); and Christopher Reid, *Imprison'd Wranglers: The Rhetorical Culture of the House of Commons, 1760–1800* (Oxford: Oxford University Press, 2012). On the expansion of the reading public, see Richard D. Altick, *The English Common Reader: A Social History of the Mass Reading Public, 1800–1900*, 2nd ed. (1957; Columbus: Ohio State University Press, 1998), 30–77. On the

The connections between law and literature in eighteenth-century Britain have attracted a great deal of attention. We have illuminating studies of writers' engagements with developments in areas such as copyright and libel law, criminal law, property law, tort law, and marriage and family law, as well as studies that consider the aesthetic and rhetorical dimensions of law and legal texts.[3] Scholars have also published a number of introductions to and overviews of law and literature, some of which touch upon the eighteenth century.[4] However, we lack a volume that

emergence of the bourgeois public sphere, see Jürgen Habermas, *The Structural Transformation of the Public Sphere: An Inquiry into a Category of Bourgeois Society*, trans. Thomas Burger with Frederick Lawrence (1989; Cambridge, MA: MIT Press, 1998).

[3] The scholarship in this area is extensive. A partial list, with an emphasis on works published in the past twenty-five years, includes: John Bender, *Imagining the Penitentiary: Fiction and the Architecture of Mind in Eighteenth-Century England* (Chicago: University of Chicago Press, 1987); Andrew Benjamin Bricker, *Libel and Lampoon: Satire in the Courts, 1670–1792* (Oxford: Oxford University Press, 2022); John Bugg, *Five Long Winters: The Trials of British Romanticism* (Stanford, CA: Stanford University Press, 2014); Mark Canuel, *The Shadow of Death: Literature, Romanticism, and the Subject of Punishment* (Princeton, NJ: Princeton University Press, 2007); Stephanie DeGooyer, *Before Borders: A Legal and Literary History of Naturalization* (Baltimore: Johns Hopkins University Press, 2022); Erin Drew, *The Usufructuary Ethos: Power, Politics, and Environment in the Long Eighteenth Century* (Charlottesville: University of Virginia Press, 2021); Melissa J. Ganz, *Public Vows: Fictions of Marriage in the English Enlightenment* (Charlottesville: University of Virginia Press, 2019); Gladfelder, *Criminality and Narrative*; Susan Paterson Glover, *Engendering Legitimacy: Law, Property, and Early Eighteenth-Century Fiction* (Lewisburg, PA: Bucknell University Press, 2006); Jody Greene, *The Trouble with Ownership: Literary Property and Authorial Liability in England, 1660–1730* (Philadelphia: University of Pennsylvania Press, 2005); Nancy E. Johnson, ed., *Impassioned Jurisprudence: Law, Literature, and Emotion, 1760–1848* (Lewisburg, PA: Bucknell University Press, 2015); Thomas Keymer, *Poetics of the Pillory: English Literature and Seditious Libel, 1660–1820* (Oxford: Oxford University Press, 2019); Sandra Macpherson, *Harm's Way: Tragic Responsibility and the Novel Form* (Baltimore: Johns Hopkins University Press, 2010); Sal Nicolazzo, *Vagrant Figures: Law, Literature, and the Origins of the Police* (New Haven, CT: Yale University Press, 2021); Cheryl L. Nixon, *The Orphan in Eighteenth-Century Law and Literature: Estate, Blood, and Body* (Farnham: Ashgate, 2011); Trevor Ross, *Writing in Public: Literature and the Liberty of the Press in Eighteenth-Century Britain* (Baltimore: Johns Hopkins University Press, 2018); Wolfram Schmidgen, *Eighteenth-Century Fiction and the Law of Property* (Cambridge: Cambridge University Press, 2002); Daniel M. Stout, *Corporate Romanticism: Liberalism, Justice, and the Novel* (New York: Fordham University Press, 2017); Kathryn D. Temple, *Loving Justice: Legal Emotions in William Blackstone's England* (New York: New York University Press, 2019); Kathryn Temple, *Scandal Nation: Law and Authorship in Britain, 1750–1832* (Ithaca, NY: Cornell University Press, 2003); Jane Wessel, *Owning Performance / Performing Ownership: Literary Property and the Eighteenth-Century British Stage* (Ann Arbor: University of Michigan Press, 2022); and Nicole Mansfield Wright, *Defending Privilege: Rights, Status, and Legal Peril in the British Novel* (Baltimore: Johns Hopkins University Press, 2020).

[4] See Kieran Dolin, *A Critical Introduction to Law and Literature* (Cambridge: Cambridge University Press, 2007), 96–119; Susan Sage Heinzelman, "Imagining the Law: The Novel," in *Law and the Humanities: An Introduction*, ed. Austin Sarat, Matthew Anderson, and Cathrine O. Frank (Cambridge: Cambridge University Press, 2010), 213–40; Bridget M. Marshall, "Romanticism, Gothic, and the Law," in *Law and Literature*, ed. Kieran Dolin (Cambridge: Cambridge University Press, 2018), 142–56; and Cheryl Nixon, "Gender, Law, and the Birth of Bourgeois Civil Society," in Dolin, *Law and Literature*, 124–41.

reflects broadly on the interplay between legal and literary developments in Britain from the Restoration to the Romantic era as well as on the place of law in eighteenth-century studies. *British Law and Literature in the Long Eighteenth Century* aims to provide such an account. Examining a range of genres and both canonical and lesser-known texts, the volume explores literary engagements with libel law, plague law, marriage and property law, naturalization law, the poor laws, the law of slavery and abolition, the theory and practice of common-law decision-making, and the evolution of the legal profession. The volume considers, too, the language and form of legal treatises and judicial decisions, as well as the role of eighteenth-century literature in the transmission of legal norms today. In doing so, the volume seeks to expand and deepen our knowledge of law and literature's mutual entanglements during a formative period of development while showing how eighteenth-century studies has contributed to and been shaped by the law-and-literature enterprise.

Law and Literature: History and Approaches

Before we consider the connections between British law and literature in the long eighteenth century, we need to examine the history and goals of the law-and-literature enterprise. As conceived by scholars in the American legal academy in the 1970s and 1980s and subsequently developed in law schools, the study of law and literature has been comprised of diverse methods and aims. Scholars early on divided the field into two main strands consisting of the study of law *in* literature and the study of law *as* literature. Where the study of law in literature focused on depictions of legal themes and characters in canonical literary texts, the study of law as literature attended to the uses of rhetoric, narrative, and interpretation in law. Like other left-leaning interdisciplinary legal movements of the late twentieth century, law and literature sought to counter the growing influence of social-scientific – especially economic – approaches to law. Proponents sought variously to instill humanistic values in lawyers, to cultivate the art of persuasion, to expose contradictions and biases in the legal system, and to advocate for justice for racial and other "outsiders."[5] Although these diverse approaches and goals generated great excitement in

[5] For early formulations of the movement and its different strands, see Guyora Binder and Robert Weisberg, *Literary Criticisms of Law* (Princeton, NJ: Princeton University Press, 2000); Peter Brooks and Paul Gewirtz, eds., *Law's Stories: Narrative and Rhetoric in the Law* (New Haven, CT: Yale University Press, 1996); Gary Minda, *Postmodern Legal Movements: Law and Jurisprudence at Century's End* (New York: New York University Press, 1995), 149–66; and Robert Weisberg,

the legal academy in the 1980s and 1990s, the movement soon gave rise to a number of critiques as scholars began to question proponents' often reductive conceptions of "law" and "literature." Renewed attention to both literary form and legal history over the past twenty-five years has revitalized the enterprise and created distinct opportunities for scholars working in eighteenth-century studies.

Scholars have long recognized James Boyd White's *The Legal Imagination* (1973) as inaugurating the study of law and literature. In his ground-breaking book, White challenged conventional views of law as a system of rules and principles and a set of policy choices. White argued that we should instead think of law as a language – a "rich and complicated system of thought and expression" – and should recognize the work of the lawyer as "an enterprise of the imagination."[6] Reading literary texts and criticism, in his view, was vital to the training of legal professionals. Conceived as a casebook for law students, *The Legal Imagination* presents thematically organized selections from classical and modern literature as well as legal, philosophical, and historical texts, along with reading and writing prompts that seek to guide readers' reflections on the value and limits of legal language and the law's conception of human nature. Responding to the ascendancy of social-scientific approaches to law, especially law and economics, White looked to literature and rhetoric to humanize legal study and practice. The underlying premise of this book as well as White's many subsequent monographs is that reading and writing about literature and attending to the rhetorical dimensions of legal

"The Law-Literature Enterprise," *Yale Journal of Law and the Humanities* 1, no. 1 (December 1988): 1–67. For more recent discussions, see Elizabeth S. Anker and Bernadette Meyler, introduction to *New Directions in Law and Literature*, ed. Elizabeth S. Anker and Bernadette Meyler (New York: Oxford University Press, 2017), 1–30; Austin Sarat, "From Charisma to Routinization and Beyond: Speculations on the Future of the Study of Law and Literature," in Anker and Meyler, *New Directions*, 59–66; and Klaus Stierstorfer, "The Revival of Legal Humanism," in Dolin, *Law and Literature*, 9–25. Some scholars considered the legal regulation of literature via libel, obscenity, and copyright laws to comprise a third strand. But the distinction between law *in* literature and law *as* literature remained central to most accounts.

6 James Boyd White, *The Legal Imagination: Studies in the Nature of Legal Thought and Expression*, 45th anniversary ed. (1973; New York: Wolters Kluwer, 2018), xxii, xxvi. Reflections on and overlaps between law and literature, of course, appeared long before the 1970s. Jane B. Baron suggests that John H. Wigmore's "A List of Legal Novels" (1908) could be said to have inaugurated the modern law-and-literature enterprise. As J. M. Balkin and others have noted, the study and practice of law as a rhetorical art, in fact, extends back to ancient Greece. See Baron, "Law, Literature, and the Problems of Interdisciplinarity," *Yale Law Journal* 108, no. 5 (March 1999): 1059–85, at 1060n4; Balkin, "A Night in the Topics: The Reason of Legal Rhetoric and the Rhetoric of Legal Reason," in Brooks and Gewirtz, *Law's Stories*, 211–24.

texts constitute essential legal training, enabling students to become ethical and empathic advocates.[7]

This approach to law and legal education prompted a flurry of work over the next two decades. Scholars took White's insights in several directions. Scholars like Richard H. Weisberg, Robin West, and Martha C. Nussbaum advocated studying depictions of law and lawyers in literary texts to enhance understandings of the value and limits of legal processes and institutions. In their view, literary texts provided a much-needed supplement and corrective to the technical, analytical, rule-bound approach that formed the mainstay of law and legal education. For Weisberg, literature added a crucial ethical dimension to legal study, exposing the limits of law and legal language.[8] In a similar vein, West maintained that storytelling in general, and fiction in particular, facilitates an "empathic knowledge of others": "the narrative voice," she explained, "can convey the subjective feel of experiences in a way that triggers understanding of others and an empathic response to their plight, thereby changing our moral beliefs and our moral assessment of law."[9] Nussbaum likewise claimed that literature "is in league with the emotions."[10] By "promot[ing] identification and sympathy in the reader," she argued, realist novels provide a "bridge both to a vision of justice and to the social enactment of that vision."[11] For Weisberg, West, and Nussbaum, as for White, reading literature served not only to humanize the law but also to open it up to critique.

Other scholars developed methods to read law *as* literature. This strand of the law and literature enterprise took several different forms. Some scholars, like Robert Cover, emphasized the rhetorical underpinning of law. In his

[7] See White, *Legal Imagination*; James Boyd White, *When Words Lose Their Meaning: Constitutions and Reconstitutions of Language, Character, and Community* (Chicago: University of Chicago Press, 1984); James Boyd White, *Heracles' Bow: Essays on the Rhetoric and Poetics of the Law* (Madison: University of Wisconsin Press, 1985); James Boyd White, *Justice as Translation: An Essay in Cultural and Legal Criticism* (Chicago: University of Chicago Press, 1990); James Boyd White, *Acts of Hope: Creating Authority in Literature, Law, and Politics* (Chicago: University of Chicago Press, 1994); and James Boyd White, *From Expectation to Experience: Essays on Law and Legal Education* (Ann Arbor: University of Michigan Press, 1999). For discussions of White's work, see Stierstorfer, "Revival of Legal Humanism," 13–16; and David Gurnham et al., "Forty-Five Years of Law and Literature: Reflections on James Boyd White's *The Legal Imagination* and Its Impact on Law and Humanities Scholarship," *Law and Humanities* 13, no. 1 (2019): 95–141.

[8] See Richard H. Weisberg, *The Failure of the Word: The Protagonist as Lawyer in Modern Fiction* (New Haven, CT: Yale University Press, 1984); and Richard Weisberg, *Poethics and Other Strategies of Law and Literature* (New York: Columbia University Press, 1992).

[9] Robin West, *Narrative, Authority, and Law* (Ann Arbor: University of Michigan Press, 1993), 10, 11; see also Robin West, *Caring for Justice* (New York: New York University Press, 1997).

[10] Martha C. Nussbaum, *Poetic Justice: The Literary Imagination and Public Life* (Boston: Beacon Press, 1995), 53.

[11] Nussbaum, *Poetic Justice*, 5, 12.

influential 1983 essay "Nomos and Narrative," Cover argued that law is part of a *nomos*, or normative universe, itself constituted by narratives. "For every constitution there is an epic," he explained, "for each decalogue a scripture. . . . Once understood in the context of the narratives that give it meaning, law becomes not merely a system of rules to be observed, but a world in which we live."[12] Law, in this view, is questioned, contested, shaped, and refined in the domain of culture. Prompted by such insights, scholars began applying the methods of literary analysis to judicial opinions, trial narratives, and victim impact statements, examining the rhetorical features of legal texts and the relationship between legal discourse and broader cultural narratives.[13]

Feminist and critical race theorists took this approach a step further, calling for lawyers and scholars to embrace legal storytelling, or "narrative jurisprudence" as it came to be known. Scholars like Kathryn Abrams, Derrick Bell, Richard Delgado, and Patricia J. Williams maintained that far from meting out impartial justice, the legal system elevated certain stories and perspectives over others, suppressing the voices of subordinated groups. Too often, they argued, judges applied seemingly neutral and abstract rules in ways that erased the particularities of human experience. In their view, crafting and recounting "oppositional narratives" – stories by and about those excluded from legal power – had the potential to revolutionize the law. Such a strategy, they maintained, would subvert the law's claims to impartiality and destabilize the idea of a single, objective "truth" while advancing the interests of marginalized groups.[14] Taken in this direction, rhetorical approaches to law ended up reifying distinctions between law and narrative, and between reason and emotion.

[12] Robert Cover, "Nomos and Narrative," in *Narrative, Violence, and the Law: The Essays of Robert Cover*, ed. Martha Minow, Michael Ryan, and Austin Sarat (Ann Arbor: University of Michigan Press, 1995), 95–172, at 96.

[13] See, e.g., Brooks and Gewirtz, *Law's Stories*; and Austin Sarat and Thomas B. Kearns, eds., *The Rhetoric of Law* (Ann Arbor: University of Michigan Press, 1994). For more recent examples of this approach, see Michael Hanne and Robert Weisberg, eds., *Narrative and Metaphor in the Law* (Cambridge: Cambridge University Press, 2018); and Peter Brooks, "Narrative Transactions – Does the Law Need a Narratology?," *Yale Journal of Law and the Humanities* 18, no. 1 (Winter 2006): 1–28. For an overview and history of rhetorical approaches to law, see Binder and Weisberg, *Literary Criticisms of Law*, 292–377.

[14] See Kathryn Abrams, "Hearing the Call of Stories," *California Law Review* 79, no. 4 (July 1991): 971–1052; Derrick Bell, "The Supreme Court, 1984 Term – Foreword: The Civil Rights Chronicles," *Harvard Law Review* 99, no. 1 (November 1985): 4–83; Richard Delgado, "Storytelling for Oppositionists and Others: A Plea for Narrative," *Michigan Law Review* 87, no. 8 (August 1989): 2411–41; Kim Lane Scheppele, "Foreword: Telling Stories," *Michigan Law Review* 87, no. 8 (August 1989): 2073–98; and Patricia J. Williams, *The Alchemy of Race and Rights: Diary of a Law Professor* (Cambridge, MA: Harvard University Press, 1991). For an overview and assessment of this approach, see Binder and Weisberg, *Literary Criticisms of Law*, 201–09, 232–60.

In the 1980s, another group of scholars began exploring a different aspect of the legal-literary nexus, focusing on the implications of literary theory for legal interpretation. The ascendancy of post-structuralism, deconstruction, and reader-response theory in literary studies led to heated debates about the meaning and authority of legal texts and the possibility of objectivity in contractual, statutory, and constitutional interpretation. Clare Dalton used the methods of deconstruction to reveal the arbitrariness of classic contract doctrine, while Sanford Levinson highlighted the multiplicity of meanings in legal texts and the role of politics in adjudication.[15] Other scholars, by contrast, sought to defend legal interpretation from the threat of nihilism. Owen M. Fiss maintained that professional standards constrained judicial discretion and enabled the objective interpretation and application of legal rules, while Ronald Dworkin likened judges to writers of chain novels working within established conventions, an analogy challenged by Stanley Fish, who nonetheless insisted on the restraining power of context.[16]

Although scholars took the law-and-literature enterprise in very different directions, they tended to agree that literature, broadly conceived, had great value for the study and practice of law. Whether to humanize the law, to cultivate rhetorical skills, to instill professional ethics, to expose contradictions and biases in the legal system, to foster empathy and respect for human difference, to advocate for legal change, or to aid in the interpretation of legal texts, scholars began to embrace the call of stories. Various incarnations of law-and-literature courses proliferated in law schools in the early to mid 1990s, and scholars produced a steady stream of books, articles, symposia, anthologies, and journal issues devoted to the field.[17]

[15] See Clare Dalton, "An Essay in the Deconstruction of Contract Doctrine," in *Interpreting Law and Literature: A Hermeneutic Reader*, ed. Sanford Levinson and Stephen Mailloux (Evanston, IL: Northwestern University Press, 1988), 285–318; and Sanford Levinson, "Law as Literature," in Levinson and Mailloux, *Interpreting Law and Literature*, 155–73.

[16] See Owen M. Fiss, "Objectivity and Interpretation," in Levinson and Mailloux, *Interpreting Law and Literature*, 229–49; Ronald Dworkin, "Law as Interpretation," in *The Politics of Interpretation*, ed. W. J. T. Mitchell (Chicago: University of Chicago Press, 1983), 249–70; Stanley Fish, "Working on the Chain Gang: Interpretation in the Law and in Literary Criticism," in Mitchell, *Politics of Interpretation*, 271–86; and Stanley Fish, "*Fish v. Fiss*," in Levinson and Mailloux, *Interpreting Law and Literature*, 251–68. For an overview of these debates, see Binder and Weisberg, *Literary Criticisms of Law*, 112–200; and Peter Leman, "Law Meets Critical Theory," in Dolin, *Law and Literature*, 26–41.

[17] Elizabeth Villiers Gemmette found that 84 law schools (80 in the United States and 4 in Canada) out of 199 schools listed in *The Association of American Law Schools Directory of Law Teachers* reported offering a law-and-literature course in the 1993–94 academic year. For an overview of these courses, see "Law and Literature: Joining the Class Action," *Valparaiso University Law Review*

The growth of law and literature, however, soon prompted a number of critiques. In the first issue of the *Yale Journal of Law and the Humanities* in December 1988, Robert Weisberg lamented the lack of sophistication in both strands of the movement; in his view, the scholarship tended to combine "overly conventional readings of literature with a complacent understanding of law" while relying upon "fuzzy grand generalities."[18] Weisberg also questioned the usefulness of the distinction between law *in* and law *as* literature, suggesting that the "best works on the two sides of the line tend[ed] to converge" and that they captured "the best insights about the relationship between the aesthetic and the political-ethical visions and forces in society."[19] A decade later, critics continued to highlight the reductive conceptions of "law" and "literature" embraced by many of the movement's proponents. Jane B. Baron, for example, argued in a 1999 essay in *The Yale Law Journal* that the movement had "failed to generate the excitement that it [was] capable of generating within the American legal academy" because it had not been sufficiently thoughtful about interdisciplinarity.[20] In particular, Baron complained, scholars depicted law as "a more or less empty," technical, and rational domain while holding up literature as a vital source of feeling and values. In doing so, scholars treated "law" and "literature" as bounded entities without considering how the boundaries were drawn.[21]

Julie Stone Peters identified similar problems in a provocative 2005 essay in *PMLA*. Literary and legal scholars ostensibly committed to bridging disciplinary divides, she argued, had instead exaggerated the differences between the disciplines. Where literary scholars yearned for "the political

29, no. 2 (1995): 665–859. For a sample of the symposia and conferences devoted to law and literature, see Baron, "Law, Literature, and the Problems of Interdisciplinarity," 1060n6, 1060n8.

18 Weisberg, "Law-Literature Enterprise," 2–3, 19.

19 Weisberg, "Law-Literature Enterprise," 5. Richard A. Posner, a conservative judge and proponent of law and economics, offered a more skeptical view of the law-and-literature enterprise in *Law and Literature: A Misunderstood Relation* (Cambridge, MA: Harvard University Press, 1988). Although Posner was receptive to the idea of applying literary insights to judicial opinions, he claimed that "the legal matter in most literature on legal themes [was] peripheral to the meaning and significance of the literature" and that "legal knowledge [was] often irrelevant to the understanding and enjoyment of literature on legal themes" (15). In the third edition of his book, he conceded that reading literature could "provid[e] jurisprudential insights, rhetorical techniques, an understanding of legal regulation of literature, and insights into social practices that law encounters," but he continued to resist the idea that literature could humanize legal professionals or provide moral instruction. See Posner, *Law and Literature*, 3rd ed. (Cambridge, MA: Harvard University Press, 2009), 7; see also 456–93.

20 Baron, "Law, Literature, and the Problems of Interdisciplinarity," 1060–61.

21 Baron, "Law, Literature, and the Problems of Interdisciplinarity," 1061, 1078–79. For a similar critique, see Binder and Weisberg's 2000 book *Literary Criticisms of Law*, a significant development and expansion of Weisberg's earlier article.

real" of law, legal scholars pined for the humanizing potential of literature. The result was a "caricatur[e] [of] disciplinary difference through each discipline's longing for something it imagined the other to possess."[22] Peters suggested, however, that scholars had finally begun to relinquish these fantasies, and that the law-and-literature movement was transforming into "something bigger and necessarily more amorphous."[23] As she saw it, the movement had started "to shed its second term and to meld into" the broader field of "law, culture, and the humanities" – the title, she noted, of "the scholarly organization that seems now to serve as home for the discipline-formerly-known-as-law-and-literature." In this way, she suggested, the movement was "erasing [and replacing] 'literature' with a new lexicon ('culture,' 'the humanities')."[24] Peters viewed this transformation as a positive development and the beginning of more genuinely interdisciplinary scholarship.

Although Peters astutely diagnosed the central problems with the law-and-literature enterprise as it had come to be theorized and taught by legal scholars, she overlooked an important development. In the late 1990s, the study of law and literature began to move beyond the institutional space of law schools. In the hands of professional literary critics, the enterprise began to take new directions. Where law and literature's earliest proponents emphasized practical dimensions of literary study for law students and lawyers, scholars in English departments, influenced by the rise of historicist approaches to literary interpretation, began to explore historically specific connections between legal and literary developments. Where legal scholars like White and Richard H. Weisberg focused on well-known texts by authors such as William Shakespeare, Charles Dickens, and Herman Melville, moreover, literary critics helped broaden the focus of inquiry. As these scholars turned their attention to legal matters, they brought the insights and methods of literary studies and legal history to bear on a wide range of texts, challenging the perceived oppositions between law and literature while moving beyond the familiar distinction between law *in*

22 Julie Stone Peters, "Law, Literature, and the Vanishing Real: On the Future of an Interdisciplinary Illusion," *PMLA* 120, no. 2 (March 2005): 442–53, at 449.

23 Peters, "Law, Literature, and the Vanishing Real," 451.

24 Peters, "Law, Literature, and the Vanishing Real," 451. For responses and critiques, see Peter Brooks, letter to the editor, *PMLA* 120, no. 5 (October 2005): 1645–46; and Richard H. Weisberg, letter to the editor, *PMLA* 121, no. 2 (March 2006): 546–47. Jack M. Balkin and Sanford Levinson were more skeptical about the influence of the humanities on legal education and practice, highlighting institutional and professional constraints that limited law's ability to draw from humanistic disciplines. See "Law and the Humanities: An Uneasy Relationship," *Yale Journal of Law and the Humanities* 18, no. 2 (Summer 2006): 155–87.

and law *as* literature.[25] A growing interest in interdisciplinary inquiry, combined with the contraction of the academic job market in the humanities, contributed to the cross-pollination of ideas and methods as students of literature increasingly turned to law and legal academia, fostering more nuanced, formally sophisticated, and historically grounded law-and-literature scholarship. Such work has proliferated over the past twenty-five years. Shaped by a renewed attention to both literary form and legal history, this work offers fresh interpretations of legal and literary texts as well as new accounts of legal and literary developments while shedding light on questions that remain of concern to this day. This scholarship, moreover, has given rise to new pedagogical approaches, especially in the undergraduate liberal-arts curriculum.[26] Far from becoming subsumed by the study of "law, culture, and the humanities," law and literature has emerged as a rich and vibrant field in its own right.[27]

Reading Eighteenth-Century British Law and Literature

Scholars of eighteenth-century British literature and culture have played an important role in the evolution of the law-and-literature enterprise. Over the past twenty-five years, scholars have examined many connections between the period's legal and literary discourses. They have approached law in the long eighteenth century not as a timeless system of rules and principles but as a set of discursive practices embedded in culture – a

[25] For discussions of these developments, see Bernadette Meyler, "Law, Literature, and History: The Love Triangle," in Anker and Meyler, *New Directions*, 160–75; and Simon Stern, "Literary Analysis of Law: Reorienting the Connections between Law and Literature," *Critical Analysis of Law* 5, no. 2 (2018): 1–8. I am sketching broad trajectories here; there are notable exceptions. Robert A. Ferguson's *Law and Letters in American Culture* (Cambridge, MA: Harvard University Press, 1984) and Alexander Welsh's *Strong Representations: Narrative and Circumstantial Evidence in England* (Baltimore: Johns Hopkins University Press, 1992), for example, anticipated the shift in methodology by several decades.

[26] For a sampling of such courses, see Austin Sarat, Cathrine O. Frank, and Matthew Anderson, eds., *Teaching Law and Literature* (New York: Modern Language Association of America, 2011).

[27] Alongside the evolution of law and literature, a rich field of law and humanities has developed, which brings legal studies into dialogue with a wide range of interpretive disciplines and includes readings of cultural texts such as films, dramatic and musical performances, visual art, material artifacts, comic books, and social media. Some of the work in this broader field, including Peters's own scholarship, has embraced the turn to history. For examples and discussions of such work, see Julie Stone Peters, *Law as Performance: Theatricality, Spectatorship, and the Making of Law in Ancient, Medieval, and Early Modern Europe* (Oxford: Oxford University Press, 2022); Greta Olson, *From Law and Literature to Legality and Affect* (Oxford: Oxford University Press, 2022); Simon Stern, Maksymilian Del Mar, and Bernadette Meyler, eds., *The Oxford Handbook of Law and Humanities* (New York: Oxford University Press, 2020); and Sarat, Anderson, and Frank, *Law and the Humanities*.

meaning-making institution itself constituted by language and narrative. This work has helped the field of law and literature move beyond the impasses of the 1980s and 1990s. Such scholarship has focused not simply on law *in* literature or law *as* literature but on the complex interactions between legal and imaginative texts. This work has also attended to the formal dimensions of law and literature. Scholars have shown how eighteenth-century legal developments shaped imaginative writing at the level of both form and theme and how literary texts intervened in and, at times, shaped the era's legal debates. Although the primary focus has been on the implications of law for imaginative writing, scholars have also highlighted the centrality of narrative and rhetoric to eighteenth-century legal discourse, challenging the idea of law as constituted solely by reason and logic.[28]

Eighteenth-century studies scholars have examined a wide range of topics. Critics showed early interest in the impact of the first modern copyright law, the 1710 Statute of Anne, on eighteenth-century literature and related questions concerning originality and authorship; in novelists' depictions of trials and the implications of changing ideas about testimony, evidence, and proof for narrative techniques; and in fictional representations of crime and punishment.[29] While these topics continue to generate important work, scholars have broadened the focus in recent decades,

[28] All the studies in note 3 above examine interactions between eighteenth-century British literature and law, albeit with an emphasis on the implications of legal developments for literature. For analyses of narrative and rhetoric in eighteenth-century law and legal discourse, see John Barrell, *Imagining the King's Death: Figurative Treason, Fantasies of Regicide, 1793–1796* (Oxford: Oxford University Press, 2000); Reid, *Imprison'd Wranglers*; Temple, *Loving Justice*; Simon Devereaux, "Arts of Public Performance: Barristers and Actors in Georgian England," in Lemmings, *Crime, Courtrooms and the Public Sphere*, 93–117; Nancy E. Johnson, "Fashioning the Legal Subject: Narratives from the London Treason Trials of 1794," *Eighteenth-Century Fiction* 21, no. 3 (Spring 2009): 413–43; Martin A. Kayman, "The Reader and the Jury: Legal Fictions and the Making of Commercial Law in Eighteenth-Century England," *Eighteenth-Century Fiction* 9, no. 4 (July 1997): 373–94; and Adam Kozaczka, "Romancing the Courtroom Anecdote: Henry Cockburn's and Walter Scott's Shared Historical Form," *Studies in Romanticism* 61, no. 4 (Winter 2022): 559–84. For similar trends in scholarship on early modern England and Victorian Britain, see Lorna Hutson, ed., *The Oxford Handbook of English Law and Literature, 1500–1700* (Oxford: Oxford University Press, 2017); and Simon Petch, "Law, Literature, and Victorian Studies," *Victorian Literature and Culture* 35 (2007): 361–84.

[29] On copyright and authorship, see Greene, *Trouble with Ownership*; Mark Rose, *Authors and Owners: The Invention of Copyright* (Cambridge, MA: Harvard University Press, 1993); Temple, *Scandal Nation*; and Simon Stern, "*Tom Jones* and the Economies of Copyright," *Eighteenth-Century Fiction* 9, no. 4 (July 1997): 429–46. On trials, evidence, and the forensic nature of eighteenth century fiction, see Jonathan H. Grossman, *The Art of Alibi: English Law Courts and the Novel* (Baltimore: Johns Hopkins University Press, 2002); Keymer, *Richardson's "Clarissa"*; and Welsh, *Strong Representations*. On crime and punishment, see Bender, *Imagining the Penitentiary*; and Gladfelder, *Criminality and Narrative*.

examining literary treatments of and responses to developments such as the use of post-publication censorship, the policing of vagrancy, the emergence of state-sponsored marriage, the campaign to abolish slavery and the slave trade, and the passage of animal-welfare legislation. Along with a greater range of topics and genres, there has been attention to a greater diversity of voices and perspectives, including literature by and about women, the poor, and people of color.[30] Recently, scholars have begun to look beyond the borders of the nation to consider literary engagements with international law, nationality law, and inter-imperial legal authority.[31]

Not surprisingly, critics have offered different accounts of the legal-literary nexus in the long eighteenth century. There have been lively disagreements about writers' stances toward the law as well as the implications of legal developments for imaginative writing. One of these debates concerns literature's response to and role in the emergence of modern contract law and related theories of contract. Legal historians have long argued that the basis of the legal system underwent a shift in this period: Where jurists previously conceived of legal obligations as grounded in birth and family, now they began treating obligations as grounded in free choice and consent.[32] Scholars have debated whether eighteenth-century literature participated in this shift. Where critics like Ian Watt, Martin A. Kayman, and John P. Zomchick maintain that novels contributed to the growth of contract logic and the celebration of the liberal individual, scholars like Wolfram Schmidgen, Sandra Macpherson, and Daniel M. Stout have pointed to the hold of older, status-based ideologies in

[30] See, e.g., Nicole N. Aljoe, *Creole Testimonies: Slave Narratives from the British West Indies, 1709–1838* (New York: Palgrave Macmillan, 2012), 93–118; Bricker, *Libel and Lampoon*; Brycchan Carey, *British Abolitionism and the Rhetoric of Sensibility: Writing, Sentiment, and Slavery, 1760–1807* (Houndmills: Palgrave Macmillan, 2005); Ganz, *Public Vows*; Keymer, *Poetics of the Pillory*; Tobias Menely, *The Animal Claim: Sensibility and the Creaturely Voice* (Chicago: University of Chicago Press, 2015); Nicolazzo, *Vagrant Figures*; Lisa O'Connell, *The Origins of the English Marriage Plot: Literature, Politics and Religion in the Eighteenth Century* (Cambridge: Cambridge University Press, 2019); Ross, *Writing in Public*; and Wright, *Defending Privilege*.

[31] See DeGooyer, *Before Borders*; Chenxi Tang, *Imagining World Order: Literature and International Law in Early Modern Europe, 1500–1800* (Ithaca, NY: Cornell University Press, 2018), 231–79; Gabriel Cervantes, "Episodic or Novelistic? Law in the Atlantic and the Form of Daniel Defoe's *Colonel Jack*," *Eighteenth-Century Fiction* 24, no. 2 (Winter 2011–12): 247–77; Marc Mierowsky, "Daniel Defoe on Naturalization," *Review of English Studies* 74, no. 313 (February 2023): 112–29; and Sharif Youssef, "Refugees and the Rise of the Novel: Trespass, Necessity, and Humanitarian Casuistry in the Long Refugee Crisis," *Humanity* 12, no. 2 (Summer 2021): 119–37.

[32] See P. S. Atiyah, *The Rise and Fall of Freedom of Contract* (Oxford: Clarendon Press, 1979); Holly Brewer, *By Birth or Consent: Children, Law, and the Anglo-American Revolution in Authority* (Chapel Hill: University of North Carolina Press, 2005); and Henry Sumner Maine, *Ancient Law: Its Connection with the Early History of Society, and Its Relation to Modern Ideas* (London: John Murray, 1861), 170.

the period's fiction, underscoring writers' investment in communal forms of ownership and corporate models of responsibility.[33]

Scholars have also debated the relationship between literary forms and state power in this period. Where John Bender maintains that eighteenth-century fiction served to supplement the law's regulatory authority, others contend that novelists' thematic concerns and formal experiments served to critique the law and to foster empathy (or "sympathy," as eighteenth-century thinkers termed it) for those on the margins of society. In Lynn Hunt's provocative account, novelists not only participated in the humanitarian reform movements of the late eighteenth century but also enabled the legal declaration of human rights.[34] Still other scholars have shown how the era's increasing regulation of speech and writing fueled literary innovation.[35] Overall, scholars have underscored the dynamic and shifting relationship between law and literature in this period.

The essays in this volume build upon and extend this body of work. Written by major scholars in the field, the chapters examine the interplay between literary forms and legal change, bringing new research and insights to bear on both familiar and unfamiliar texts. Specifically, the chapters read political satire, sentimental and historical fiction, pamphlets, poems, periodical essays, slave narratives, and judicial decisions alongside developments in common law, statute law, equity, and jurisprudence. Some of the writers under consideration – such as Fielding, Richardson, and Scott – had formal legal training or professional connections in the legal world; others, like Sir Humphrey Mackworth and Mary Prince, found themselves thrust into legal disputes or subjected to legal wrongs. Broadly speaking, the chapters examine the role of literature and rhetoric in the modernization of British law: They trace a shift, though at times uneven and contested, from older forms of legal and political organization to newer ones, from relationships grounded in birth and status to those grounded in individual choice and consent. At the same time, the chapters show how writers and jurists alternately contributed to and challenged inequalities that continued to permeate the legal system.

33 See Ian Watt, *The Rise of the Novel: Studies in Defoe, Richardson, and Fielding*, 2nd ed. (1957; Berkeley: University of California Press, 2001); Kayman, "Reader and the Jury"; John P. Zomchick, *Family and the Law in Eighteenth-Century Fiction: The Public Conscience in the Private Sphere* (Cambridge: Cambridge University Press, 1993); Schmidgen, *Eighteenth-Century Fiction*; Macpherson, *Harm's Way*; and Stout, *Corporate Romanticism*.

34 See Bender, *Imagining the Penitentiary*; Gladfelder, *Criminality and Narrative*; and Lynn Hunt, *Inventing Human Rights: A History* (New York: W. W. Norton, 2007).

35 See Bricker, *Libel and Lampoon*; Bugg, *Five Long Winters*; and Keymer, *Poetics of the Pillory*.

Written by scholars with diverse backgrounds and orientations – some based in English departments and others in law schools – the chapters approach the study of law and literature in different ways. Some of the contributors offer new readings of imaginative texts, while others focus on the language and form of legal writing. Still others complicate and transcend the traditional taxonomy, examining formal and rhetorical dimensions of – and interactions between – legal and literary texts. Methodologically, the chapters employ historicist approaches, probing legal and literary developments at different points in the long eighteenth century. While the chapters share an historicist orientation, however, the volume does not suppress disagreement. Rather, the volume showcases debates about the law's role in rectifying injustice and regulating society, as well as the extent to which imaginative writing resists, stands apart from, and/or is complicit in legal wrongs. The chapters ultimately show the centrality of eighteenth-century British law and literature to legal, political, and ethical debates that remain of concern to this day.

The chapters are arranged roughly chronologically and can be read either separately or sequentially. Each chapter offers a broader context to situate its close readings or uses a specific case to consider broader historical or theoretical issues. The volume begins with Andrew Benjamin Bricker's chapter, "'Every Common Reader': Satire, Libel Law, and the Emergence of Objective Interpretive Procedures, ca. 1670–1730," which takes up foundational questions about legal and literary interpretation. The chapter examines two related developments: the growth of verbal ambiguity in satire, especially the use of irony, circumlocution, and allegory; and the emergence and refinement of doctrines for the courtroom interpretation of ambiguous language in prosecutions for libel. Between the late seventeenth and the early eighteenth centuries, Bricker shows, English common-law courts responded to the new forms of verbally evasive satire employed by authors such as John Dryden, Aphra Behn, Jonathan Swift, and Alexander Pope by instituting or refining supposedly "reasonable" or "objective" interpretive standards in libel trials. These innovations required jurors to reject their subjective understandings of libelous statements in favor of a sociocentric interpretation – the interpretation of a theoretical community of average or typical readers who responded in predictable and normative ways. Such readers were thought to be able to deduce a satirist's intended meaning from a set of shared beliefs about the primary denotations and connotations of words and idioms. The new doctrines enabled the crown to defer to jurors in the abstract while effectively displacing the interpretive latitude of jurors in practice. Bricker shows how courts refined these doctrines in two trials for seditious libel: *R. v. Browne* (1706) and *R. v. Clerk* (1728/29). He suggests that the doctrines not only had a pronounced effect on the courtroom interpretation of ambiguous language in libel trials in this period but also provided a model of "objective" standards and jury instructions that would later be used in other areas of law. The new standards also had important implications for imaginative writers. Far from constraining literary expression, the legal doctrines prompted satirists to continue experimenting with techniques of verbal indirection, techniques that remain a defining feature of satire today.

The second chapter turns from jurists' attempts to regulate and interpret literature to the role of law in Britain's industrial economy. In the late seventeenth and early eighteenth centuries, Britain saw an unprecedented growth of transport infrastructure. The turnpikes, canals, and railways that appeared throughout the realm frequently crossed one another, requiring individuals to decide how different directions of traffic should negotiate the spaces they shared. In "Perpendicular Publics: Contesting Infrastructure at Early Eighteenth-Century Rail Crossings," David Alff examines the conflicts occasioned by one such crossing in the South Wales town of Neath. In 1705 Sir Humphrey Mackworth laid wooden tracks across the king's highway to transport coal between his mines and a canal. A rival coal magnate, Edward Mansell, promptly accused Mackworth of erecting a nuisance and dispatched a crew to smash his rails. Where Mansell claimed that the tracks spoiled the king's highway, Mackworth asserted in the Great Sessions that his "wagonway," as it was known, delivered public benefits by employing artisans, distributing coal fuel, and generating customs revenue. Mackworth also published two pamphlets detailing and defending his actions. Combining rhetorical analysis with recent insights from infrastructure studies, Alff examines how Mackworth used both the language and process of the law to define the conditions under which public works could exist. The chapter focuses on the conciliatory rhetoric that Mackworth employed to counter Mansell's violence. Alff shows how early modern public works emerged not through sovereign imposition or as "an unthought material stratum" but as a call to arbitration and an occasion to weigh the costs and benefits of national amenities. Alff suggests that cases like Mackworth's laid the groundwork for legislation later in the century that established the use of the railway as a private work conducive to public interest.

In Chapter 3, "Ambivalence, Survival, and Law in Defoe's *Journal of the Plague Year*," Kathryn D. Temple considers another manifestation of the conflict between private interest and public welfare in early eighteenth-century Britain, focusing on Defoe's treatment of the law's failed response to the outbreak of bubonic plague. Defoe's novel, Temple suggests, points toward the recognition of what critical-legal scholar Duncan Kennedy has termed the "fundamental contradiction" between our autonomy needs and our reliance upon other people. This contradiction manifests as a profound ambivalence about the law and its regulations. At the very moment when Defoe's protagonist, H.F., needs to isolate and function as a free and self-reliant individual to prevent contagion, he also needs to function as part of the larger community. Building upon scholarship addressing law and the emotions, Temple argues that feelings of ambivalence become central to both the plot and the form of the novel, and that H.F.'s embodied ambivalence aids his survival. As Temple shows, H.F. operates on a continuum, neither completely abiding by nor defying the law. Given the misguided and ineffectual nature of the legal regulations, H.F.'s lack of compliance proves beneficial. His ambivalence prompts him to strike a protective balance between isolation and interaction, providing him with the stories he needs to construct his narrative and to maintain a sense of purpose in the face of chaos. In Temple's reading, the novel ultimately shows the limits of the plague regulations while illuminating the irreconcilable conflict between individuals' resistance to and desire for the rule of law during periods of crisis. Temple's analysis has implications not only for law-and-literature and law-and-emotions scholarship but also for our understanding of legal responses to outbreaks such as the COVID-19 pandemic.

The next three chapters examine the developing legal profession and the practice of judging in mid-eighteenth-century England. In Chapter 4, "The Court of Justice and the Court of Conscience: Legal Ethics in *Tom Jones*," Suzanna Geiser reads Fielding's 1749 novel as a meditation on the problems created by the era's lax standards for legal professionals. In doing so, she shows the value of exploring literature's historical contributions to professional legal education. Written by a barrister-turned-magistrate and published decades before the law became a closely regulated profession, *Tom Jones* makes the case for educational and ethical mandates in the field. The novel's legal subplots and intercalary chapters on legal authority, Geiser argues, reveal a profession corrupted by both England's class system and the period's rising devotion to the individual and his self-interest. Yet the novel does not simply decry the law's ethical failures; it also examines the field's possibilities. Geiser suggests that Fielding considers the value and limits of three ethical theories circulating in nascent or full form at mid century: deontology, consequentialism, and virtue ethics. Ultimately,

Geiser argues, the novel reveals the limits of each construct, offering in its place a hybrid philosophy that combines the strict rules symbolized by the court of justice with the more subjective judgments associated with the court of conscience. This philosophy reveals the importance of encoded duty and obligation for a principled and self-regulating professional body while recognizing the role that individual virtue plays in developing a professional identity committed to the law's core values of truth and justice.

My chapter, "'A Higher Tribunal': Equity, Law, and the Family in *Sir Charles Grandison*" (Chapter 5), turns to the work of Fielding's rival novelist. The chapter reads the scenes of judging and judgment in Richardson's 1753–54 novel in the context of debates about the nature and scope of equity as well as the value and limits of England's laws regulating familial relations. Equity emerged in the medieval period as a court of conscience to remedy the failings of the common law. England's prerogative courts – including, most importantly, the Court of Chancery – assumed jurisdiction over these cases in the late fourteenth century. By the early seventeenth century, however, disputes had emerged over the subjective nature of the court's rulings. Richardson's novel, I argue, not only affirms the value of equity as the basis for judgments in the Court of Chancery but also shows the need to apply equitable principles to everyday life. Like many jurists in his day, Richardson seeks to correct the common-law courts' harsh judgments without substituting arbitrary and subjective rulings in their place. The eponymous hero, who routinely considers perspectives other than his own, serves as the primary embodiment of equity, but Harriet Byron (later Lady Grandison) further demonstrates the value of fair and flexible judgment. Both Sir Charles and Harriet adopt an impartial stance when mediating familial conflicts, and they prioritize mercy and forgiveness over strict legal justice. Through their interventions in disputes concerning marriage, custody, and inheritance, Richardson critiques the patriarchal principles that underpin English common and statutory law. Richardson's commitment to equity shapes his experiments with epistolary form: By presenting competing accounts of the conflicts, the novel prompts readers to consider the disputes from multiple points of view. Through the novel's thematic concerns and formal experiments, Richardson responds to critics' concerns about the subjective nature of equity while showing the need to extend the era's equity jurisprudence to rectify injustices in familial life.

Mid-eighteenth-century Britons witnessed developments not only in fictional representations of lawyers and judges but also in the reporting of legal decisions. Law-and-literature scholars have analyzed the rhetoric and form of contemporary US Supreme Court decisions, but few have looked closely at the origins of the genre. In "Mansfield, Burrow, and the Reformulation of the Legal Decision" (Chapter 6), Simon Stern takes up the changing form of the judicial opinion in English common-law courts. Until the last few decades of the eighteenth century, legal decisions were not routinely written with the expectation that they would appear in print. Judges did not typically summarize at the outset the points in contention, nor did decisions routinely begin with a statement of the relevant facts before moving on to a section applying the law to those facts. Stern examines the role played by William Murray, Lord Mansfield, Chief Justice of the Court of King's Bench from 1756 to 1788, and Mansfield's law reporter James Burrow in helping to shift the judicial decision toward its modern form. Stern argues that Mansfield was more explicit and self-conscious than most of his contemporaries in marking his decisions and the rulings in them as precedents that would govern future disputes. To make the holdings legible and portable, Mansfield explained the legal principles and drew on previously decided cases more directly than was customary at the time. He was aided in this endeavor by Burrow, whose published case reports used various formal and typographical features that complemented Mansfield's efforts, drawing readers' attention to the holdings of cases and identifying significant legal points by setting them off visually. Stern suggests that Burrow's work as a member of the Royal Society, which had a long tradition of publishing scientific cases, helps explain many of his ideas about the structure of legal decisions. Through a close examination of the formal features of selected decisions and their appearance on the printed page, Stern highlights the role that Mansfield and Burrow played in the modernization of the legal decision and the development of precedential reasoning.

The second half of the century also saw developments in and debates about the constitution of the British nation and the nature and reach of British law. The next two chapters consider the implications of these debates for prose fiction. In Chapter 7, "Novel Subjects: Naturalization in Richardson and Edgeworth," Stephanie DeGooyer examines literary responses to and engagements with ideas about naturalization, focusing especially on the debates surrounding the 1753 Jewish Naturalization Act, which allowed Jewish persons to become naturalized by application to Parliament without a test of sacrament. In the end, the act barely passed the House of Commons before being repealed in the wake of anti-Semitic outcry from the public. Yet, DeGooyer shows, the bill and the debates it sparked about naturalization were subsequently taken up by novelists. Although the seventeenth-century legal dream of a "general naturalization bill" that would enable the admission of all persons regardless of religion or ethnicity ultimately failed in the legal sphere, imaginative writers carried on the experiment, using prose fiction as a creative form for imagining the reception, acculturation, and legal protection of foreigners in England. DeGooyer focuses on the treatment of these questions in Richardson's *Grandison* and Maria Edgeworth's *Harrington* (1817). Where Richardson looks back to an older view of naturalization as a return to an original common human nature expressed in natural law, Edgeworth embraces a newer approach, advanced by John Locke, who maintained that national allegiance could be altered by parliamentary statute. In refusing to incorporate Jewish and Catholic characters into the English nation, Richardson's novel ultimately betrays the promise of the older approach. Edgeworth's gimmicky ending, which reveals the novel's Jewish heroine to be also Christian, likewise speaks to fears about the idea of converting foreigners into political subjects based on will alone. At the same time, however, Edgeworth's novel reveals the radical potential of the new theory of naturalization and the creative power of fiction as a form of subject creation.

In "Common Law and Cultural Difference in Scott's *Ivanhoe* and *Chronicles of the Canongate*" (Chapter 8), Anne Frey examines Scott's more pessimistic account of the justice meted out to different ethnic groups in Britain and its overseas empire. Although the 1707 Act of Union combined the Parliaments of England and Scotland, the statute largely permitted Scotland to retain its own, separate legal system. Scots law thus became a source of national pride. The multiplicity of legal systems, however, created difficulties. In *Ivanhoe* (1819) and *Chronicles of the Canongate* (1827), Frey argues, Scott interrogates the fiction that the common law derives its legitimacy from locally shared traditions. Although Scott values the stability and continuity of customary law, he questions whether such law can fairly govern a multi-ethnic community. Again and again in these texts, Scots get caught up in legal systems that do not recognize their distinctive customs and traditions. Through these plots, Scott highlights two main problems with the common law: He suggests that laws that tie legitimacy to place belie the fact that people are hybrid and mobile, and he shows that even when judges possess knowledge of local traditions, they are often more interested in asserting their own power than in meting out justice. In *Ivanhoe* Scott suggests that memories of state violence eventually fade over time, but in *Chronicles of the Canongate* he presents the imposition of common law as a series of tragedies.

During this period, Britons also debated the law's role in maintaining and rectifying economic inequalities. In "The Legal Character of Paupers in Early Nineteenth-Century England" (Chapter 9), Mark Schoenfield examines representations of and responses to the legal regulation of poverty. The chapter explores the legal discourse that governed metropolitan paupers and that some paupers themselves deployed in the service of self-representation. Schoenfield draws from a wide range of sources, including poems by Thomas Hood and William Wordsworth, periodical essays, legislative reports, legal cases, and biographical sketches, considering how writers alternately affirmed and interrogated the law's efforts to strip paupers of agency. Schoenfield argues that many writers cast beggary as a professional mode characterized by inventiveness and effort, the very qualities that paupers were thought to lack. He shows how both imagined and actual beggars mobilized the theatricality of which they stood accused to contest the law's regulations and to highlight the similarities between the capitalist's reliance on credit and the beggar's reliance on credulity.

In "Liberty in 'Parenthesis': The Case of *The Slave, Grace* (1827) and Antislavery Satire in *The History of Mary Prince* (1831)" (Chapter 10), Sarah Winter examines another site of conflict over freedom and agency in the early nineteenth century, turning to the law and literature of slavery. In *Somerset v. Stewart* (1772), Lord Mansfield famously held that individuals could not be detained in England against their will or sent out of the country for sale and re-enslavement, a judgment that many viewed as outlawing slavery on English soil. In the case of *The Slave, Grace*, however, William Scott, Lord Stowell, Chief Justice of the English High Court of Admiralty, clarified the limits of Mansfield's decision, holding that the petitioner, Grace James, reverted to her enslaved status when she returned to Antigua, even though she had enjoyed the status of a free person during her residence in England. Winter reads published and unpublished legal opinions and correspondence concerning the case, highlighting the contradictions in the law's conception of English liberty. She also examines responses in the popular press, emphasizing that some commentators read the decision as auto-satire – that is, as an inadvertent critique and satire of its own contradictions. Winter then turns to Mary Prince's *History*, the only known published narrative by a woman enslaved in the British West Indies. Scholars have long emphasized abolitionists' sentimental appeals to readers; Winter, by contrast, highlights the satirical dimensions of Prince's account. Read alongside James's case, Prince's narrative accrues new evidentiary value, offering insight into the experiences, perspectives, and agency of enslaved women caught up in the contradictory laws regulating slavery in the British Empire.

Eighteenth- and early nineteenth-century writers' treatments of human rights remain highly contentious today. In the volume's final chapter, "Yearning for Restriction in the Romantic Novel: Propagating Conservative Legal Norms in Right-Wing Literary Podcasts and Religion-Centered Editions of Works by Jane Austen and Mary Shelley," Nicole Mansfield Wright considers how right-wing editors and podcasters have commented on struggles for liberty and autonomy in Romantic-era fiction. In the past several decades, conservative publishers and podcasters in the United States have sought to counter what they view as progressives' institutional capture of higher education by presenting the long eighteenth century as a wellspring of resources for right-wing legal and social thought. Wright examines two such initiatives: the Ignatius Press's Ignatius Critical Editions, which reprint major works of British and American literature, and the *National Review*'s "Great Books" podcast. She focuses on three novels polemicized by these ventures: Austen's *Pride and Prejudice* (1813) and *Mansfield Park* (1814) and Shelley's *Frankenstein; or, The Modern Prometheus* (1818). Wright shows how the editions and podcasts reflect conservatives' long-term campaign to reshape popular and academic discourse on legal norms and conceptions of justice. In particular, she argues, the editors and podcasters claim to present interpretations of the texts that are faithful to the periods in which the novels were written. In fact, however, the editors and podcasters reinterpret Austen's and Shelley's depictions of freedom and personal autonomy in a manner consistent with the political priorities of today's Christian right, extolling restrictions on choice – especially for members of subordinate groups – as conducive to contentment and true freedom. Specifically, Wright shows how the editors and podcasters use the novels to hold up restrictions on women's sexual and legal freedom, social and economic freedom, and readers' interpretive freedom. She highlights the importance of attending to such efforts, showing how their politically freighted renditions alter our understandings of Austen's and Shelley's texts.

Together, these chapters reveal the complex interplay between British law and literature in the long eighteenth century, the centrality of narrative and rhetoric to eighteenth-century legal discourse, and the continuing relevance of the era's legal debates today. The chapters uncover a range of views about the law in the period's literature. Many writers contest the gendered, racial, religious, and class-based inequalities that permeate the legal system. But these critiques are not always or entirely consistent. DeGooyer and I show how Richardson and Edgeworth present sentimental fiction as a legal supplement and a forum for equitable judgment. Yet, as I argue, while Richardson goes far in challenging the patriarchal underpinning of English marriage, custody, and inheritance laws, there are limits to his critique. DeGooyer likewise highlights Richardson's reluctance to extend English subjecthood to Jews and Catholics, and Frey suggests that Scott's fiction implicitly resists and yet also encodes the legal inequities experienced by Scots in Britain's multi-ethnic society. We find sharper critiques of the law in texts authored by those who were themselves disenfranchised by it: Winter highlights the ways in which formerly enslaved people used literary forms to assert their agency and contest the law's denial of their rights, while Schoenfield reveals how some paupers deployed legal rhetoric on their own behalf. As Winter shows, writers like Prince convey their critiques not by appealing to readers' sympathies but by employing satire. Overall, the chapters reveal that writers used a range of techniques to expose and contest the law's inequalities during this period.

The relationship between law and literature, however, is not always marked by opposition. Legal developments also contributed to and fueled literary experimentation, while litigants and jurists used language and rhetoric in creative ways. Bricker shows that the crown's attempts to regulate libelous statements sparked innovations on the part of satirists, and Stern demonstrates how Mansfield and Burrow employed rhetorical, stylistic, and typographical devices to develop the law's precedential reasoning. Alff, for his part, suggests that early industrialists looked both to legal processes and legal rhetoric to sustain economic progress, and DeGooyer shows how legal fictions could be a form of subject creation. Temple, meanwhile, highlights Defoe's ambivalent treatment of England's plague regulations, exploring both the value and the limits of abiding by the law during periods of crisis. We find, then, a range of responses to and disagreements about the law at the level of both form and theme, underscoring the complex interactions between legal and literary discourses throughout the period.

The chapters showcase, too, debates about the nature of legal and literary interpretation and the tension between objective and subjective standards of judgment. Geiser, Frey, and I consider novelists' examinations of the law's reliance upon strict rules and precedents as opposed to discretionary modes of justice. Although objective standards may provide stability and predictability, the chapters show, such standards lead to problems when judges attempt to impose universal rules on diverse subjects without considering their individual circumstances and histories. As Bricker emphasizes, such efforts can also result in highly constrained and politically motivated interpretations. Writers attempt to resolve these problems in different ways. Fielding holds up a hybrid philosophy for legal professionals that combines external standards with the dictates of the individual conscience and the needs of the community, while Richardson shows the need to build in checks on equitable judgment by considering multiple points of view. Scott, for his part, suggests that British and English courts ought to consider the customs and histories of everyone they presume to judge.

These questions also emerge in Wright's analysis of recent efforts by right-wing Christian groups to reinterpret and market Austen's and Mary Shelley's novels for conservative audiences. As Wright shows, the editors of the Ignatius Critical Editions and the producers of the *National Review*'s "Great Books" podcast claim to offer objective interpretations of the texts even as they flatten the meanings of the novels and misrepresent the contexts in which the authors wrote and published. The interest in Austen's and Shelley's novels on the part of such groups, of course, reaffirms the texts' continuing relevance. Ultimately, Wright's chapter, like the others in the volume, underscores the political and ethical stakes of reading eighteenth-century literature. In different ways, all the contributors remind us of the value of attending to the interplay between law and literature in the long eighteenth century as well as the legacy of eighteenth-century legal and literary developments today.

Future Directions

While this volume aims to cover a range of texts and topics, the authors discussed in the pages that follow are necessarily selective. The chapters do not convey the full scope of writers who engaged with the law in the long eighteenth century, and they touch upon only a few of the jurists and litigants who experimented with narrative and rhetoric in this period. The chapters seek rather to showcase different approaches to and points of intersection between law and literature while opening up new avenues for research. Further work should be undertaken not only on the writers examined in this volume but also on legal dimensions of texts by authors such as Delarivier Manley, Jonathan Swift, Tobias Smollett, Eliza Haywood, Elizabeth Inchbald, Charlotte Smith, Joanna Baillie, Ottobah Cugoano, and Robert Wedderburn. Analyses of recent adaptations and interpretations of works by these and other authors, moreover, can help illuminate the significance of such texts for legal, political, and ethical debates today.

The novel has proved to be an especially fruitful site for law-and-literature analysis, and much work remains to be done on this influential and capacious genre. But, as Schoenfield and Winter suggest, more attention should also be paid to the legal dimensions of poetry, periodical essays, and life-writing. The legal dimensions of Restoration and eighteenth-century drama, theater, and performance would likewise benefit from further analysis. David Francis Taylor's study of the relationship between Richard Brinsley Sheridan's parliamentary and theatrical careers offers an excellent example of this type of work, as does Peters's analysis of Sheridan's *Pizarro* (1799) and the impeachment trial of Warren Hastings, Regina Hewitt's and Victoria Myers's work on Baillie's drama and criminal justice, and Jane Wessel's study of disputes over literary property in stage performances prior to the legal recognition of such rights.[36]

More work, finally, should be undertaken on the rhetorical and formal dimensions of eighteenth-century legal texts, including trial narratives, last dying speeches, legal treatises, parliamentary debates, statutes, and judicial opinions. Building upon the analyses offered by Bricker, Alff, and Winter, scholars might examine the evolution and logic of legal doctrines, the rhetoric of popular legal tracts, or the contradictions and inconsistencies of specific cases. More work should also be undertaken on the formal features of both common-law and equity case reports, along the lines of Stern's analysis. A host of digital archives including Eighteenth-Century Collections Online; The Making of Modern Law; The Proceedings of the Old Bailey, 1674–1913; Legal London; the Early Caribbean Digital Archive; and Runaway Slaves in Britain have made such materials more accessible. In the wake of the curtailing of legal rights and the renewed calls for legal and social justice in the United States, in the United Kingdom, and around the world, the study of law and literature has taken on new urgency. As the following chapters show, analyses of the legal dimensions of British literature and the rhetorical features of legal texts in the long eighteenth century can ultimately help us understand not only the entanglements of law and literature in the past but also the role of literature, writing, and rhetoric in the pursuit of justice today.

[36] See David Francis Taylor, *Theatres of Opposition: Empire, Revolution, and Richard Brinsley Sheridan* (Oxford: Oxford University Press, 2012); Julie Stone Peters, "Theatricality, Legalism, and the Scenography of Suffering: The Trial of Warren Hastings and Richard Brinsley Sheridan's *Pizarro*," *Law and Literature* 18, no. 1 (Spring 2006): 15–45; Regina Hewitt, *Symbolic Interactions: Social Problems and Literary Interventions in the Works of Baillie, Scott, and Landor* (Lewisburg, PA: Bucknell University Press, 2006), 77–103; Victoria Myers, "Joanna Baillie and the Emergence of Medico-Legal Discourse," *European Romantic Review* 18, no. 3 (July 2007): 339–59; and Wessel, *Owning Performance*.

CHAPTER 1

"Every Common Reader"

Satire, Libel Law, and the Emergence of Objective Interpretive Procedures, ca. 1670–1730

Andrew Benjamin Bricker

This chapter studies the reciprocal relationship between English satire and libel law between roughly 1670 and 1730. I take up the growth of verbal ambiguity and especially the increasing use of irony, circumlocution, and allegory among satirists, and demonstrate, in turn, how the courts, through the refinement of doctrines for the interpretation of language, responded to the problem of verbal ambiguity in prosecutions for libel. I track this interaction across a series of trials in the common-law courts of England during the later seventeenth and early eighteenth centuries. In each case, the courts further refined the supposedly "objective" interpretive standards to be used by jurors. Such interpretive doctrines were important because they created a theoretically reasonable means of assessment based on the assumption that an average or so-called common reader exists, one who ought to be able to deduce a satirist's intended meaning from a shared set of beliefs about the primary denotations and connotations of a word, locution, or idiom.[1]

Such objective interpretive standards had two goals: to create mechanisms for delimiting verbal ambiguity, which had come to saturate satire during its so-called Golden Age and which troubled libel prosecutions; and to limit the interpretive latitude of recalcitrant jurors so that they might read ambiguously libelous language in more predictable and less idiosyncratic ways. Over time, the courts expanded these standards – from "common intendment" in 1671 to "the generality of readers" in 1729 – which permitted the crown to defer to jurors in the abstract while effectively displacing the capricious interpretations of actual jurors in practice. These innovations required jurors to reject their personal understanding of a libelous statement in lieu of a rational projection: a community of theoretical readers around whom semantic consensus could be built. As a

[1] See, e.g., "The Trial of Mr. Richard Francklin" (1731), in William Cobbett et al., *Complete Collection of State Trials*, 21 vols. (London, 1809–26), 17:666–68.

result, by relying upon a sociocentric interpretation of language, such rules also permitted the crown to skirt a series of technical linguistic issues, such as how a prosecutor might demonstrate the intended meaning of an ironic compliment or the tenor of an allegorical narrative in the absence of internal textual evidence.

This chapter's focus on objective interpretive procedures belongs to a growing body of scholarship on the relationship between eighteenth-century satire and libel law.[2] That research has helped to make the law central to our understanding of satire's development by showing how legal pressures shaped satiric production. I have been especially drawn, both here and in my previous work, to the manifold and sometimes unpredictable ways in which satirists and their booksellers both interpreted and responded to the law. Libel laws from this period were not "crystalline," to borrow Carol M. Rose's terminology, but "muddy."[3] In radically revising libel laws and developing new interpretive doctrines, the courts frequently produced confusion among satirists about their precise liabilities, leading to a form of what Naomi Mezey has called slippage: the "inconsistencies between the production of legal meaning and its cultural reception."[4] In this chapter, I identify these moments of doctrinal muddiness in eighteenth-century libel law and track instances of slippage in lay legal interpretation, showing how this disconnect between legal theory and literary practice helped to produce what Simon Stern has called the "enabling conditions" that bridge the spheres of law and literature.[5]

This chapter begins with a brief discussion of libel law and shows how developments in satiric practice in the late seventeenth and early eighteenth centuries, and especially the sustained use of verbal evasion, troubled

[2] Thomas Keymer, *Poetics of the Pillory: English Literature and Seditious Libel, 1660–1820* (Oxford: Oxford University Press, 2019); Andrew Benjamin Bricker, "Libel and Satire: The Problem with Naming," *English Literary History* 81, no. 3 (Fall 2014): 889–921; Andrew Benjamin Bricker, "After the Golden Age: Caricature, Libel, and the Deverbalization of Satire," *Eighteenth-Century Studies* 51, no. 3 (Spring 2018): 305–36; Joseph Hone, "Legal Constraints, Libellous Evasions," in *The Oxford Handbook of Eighteenth-Century Satire*, ed. Paddy Bullard (Oxford: Oxford University Press, 2019), 525–41; and Roger Lund, "'An Alembick of Innuendos': Satire, Libel, and *The Craftsman*," *Philological Quarterly* 95, no. 2 (Spring 2016): 243–68. This chapter draws from a throughline in my book *Libel and Lampoon: Satire in the Courts, 1670–1792* (Oxford: Oxford University Press, 2022). For an expanded discussion of the cases and issues presented here, see chaps. 1, 3, and 5.

[3] Carol M. Rose, "Crystals and Mud in Property Law," *Stanford Law Review* 40, no. 3 (February 1988): 577–610.

[4] Naomi Mezey, "Law as Culture," in *Cultural Analysis, Cultural Studies, and the Law: Moving beyond Legal Realism*, ed. Austin Sarat and Jonathan Simon (Durham, NC: Duke University Press, 2003), 39–72, at 54.

[5] Simon Stern, "Literary Analysis of Law: Reorienting the Connections between Law and Literature," *Critical Analysis of Law* 5, no. 2 (2018): 1–8, at 3.

the extant procedures of the law. Over the succeeding two sections, I move to my central cases. I focus first on the legal groundwork that led to the emergence of objective procedures for the courtroom interpretation of defamatory language, before exploring two separate trials, one on irony in 1706 and another on allegory in early 1729, which modeled the bench's directions to juries across the seventeenth and eighteenth centuries and refined procedures for the courtroom interpretation of defamatory language. Taken together, these rulings were part of a more general revision to libel laws during this period. Those refurbished laws furnished the government with its primary means of regulating the press across the eighteenth century through post-publication prosecutions.[6] In closing, I take up this reciprocal back-and-forth between law and literature across these decades: how the crown responded to the growth of verbally ambiguous satire and sought to regulate and interpret such works in the courts; and how satirists, in turn, refined verbal evasions that purposely troubled those emerging interpretive procedures. This interaction between libel law and satire also had several long-term consequences for both legal procedure and logic and the language and rhetoric of satire – consequences that extend well beyond the eighteenth century and that continue to shape legal and literary practice today.

Libel Law and the Evolution of Satire

To begin, it is worth stepping back and considering what defamation was and how it worked in the seventeenth and eighteenth centuries. Defamation was a capacious and ever-expanding umbrella category that encompassed not only libel (written defamation) and slander (oral defamation), but also seditious libel (a loosely defined category of political and opposition writings), blasphemous (religious) libel, and obscene (pornographic) libel.[7]

To prove defamation, a private complainant or crown prosecutor had to establish two facts. First, they had to show that there was a clearly identifiable victim. The ease or difficulty of establishing the victim of an ambiguous attack has proved a point of contention among legal and literary historians, especially in works of satire where the victim's name

[6] Philip Hamburger, "The Development of the Law of Seditious Libel and the Control of the Press," *Stanford Law Review* 37, no. 3 (February 1985): 661–765.

[7] For a useful overview of libel law in the eighteenth century, see James C. Oldham, *English Common Law in the Age of Mansfield* (Chapel Hill: University of North Carolina Press, 2004), chap. 10.

has been partially obscured through "emvowelment" or "gutted" names, such as J--- S---- for John Smith.[8] Such naming practices were extremely common in eighteenth-century printed satire, and the theory went at the time, at least among satirists and their booksellers and even among some victims of satire, that such gutted names provided at least a degree of legal protection.[9] However, as I have argued elsewhere, naming was a problem that was often handled quickly by courts in the seventeenth century and then was formally addressed and dismissed in a 1713 trial over the verse satire "The British Embassadress's Speech to the French King."[10] In his ruling on the case, Lord Chief Justice Thomas Parker argued that missing letters were nothing more than "trifling Evasions," which could be supplied by the court.[11]

Interestingly, although gutted names therefore served no formally recognized legal function, they remained a common feature of printed satire across the eighteenth century. One reason why these textual lacunae proved so resilient is that they served as an irresistible stimulant to readerly acts of participation, deduction, and identification. The thousands of copies of eighteenth-century printed satires, bedaubed in contemporary hands with the missing names of satiric victims and held today in research libraries across the world, are ample testament to the eagerness with which readers literally filled in these onomastic crosswords. These naming practices also endured for another reason. For satirists, gutted names were part of the pseudo-ethical practice of satire itself, a way to name victims without naming them directly, thereby creating a semi-plausible deniability through often playful typographic effects.

In any case, the identity of the victim was only one matter that complainants and prosecutors had to establish in trials for libel. In addition, they needed to demonstrate that the imputations in the writing were defamatory rather than simply offensive, unkind, or

[8] "Emvowel" does not appear in the *Oxford English Dictionary*, but the term was seemingly common in the eighteenth century. See, e.g., Henry Fielding, *The Jacobite's Journal and Related Writings*, ed. W. B. Coley (Middletown, CT: Wesleyan University Press, 1975), 96.

[9] Gregory Colomb, *Designs on Truth: The Poetics of the Augustan Mock-Epic* (University Park: Pennsylvania State University Press, 1992), 63; C. R. Kropf, "Libel and Satire in the Eighteenth Century," *Eighteenth-Century Studies* 8, no. 2 (Winter 1974–75): 159; and Edward Nathan, "The Bench and the Pulpit: Conflicting Elements in the Augustan Apology for Satire," *English Literary History* 52, no. 2 (Summer 1985): 387.

[10] Bricker, "Libel and Satire," 895–96; and "The British Embassadress's Speech to the French King," in *Poems on Affairs of State: Augustan Satirical Verse, 1660–1714*, vol. 7, *1704–1714*, ed. Frank H. Ellis (New Haven, CT: Yale University Press, 1975), 590–96.

[11] See William Hawkins, *A Treatise of the Pleas of the Crown*, 2 vols. (London, 1716), 1:194.

impolite.[12] Two types of defamatory imputations existed. The first were imputations that were defamatory per se, which were first formally established and brought together in a case from 1670.[13] These included accusations of criminality, communicable disease, and professional misconduct. To modern eyes, these might seem like a grab bag of imputations, but all these accusations could jeopardize an individual's public standing and thus their capacity to carry on their trade. The second type of defamatory accusation was simply contextual.[14] For instance, I might innocently accuse someone of being an "ambidexter" (that is, a double-dealing hypocrite or someone who takes bribes from both sides).[15] Not nice, of course, but not strictly defamatory by itself. However, that same accusation made against an attorney would speak directly to one's professional competence and trustworthiness, thus qualifying as potentially defamatory.

To understand how satiric works raised these interpretive questions concerning the identity of the victim and the nature of the imputation, we also need to understand how satire changed during the later seventeenth century and the eighteenth century. Medieval and early modern satires were often openly defamatory, attacking their victims by name and directly in the language of criminal wrongdoing.[16] It was precisely these Juvenalian works that the authorities were most eager to suppress through the 1599 Bishops' Ban.[17] It was this libelous culture of satire that the English inherited at the Restoration in 1660, when manuscript verse

[12] Sir William Holdsworth, *A History of English Law*, 2nd ed., 10 vols. (London: Methuen, 1937), 8:370–71.

[13] *King v. Lake*, (1670) 145 Eng. Rep. 552.

[14] John H. Baker, *An Introduction to English Legal History*, 4th ed. (Oxford: Oxford University Press, 1995), 444; *Smale v. Hammon*, (1610) 80 Eng. Rep. 743; and *Anon.* (1580), Misc. MS 488/76, Lincoln's Inn, reprinted in *Sources of English Legal History: Private Law to 1750*, ed. J. H. Baker and S. F. C. Milsom (London: Butterworths, 1986), 638–39.

[15] *Oxford English Dictionary*, s.v. "ambidexter (n. & adj.)," September 2024, https://doi.org/10.1093/OED/4514941483.

[16] A. R. Heiserman, *Skelton and Satire* (Chicago: University of Chicago Press, 1961); Alvin Kernan, *The Cankered Muse: Satire of the English Renaissance* (New Haven, CT: Yale University Press, 1959); John Peter, *Complaint and Satire in Early English Literature* (Oxford: Clarendon Press, 1956); Laura Kendrick, "Medieval Satire," in *A Companion to Satire*, ed. Ruben Quintero (Malden, MA: Blackwell, 2007), 52–69; and John N. King, "Traditions of Complaint and Satire," in *A New Companion to English Renaissance Literature and Culture*, ed. Michael Hattaway, 2 vols. (Malden, MA: Blackwell, 2010), 2:326–40.

[17] Cyndia Susan Clegg, *Press Censorship in Elizabethan England* (Cambridge: Cambridge University Press, 1997), chap. 9; Debora K. Shuger, *Censorship and Cultural Sensibility: The Regulation of Language in Tudor-Stuart England* (Philadelphia: University of Pennsylvania Press, 2006), 85; William R. Jones, "The Bishops' Ban of 1599 and the Ideology of English Satire," *Literature Compass* 7, no. 5 (2010): 332–46; and Richard A. McCabe, "Elizabethan Satire and the Bishops' Ban of 1599," *Yearbook of English Studies* 11, no. 2 (1981): 188–93.

lampoons began to circulate in staggering numbers.[18] Such satires did little to upset the literary-legal nomenclature of this period, when they were known almost uniformly as "libels."[19]

During this same era, licensing – the pre-publication submission of manuscripts to government censors – remained the main mechanism of press regulation both in England and across Europe. Licensing, though, had its limits. It worked only on texts voluntarily submitted for authorized publication, a situation which led to a flourishing world of underground publishing, and scholars estimate that perhaps as many as half of all publications during this period were issued without a license.[20] Licensing also led to the growth of manuscript publication, especially for verse satires, thousands of which circulated by hand in the latter half of the seventeenth century.[21] It is worth noting that manuscript publication was a purely material rather than rhetorical form of evasion. The medium of circulation, rather than the verbal qualities of the satire, provided the protection.

Throughout the decades that followed the Restoration, however, two trends were on a collision course: the growth of verse libels as a wellspring of personal satire and political opposition; and the refinement of the law, and especially of libel laws, to police written works. In short, satire needed to change if it was going to circulate broadly in print. Writers like John Dryden responded by developing new satiric models, often structured around sustained irony and comic circumlocution, which came to inform satiric practice in the early eighteenth century, when we see a veritable explosion of printed satires by writers still familiar today: Jonathan Swift, Alexander Pope, John Gay, and Daniel Defoe. Later in his career, Dryden would also write a history and theory of satire that came to inform not only theoretical but also practical understandings of what satire is and how it ought to be written. His goal in part was to elevate and legitimize satire, precisely by distancing what he called "true Satires" from those nasty, direct, and artless manuscript lampoons. The well-mannered style that he defined – the tonal feature of disinterestedness, of dissembled

[18] See *Poems on Affairs of State: Augustan Satirical Verse, 1660–1714*, ed. George deF. Lord et al., 7 vols. (New Haven, CT: Yale University Press, 1963–75); and *Court Satires of the Restoration*, ed. John Harold Wilson (Columbus: Ohio State University Press, 1976).

[19] Harold Love, *English Clandestine Satire, 1660–1702* (Oxford: Oxford University Press, 2004), 7.

[20] Fredrick Seaton Siebert, *Freedom of the Press in England, 1476–1776: The Rise and Decline of Government Control* (Urbana: University of Illinois Press, 1965), 243; and D. F. McKenzie, *Making Meaning: "Printers of the Mind" and Other Essays*, ed. Peter D. McDonald and Michael F. Suarez (Amherst: University of Massachusetts Press, 2002), 131.

[21] *Poems on Affairs of State*, 1:xxvi.

indifference – came to mark and define the irony of eighteenth-century satire.[22] What we begin to witness, between the verse lampoons of the mid seventeenth century and the much more verbally ambiguous satires that followed, is a radical rhetorical break as verbal rather than material forms of evasion came to typify the satire that found its way into print.

The Foundations of Objective Interpretive Procedures

Drydenian irony posed a specific problem for the courts. Prosecutors and plaintiffs were suddenly forced to prove the seemingly impossible: that a bland compliment could be just as libelous as a defamatory accusation. Over the next two sections, I lay out how the courts came to navigate the problems posed by verbally evasive satire. I focus especially on the development of objective procedures for the courtroom interpretation of defamatory language. In response to satiric forms of verbal evasion, the crown developed a new strategy in the courts: a new courtroom hermeneutics with new protocols of reading.

This interpretive approach to verbal ambiguity was developed through a series of cases and rulings between roughly 1670 and 1730. One of the most important early cases was *King v. Lake* in 1671 under Justice (later Chief Justice) Sir Matthew Hale. This case was merely one in a series of lawsuits between the 1660s and 1670s between Edward King and Sir Edward Lake.[23] The significance of the 1671 case is surprising. At the heart of the trial was not an ambiguously libelous satire but on an overtly defamatory private letter that Lake had written and sent to Anne, Countess of Lincoln, in which he called King, a counsellor at law, "a griping lawyer" who would "milk [her] purse" in a "vexatious suit."[24] On its surface, then, *King v. Lake* has nothing to say directly about satire. But the justices' contemplation of the procedural and interpretive issues that defamatory language poses, whether such imputations were ambiguously idiomatic or

[22] John Dryden, *Discourse concerning the Original and Progress of Satire*, in *The Works of John Dryden*, vol. 4, *Poems 1693–1696*, ed. A. B. Chambers, William Frost, and Vinton A. Dearing (Berkeley: University of California Press, 1956–90), 9; Margaret Anne Doody, *The Daring Muse: Augustan Poetry Reconsidered* (Cambridge: Cambridge University Press, 1985), 211; and Steven N. Zwicker, "Dryden and the Invention of Irony," in *Swift's Travels: Eighteenth-Century Satire and Its Legacy*, ed. Nicholas Hudson and Aaron Santesso (Cambridge: Cambridge University Press, 2008), 74–90, at 75.

[23] For the earlier cases, see *King v. Lake*, (1664) 145 Eng. Rep. 499; *King v. Lake*, (1664) 145 Eng. Rep. 511; *King v. Lake* (1667), in Baker and Milsom, *Sources of English Legal History*, 652–54; *King v. Lake* (1668), in *A Source Book of English Law*, ed. A. K. R. Kiralfy (London: Sweet and Maxwell, 1957), 154–63; and *King v. Lake*, (1670) 145 Eng. Rep. 552.

[24] *King v. Lake*, (1671) 89 Eng. Rep. 12, 12. See also *King v. Lake*, (1671) 86 Eng. Rep. 289.

purposefully evasive, opened up a larger discussion of how to delimit the deliberations of jurors.

In the first place, the justices' ruling in the case further eroded and actively displaced *mitior sensus*, a doctrine traditionally used to guide the jury's interpretation of defamatory language.[25] According to this rule, jurors were encouraged to understand ambiguously defamatory language in its lesser, more innocuous sense.[26] Such an interpretive procedure created an opening for defendants. For instance, to claim that a man was a "murderer" might be defamatory, though this might only mean, in *mitiori sensu*, as Hale's colleagues reasoned, that he was a murderer of "hares."[27] The doctrine of *mitior sensus* was not officially abolished until 1714, but by the 1670s it was under intense judicial scrutiny. *King v. Lake* provided an opportunity for Hale and his colleagues to revisit the doctrine and to demonstrate the pressing need for more objective standards of interpretation.

King v. Lake also led to a critical revision to trial procedure in actions for defamation. With *mitior sensus* and its generous accommodation of far-fetched defenses set aside, the justices were able to install a theory of "common intendment." By the 1670s, common intendment already had a long history at law, especially in discussions of contracts and wills, and had been invoked in earlier trials for defamation.[28] However, common intendment became a feasible candidate for guiding the interpretation of defamatory language only at mid century, when judicial opposition to the older doctrine of *mitior sensus* had gained ground.[29] Where *mitior sensus* mandated that jurors always defer to the lesser, non-defamatory meaning of words, under common intendment jurors were instructed to interpret those same words in their most natural sense given the context of their utterance. It was precisely this theory that allowed the bench, and later crown prosecutors, to formulate a theoretically objective means of

25 Richard H. Helmholz, *The Oxford History of the Laws of England*, vol. 1, *The Canon Law and Ecclesiastical Jurisdiction from 597 to the 1640s* (Oxford: Oxford University Press, 2003), 577.

26 See *Morrison v. Cade*, (1607) Cro. Jac. 162; *Foster v. Browning*, (1624) 79 Eng. Rep. 596; and *Kilvert v. Roe*, (1625) 73 Eng. Rep. 1022.

27 *King*, 89 Eng. Rep. at 12.

28 See, for instance, Sir Thomas Littleton (or de Littleton), *Littleton's Tenures in English*, trans. Eugene Wambaugh (Littleton, CO: Rothman, 1985), sec. 646; and John Cowell, *The Interpreter: Or Booke, Containing the Signification of Words* (London, 1637), [I3]. See also Roger T. Simonds, *Rational Individualism: The Perennial Philosophy of Legal Interpretation* (Amsterdam: Rodopi, 1995); *Stamp v. White*, (1621) 79 Eng. Rep. 513; and *Peard v. Jones*, (1635) 79 Eng. Rep. 934.

29 See Henry Rolle, *Un Abridgment des Plusieurs Cases et Resolutions del Common Ley* (London, 1668), quoted in Baker, *Introduction to English Legal History*, 443.

assessment: a supposedly average or typical reader in lieu of a potentially idiosyncratic and unpredictable juror.

Over time, the courts expanded the use of these reasonable standards.[30] In 1694, for instance, Chief Justice Sir John Holt ruled that all words, no matter how ambiguous, should be understood in sociocentric terms. They should be taken, that is, "in a common sense according to the vulgar intendment of the by-standers."[31] It is worth noting, again, the standard being pointed to by the bench. When presented with a potentially defamatory statement, jurors were asked not what they individually and personally believed that statement to mean; instead, they were asked to imagine and conceptualize a rational abstraction: How might an ideal or typical English reader most commonly understand that statement?

The bench's theorization of this abstraction posed its own legal, conceptual, and practical problems. First, as Hale's colleagues on the bench readily conceded, common intendment failed wholly to isolate defamatory language. Words that seemed explicitly defamatory might still be deemed innocent given their immediate context. As the justices observed, even an apparently absurd defense in the abstract might prove entirely reasonable, justifiable, and obvious if "the circumstances do evince it."[32] Equally interesting was the willingness of later judges to cite the doctrine despite the dubious socio-linguistic assumptions built into any notion of linguistic commonality. In the courts, for instance, common intendment was understood as simply "common meaning."[33] But "common" could also possess a specific legal definition: a form of meaning or intention at common law; or a customary or reasonable interpretation, as determined by the law.[34] What exactly was "common" about those forms of intentionality or meaning, however, was harder to pin down. For instance, when applied to the interpretation of language, "common" by extension pointed to a broader sociological application: what was commonly, or generally, held to be the most obvious meaning of a given phrase among a group of listeners or readers. This was precisely the important legal-hermeneutic function the doctrine performed: that meaning was directly accessible precisely because

[30] For the codification of sociocentric doctrines of interpretation, see *State Law: Or, the Doctrine of Libels, Discussed and Examined*, 2nd ed. ([London], [1730]), 59–62, 74–76.

[31] *Somers v. House*, (1694) 90 Eng. Rep. 919, 919. [32] *King*, 89 Eng. Rep. at 12.

[33] John Rastell, *Les Termes de la Ley: Or, Certain Difficult and Obscure Words and Terms of the Common and Statute Laws of this Realm*, in *An Exposition of Certaine Difficult and Obscure Words* (1579) (London, 1721), 147. For this sense of the phrase, see the entry for "Domus instructa" in William Fulbecke, *A Direction or Preparative to the Study of the Lawe* (London, 1600), n.p.

[34] *Oxford English Dictionary*, s.v. "intendment (n.)," September 2023, https://doi.org/10.1093/OED/7178984602.

an entity known as the linguistically typical English listener or reader could be conceptualized and invoked in jury deliberations.

It is worth pausing to emphasize that these critical interventions in courtroom procedure and their consequences for both jury directions and works of satire were largely unintentional. At that moment, the judges were not seeking a mechanism to understand ambiguous works of satire. As Philip Hamburger has shown, it was only after licensing lapsed in 1695, when unregulated print including works of satire began to flourish, that the crown turned to newly repurposed libel laws as the primary means of regulating the press.[35] Nonetheless, *King v. Lake* was important because it helped to establish the government's post-licensing regulatory strategy both in modeling the bench's directions to juries across the seventeenth and eighteenth centuries and in formulating an interpretive abstraction for the courtroom interpretation of libelous language in works of satire that the bench would return to, expand, and refine again and again in the coming decades.

Satire in the Courts and the Refinement of Objective Interpretive Procedures

Among the rhetorical evasions that came to typify eighteenth-century satire, none was quite as effective and pervasive as verbal irony: to say one thing and yet simultaneously mean something else. It was also one of the most useful tools for complicating courtroom interpretive procedures for both the authorities and the courts. Ironic materials posed difficulties precisely because they necessitated the interpretation of the writer's (or defendant's) intentions. The libelous interpretation of ironic writings, that is, always turned on the disparity between an innocent surface meaning and a potentially defamatory or seditious intended meaning. This tension between the demands of the law and the interpretive requirements posed by irony came to a head in a trial for seditious libel in 1706.

The trial focused on a short mock-encomiastic poem published (though perhaps not written) by Dr. Joseph Browne. In the poem, entitled *The Country Parson's Honest Advice to the Judicious Lawyer, and Worthy Minister of State, My Lord Keeper*, the speaker, a straight-talking country parson,

[35] Hamburger, "Development of the Law of Seditious Libel," 724–25. On licensing, see Raymond Astbury, "The Renewal of the Licensing Act in 1693 and Its Lapse in 1695," *The Library*, 5th series 33, no. 4 (1978): 296–322; and "Commons' Reasons for not Renewing the Licensing Act, 1695," in *The Eighteenth-Century Constitution, 1688–1815: Documents and Commentary*, ed. E. Neville Williams (Cambridge: Cambridge University Press, 1960), 399–401.

praises eighteen noble lords, each for a different virtue, all ostensibly to lay out the best possible example for William Cowper, the Whig MP who had recently been nominated to the position of Lord Keeper of the Great Seal. The speaker advises:

> Be Wise as *Somerset*, as *Somers* Brave,
> As *Pembroke* Airy, and as *Richmond* Grave;
> Humble as *Orford* be; and *Wharton*'s Zeal;
> For Church and Loyalty wou'd fit thee well;
> Like *Sarum*, I wou'd have thee love the Church;
> He scorns to leave his Mother in the Lurch.
> For well governing your Family,
> Let pious *Haversham* thy Pattern be:
> And if it be thy Fate again to Marry,
> And *Seymour*'s Daughter will thy Year out tarry,
> May'st thou use her as *Mohun* his tender Wife,
> And may she lead his virtuous Lady's Life.
> To sum up all; *Devonshire*'s Chastity,
> *Bolton*'s Merit, *Goldolphin*'s Probity,
> *Halifax* his Modesty, *Essex*'s Sense,
> *Montague*'s Managment, *Culpepper*'s Pence,
> *Tenison*'s Learning, and *Southampton*'s Wit,
> Will make thee for an able States-man fit.[36]

Three hundred years later, one might be hard pressed to call *The Country Parson's Honest Advice* a masterpiece of early modern satire. Its value lies, instead, not only in the trial that resulted from its publication, but also in the ironic method the poem employs. Most notable is the poem's encomiastic plainness and consistency, an ironic system of wholesale inversion. The virtue associated with each lord points precisely to the quality each man was thought painfully to lack. "Pious" (line 8) John Thompson, Lord Haversham, for instance, was a notorious adulterer and occasional conformist; William Cavendish, Fourth Earl and First Duke of Devonshire, a man "famous for Debauchery [and] Lewdness," was hardly known for his "Chastity" (line 13).[37] Without the necessary local knowledge about these lords, it would have been very hard, at a textual level, to detect the irony here – that key disparity between the surface meaning (mere praise) and the intended meaning (a series of cutting insults). At the time,

[36] [Joseph Browne?], *The Country Parson's Honest Advice to the Judicious Lawyer, and Worthy Minister of State, My Lord Keeper* (London, 1706), reprinted in *Poems on Affairs of State*, 7:156–59.

[37] John Dunton, *The Hazard of a Death-Bed Repentance* (London, 1708), 38; and Thomas Hearne, *Remarks and Collections*, 11 vols., ed. C. E. Doble et al. (Oxford: Clarendon Press, 1885–1921), 2:39–40.

contemporaries saw the work exactly for what it was.[38] As Thomas Hearne observed, the poem "severely reflects (but Ironically) on divers Great Men."[39] Again, though, it is worth pointing to why such a form of irony proved so difficult for the courts. Despite Browne's irony being obvious – it was, as Thomas Keymer has put it, a "blatant sarcasm" to its first readers – *The Country Parson's Honest Advice*'s epideixis remained unambiguously positive at a purely semantic or linguistic level.[40] That surface quality hardly hindered lay interpretation, but it did trouble courtroom procedures that early on remained focused on surface rather than intended meanings.

When Browne and the poem were finally put on trial for seditious libel in 1706, irony became the focus of the case. The other facts of the prosecution were quickly established. Browne's printer, Hugh Mear, had earlier identified him, and Browne himself admitted in his deposition to Erasmus Lewis, the undersecretary of state, that he had given the poem over to Mear to be printed and sold and thus made public.[41] (While awaiting trial, Browne had foolishly made similar concessions in a tongue-in-cheek public letter to the secretary of state, Robert Harley, for which he later faced a second prosecution for seditious libel.[42]) Those were the easy facts to establish.

However, in order for the poem to be interpreted as a seditious libel, the crown also needed to demonstrate to the jurors, who were charged with determining the meaning of the poem, that it was in fact ironic insults rather than mere praise.[43] This entailed its own problems. Take the poem's opening line: "Be Wise as *Somerset*." It was up to the jury to decide whether this ought to be interpreted strictly – that is, that the line simply means that Somerset is wise – or interpreted ironically (i.e., that Somerset is dimwitted).[44] Moreover, by putting this issue of fact to the jury, the crown was inevitably dragging in questions of malice and intent that the

[38] Keymer, *Poetics of the Pillory*, 124.
[39] Hearne, *Remarks and Collections*, 1:176.
[40] Keymer, *Poetics of the Pillory*, 99.
[41] Historical Manuscripts Commission, *Manuscripts of the Duke of Portland*, 10 vols. (London: Her Majesty's Stationery Office, 1899), 4:282.
[42] Joseph Browne, *A Letter to the Right Honourable Mr. Secretary Harley, by Dr. Browne* (London, 1706).
[43] Richard H. Helmholz, "Civil Trials and the Limits of Responsible Speech," in *Juries, Libel, and Justice: The Role of the English Juries in Seventeenth- and Eighteenth-Century Trials for Libel and Slander* (Los Angeles, CA: William Andrews Clark Memorial Library, 1984), 3–36.
[44] Richard H. Helmholz, *Select Cases on Defamation to 1600* (London: Selden Society, 1985), xcii–xcv; Knightley D'Anvers, *A General Abridgment of the Common Law* (London, 1722–25), 1:140; and William Sheppard, *Action upon the Case for Slander*, 2nd ed. (London, 1674), 20.

court's chief justice, Sir John Holt, had deemed immaterial to the crime in a series of earlier cases.[45]

In court, Browne's defense proved a shambles. Once the prosecution established the lone necessary question of fact – that Browne had copied the libel down – the case was open and shut, and the jury found Browne guilty. His counsel, however, submitted a motion in arrest of judgment, claiming that Holt had denied the jury the opportunity to speak to a separate question of fact: whether the poem meant what the prosecution claimed it to mean. The words of the poem, they argued, "did not import a scandal, but, in their natural signification, carry a credit."[46] The Attorney General responded that the jury had already spoken to that fact, and that it had been incumbent on the defense to demonstrate that the poem was innocuous praise. The poem "gives every lord a character ironically," he argued, "and so 'tis set forth in an information, and the jury find him guilty."[47] As the Attorney General continued, Browne "ought to have shewed at the trial that he did not intend to scandalize them."[48] Interestingly, in claiming that the work was written ironically, the crown was shifting the burden of proof from the prosecution to the defense. Chief Justice Holt agreed. Defendants needed to demonstrate that seemingly ironic phrases were wholly innocent. But he also took this argument a step further, ruling that "it was answered and resolved by the Court, that this [poem was . . .] ironical, and whether 'twas so or not, the jury were judges; they found it so."[49] In short, the prosecution could raise the possibility of irony and the jurors were tasked with confirming it.

Holt's decision to defer to the jury was undergirded by a clear sense that ironic meaning was produced by a community of readers, rather than a mechanistic set of verbal signals. In this way, Holt might be thought of as a kind of Fishian *avant la lettre*.[50] This "sociocentric" view of ironic interpretation holds that readers are ultimately responsible for ironic meaning, and that interpretation is a learned set of conventions produced by the institutions that have authorized them.[51] Putting it slightly

[45] *R. v. Paine*, (1696) 87 Eng. Rep. 584; *R. v. Bear* [sic], (1698) 90 Eng. Rep. 1132; *R. v. Bear* [sic], (1699) 91 Eng. Rep. 363; and *R. v. Beare*, (1698) 91 Eng. Rep. 1175. See Hamburger, "Development of the Law of Seditious Libel," 703–08, 726–33.

[46] *R. v. Brown* [sic], (1706) 88 Eng. Rep. 911, 911.

[47] *R. v. Browne*, (1706) 90 Eng. Rep. 1134, 1134.

[48] *Brown*, 88 Eng. Rep. at 912.

[49] *Browne*, 90 Eng. Rep. at 1134.

[50] Stanley Fish, "Short People Got No Reason to Live: Reading Irony," *Daedalus* 112, no. 1 (Winter 1983), 175–91, at 189.

[51] Wayne C. Booth, "A New Strategy for Establishing a Truly Democratic Criticism," *Daedalus* 112, no. 1 (Winter 1983): 193–214, at 197.

differently, we understand locutions as ironic not because they contain simple ironic signals that all (or at least most) readers should be able to identify and decode, but because our entire practice of reading and interpretation is a product of habits authorized by the institutions within which we read. More importantly, Holt saw the potential hazards of allowing irony as a defense. "If this were not a crime," he explained, then any writer "might by contraries libel any person." As Holt concluded, "An information will lie for speaking *ironically*."[52] Satirists, once seemingly liberated by irony – its curious reversals in meaning, its susceptibility to both innocuous and lacerating interpretations – were now its clearest victims. Prosecutors needed only to assert its mere existence, forcing the defendant to prove that a dubious locution was perfectly innocent.

The ruling was confirmed – Browne was found guilty – and, in the process, the law was revised. *R. v. Browne* was simply one ruling in a series that sought to constrain the subjectivity of jurors, who had tremendous discretion in trials for libel and often bucked the directions of the bench.[53] As we saw earlier, "common intendment" held that jurors were expected to interpret words in their most natural sense given the context of their utterance.[54] In Browne's case, the courts extended this line of thought to ironic materials. As Holt had earlier argued, words should be taken "in a common sense according to the vulgar intendment of the by-standers."[55] That is, interpretation should rely on an abstract "common reader" – how a juror believed most people would have understood a phrase, rather than merely the way an individual juror did.[56] Such a rule in practice meant that the courts could defer to the jury in the abstract while effectively displacing the capricious interpretations of actual jurors in practice. The result was a hypothetical juror, who read in more coherent, more reasonable, and more predictable ways.

This legal logic was extended just over two decades later, when the courts finally turned to allegory, a satiric tool that had flourished especially in the satiric secret histories authored by Aphra Behn and Delarivier Manley and in the genres of parallel history and fake news from abroad employed in the growing periodical press of the 1710s and 1720s. The courts took up allegory directly in a trial for the so-called Persian Letter, a Jacobite allegory that had appeared in *Mist's Weekly Journal*, one of the

[52] *Browne*, 90 Eng. Rep. at 1134.

[53] J. M. Beattie, *Crime and the Courts in England, 1660–1800* (Princeton, NJ: Princeton University Press, 1986), 400–49; and Baker, *Introduction to English Legal History*, 143–44, 151.

[54] *King*, 89 Eng. Rep. at 12. [55] *Somers*, 90 Eng. Rep. at 919.

[56] "Trial of Mr. Richard Francklin," 666–68.

most popular political periodicals of this period.[57] The letter seemingly describes a foreign usurpation, but it was clear to both the authorities and onlookers that Persia and its politics were nothing more than winking Jacobite stand-ins for the graft and sleaze of the Walpole government and the royal family. Persia, the letter states, had long been governed by the "old Usurper *Meryweis*" (George I), before being handed over to the ham-fisted mismanagement of "*Esreff*, the present Usurper" (George II). Apparently, Esreff was illegitimate, a fact disclosed by two secret "Writings" held in the possession of a "High Priest" and Meryweis's "Favorite Concubine" (the Duchess of Kendall, George I's former mistress). The "Chief Scribe" (Sir Robert Walpole), however, had gained access to the writings, and was using the secret to "purchase [Esreff's/George I's] Friendship"; the Chief Scribe was also being "*screened* by *Esreff*'s Authority, from the Cries of the People, who were groaning under the Load of his Depredations." Esreff, who is all "Avarice," "Ambition," and "Vanity," is a "Tyrant" who has displaced "the lawful Sophi" (James Francis Edward Stuart). Sophi, nonetheless, retains his "Patience," knowing providence will set the kingdom right.[58]

The Persian Letter was widely read as a coded Jacobite attack on the crown. As the pro-ministry *London Journal* sneered, it was nothing more than "High Treason among the People against their King and Country."[59] Nonetheless, there was little the authorities could do to either the letter's pseudonymous author, Amos Dudge (actually Philip, Duke of Wharton, a wishy-washy Jacobite living abroad in exile), or the journal's editor-proprietor, Nathaniel Mist, who had gone into hiding.[60] Instead, the government sought to dismantle the journal's operations, arresting some twenty pressmen, printers, hawkers, and booksellers tied to *Mist's*, which led to further arrests and grand jury indictments in Middlesex, Westminster, and Bristol.[61] The government initiated prosecutions against at least eight of Mist's stationers, four of whom were eventually found guilty of seditious libel.[62]

57 See Matthew Thomas Symonds, "Grub Street Culture: The Newspapers of Nathaniel Mist, 1716–1737" (Ph.D. diss., University College London, 2007), chap. 7.

58 *Mist's Weekly Journal*, no. 175 (August 24, 1728).

59 *London Journal*, no. 477 (September 21, 1728).

60 See Lawrence B. Smith, "Wharton, Philip James, Duke of Wharton and Jacobite Duke of Northumberland (1698–1731)," *Oxford Dictionary of National Biography* (2004), https://doi.org/10.1093/ref:odnb/29171.

61 "Trial of Mr. Richard Francklin," 666–67n.; and Paul Chapman, "Mist, Nathaniel (d. 1737)," *Oxford Dictionary of National Biography* (2004), https://doi.org/10.1093/ref:odnb/18822.

62 *Monthly Chronicle*, November 28, 1728, reprinted in *Monthly Chronicle* ([London,] [1728–32]), 1:247, and *Monthly Chronicle*, February 25, 1729, reprinted in *Monthly Chronicle*, 2:33.

The most useful of these trials to the crown was the ruling in the case against a printer for Mist, John Clarke (rather than Clerk, as he is known today in the decision on the case).[63] In Clarke's case, the crown knew that it was facing the procedural conundrum always posed by allegory. How was one to demonstrate legally that this supposedly innocent letter from Persia was actually a Jacobite screed confected from "odious Parallels"?[64] In their correspondence on the trial, both the Attorney General and the Solicitor General pointed to this problem, noting that "the whole paper is Allegorical" and that they must demonstrate to *whom* the libel actually referred. That meant convincing "a Jury that the name *Sophi*," for example, "was intended by the persons concern'd in printing to signify the Pretender[,] . . . a term never used for him before."[65] Nonetheless, they remained confident that the crown would be able to prove that "several of the Royal Family" had been "scandalously traduced under borrowed names."[66]

When Clarke went to trial on February 25, 1728/29, he was defended by William Hawkins. A serjeant-at-law, Hawkins knew the difficulties the crown faced. As he wrote years earlier, "I have heard it agreed in the Court of King's Bench" that "no Writing whatsoever is to be esteemed a Libel, unless it reflect upon some particular Person."[67] During Clarke's case, he raised this issue, arguing that the Persian Letter could not be construed as a reflection on either Walpole or George II. Hawkins asserted that there was a stark disparity between those ostensibly depicted in the letter and their reputations in real life.[68] In short, how could honest, upstanding Walpole ever be equated with the crafty High Scribe, who was shielding an illegitimate monarch, whom the crown, incredibly, claimed to be the wholly lawful King George II?

Interestingly, this reasoning enabled the Attorney General to demonstrate the tenor of the allegory. On its surface, Hawkins's argument was old hat. He was pushing the crown not simply to decode the allegory – to state that George II was Esreff – but also to demonstrate *how* the text corresponded with a public perception of George II as an illegitimate tyrant. In so doing, however, Hawkins was also returning to a defense that had failed more than twenty years earlier in Browne's trial – a case he knew

[63] *An Account of Persons Held to Bail to Answer in the Court of King's Bench for Libels, from 1 Anne to 57 Geo. 3 Both Inclusive*, ed. E. H. Lushington (March 3, 1818), 10, entry 74, KB 33/24/2, The National Archives, Kew, United Kingdom.
[64] *Monthly Chronicle*, February 25, 1729, reprinted in *Monthly Chronicle*, 2:32.
[65] SP 36/151/56–57, The National Archives, Kew.
[66] *R. v. Clerk* [sic], (1728/29) 94 Eng. Rep. 207, 207.
[67] Hawkins, *Treatise of the Pleas of the Crown*, 2:195.
[68] *Clerk*, 94 Eng. Rep. at 207.

well[69] – by wrongly claiming that irony prohibited jurors from reading ostensibly innocent constructions in a defamatory manner.

Chief Justice Raymond picked up immediately on Hawkins's claim and rejected it, citing the earlier ruling in *R. v. Browne*. This is why we might think of Hawkins's defense as an argumentative gaffe. In denying the justness of representing George II as a hapless Persian tyrant, Hawkins was also pointing directly to the form of ironic inversion that had permitted the conviction of Browne – a kind of distorted satiric mirroring, in which one's virtues were one's vices. Hawkins was revealing, that is, how one could arrive at a libelous reading of the allegory. There was not a *direct* allegorical correspondence between the satiric representation and the real-world victim; there was, instead, an *inverse* correspondence between the two. We know that the tyrannical Esreff is George II not because George II is tyrannical, but precisely because he is *not*.

This misstep opened the door for the Attorney General to pursue a new argument, at least as it pertained to allegory, one that drew on the sociocentric interpretation of verbal irony. As the Attorney General argued, "it lies upon the counsel for the King only to shew, that this construction, which they've put upon the paper, is such, as the generality of readers must take it in according to the obvious and natural sense of it." The crown, that is, was obliged only to assert the allegorical meaning of the text, based on a theoretical community of idealized readers. The jury, in turn, had only to agree that this hypothetical "generality of readers" would, indeed, read the allegory in this manner. Chief Justice Raymond also "agreed the law to be so," pointed to *R. v. Browne*, and noted that "the Crime was even greater for making the Parallel."[70]

Such a rule in practice meant that the crown could defer to the jury in the abstract while effectively displacing the capricious interpretations of actual jurors in court. In this sense, the decision in *R. v. Clerk* belongs to an important series of eighteenth-century rulings that sought to neutralize jurors, who often had tremendous discretion in trials for libel and who often fought the directions of the bench, especially in trials for seditious libel.[71] The crown could not stop jurors from interpreting the text, but it could control the heuristic of their interpretation.

69 Hawkins, *Treatise of the Pleas of the Crown*, 1:194.

70 *Clerk*, 94 Eng. Rep. at 207; *Monthly Chronicle*, February 25, 1729, reprinted in *Monthly Chronicle*, 2:33.

71 Thomas A. Green, *Verdict According to Conscience: Perspectives on the English Criminal Trial Jury, 1200–1800* (Chicago: University of Chicago Press, 1985), chaps. 7 and 8, esp. 249, 329.

Of the many trials that resulted from the Persian Letter, the ruling in *R. v. Clerk* proved a major advancement in the government's ongoing efforts to develop courtroom procedures for fixing verbal ambiguity in potentially defamatory and seditious publications. The government had solved the problem of "*libellous Parallels*";[72] eventually this notion of the "generality of readers" became a commonly accepted doctrine.[73] Just a few years later, for instance, Attorney General Sir Philip Yorke pointed to the ruling in his final statement to the jury in the prosecution of Richard Francklin. As he argued then, "fictitious names" should be "plainly . . . understood as if their names were particularly mentioned." They should, in short, be "understood . . . as every common reader would" understand them.[74] This is why the supposedly reasonable and objective standards proved so important. The construction of a purely hypothetical community of readers, who read in predictable and normative ways, became a potent tool for mitigating jury recalcitrance that slowly eroded the interpretive latitude of jurors themselves. Moreover, the "common reader" was not built on a *linguistic* theory (that is, how, technically, irony or allegory signifies), but was fashioned from a sociocentric understanding: how communities of readers coalesce around a *collective* understanding of a given verbal object, statement, or idiom.

Libel, Satire, and the Growth of Objective Means of Assessment

In theorizing this purely hypothetical community of readers who might read in predictable and normative ways, the crown and the courts leapt out ahead of the literary field in their legal attempts to redress the question of semantic doubling in works of irony and allegory. Early modern forms of literary criticism struggled well into the eighteenth century to explain how readers went from a text's innocent surface meaning to the latent and yet somehow accessible intended meaning.[75] Verbal irony was particularly difficult. Not until the 1720s and 1730s did irony start to feature more prominently in early works of literary theory. Even then, though, critics often fell back on a stock formulation, one that did little to explain how readers moved from a surface meaning to an intended one: irony was

[72] *The Craftsman*, no. 140 (March 8, 1728/29).

[73] Laurence Hanson, *Government and the Press, 1695–1763* (Oxford: Clarendon Press, 1967), 24. See *State Law*, 57.

[74] "Trial of Mr. Richard Francklin," 666–68.

[75] Norman Knox, *The Word Irony and Its Context, 1500–1755* (Durham, NC: Duke University Press, 1961), 141.

saying the contrary, or opposite, of what one means.[76] Perhaps most interestingly, critics claimed that the easiest way to detect irony was not verbally but typographically, by "print[ing] some ambiguous Words in significant *Italick* Characters."[77]

The long-term consequences of this interaction between libel law and satire were significant. For the law, these new interpretive doctrines had a pronounced effect on both the courtroom interpretation of ambiguous language and the relationship between the jury and the bench. Objective interpretive procedures proved a useful model for jury directions more generally and an important precursor to later "reasonable man [or person]" standards, first established in 1837, particularly in their shared implicit appeal to standardized mechanisms of assessment.[78] Such interpretive doctrines did not directly influence the emergence of the reasonable-person standard, but they helped to develop a line of legal logic in their implicit recourse to objective personifications (whether the reasonable person on the one hand, or the common reader on the other).[79] As a result, we can identify in these cases the growth of supposedly objective means of assessment in the courts' appeal to an abstract standard, one that continues to influence jury directions in Anglo-American law today.[80]

We might point to equally long-term consequences for literature. The reliance of eighteenth-century satirists on verbal indirection – particularly in the forms of sustained irony and allegory – was largely the product of legal pressures. Verbal evasion sought to trouble extant courtroom procedures, which often had great difficulty in making sense of implicit, inverse, or obscure meanings. It was these verbal evasions that objective interpretive procedures directly targeted, often successfully, especially during the first few decades of the eighteenth century. Eventually, over the course of

[76] Knox, *Word Irony*, 30. In his *Dictionary* (London, 1755), for instance, Samuel Johnson calls it a "mode of speech in which the meaning is contrary to the words."

[77] Thomas Gordon, *The Humourist* (London, 1725), 2:99–102. See also [Thomas Gordon], *The Art of Railing at Great Men* (London, 1723), 16; *The Craftsman*, no. 580 (September 12, 1730); and [Francis Squire], *A Faithful Report of a Genuine Debate concerning the Liberty of the Press* (London, 1740), 18.

[78] *Vaughan v. Menlove*, (1837) 173 Eng. Rep. 232. See also Baker, *Introduction to English Legal History*, 414; [Francis Buller], *An Introduction to the Law Relative to Trials at Nisi Prius* (London, 1767), 25; William Jones, *Treatise on the Law of Bailments* (London, 1781), 6; and *Jones v. Bird*, (1822) 5 B. & Ald. 845.

[79] Simon Stern, "*R v Jones* (1703)," in *Landmark Cases in Criminal Law*, ed. Phil Handler, Henry Mares, and Ian Williams (Oxford: Hart, 2017), 59–79; and Alan D. Miller and Ronen Perry, "The Reasonable Person," *New York University Law Review* 87, no. 2 (May 2012): 323–92.

[80] Mayo Moran, *Rethinking the Reasonable Person: An Egalitarian Reconstruction of the Objective Standard* (Oxford: Oxford University Press, 2003), 1.

the succeeding decades and centuries, legal pressures gradually diminished as ever broader definitions of press freedom emerged. In turn, satirists were increasingly able to criticize both their victims and the government more directly. Nonetheless, verbal ambiguity had become such a fundamental feature of satire that satirists themselves continued, and continue today, to employ these same verbal evasions in spite of the absence of the regulations that helped to produce them. Such a consideration of satire and libel law shows how this interplay between two fields, often siloed off in higher education and scholarship alike, had reciprocal effects in both domains, the consequences of which can still be seen and felt today.

CHAPTER 2

Perpendicular Publics

Contesting Infrastructure at Early Eighteenth-Century Rail Crossings

David Alff

In the second book of his *Wealth of Nations* (1776), Adam Smith explains how banks turn society's idle cash reserves into "tools to work with" and "subsistence to work for."[1] Before they are deposited in a bank, the merchant's gold and silver coins resemble a "highway [that] carries to market all the grass and corn of the country, [but] produces not a single pile of either."[2] Smith's simile reveals how minted metal absorbs some of the value it bears, like a road that conveys harvests by occupying tillage. "The judicious operations of banking," Smith continues, displace wealth from frozen species into promissory notes, "providing, if I may be allowed so violent a metaphor, a sort of wagon-way through the air, enabling the country to convert, as it were, a great part of its highways into good pastures, and corn fields, and thereby to increase, very considerably, the annual produce of its land and labour."[3] Paper notes circulate wealth without locking it into the exchange medium, a convenience that Smith likens to land that is both fertile and traversable. Cultivation and conveyance become simultaneously possible thanks to banking's "wagon-way through the air," a feat of metaphorical engineering that Smith's readers have pictured as a skyway lofting over georgical abundance and the hard realm of monetary trade-offs.[4]

Eager to understand the figure's tenor (banking), we presume to recognize its vehicle (wagon-way). But what was a wagon-way, exactly, and how might one sail "through the air"? In 1776, the term "wagon-way" – or "wagonway," as it was often printed – could refer to any road suitable for

[1] Adam Smith, *The Wealth of Nations*, ed. Edwin Cannan (1776; New York: Modern Library, 2000), 349.

[2] Smith, *Wealth of Nations*, 349.

[3] Smith, *Wealth of Nations*, 349.

[4] Gavin Kennedy writes, "The eighteenth-century reader was immediately struck by a vivid image of something she had never seen nor probably had even imagined, but she knows immediately from having seen real wagons pulled by horses guided by their drivers, trundling along country roads loaded with hay or corn." *An Authentic Account of Adam Smith* (Edinburgh: Springer International, 2018), 52.

Figure 2.1 John Buddle, "A Representation of a Coal Waggon," in *General Magazine of Arts and Sciences* 14, no. 6 (June 1764). From the British Library archive.

wagons: A "highway," suggests Maria Pia Paganelli, or the "high road" that Smith mentions in his lectures on jurisprudence, claims Hugh Rockoff.[5] It is possible that Smith had such a cart path in mind, though his interest in transportation technology suggests a more precise referent. In the eighteenth century, a wagonway usually signified wooden tracks that British miners laid across land to carry coal from hillside pits to river ports. Wagonways consisted of rails, often oak, pinned to beech-beam ties sunken into beds of ship ballast, which together formed a makeshift track. This track hosted wagons: horse-drawn, flange-wheeled hoppers heaped with bituminous piles (Figure 2.1). Daniel Defoe described this assemblage of landscaping and carpentry as a "great machine" and "artificial road" to distinguish the wagonways he observed in Newcastle and Bath from England's existing scramble of grass lanes and dirt paths.[6] Wagonways are today recognized as an equine-powered ancestor of the modern railway.

[5] Maria Pia Paganelli, "Vanity and Daedalian Wings of Paper Money in Adam Smith," in *New Voices on Adam Smith*, ed. Eric Schlieser and Leonidas Montes (London: Routledge, 2006), 271–90, at 276; Hugh Rockoff, "Parallel Journeys: Adam Smith and Milton Friedman on the Regulation of Banking," in *Beyond Liquidity: The Metaphor of Money in Financial Crisis*, ed. Brad Pasanek and Simone Polillo (London: Routledge, 2013), 24–52, at 25–26.

[6] Daniel Defoe, *The Complete English Tradesman*, 2 vols. (London: Charles Rivington, 1727), 2:29.

As an economist who extolled roads, canals, and river navigations as the "greatest of all improvements" for their capacity to "put the remote parts of the country more nearly upon a level with those in the neighborhood of the town," Smith appreciated the special importance of coal trams to Britain's industrial development.[7] He would have employed the term "wagon-way" with according exactitude. Having grown up east of the Dunfermline coalfields and having subsequently lived in the coal entrepôts of Edinburgh and Glasgow, Smith would have encountered wagonways, real and projected, throughout his life.[8] Indeed, *The Wealth of Nations* appears to reference railed transport itself when it describes a miner who "employs in sinking his shafts, in erecting engines for drawing out the water, in making roads and wagon-ways."[9] That Smith distinguishes "roads" from "wagon-ways" implies that he recognized the latter as a distinct form of freight conveyance.

Coal transport gave Smith a metaphor for banking's rejuvenation of dead stock. That Smith calls this trope "violent" implies he knew that his trope strained the relationship it posits. Wagonways seldom flew through the air. To the contrary, they crossed at ground level whatever land happened to lie between a pithead and the river docks where coal was chuted onto lighters. Before conveying coal, miners had to obtain permission to lay tracks over a checkerboard landscape of fields, pastures, parks, estates, and wastes – disparate grounds held by bishops, corporations, farmers, the crown, and, sometimes, inopportunely, rival coal magnates. In an era before Parliament routinely condemned property to establish legal ways for transportation projects, surveyors, landholders, and their lawyers disputed where wagonways could go – where, in the language of *The Wealth of Nations*, the circulation of "grass and corn" would be permitted to diminish its cultivation. Smith's knowing catachresis at once references and ignores a long history of conflict.

As early modern wagonways expanded to service Britain's appetite for fuel, they encountered not only tillage but roads. Except in the rare instances where wagonways bridged over or burrowed under highways,

7 Smith, *Wealth of Nations*, 170. In her 1733 *Description of Bath*, poet Mary Chandler similarly marvels at a "new made Road, and wonderful machine," the wagonway that Ralph Allen built to carry limestone from mines through his Prior Park estate and onto barges in the River Avon. See *Description of Bath* (Bath: James Leake, 1736), 16.

8 The Tranent Colliery Waggonway, outside Edinburgh, cut through the battlefield of Prestonpans, site of Jacobite victory during the 1745 uprising. In 1770, Smith's friend James Watt published his design of a wagonway to draw coal from barges on his projected Monkland Canal up into central Glasgow. See *A Scheme for Making a Navigable Canal from the City of Glasgow to the Monkland Coalierys* (Glasgow, 1770), 9.

9 Smith, *Wealth of Nations*, 334.

the meeting of rail and road generated a level crossing. The phrase "level crossing" describes any place where rails overlay road, and in so doing extend a right of way to two or more streams of transverse traffic. The rail–road crossing's permissory overlap engenders what John Stilgoe calls a "micro-environment" that meshes "two landscapes into something new."[10] This literal "intersection of the mobile elements" (to borrow Michel de Certeau's phrase) confronted travelers with inconvenience and hazard.[11] One might wait at an intersection, or crash. Such contingencies posed difficult questions for the authors and interpreters of common law: What vehicles should take priority and when? What forms of traffic bolstered and vitiated the common good? What conduits warranted the status of public work, and which could be considered equipment for private gain?

These problems stem from the crossing's unavoidable – even archetypal – ambivalence, its conflation of the "multiple, overlapping, or nested forms of sovereignty" that Keller Easterling finds intrinsic to infrastructural space.[12] Crossings result from people moving themselves and their things from one place to another. They manifest movement "not [as] a casting about the hard surfaces of a world in which everything is already laid out," claims Tim Ingold, "but [as] an issuing along with things in the very process of their generation."[13] As topographical residue of the traffic they route, crossings tell a "simultaneity of stories-so-far" in Doreen Massey's phrase.[14] Their "coexisting heterogeneity" attests to infrastructure's intensification – whereby one plot of earth carries multiple forms of traffic – as well as a border at which the traveler's expectation of continuous progress runs into contravening matter.[15] Crossings mark infrastructure's overabundance and dearth, what S. I. Johnston calls "liminal points or transitional gaps between defined, bounded areas, that is, between roads or between the areas of land that roads define."[16]

[10] John Stilgoe, *Metropolitan Corridor: Railroads and the American Scene* (New Haven, CT: Yale University Press, 1985), 167, 188.

[11] Michel de Certeau, *The Practice of Everyday Life* (Berkeley: University of California Press, 1984), 117.

[12] Keller Easterling, *Extrastatecraft: The Power of Infrastructure Space* (New York: Verso, 2016), 15.

[13] Tim Ingold, *Being Alive: Essays on Movement, Knowledge, and Description* (London: Routledge, 2011), 12.

[14] Doreen Massey, *For Space* (London: Sage Publications, 2005), 9.

[15] Massey, *For Space*, 9.

[16] S. I. Johnston, "Crossroads," *Zeitschrift für Papyrologie und Epigraphik* 88 (1991): 217–24, at 218. Bernard Dionysius Geohegan also employs the language of "gap" to describe those instances "where an infrastructure only partially fulfills the promise of smooth and continuous transitions among heterogeneous parts and sites," resulting in a "slight rupture or assonance." "Mind the Gap: Spiritualism and the Infrastructural Uncanny," *Critical Inquiry* 42, no. 4 (2016): 899–922, at 900.

The level crossing's vacillation between convergence and rupture made it a rich subject for literary meditation. The "intrinsically ambivalent and polymorphous" deity Hecate presides over intersections in Greek mythology.[17] Crossings famously cause collisions, as at the "crossing of three ways" where the rash and slighted Oedipus Rex slays his father, unwittingly fulfilling the oracle foretelling his own doom.[18] Crossings also confounded heroes of seventeenth- and eighteenth-century fiction, like Christian of *Pilgrim's Progress* (1678), who, along with his traveling companion, Hopeful, strays from the right road at a junction where "a way put itself into their way, and seemed withal to lie as straight as the way which they should go."[19] London's tortuous Seven Dials intersection likewise bewilders the London tourist who "with enquiring face / Bewilder'd, trudges on from place to place" in John Gay's burlesque manual of pedestrianism, *Trivia: Or the Art of Walking the Streets of London* (1716).[20]

Where literary authors staged crossing conflicts in drama, poetry, and fiction, this chapter focuses on the forms of writing that emerged from legal disputes about wagonways in the early eighteenth century. Combining the methods of law and literature with recent insights from infrastructure studies, I examine the "stories, explanations, performances, [and] linguistic exchanges" that coalesced around one violently contested wagonway intersection.[21] I show how this crossing spurred an outpouring of legal writing that struggled to fix the relationship between private freight conduits and the public's interest in unencumbered roads. This fight took place during the summer of 1705 at the intersection of the Gnoll Hill colliery wagonway and the king's highway in the Glamorganshire vale of Neath. Extant accounts of the conflict reveal how early modern public works emerged not simply through sovereign imposition or as an

[17] Simon Hornblower and Antony Spawforth, eds., *The Oxford Classical Dictionary* (New York: Oxford University Press, 1996), 671. These ghostly grounds became sites of parochial abjection, "among the few appropriate places to leave materials expelled from society." Johnston, "Crossroads," 220. These ejected materials included the bodies of suicide victims, who were customarily buried beneath the signposts that helped travelers navigate intersections. When Samuel Richardson's Pamela contemplates suicide, she wonders whether her captor Mr. B. would "order me a decent Funeral, and save me, or rather this Part of me, from the dreadful stake, and the Highway Interment." *Pamela; or, Virtue Rewarded*, ed. Thomas Keymer and Alice Wakely (1740; Oxford: Oxford University Press, 2001), 173.

[18] Sophocles, *Oedipus: King of Thebes*, ed. Gilbert Murray (New York: Oxford University Press, 1911), 42.

[19] John Bunyan, *The Pilgrim's Progress*, ed. Roger Sharrock (1678; New York: Penguin, 1987), 115.

[20] John Gay, *Trivia: Or the Art of Walking the Streets of London* (London: Bernard Lintott, 1716), 16.

[21] Paul Gewirtz, "Narrative and Rhetoric in the Law," in *Law's Stories: Narrative and Rhetoric in the Law*, ed. Peter Brooks and Paul Gewirtz (New Haven, CT: Yale University Press, 1996), 2–13, at 2.

unthought material stratum – as infrastructure is sometimes construed today – but as a call to arbitration, an occasion for people to decide upon the costs and benefits of national amenities.

If "infrastructures are matter that enable the movement of other matter," as Brian Larkin claims, this chapter parses an instance in which eighteenth-century industrialists tried to account for one form of mobilized matter's interference with another.[22] I show how this accounting employed legal diction, specifically the rhetoric of "nuisance" and "riot," to describe the crossing's potential intrusion on public prerogative. Answering Marian Valverde's lament that "legal scholarship has not played much of a role in the so-called infrastructure turn," this chapter shows how writers debating infrastructural intersections used the rhetoric and process of the law to define the conditions under which an eighteenth-century public work could exist.[23] This appropriation of legal lexicon constitutes one early attempt at defining infrastructure itself not as a material category but as a battery of mutual obligations.

Crossing Neath

In 1686, the Shropshire lawyer Sir Humphrey Mackworth married Mary Evans, Welsh heiress to an estate in Neath, a market town upriver from Swansea Bay. The second son of a parliamentary representative and the grandson of a Cromwellian colonel, Mackworth spent six months at Magdalen College, Oxford, before entering London's Middle Temple. In 1697, Mackworth assumed the leases of several abandoned coal mines on Gnoll Hill, a steep prominence outside Neath, and began preparing them for extraction. For decades, Gnoll Hill had languished as a bituminous waste where town burgesses "conversant only with the methods that were already old-fashioned" fetched coal from the near surface.[24] Mackworth lamented how each burgess sank "a Pit for himself, till at last they came to cross one another's Works, which caused a great Difference and several Law-suits."[25] Using his inheritance to consolidate and improve upon these haphazard efforts, Mackworth installed ventilation shafts that

[22] Brian Larkin, "The Politics and Poetics of Infrastructure," *Annual Review of Anthropology* 42 (October 2013): 327–43, at 329.

[23] Marian Valverde, *Infrastructure: New Trajectories in Law* (Abingdon, Oxon: Routledge, 2022), 6.

[24] D. Rhys Phillips, *The History of the Vale of Neath* (Swansea: D. Rhys Phillips, 1925), 233.

[25] [Sir Humphrey Mackworth?], *Affidavits, Certificates, and Presentments; Proving the Facts Mentioned in the Case of Sir Humphry Mackworth, and the Mine-Adventurers* (London, 1705), 35.

allowed workers to toil deeper underground and coffers that stopped mine floors from flooding.[26]

Mackworth also laid a wooden wagonway down Gnoll Hill to the center of Neath, where one track branched off to a metal-smelting plant he erected in Melincryddan and another extended across the king's highway to a wharf he built on the River Neath.[27] Mackworth modeled his "artificial road" after those of the Tyneside (whose mechanics were adopted by miners in his native Shropshire) and recruited seasoned drivers from coal belts in Newcastle, Shropshire, and Germany to pilot wagons.[28] For a brief period, Mackworth tried to take advantage of the Welsh coast's prevailing ocean winds by introducing "Sailing wagons" by which "one Horse does the Work of ten at all times; but when any Wind is stirring (which is seldom wanting near the Sea)."[29] The panegyrist Thomas Yalden commended Mackworth's invention in a series of doggerel couplets: "thy speedy Sailes, and useful Engine show, / A genius richer than Mines below."[30] When wind proved an unreliable propellent for coal-laden wagons, Mackworth reverted to ordinary horsepower but retained his reputation as an intrepid inventor.

Mackworth bolstered his local standing in 1698 by becoming deputy governor for the Company of the Mine Adventurers, a joint-stock effort to recuperate Cardiganshire lead mines that he claimed would prove "Advantagious for the Publick Good, Charitable to the Poor, and Profitable to every Person who shall be concerned therein."[31] The company used Mackworth's Neath wharf, wagonway, and Melincryddan plant to smelt lead, copper, and silver mined from North Wales and Cornwall.[32]

26 William Waller, "The Epistle Dedicatory to Sir Humphry Mackworth," in *An Essay on the Value of the Mines, Late of Sir Carbery Price* (London, 1698), [i–xxi], at [vii–viii].

27 Mackworth, *Affidavits*, 36.

28 Philip Jenkins, *The Making of a Ruling Class: The Glamorgan Gentry 1640–1790* (Cambridge: Cambridge University Press, 1983), 59; Phillips, *The History of the Vale of Neath*, 233.

29 Waller, "Epistle Dedicatory," [viii]. Waller claimed that the invention "could not fail of Bishop Wilkins's Blessing . . . in case he were in a Capacity to bestow it," which he was not, the Royal Society co-founder having died in 1672 ([ix]). Waller's comment reflected scientific interest in wagonways, including from J. T. Desaguliers, whose *Course of Experimental Philosophy* (1734) includes an essay by Charles de Labelye, which diagrams a wagonway. See "A Description of the Carriages Made Use of by Ralph Allen, Esq; to Carry Stone from His Quaries, Situated on the Top of a Hill, to the Water-side of the River Avon, near the City of Bath," in *A Course of Experimental Philosophy* (London, 1734), 1:274–77, at 275.

30 Thomas Yalden, *A Poem on the Mines Late of Sir Carbery Price* (London: J. Nutt, 1701), 5.

31 Sir Humphrey Mackworth, *The Mine-Adventure; or an Undertaking Advantageous for the Publick Good, Charitable to the Poor, and Profitable to Every Person Who Shall Be Concerned Therein* (London], 1698), 1.

32 William P. Griffith, "Mackworth, Sir Humphrey (1657–1727)," *Oxford Dictionary of National Biography* (2004), https://doi.org/10.1093/ref:odnb/17631.

The wagonway served both the Gnoll Hill mine and the Mine Adventurers by integrating extraction, metalwork, and export along a single mechanized conduit. Neath became the nucleus of a regional operation.

Mackworth's rapid and ballyhooed success incensed a rival coal clan, the Mansells of Margam and Britton Ferry. Mackworth struck Glamorgan's most venerable, wealthy, and influential Welsh gentry family as an upstart virtuoso and English invader.[33] Proximity to one another on the banks of the River Neath made Mackworth and miner Edward Mansell natural rivals. International affairs made the men political enemies: Where the moderate Tory Mansell supported England's participation in the War of the Spanish Succession, the high Tory Mackworth opposed Britain's intervention in what he regarded as a wasteful foreign conflict.[34]

In 1705 Mansell initiated a war of his own, exploiting his powers as justice of the peace to terrorize Mackworth's employees, vandalize his facilities, and ultimately destroy his wagonway at its intersection with the king's highway. Mackworth answered these attacks by wielding his own authorities as justice of the peace, constable, lord, and MP for Glamorganshire. Beyond his offices, Mackworth rallied public sympathy for his plight by drafting polemical tracts. A prolific pamphleteer, Mackworth had already published essays on topics ranging from parliamentary prerogative and the formation of a national bank to religious conformity, the immorality of alehouses, and the fortunes of his Company of the Mine Adventurers.[35] Many of these compositions attuned an influential London audience of investors, legislators, and crown officials to business opportunities and happenings in the Welsh hinterlands.

Most of what we know about the Mansell–Mackworth battle derives from two anonymous tracts: *The Case of Sir Humphry Mackworth, and of the Mine-Adventurers* (1705) and its companion source book, *Affidavits, Certificates, and Presentments; Proving the Facts Mentioned in the Case of Sir*

[33] Jenkins, *Making of a Ruling Class*, 28.

[34] C. D. J. Trott, "Coal-Mining in the Borough of Neath," *Morgannwg Transactions of the Local History Society* 13 (1969): 47–74, at 68. Mackworth's chronicler William Waller salutes the "native Wealth" of Neath coal as a "Welsh Potozi" that might, he warily suggests, fund the "long expences of our Gallick War." See *Essay on the Value of the Mines*, 12. Mackworth himself characterized the Company of the Mine Adventurers as an enterprise that would "replenish the publick Treasury of the Kingdom, after so great Losses and Expences in the late War." *Mine-Adventure*, 1.

[35] See [Sir Humphrey Mackworth], *A Vindication of the Rights of the Commons of England* (London: J. Nutt, 1701); [Sir Humphrey Mackworth], *England's Glory; or, The Great Improvement of Trade in General, by a Royal Bank, or Office of Credit, to Be Erected in London* (London: Tho. Bever, 1694); Sir Humphrey Mackworth, *A Treatise concerning Providence; By Way of Dialogue* (London: George Strahan, 1704); H.M., *Down with the Mug: Or, Reasons for Suppressing the Mug-Houses* (London: John Morphew, 1717); Mackworth, *Mine-Adventure*.

Humphry Mackworth, and the Mine-Adventurers (1705). Both pamphlets portray the dispute from the vantage of Mackworth, who most likely wrote them. Given their bias, these accounts do not allow us to adjudicate the conflict retrospectively. They do, however, preserve the polemical diction and conceptions of public utility that miners employed to justify their incursion on roads. Attention to these formal mechanics reveals that while Mackworth and Mansell disputed virtually every single fact of their case, they sought remedies from the same sources of judicial authority and even advanced similar formulations of rights of way. Where Mackworth claims that Gnoll Hill's wagonway supports the production and provisioning of heating fuel in west Britain, Mansell construes it more narrowly as an obstacle to sanctioned traffic.

Mansell first objected to Mackworth's recruitment of "Strangers and Idle Persons, without Certificates or Testimonials of their last legal Settlements."[36] Mansell resented the hiring of "strangers" to toil for Mackworth (himself a stranger in the eyes of Glamorganshire's rank-and-file gentry) and claimed that such hiring deprived the crown of soldiers to fight in the War of the Spanish Succession. As a justice of the peace, Mansell possessed broad discretionary power to arrest those of Mackworth's employees he deemed vagrants and have them conscripted in the military. Mansell even threatened to "press the Seaman that came to [Mackworth's] Coal-works" to conduct business.[37] Mackworth's *Affidavits, Certificates, and Presentments* documents Mansell's repeated attempts to detain coal workers with the perfunctory repetition of a modern police blotter: "Thomas Jones, smelter of Lanartheny, listed as Soldier by Edward Mansell, Thomas Mansell, and Thomas Popkins"; "John Bynon, carrier to the mills, sent away to serve Her Majesty in the Land Forces."[38] *The Case of Sir Humphry Mackworth* asserts that these victims were "Men of a Lawful Calling and Employment," while reminding readers that the self-interested "Justices had Coal-Works of their own."[39]

Affidavits also complained that Mansell's indictments coerced some of Mackworth's personnel to flee "their Works, the Lead and Silver, in the Furnaces, were left unwrought, the Furnaces thereby Damnified, the Coal-works were stopt, several Ships lying in the River and waiting for Coals, or other Freight from the Said Sir Humphry Mackworth, or the said

[36] Edward Mansell, *The Case of John Morgan and Others* (1705), quoted in Trott, "Coal-Mining in the Borough of Neath," 64.

[37] [Sir Humphrey Mackworth?], *The Case of Sir Humphry Mackworth, and of the Mine-Adventurers* (London, 1705), 4.

[38] Mackworth, *Affidavits*, 17, 19.

[39] Mackworth, *Case of Sir Humphry Mackworth*, 5

Company, were then disappointed and delayed."[40] This chain of agentless passive verbs ("unwrought," "Damnified," "stopt," "disappointed," "delayed") reveals how metal-making and regional shipping depended upon those "strangers" that Mackworth employed and Mansell scared off. The reference to "Lead and Silver" reminds readers that Mackworth's Neath wagonway conveyed not only his estate's coal, but the Cardigan and Cornish ores that his Melincryddan plant purified. In describing Mansell's insidious attacks, *The Case of Sir Humphry Mackworth* delivers an appreciative inventory of Mackworth's intricate operations, which employed German diggers and Tyneside wagoners to create markets for Welsh metal on both sides of the Bristol Channel.

Mansell further confounded Mackworth's operations by dispatching gangs to rip down his fences and steal his coal, and by spreading rumors on the Swansea docks, as *The Case of Sir Humphry Mackworth* put it, "to disparage the said Coal, and the Port of Neath, and discourage Merchants and Masters of Vessels from coming or trading to that Port; sometimes giving out, that the Coal was not good; at other times that the Works were discontinued, or else that the same would in a short time be destroyed."[41] This smear campaign apparently failed (perhaps owing to Mackworth's facility with self-promotion in the print medium and respected standing around Swansea Bay), for in the summer of 1705, Mansell began attacking the conduit that synchronized extraction, smelting, and transshipment operations around Neath. Mansell had already impressed wagon pilots "who by long continuance were become Skillful in bringing forth Coal."[42] According to affidavits presented at the 1705 Quarter Sessions, he now questioned the wagonway's fundamental legality. Mansell particularly scrutinized the stretch of track that ran through Neath center over a commons that Mackworth leased from the town burgesses, and across the king's highway at what is today the intersection of lower Cimla and Eastland Roads. In the August sessions, Mansell conspired to have Mackworth indicted for "erecting a Nusance across the Highway."[43]

A nuisance, according to the eighteenth-century jurist William Blackstone, could be anything that "obstructed or annoyed such things as are of daily convenience and use."[44] Nuisance derived from the medieval notion of purpresture, infringement upon lands to which others hold

[40] Mackworth, *Affidavits*, 22. [41] Mackworth, *Case of Sir Humphry Mackworth*, 4.
[42] Mackworth, *Case of Sir Humphry Mackworth*, 5.
[43] Trott, "Coal-Mining in the Borough of Neath," 72.
[44] William Blackstone, *Commentaries on the Laws of England*, ed. Wilfrid Prest, bk. 3, *Of Private Wrongs*, ed. Thomas P. Gallanis (1768; Oxford: Oxford University Press, 2016), 3.

rights, including rights of passage. According to Valerie Allen and Ruth Evans, the term covered "damage to the common good and damage to royal property," and most frequently addressed obstructions to the king's highway.[45] So injurious was a nuisance, Blackstone asserts, that it required "immediate remedy" and "[could not] wait for the slow progress of the ordinary forms of justice."[46] He reasons that if a "gate be erected across the public highway, any of the king's subjects . . . may cut it down."[47] A nuisance indictment in Glamorganshire would authorize Mansell's agents to remedy what they construed to be an intrusion upon public land without having to wait for "ordinary forms of justice." The charge alone licensed them to act.

Mackworth had little time to discern, and less to fend off Mansell's plot, which used the pretext of nuisance to justify vigilante justice. Mackworth frantically sought witnesses to help him quash the indictment, but the presiding justice, Thomas Popkins, an established gentry man and Mansell partisan who was complicit in the arrest of Gnoll Hill coal workers, deferred his hearing to the next session.[48] By the double maneuver of indictment and delay, Mansell's agents "had their Design."[49] On the evening of September 14, a crew led by one John Morgan used pickaxes, iron bars, and shovels to dismember the wagonway where it crossed the king's highway. The crew sawed apart the wooden rails and chopped wheels from wagons. When confronted by Mackworth's employees, the saboteurs answered nonchalantly that they "would justify what was done" at the next session.[50] Mansell and Popkins went so far as to issue warrants of arrest for any Mackworth workers who tried to "prevent the said John Morgan and his Confederates from digging up and destroying the Waggon-way," asserting that Mackworth's men were the ones inhibiting justice.[51]

Following the attack, Mackworth restored the wagonway crossing by laying new tracks across the road – ensuring that the rails did not hinder carriage traffic – and awaited vindication in the next session. Mansell's men returned a few nights later and dismantled the wagonway with the same casual certitude they displayed during the first assault. Mackworth again reassembled the railway and resumed running coal wagons from Gnoll Hill to Neath wharf. Again, Mansell's nocturnal crew appeared, and

[45] Valerie Allen and Ruth Evans, "Introduction: Roads in Writing," in *Roadworks: Medieval Britain, Medieval Roads*, ed. Valerie Allen and Ruth Evans (Manchester: Manchester University Press, 2016), 1–32, at 16.

[46] Blackstone, *Commentaries*, 3:3.

[47] Blackstone, *Commentaries*, 3:3.

[48] Jenkins, *Making of a Ruling Class*, 59; Mackworth, *Affidavits*, 17, 42.

[49] Mackworth, *Case of Sir Humphry Mackworth*, 11.

[50] Mackworth, *Case of Sir Humphry Mackworth*, 11.

[51] Mackworth, *Affidavits*, 42.

again they prised up the line where it met the road. The crossing would be obliterated and restored several more times over the coming weeks before Mackworth's drivers realized that they could simply drag coal wagons across the trackless intersection and reset them on rails on the other side. Mansell's agents punished this improvisation by digging a pit in the road – burrowing out the thoroughfare they were ostensibly ridding of nuisance.

In an affidavit, Neath highway surveyor Philip Gregory swore that on September 8, he saw "John Morgan and Phillip William of Neath aforesaid, Laborers, digging up Her Majesty's High-way between Neath and Mellingrythan with force and Arms in a riotous manner."[52] Neath constable James Hall also reported seeing Mansell's men "breaking up the High-way between Neath and Mellingrytham within the said Parish with Force and Arms in a Riotous manner."[53] Gregory and Hall accused Mansell of riot, a disturbance of the peace tinged with associations of wanton excess. Where the nuisance charge blamed Mackworth's wagonway for upsetting "daily convenience," riot implicated Mansell's agents, who, having dug up the road, could no longer sustain the fiction that they were protecting the king's traffic. Gregory appealed to the Glamorgan justice of the peace, Thomas Popkins, a Mansell supporter who predictably declined his request for a warrant.[54] Employing his own power as justice of the peace, Mackworth "issued forth his warrants."[55] When the Grand Sessions convened in October, those Mansell employees accused of behaving in a "riotous manner" faced charges of "breaking and spoiling the said High-way." They were convicted of harming the road, but they succeeded in their mission of weakening Mackworth's operations.[56]

52 Mackworth, *Affidavits*, 42.

53 Mackworth, *Affidavits*, 44. Valerie Allen notes that "One of the oldest legal terms in the language for damage done to roads is *stretbreche* (street-breaking), which the twelfth century *Leges Henrici Primi* identify as what happens when someone 'destroys a road by closing it off or diverting it or digging it up.'" "When Things Break: Mending Roads, Being Social," in Allen and Evans, *Roadworks*, 74–96, at 75.

54 Mackworth, *Affidavits*, 43. 55 Mackworth, *Affidavits*, 48.

56 Mackworth also denounced Mansell's attacks in Parliament in December 1705. The Commons *Journals* record a

> Complaint being made to the House, that several Persons, viz. Tho. Popkins, Esquire, Captain Bussy Mansell, William Wilson, Serjeant, John Jones, Corporal of the Company of the said Captain Mansell, Watkin Reynold, Howell Thomas, William John and Hopkin David, have pressed, imprisoned, and detained Griffith Evans, William Blower, and Edward John, Servants of Sir Humphrey Mackworth (a Member of this House) in Breach of the Privilege of this House.

This complaint and two similar ones were "referred to the Committee of Privileges and Elections," though the records contain no subsequent mention of either. *Journals of the House of Commons* (London: Her Majesty's Stationery Office, 1803), 15:75.

Mackworth claimed that Mansell's disturbance of local peace undermined a national economy dependent on the free passage of coal wagons through Neath. In a 1694 tract, Mackworth had touted Britain's capacity to "live within itself, as any Nation; having not only all things necessary for the Life of Man, but also Abundance, Materials, and Stores," including "Coals inexhaustible."[57] To illustrate how the Gnoll Hill wagonway converted natural resources into state amenity, *The Case of Sir Humphry Mackworth* records the testimony of portreeves, aldermen, and burgesses, who certified that the "West part of England is chiefly supplied with Coal from Neath, and other places in the County of Glamorgan." By investing "several Thousand Pounds" of his own, these officials attested that Mackworth almost singlehandedly revived a coal trade that had been "almost totally lost at Neath, during the space of Thirty Years and upwards."[58] Mackworth's private enterprise, the pamphlet suggested, rendered the public good of energy export.

Mackworth explained that by furnishing the kingdom with heating material, he also rendered the tertiary benefit of filling royal coffers. The portreeve's testimony asserted that the wagonway carried not just coal but customs revenue: "The said Coal-works, without the Conveniency of this Foot-rid and Waggon-way, could not be carried on to any Profit; but by means thereof great quantities of Coal are brought forth and sold to Sea, whereby her Majesty and the Public receive annually for the Duty of these Coals, the Sum of 1500 *l.* and upwards."[59] These nested prepositions ("without," "on," "to," "by," "for," "of") forge a causal chain that identifies Mackworth's wagonway as a catalyst for regional growth and treasury income. Where Mansell assumed that wagonways hindered the public's expectation of passage on the king's highway merely to enrich Mackworth, the pamphlet identifies an alternative form of the public good in state revenue.

57 Mackworth, "The Epistle Dedicatory," in *England's Glory*, [i–v], at [i–ii]. In this passage Mackworth appears to plagiarize an earlier improvement-minded pamphleteer, Carew Reynel. See Preface to *The True English Interest: or, An Account of the Chief National Improvements in Some Political Observations* (London: Giles Widdowes, 1674), [i–vxi], at [i–ii].

58 Mackworth, *Case of Sir Humphry Mackworth*, 3. In later pamphlets justifying his involvement with the Mine Adventurers, Mackworth would assert his "constant zeal to promote their common interest." Sir Humphrey Mackworth, *A Short State of the Case and Proceedings of the Company of Mine-Adventurers; with an Abstract of the Defence of the Deputy Governor and Directors* (London, 1710), unpaginated.

59 Mackworth, *Case of Sir Humphry Mackworth*, 4. In consulting the Port Books, Trott concludes that despite Mackworth's boasts that large quantities of Neath coal sailed abroad, "only small quantities of Neath coal reached Ireland, the Channel Islands, Breton ports, and San Sebastian and Bilbao in Spain." Trott, "Coal Mining in the Borough of Neath," 67.

By compiling the testimony of miners, smelters, refiners, shippers, carriers, and joiners, Mackworth's *Affidavits* also reminds readers that his mines have occasioned and remunerated diverse forms of craft labor. The roster of deponents fashions Mackworth as a wage provider from whom the "Inhabitants of the said Town of Neath and Country thereabouts, receive great Advantage."[60] The pamphlet transcribes testimony from one Robert Evans, who suggests that Melincryddan copperworks alone employed "an Hundred Men and upwards."[61] From this occupational vantage, attacks upon Mackworth's employees and wagonway constituted not only corporate sabotage but a categorical wrong inflicted on laborers. According to *Affidavits*, such violence harmed recipients of Mackworth's munificent personal charity, which included his hiring of a schoolmaster to instruct local children (including those of his workers) and his co-founding of the Society for Promoting Christian Knowledge.[62] Already regarded as a successful industrialist by his associates, Mackworth was now commended for his "frank and generous Disposition for the publick Good."[63]

After reviewing the wagonway's economic and philanthropic benefits, *Affidavits* contests Mansell's basic empirical premise that the coal tram hindered road traffic. Where Mansell's indictment alleged that the wagonway created a ten-foot embankment in the middle of the road "to the great annoyance of her Majesty's Subjects," *Affidavits* cites a surveyor who measures a gentler rise of three feet and two inches over twenty-six lateral feet. *Affidavits* asserts that this mild slope actually improved the road by facilitating drainage. The Neath segment was "formerly a pool of Water and Dirt," claims the pamphlet, until Mackworth "did at his own expence fill up the said Pool, and with Gravel, Slaggs, Cinders, and Rails of Wood four Inches Square, did make the same a good and firm way for all Persons to pass over."[64] The surveyor concludes that the crossing constitutes the best stretch of road for "all sorts of carriages" between Swansea and Cardiff.[65]

60 Mackworth, *Affidavits*, 29. In *England's Glory*, Mackworth described the deleterious impact of unemployed subjects who "are as Catterpillers to Plants, and Worms to Woods, that only waste the Product of Industrious Hands" (20).

61 Mackworth, *Affidavits*, 17.

62 Trott, "Coal-Mining in the Borough of Neath," 57.

63 Waller, "Epistle Dedicatory," [vii]. According to Koji Yamamoto, Mackworth's case demonstrates how profit-seeking enterprise could "operate in a state of symbiosis with charitable missions." *Taming Capitalism before Its Triumph: Public Service, Distrust, and "Projecting" in Early Modern England* (Oxford: Oxford University Press, 2017), 248.

64 Mackworth, *Affidavits*, 52. Such a claim would have resonated with Londoners, who assumed that early modern Welsh roads laid in a deplorable estate. Philip Jenkins asserts that while "an unwary traveller might find himself in mortal danger" west of Swansea until the late eighteenth century, the way between Swansea and Wales was relatively good. *Making of a Ruling Class*, 7.

65 Mackworth, *Affidavits*, 52.

Mackworth's wagonway did not fly through the air in the dramatic fashion that *Wealth of Nations* described, but it may have improved the way in which it shared a small plot of earth. According to *Affidavits*, the tram's embanked rails, ties, and ballast glued together an otherwise founderous road. Where an aerial wagonway represented the salutary evasion of conflict for Smith, Mackworth conceives the intersection as a site of mutual benefit. His conciliatory approach to grade crossings concretizes an economic philosophy that rationalizes private freight's position within the kingdom's multi-modal logistical network. Where Mansell conceived the Neath crossing as a zero-sum sacrifice of public good to private accumulation, Mackworth identifies crossings as sites of potential cooperation, where the intersection of mobile elements facilitates mobility.

At the bare minimum, *Affidavits* claims that Mackworth's wagonway harmed no one. Testimony from the parish road surveyor confirms that the Neath crossing had "been quietly enjoyed for eight Years" without incident until the summer of 1705, when Mansell's crew dug it up. The pamphleteer insinuatingly wonders what attracted Mansell to this commonly "enjoyed" plot of land at a time when Glamorganshire's local roads remained "out of repair in several other places."[66] Listing various jury presentments for residents who breached or muddied the road, or were otherwise derelict in their statutory maintenance obligations, *Affidavits* accuses Justice Mansell of abusing public office to settle a personal score while neglecting his parochial duties elsewhere.[67] The unwavering personal animus at the heart of the Mackworth–Mansell conflict is confirmed by its conclusion: C. D. J. Trott notes that the battle over the Gnoll Hill wagonway ceased with Mansell's death in January 1706.[68]

By the time Mansell died, the Neath crossing was the least of Mackworth's worries. In 1705, the Mine Adventurers consortium collapsed. Mackworth tried to raise money and save public face by selling unbacked shares, a "notorious and scandalous fraud" that precipitated his dismissal from the company.[69] Mackworth reorganized his mining assets in 1713 under a new company, the Mineral Manufacturers of Neath, but this too failed under a cloud of scandal. Mackworth fell into debt and received formal censure from his colleagues in the House of Commons. Until his death in 1727, Mackworth continued to issue pamphlets

66 Mackworth, *Affidavits*, 53–54. 67 Mackworth, *Affidavits*, 52–53.
68 Trott, "Coal-Mining in the Borough of Neath."
69 Quoted in Mary Ransome, "The Parliamentary Career of Sir Humphry Mackworth: 1701–1713," *University of Birmingham Historical Journal* 1 (1948): 232–54, at 234.

exculpating himself from charges of deceit. One tract touted his good character in erecting various mining facilities "at his own Charge."[70] Among his furnaces, cranes, bridges, wharves, and canal, Mackworth mentioned "the Waggon way from the Gate to the Waterside."[71] The coal tram that Mackworth had defended so vigorously – and by so many disparate criteria – was now made to return the favor by attesting the author's "[c]onstant Zeal to promote [the Company of the Mine Adventurers'] Common Interest."[72]

Legislating Crossings after Neath

Neath's was neither the first nor the last wagonway crossing to provoke violence. The Mackworth–Mansell dispute's focus on nuisance (an interruption of public peace authorizing immediate redress) and riot (an illicit means of redress) busied courts in coal export centers throughout South Wales, Shropshire, Scotland, and Tyneside. Wagonways hovered between legitimate conduit and indictable annoyance until 1714, when certain Newcastle landowners advanced a series of test cases meant to effect the closure of all level crossings. This challenge backfired, according to wagonway historian M. J. T. Lewis, solidifying the lawfulness of coal trams.[73] Subsequent parliamentary statutes ratified the wagonway as a private work conducive to the public good. The Northumberland Roads Act of 1748, for example, reserved for miners a "[l]iberty to make, repair, and use such Waggonway and Waggonways, in, along, or cross the said Road, as they, or any of them could or might have been done."[74] The level crossing here finds protection in the prepositions that sanction its overlap with shire highways.

One year later, another bill provided for the rehabilitation of a specific Northumberland road between west Cowgate and Kenton by placing it under the supervision of a turnpike trust authorized to toll passengers to raise repair funds. In relinquishing the public way to a private trust, the framers included a proviso protecting wagonways: "nothing in this Act contained" shall prevent miners from "laying a Waggon-way or Ways along or cross any Part of the Said Road" or to "make, repair, and use such Waggonway and Waggon-ways in, along, or cross the said Road."[75]

70 Mackworth, *Short State of the Case*, 27.
71 Mackworth, *Short State of the Case*, 27.
72 Mackworth, *Short State of the Case*, 64.
73 M. J. T. Lewis, *Early Wooden Railways* (London: Routledge, 1974), 159.
74 Northumberland Roads Act, 22 Geo. II Public Acts c. 7.
75 *A Bill for Repairing the Road from the West Cowgate near the Town of Newcastle upon Tyne* (London, 1749), 7.

This bill protected the wagonway from the road itself, now controlled by profit-minded trustees who might try to increase toll revenues by removing the obstacle of tracks and wagons. The Transportation Act of 1768 protected wagonways from criminal interference by making a transportable felon of anyone who would "willfully or maliciously set fire to, burn, demolish, pull down, or otherwise destroy or damage" mining facilities, including "waggonway[s] or trunk[s]."[76]

Subsequent statutes affirmed the legitimacy of rail crossings but compelled their operators to take measures to protect road traffic. When Parliament authorized the construction of the Penclawdd Tramroad in Glamorgan in 1811, it required that the rails "run in a Groove . . . in such a way that Carriages of all Kinds may easily pass over the same."[77] Should the tracks render a way impassible, the Penclawdd projectors would be required to lay out a new "good and sufficient Carriage or Horse Road."[78] The Highway Act of 1839 made railway owners erect gates across intersections and employ "good and proper Persons" to serve as gatekeepers.[79] In a sign of the railway's increasing political might, the Railway Regulation Act of 1844 clarified that crossing gates could remain closed until traffic approached on the road.[80] In more recent years, the Level Crossings Act of 1983 empowered the secretary of state to order railways to install "barriers or other protective equipment" to protect rail and road passengers.[81] Legislators have made railways responsible for the safety of highway passengers, but no one questions their right to lay tracks at grade.

Where Mackworth struggled to disentangle his wagonway from the crime of purpresture, later legislators endowed coal trams with protections that Parliament had for centuries conferred upon the high roads. Parliamentary statutes made it increasingly possible for railed freight to claim space for itself against other land uses and forms of traffic. Accounts of legal conflicts like *The Case of Sir Humphry Mackworth* and *Affidavits* track the evolution by which the wagonway's legal status caught up to the self-evidence of its material form. This literature shows how wagonways that had for centuries existed under the guise of temporary easements

[76] 8 Geo. III c. 15, quoted in George Wilson's abridgement of *Historia Placitorum Coronae: The History of the Pleas of the Crown*, ed. Sollum Emlyn (London: T. Payne, 1778), 1:725.

[77] 51 Geo. III. c. 106. [78] 51 Geo. III. c. 106.

[79] Highway (Railway Crossings) Act 1839, 2 & 3 Vict. c. 45. This act made compulsory the practices of many seventeenth-century wagonway operators, whose easements required that they erect gates, hire attendants, and build gatehouses to shelter attendants. See Jack Simmons and Gordon Biddle, eds., *The Oxford Companion to British Railway History: From 1603 to the 1990s* (Oxford: Oxford University Press, 1993), 261.

[80] 7 & 8 Vict. c. 85. [81] Level Crossings Act 1983 c. 16.

hammered out between individual miners and landowners found lasting recognition (and increasingly stringent regulation) in the language of legislation.

Wagonways, like all infrastructures, obtained their life from law: their license, land, and operating protocols. Mackworth's pamphlets address an audience that conceived public works in terms of the legal responsibilities that their authors bore to society. The wagonway's nonpossessory use of a strip of the king's highway belongs neither wholly to a realm of public benefit nor to a sphere of private accumulation. The relationship can be more productively thought of along the lines of what Erin Drew calls "chains of obligation" that early modern agrarians used to distinguish between "just and legitimate uses of land and power and unjust and illegitimate ones."[82] Law spells out these obligations when conflict arises, as it did, inevitably, paradigmatically at grade crossings. When the Glamorgan Quarter Sessions justices adjudicated charges of nuisance and riot, they were simultaneously specifying what, where, and when a public work could occur.[83] Such works were never fully formed positivist objects "in which everything is already laid out."[84] Rather, these works emerged contingently through deliberation.

Whether Mackworth constructed a nuisance or a public work was a matter of judicial opinion, a perspectival formation that anticipates Antina von Schnitzler's definition of infrastructure as an "epistemological vantage point."[85] Inversely, crossings reveal how legislation and jurisprudence never functioned as uniform extrinsic forces acting, in Valverde's phrase, "on the world from outside and/or from above," but instead constituted an immanent interpretive process that elaborated itself in response to the facts it addressed.[86] Writings about the Neath crossing record the "jostling, colliding, and overlapping of social, cultural, technological, and natural forms" that compel for Caroline Levine the hermeneutical recalibration called "infrastructuralism" – a renewed attention to form that can, in this

[82] Erin Drew, *The Usufructuary Ethos: Power, Politics, and Environment in the Long Eighteenth Century* (Charlottesville: University of Virginia Press, 2021), 4.

[83] On the temporal nature of infrastructure, see Susan Leigh Star and Karen Ruhleder, who ask, "[w]hen is an infrastructure?" in "Steps toward an Ecology of Infrastructure: Design and Access for Large Information Spaces," *Information Systems Research* 7 (March 1996), 111–34, at 112. See also Ina Bloom, "'And Follow It': Straight Lines and Infrastructural Sensibilities," *Critical Inquiry* 45, no. 4 (Summer 2019): 859–83, at 861.

[84] Ingold, *Being Alive*, 12.

[85] Antina von Schnitzler, "Infrastructure, Apartheid Technopolitics, and Temporalities of 'Transition,'" in *The Promise of Infrastructure*, ed. Nikhil Anand, Akhil Gupta, and Hannah Appel (Durham, NC: Duke University Press, 2018), 133–54, at 147.

[86] Valverde, *Infrastructure*, 113.

case, account for the capacity of works like wagonways to adjust the public institutions that commissioned them.[87]

The "jostling, colliding, and overlapping" movement of people and materials never played out on a frictionless plain of improvement where, in *Wealth of Nations*, one form of traffic simply vaults "through the air." To the contrary, fights over small but intensively used strips of land reveal the hierarchies of decisions that made public work a political category. The ever "jostling" – ever ongoingly gerundial – intersection shakes us out of what Larkin identifies as an unthinking "belief that, by promoting circulation, infrastructures bring about change, and through change they enact progress, and through progress we gain freedom."[88] The possibility and membership of such a "we" is precisely what Mackworth and Mansell debate. *The Case of Sir Humphry Mackworth* and *Affidavits* invite us to consider whether certain forms of circulation must always come at the cost of others in a world where interference is inevitable, or whether such sites might function as zones of noninterference or even mutual benefit.

[87] Caroline Levine, "Infrastructuralism, or the Tempo of Institutions," in *On Periodization: Selected Essays from the English Institute*, ed. Virginia Jackson (English Institute, 2010), www.fulcrum.org/epubs/ws859g78b?locale=en#/6/20[div1_c02]!/4/2[div1_c02]/2/2/1:0.

[88] Larkin, "Politics and Poetics of Infrastructure," 332.

CHAPTER 3

Ambivalence, Survival, and Law in Defoe's Journal of the Plague Year

Kathryn D. Temple

Daniel Defoe's *A Journal of the Plague Year* (1722) recounts one man's experience of the bubonic plague of 1665 as it gradually gathers force and comes to dominate London life (and death), killing almost 100,000 of the city's 460,000 population.[1] In Defoe's narrative, the protagonist, H.F., details the suffering of many who die horribly. For generations, critics have debated the truth value of *Plague Year*. Did H.F. actually exist and, if he did, was *Plague Year* his work? How accurate are the details in the narrative? How does it compare with other primary texts describing the London plague? The current understanding, of course, is that this is a text that teeters on the edge of truth and fiction, a "faction" rather than fiction or fact.[2] Its value lies not in its historical accuracy but in its representation of what Richard Barney and Helene Scheck have argued is typical of plague narratives: "disruption," particularly disruption that connects the socio-legal, the political, and the biological.[3] *Plague Year* is exemplary in this regard. As Margaret Healy asserts, it offers "a complex texture of interwoven relationships between the subjective and the social, the private and the collective."[4] Defoe develops this "complex texture" in a number of ways, through plot, commentary, description, historical references, and

[1] These figures are uncertain. Estimates range from about one-fourth to one-third of London's population. For an estimate of "more than 97,000" see Paula R. Backscheider, "Daniel Defoe: A Chronology," in Daniel Defoe, *A Journal of the Plague Year*, ed. Paula R. Backscheider (1722; New York: W. W. Norton, 1992), 356–59, at 356. The United Kingdom National Archives' website suggests that the more accurate number is over 100,000 and also notes that 68,596 deaths were actually recorded by the city. See "Great Plague of 1665–1666," https://www.nationalarchives.gov.uk/education/resources/great-plague/.

[2] For *Plague Year*'s reception history, see Robert Mayer, "The Reception of *A Journal of the Plague Year* and the Nexus of Fiction and History in the Novel," *ELH* 57, no. 3 (Fall 1990): 529–55.

[3] Richard A. Barney and Helene Scheck, "Introduction: Early and Modern Biospheres, Politics, and the Rhetorics of Plague," *Journal for Modern Cultural Studies* 10, no. 2 (Fall/Winter 2010): 1–22, at 10–12.

[4] Margaret Healy, "Defoe's *Journal* and the English Plague Writing Tradition," *Literature and Medicine* 22, no. 1 (Spring 2003): 25–44, at 40.

formal devices, to name only a few. But a crucial connective thread undergirding these themes is Defoe's representation of the affective and emotive reactions that accompany juridical efforts to control the spread of the plague. This is an area that a faction is ideally suited to examine precisely because factions make claims on both fiction and history, and in the case of *Plague Year* on legal history.[5]

Given the devastating circumstances that Defoe narrates, we might expect that horror, fear, and grief would be prominent emotions in *Plague Year* and they are. However, the emotion that most clearly frames the work and motivates the protagonist is ambivalence, an under-explored emotion in both law-and-literature and law-and-emotions scholarship.[6] Ambivalence in *Plague Year* is not the nagging, low-level drag that it is often portrayed to be but rather an energizing force, one that impels Defoe's narrator and

[5] For a discussion of the relevance of literature and literary study to the history of emotion, see Sarah McNamer, "The Literariness of Literature and the History of Emotion," *PMLA* 130, no. 5 (2015): 1433–42. Affect and emotion operate along a continuum from the nonconscious transmissible reactivity and intensity we associate with "affect" to what we tend to define as the socially constructed "emotion" that can be articulated and identified. See Melissa Gregg and Gregory J. Seigworth, eds., *The Affect Theory Reader* (Durham, NC: Duke University Press, 2010). For the scholarly preference for the use of the word "passions" instead of "emotions" when referencing the early eighteenth century and the response to that preference, see Geoffrey Sill, *The Cure of the Passions and the Origins of the English Novel* (Cambridge: Cambridge University Press, 2001); and Joel P. Sodano, "Semblances of Affect in the Early English Novel: Narrating Intensity," in *Affect Theory and Literary Critical Practice*, ed. Stephen Ahern (Cham, Switzerland: Palgrave, 2019), 65–82. For a discussion of issues involving the use of the word "emotion," see Thomas Dixon, "'Emotion': The History of a Key Word in Crisis," *Emotion Review* 4 (2012): 338–44. Attachment theory and theories of group identity are both significant for this project, although outside the scope of this chapter.

[6] Defoe is probably the most prominent of those early eighteenth-century authors who explored ambivalence, but there are many precursors, especially in romances by women writers like Delarivier Manley. For the argument that ambivalence is related to the "historical juncture" between the Middle Ages and modernity when science as natural philosophy is tested and found wanting, see David Brooks, "Daniel Defoe's *A Journal of the Plague Year*," in *Disasters: Images and Contexts*, ed. Peter Hinton (Sydney: Sydney Studies, 1992), 167–85. For a brief mention of ambivalence, see Emmanuelle Peraldo, "Telling Figures and Telling Feelings: The Geography of Emotions in the London of Defoe's *Journal of the Plague Year* and *Due Preparations for the Plague (1722)*," *Revue de la Société d'études anglo-américaines des XVII et XVIII siècles*, no. 69 (2012): 167–83. The robust discussion of ambivalence in colonized subjects generated by Homi K. Bhabha in the 1990s does not seem to have influenced scholarship in the early eighteenth-century history of emotions around legality. For this approach, see Bhabha, "Signs Taken for Wonders," *Critical Inquiry* 12, no. 1 (Autumn 1985): 144–65. For the treatment of emotions in law-and-emotions scholarship, see Susan Bandes, ed., *The Passions of Law* (New York: New York University Press, 1999); and Susan Bandes, Jody L. Madeira, and Kathryn D. Temple, eds., *Research Handbook on Law and Emotion* (Northampton, MA: Edward Elgar Publishing, 2021). For a discussion of ambivalence in law and the ambivalence of the rule of law, see Amalia Amaya, "Epistemic Ambivalence in Law," *Philosophical Issues*, no. 31: (2021): 7–23; and Jill Stauffer, "The Rule of Law and Its Shadow: Ambivalence, Procedure, and the Justice Beyond Legality," *Law, Culture and the Humanities*, no. 3 (2007): 225–43.

others to move restlessly along a continuum between two poles even as it aids survival. At one end of the continuum, we find cautious, law-abiding, God-fearing, community-oriented citizens. Many of these people died when they obeyed the law and sheltered at home, a useless gesture since the plague was spread in part by fleas. At the other end of the continuum, Londoners are represented as risk-takers and lawbreakers who respect no one and care nothing for God, king, or the law, even committing suicide, one of the most egregious departures from the authority of church and state. The ambivalent characters, most prominently H.F., operate along this continuum. Throughout the narrative, Defoe places his representations of embodied ambivalence into conversation with a prominent symbol of the social, the political, and the collective, that of the English legal system and what Greta Olson refers to as "legality." For Defoe, legality comprises the various norms and expectations we associate with the law, whether obvious symbols of normative legality such as the court, the king, and God, or the broader concept of the collective and the collective good.[7] This ambivalent movement between two sorts of commitments, the individual and the collective, enacts what legal scholar Duncan Kennedy has famously termed the "fundamental contradiction" between our autonomy needs and our reliance on community for survival.[8] Reading *Plague Year* through this lens

[7] Greta Olson uses "legality" expansively to include the "'living law,' or the codes of behavior and rules for ordering conflicts that precede and extend beyond book law." *From Law and Literature to Legality and Affect* (Oxford: Oxford University Press, 2022): 6–7. On the importance of emotions to law, legal institutions, and human responses to them, see Tom R. Tyler, *Why People Obey the Law: Procedural Justice, Legitimacy and Compliance* (New Haven, CT: Yale University Press, 1990) and Tyler, *The Expressive Powers of Law: Theories and Limits* (Cambridge, MA: Harvard University Press, 2017). For a "holistic" approach to law and the emotions, see Julia J. A. Shaw, *Law and the Passions: Why Emotion Matters for Justice* (Abingdon, Oxon: Routledge, 2020). For contemporary and historical approaches to law and emotion and an overview of the field, see Bandes et al., *Research Handbook on Law and Emotion*. For a discussion of the issues involved in the history of emotions around law, see Merridee L. Bailey and Kimberley-Joy Knight, "Writing Histories of Law and Emotion," *Journal of Legal History* 38, no. 2 (2017): 117–29.

[8] Duncan Kennedy, "The Structure of Blackstone's Commentaries," *Buffalo Law Review* 28, no. 2 (1979): 205–382. In 1984, Kennedy rejected the fundamental contradiction as a "lifeless slogan," a "reified abstraction," that encouraged activists to give up hope. Kennedy argued that "the goal is not to convince people by lucidity . . . and the beauty with which we get at the real structure of reality. But rather to operate in the interspace of artifacts, gestures, speeches and rhetoric, histrionics, drama, all very paradoxical." See Peter Gabel and Duncan Kennedy, "Roll Over Beethoven," *Stanford Law Review* 36, no. 1 (January 1984): 1–55, at 9. Despite this repudiation and the supposed death of critical legal theory, these concepts have a continuing influence on legal theory. See Elaine McArdle, "The Influence of Critical Legal Studies," *Harvard Law Bulletin*, Summer 2021, https://hls.harvard.edu/today/the-influence-of-critical-legal-studies/. Paul Baumgardner has argued that the fundamental contradiction is undergoing a revival in legal and political scholarship. See "The Fundamental Contradiction Redux? Liberty, Coercion, and American Legal Development," *Law and Social Inquiry* 42, no. 3 (Summer 2017): 924–42.

reveals the value of ambivalence under survival conditions while also increasing our understanding of how and why people follow or resist the law in everyday life.

Defining Ambivalence

Although ambivalence has always been part of our emotional repertoire, the word "ambivalence" did not appear until 1910, when Eugen Bleuler began using it to describe his patients' behaviors. Although Bleuler's "ambivalence" differs from current understandings, his description of what had previously been an inchoate affect, something felt almost atmospherically, initiated efforts to construct a defined emotion capable of explaining the human tendency to vacillate. Although a full discussion of this development is beyond the scope of this chapter, the naming and defining of ambivalence seems related to other developments we associate with modernity. Michael Hviid Jacobsen has argued, for instance, that we had no need to categorize certain emotive-cognitive behaviors as "ambivalent" until the rise of modernity. With modernity's increasing complexity combined with its insistence on classifications, predictability, and progress, on productivity, and more recently on "time management," ambivalence was initially constructed as a problem.[9] To refuse commitment to one course of action, one ideology, or one mode of behavior is to challenge modernity's "power to divide, classify and allocate," as Zygmunt Bauman has commented.[10] Ambivalence in both Bleuler's and the modern sense is more than indecisiveness. As Michael Hviid Jacobsen has put it, "Feeling ambivalent is about trying to have it or feel it both ways at the same time or being unable to reconcile certain contradictory or conflicting emotions but also knowing all too well that this is not really possible."[11] Thus ambivalence, though sometimes confused with "indifference" or seen as a struggle to resolve ambiguity, involves strong but conflicting emotions. It is both a personal, "owned" emotion and a sociological one, constructed by the impossible choices that modernity asks us to make, by "structural arrangements beyond our immediate reach and control."[12]

Emotional-cognitive ambivalence developed a bad reputation in some circles as the cause of anxiety, paralysis, and passivity in victims who swing

[9] Michael Hviid Jacobsen, "Ambivalence: Exploring a Mixed Emotion," in *Emotions in Culture and Everyday Life: Conceptual, Theoretical and Empirical Explorations*, ed. Michael Hviid Jacobsen (London: Routledge, 2022): 232–52.

[10] Zygmunt Bauman, *Modernity and Ambivalence* (Cambridge: Polity Press, 1991), 15.

[11] Jacobsen, "Ambivalence," 237.

[12] Jacobsen, "Ambivalence," 242.

back and forth between alternatives, unable to act.[13] However, in a recent shift, psychologists and sociologists have begun to recognize not only ambivalence's ubiquity but also its positive valence for decision-making and human relations.[14] Many scholars now argue that it has both positive and negative implications: As Jacobsen sums it up, "there is always a delicate balance between gains and losses, possibilities and limitations, certainty and ambivalence."[15] Those who advocate for ambivalence suggest that it may be especially useful in times that might otherwise incite despair because in difficult situations where reliable information is scant, ambivalence can increase information-seeking, creative problem-solving, and determination and lend meaning to our decisions.[16] The current construction of ambivalence also emphasizes its role in supporting our feelings of autonomy. As Emily Abbey puts it, "the ebb and flow of ambivalence drives the process of meaning construction," whereas the adoption of certainty places meaning in the hands of another as "certainty" itself becomes a law of sorts that the person cannot disobey.[17]

Given its focus on both "structural arrangements" and their failure, *Plague Year* offers an opportunity to study the prehistory of ambivalence under what John Richetti has described as conditions of "total uncertainty."[18] Such conditions seem likely to evoke ambivalence since, by definition, they yield no easy answers. In *Plague Year*, Defoe relies on representations of ambivalent characters contained in a narrative structure that amplifies this theme. In doing so, he demonstrates the efficacy of ambivalence in situations where law fails to respond to life's difficulties or complexity.

Ambivalence in *Plague Year*

Plague Year has often been read either as a story about the state lapsing into chaotic lawlessness or as one about the state exerting total panoptic control

[13] Brooks, "Daniel Defoe," 173.

[14] See, for example, Christina Ting Fong, "The Effects of Emotional Ambivalence on Creativity," *Academy of Management Journal* 49, no. 5 (October 2006): 1016–30.

[15] Jacobsen, "Ambivalence," 237.

[16] Jacobsen, "Ambivalence," 237; Emily Abbey and Jaan Valsiner, "Emergence of Meanings through Ambivalence," *Forum: Qualitative Social Research* 6, no. 1 (2005), www.qualitative-research.net/index.php/fqs/article/view/515/1115.

[17] Emily Abbey, "Ambivalence and Its Transformations," in *The Handbook of Culture and Psychology*, ed. Jaan Valsiner (Oxford: Oxford University Press, 2012), 989–97, at 995. Recent scholarship on the value of ambivalence is extensive and interdisciplinary. For some representative examples from literary theory and philosophy, see Jackie Stacey, "Wishing Away Ambivalence," *Feminist Theory* 15, no. 1 (2014): 39–49; and Hili Razinsky, *Ambivalence: A Philosophical Exploration* (Lanham, MD: Rowman and Littlefield, 2016).

[18] John J. Richetti, "Epilogue: *A Journal of the Plague Year* as Epitome," in Defoe, *Journal of the Plague Year*, 295–301, at 296.

over its citizens. In his 1975 lectures, Michel Foucault lays out these two views (or what he calls "dreams"), arguing first that "there is a literature of plague that is a literature . . . when the law is forgotten" and secondly that there is a "political dream" when "political power is exercised to the full."[19] While Foucault does not discuss *Plague Year,* the novel clearly shifts uneasily between these two poles – in part through its treatment of reactions to governmental measures to limit contagion, and in part through chronicling the intensity with which both H.F. and the general population vacillate between a positive desire for various forms of governmental control and their rejection of such efforts. Martin Wagner details H.F.'s shifting analysis of governmental measures – particularly the shutting-up of houses – noting that at certain times H.F. praises the governmental response while at others he criticizes it. The governmental response to the plague, though more developed and enforced than Defoe acknowledges in *Plague Year*, was in fact inadequate. The many rules and regulations that constituted legality in relation to the plague were unenforceable and, in any case, no match against the high communicability of bubonic plague. In *Plague Year*, Foucault's dream of "spatial partitioning and subdivision of a population taken to its extreme point" was just a dream.[20]

This is not to understate the restrictive nature of the legal regulations related to the plague. Plague law, both before 1665 and after, included any number of restrictions: travel restrictions, trade restrictions, and quarantine orders, as well as the mass appointment of "watchers" (actually guards meant to enforce quarantines), orders for the establishment of special hospitals, and numerous laws governing the disposition of bodies.[21] The government used its established authority to quarantine suspected victims in their houses, with at one point as much as 50 percent of the population either ordered into or actually enduring some form of lockdown.[22] Entertainments and gatherings were prohibited, and citizens required passports in order to leave the city. Travis Chi Wing Lau points out that during the time Defoe wrote *Plague Year*, plague law became even more restrictive. For example, while the Quarantine Act of 1710 "enabled the

[19] See Martin Wagner, "Defoe, Foucault and the Politics of the Plague," *Studies in English Literature 1500–1800* 57, no. 3 (Fall 2017):501–19 for a succinct summary of this argument.

[20] Michel Foucault, *Abnormal: Lectures at the Collège de France*, trans. Graham Burchell, ed. Valerio Marchetti and Antonella Salomoni (New York: Picador, 1999), 47.

[21] Ernest B. Gilman, "The Subject of the Plague," *Journal for Early Modern Cultural Studies* 10, no. 2 (Fall/Winter 2010): 23–44, at 40.

[22] Ian Ward, "Henry Foe's Dilemma," *International Journal of Law in Context* 18, no. 2 (June 2022): 175–95, at 179.

surveillance and detention of all vessels arriving from reportedly infected areas for forty days," in 1721 more aggressive measures were taken by an act that prohibited trade for a year with countries thought to be infected with the plague.[23] As Graham Hammill argues, "plague legislation … shaped understandings of national community, sovereignty, and the role of violence in enacting political reform."[24]

In Defoe's account, the plague, in concert with these legal prohibitions, turns London into an emotional pressure cooker where the effects of stress on a city can be closely observed. Increasing the stakes is Defoe's observation that as with any natural disaster, the plague involved a general exodus of the wealthy and privileged, including the king and his court. Defoe focuses on those who remain, on the poorer, less privileged members of the population. *Plague Year* offers an extended meditation on the emotions that a panicked population with few options and limited resources feels when the legal system and other sources of authority meant to protect it fail. Plague, as Foucault and others have pointed out, throws "the limits and responsibilities of government into sharpest relief," but it also brings the emotions of the populace regarding law and government to the foreground.[25]

Wagner observes that Defoe presents "side-by-side accounts of the government's efforts to instill order as both very successful and completely futile." He suggests that this represents "an unresolved conflict in the novel."[26] Valiantly attempting to resolve this "unresolved conflict" by offering a third possible reading, Wagner interprets Defoe's stories of citizens who prudently shut themselves up in "voluntary self-confinement" as representing a new and different model of "autonomous bourgeois identity."[27] These families supposedly "escape the administration's measuring gaze" *by obeying the law*, in Wagner's view demonstrating a form of agency that is "surprisingly subversive" and one that is significant for the development of individualism in its indication of how "lawful behavior now also becomes contingent on the individual."[28] Wagner's interesting reading offers a handy exit from the usual panopticon/chaos binary, and

[23] Travis Chi Wing Lau, "Defoe before Immunity: A Prophylactic *Journal of the Plague Year*," *Digital Defoe: Studies in Defoe and His Contemporaries* 8, no. 1 (Fall 2016): 23–39, at 25.

[24] Graham Hammill, "Miracles and Plagues: Plague Discourse as Political Thought," *Journal for Early Modern Cultural Studies* 10, no. 2 (Fall/Winter 2010): 85–104, at 85.

[25] Alan McKinlay, "Foucault, Plague, Defoe," *Culture and Organization* 15, no. 2 (June 2009): 167–84, at 181.

[26] Wagner, "Defoe, Foucault," 509. [27] Wagner, "Defoe, Foucault," 509.

[28] Wagner, "Defoe, Foucault," 513.

yet it does so by downplaying how much of the text is devoted not to the law-abiding or to criminals but rather to those, including the narrator, who simply cannot make up their minds. These characters obey and then disobey, obey, and disobey again as their ambivalence pulls them first in one direction, then in another. Meanwhile the text itself reflects this ambivalence through formal devices that undergird the ambivalence of the characters, and especially the narrator. What happens to our reading of *Plague Year* if, instead of trying to dispense with this "unresolved conflict in the novel," we foreground the contradiction while recognizing that it is ambivalence rather than adhesion to one or the other of these binary possibilities that dominates Defoe's account?

Defoe, I suggest, is wrangling with one of the big questions that modern democratic societies face. As Wagner puts it, "how can one act independently in a law-governed society without having to break the law?"[29] This question has been put a number of different ways, of course, but critical legal theorist Duncan Kennedy has framed it particularly eloquently. Kennedy, rather than trying to resolve the question, labels it "the fundamental contradiction." He argues that it is one that all humans face, that of the incompatibility of our desire for personal freedom with our absolute dependence on others for species and personal survival. In this schema, "freedom" maps onto individuality but also onto lawlessness while "dependence on others" maps onto community, established religion, and the acceptance of one's legally defined subjectivity. As Kennedy puts it, "the goal of individual freedom is at the same time dependent on and incompatible with the communal coercive action that is necessary to achieve it."[30] Kennedy might as well have been describing plague conditions when, in a quite dark take on this problem, he says, "at the same time it forms and protects us, the universe of others ... threatens us with annihilation and urges upon us forms of fusion that are quite plainly bad rather than good ... Numberless conformities, large and small abandonments of self to others, are the price of what freedom we experience in society."[31] This is at base both a legal and political issue and an *emotional* issue involving the intersection between our individual ("selfish" and survival-oriented) desires and our attachment needs. As Kennedy says, we are driven by "our *feelings* that ... the collective is a threat."[32] The "assurances of reason" cannot resolve the fundamental contradiction because the conflict is driven by survival emotions: the desire for liberty

[29] Wagner, "Defoe, Foucault," 514. [30] Kennedy, "Structure," 212.
[31] Kennedy, "Structure," 212. [32] Kennedy, "Structure," 257 (emphasis added).

from the tyranny of the crowd and our inability to survive in isolation work hand in hand to maintain the contradiction. And these feelings – residing on the affect-emotion continuum – are embodied, experienced both as articulated concerns and in physical urges. Kennedy comes to a depressing conclusion, arguing that our judicial systems and conceivably all social organizations including the church and state falsely operate to occlude this fundamental contradiction. If we think we are enacting justice, he argues, we are deluded, acting in bad faith, and either engineering or being used to engineer the cover-up. The pomp and circumstance of our institutions, as well as their claims to justice and reason, merely serve to blind us to this charade. Jessie Allen flips this despairing take on its head, suggesting that the law serves an essential function in providing performative legal rituals capable of reconciling the fundamental contradiction while recognizing that such a reconciliation is never complete.[33] Extrapolating from Allen's view, legal rituals, symbols and visible efforts to enforce the law as well as various emblems of legality are crucial to our sense of security whether they are successful or not. Rather than cloaking the fundamental contradiction, they offer dynamic representations of a system in flux and in a somewhat contradictory manner serve to stabilize it.

Plague Year provides a sort of sealed laboratory for exploring the value of ambivalence in a world where these symbols have left town and the remnants of legality have limited effectiveness. In *Plague Year* there are no good decisions to be made. No one knows what causes the plague; those who obey the unenforceable laws and self-isolate are as likely to be infected as those who do not. The causes are thought to be legion: steam, fumes, breath, sweat, stench, exposure to sores, or possibly, as Defoe puts it, "an immediate Stroke from Heaven."[34] Often people who appear to be well are "all that while carrying Death with them into all Companies which they come into" (159). H.F. tells us that doctors are baffled and people both seek and flee them, putting their faith in magic charms and quack cures, "mad, upon their running after Quacks, and Montebanks, and every practicing old woman" (29). People may wish for but cannot trust governmental regulation since the authorities isolate non-infected people with infected people, prohibit travel to less dangerous areas, and, at the same time, fail to provide measures such as appropriate burial procedures, ensuring many unnecessary deaths. Ambivalence in *Plague Year* can thus be seen as a "natural" and even pragmatic response to the crisis as well as a

[33] See Jessie Allen, "Performing Justice," *Emotions: History, Culture, Society* 2, no. 1 (2018): 52–70.
[34] Defoe, *Journal of the Plague Year*, 64. Hereafter cited parenthetically in the text.

form of resistance to modernity's efforts to categorize and routinize a population. Defoe's characters are uncertain whether to leave or stay, terrified of exposure and yet reluctant to submit to enforced isolation. Their movement throughout the city and various escapes from the city become signs of this ambivalence.

Defoe's faction is an emotionally saturated text, as one might expect given the experiences H.F. describes. "No one can account for the possession of fear when it takes hold of the mind," Defoe's protagonist H.F. says. "Sorrow and Sadness sat on every Face . . . . [T]he Voice of Mourning was truly heard in the Streets; the shrieks of Women and Children at the Windows . . . were so frequent to be heard . . . that it was enough to pierce the stoutest Heart in the World" (18). Words like "Grief," "Agony," "Sorrow," "Terror," and "Desolation" appear throughout the narrative. People are "roaring, and crying, and wringing their Hands" (85). We may find no better description of embodied grief in literature than that of Defoe's sinking head man, who "was so absolutely overcome with the Pressure upon his Spirits, that by Degrees, his Head sunk into his Body, so . . . that the Crown of his Head was very little seen above the Bones of his Shoulders" and "his Face . . . lay against his Collar-Bone, and cou'd not be kept up otherwise, unless held up by the Hands of other People" (98). Eventually H.F. seems to tire of these terrifying, emotionally wrenching stories, commenting on his own narration:

> [A]fter I have told you, as I have above, that One Man being tyed in his Bed, and finding no other Way to deliver himself, set the Bed on fire with his Candle . . . and Burnt himself in his Bed, . . . What can be added more? What can be said to . . . give [you] a more perfect Idea of a complicated Distress? (140)

What can be said to attain "a more perfect Idea of a complicated Distress" involves both reading for overt expressions of emotion and reading for structure and form to examine the ambivalence that appears both on the surface level and in the deep structure of the text. Defoe's characters hover somewhere between affect and emotions, sometimes reacting viscerally to stimuli and unknowingly participating in a world of intensities interacting with each other, while at other times clearly articulating emotions as mediated by cultural, social, and legal contexts. The general tenor can be traced at the level of the word or phrase. What Frank H. Ellis views as "most annoying," H.F.'s repetition of qualifying phrases like "I say I could wish" and "I must go back" suggests a sort of narrative ambivalence, in that Defoe arranges the narrative, not in chronological order, but in a convoluted and repetitive, even circular order that, as Ellis points out, rarely meets readers' expectations for a plague narrative.[35] Words and phrases, narrative details, and the direct expression of emotions are, of course, of crucial importance for understanding the representation of emotions in historical periods. However, scholars like Kathryn de Luna, Eugenie Brinkema, and myself, among others, have argued that if we wish to study the history of emotion we need to move beyond the direct expression of emotions and also consider the structure, style, mode, and mood of the texts we rely upon.[36]

In *Plague Year* intense emotional reactions are channeled through and subordinated to H.F.'s descriptions of his own and others' ambivalence, signified by problems in making decisions, by a lack of congruence between intentions and acts, and by the restless movements – both physical and emotional – exhibited not only by H.F. but by multiple other characters and by the text itself. Inconsistency drives the narrative to an extent that is almost comic. To offer one example, H.F. tells us that "the best Preparation for the Plague [is] to run away from it" (12). However, the movement of most of the characters, including the protagonist, is surprisingly not directed toward an escape from London or "running away from it" but is instead impulsive and wandering as citizens attempt to escape their household confinement, gather in groups at churches and taverns, leave and return to their homes, loot other citizens, observe people's traumas, and engage in all forms of movements in and around the city. The text contains many scenes in which ambivalence is figured through some combination of physical movement and expression. To offer only two examples: H.F. checks on his brother's business, where he encounters a bizarre spectacle of women trying on "High Crowned Hats" (73) as if unconcerned by the death of those around them (or by ownership interests for that matter), and in another long, interpolated tale, he meets, follows, and questions "the boatman," a selfless character who is sacrificing all for his family, self-isolating so that he can work and provide them with food and thus denying himself the very company that H.F.

35 See Frank H. Ellis, review of Defoe's *Journal of the Plague Year*, ed. Paula R. Backscheider, *Review of English Studies* 45, no. 177 (February 1994): 76–82, at 77–78. In this entertaining review, Ellis lists hundreds of like phrases and discusses Defoe's use of repetition in detail as a factor that diminished the popularity of *Plague Year* when it was published and irritated Ellis when he wrote the review.

36 Eugenia Brinkema, *The Forms of the Affects* (Durham, NC: Duke University Press, 2014); Kathryn D. Temple, *Loving Justice: Legal Emotions in William Blackstone's England* (New York: New York University Press, 2019); Kathryn DeLuna, unpublished lecture, Society for the History of Emotion Conference, Rome, summer 2022. In her most recent book, *Life-Destroying Diagrams* (Durham, NC: Duke University Press, 2022), Brinkema argues that reading form for anything other than taking pleasure in form itself diminishes the value of formalism.

seems compelled to seek out. Multiple ironies accompany these narratives, and the text often seems to display an ironic ambivalence itself, in that H.F. relates behaviors so contradictory that they (almost) become humorous even as they are being described with utmost seriousness. For example, H.F. often notes complaints about others who leave their homes seemingly without symptoms and yet spread the disease. Yet when he encounters the boatman, he claims rather insistently to be healthy himself so that he can enjoy a ride down the Thames and thus indulge his "Curiosity" (92). The story becomes a narrative exploration of the workings of ambivalence as H.F. both ignores and recognizes his own hypocrisy: "[H]ow much less is my Faith than thine? . . . [H]ow much better this Poor Man's Foundation . . . than mine . . . he used all possible Caution for his Safety" (90). Of course, the boatman has not used "all possible caution," but has instead allowed H.F. to accompany him.

Defoe amplifies this effect by organizing a set of nested narratives, each of which energetically intersects with the others. He opens the narrative with an account of the restless movement of the plague itself – from Holland, perhaps Cyprus, to France, and then to London – then shifts quickly to H.F.'s lengthy and ambivalent ruminations. How should he deal with the plague? Should he stay or should he go? H.F. has his doubts: "I now began to consider seriously with my Self . . . that is to say, whether I should resolve to stay in London, or shut up my House and flee" (11). Reading these episodes through Kennedy's lens suggests that the fundamental contradiction is hard at work here. H.F. vacillates between commitment to the larger community, as represented by law, whether the law of the state or of God, and the desire for independent action, a yearning for liberty, the liberty to disobey the law, abandon the community, and flee London. At first, H.F. seems quite pragmatic as he weighs the maintenance of his business against the preservation of his life. The juxtaposition of such unequal concerns, trade against "Life" (11), offers a comic moment, but trade here represents a healthy and engaged community, and to abandon it is to reject the common good. More seriously, H.F. ponders whether God would prefer him to flee or stay, an ambivalence that results in his brother's mocking comment: "Master save thy self" (12). This is no light moment for H.F., however. "Master save thy self" is what was said to Christ on the cross, and H.F. immediately leaps to the conclusion that he, like Christ, should remain on the cross of London and give himself up to God's will. Does Defoe hint at humor here in that H.F. is now comparing his own sacrifice to that of Christ? H.F. then embarks on a lengthy description of his internal decision-making process, in part through describing further discussions with his brother – who points out that God might as well protect H.F.'s business as protect his body – and in part through a process of self-questioning. Are various delays caused by trivial factors signs from God that he should stay in London? His brother finds it ridiculous that God would communicate through commonplace events like a servant quitting or the lack of a ready horse. At one point, his brother compares H.F.'s faith in a God who will save him to that of the Turks who "would go unconcern'd into infected Places, and converse with infected Persons, by which Means they died at the Rate of Ten or Fifteen Thousand a Week" (14). But being compared to infidels has only a temporary effect on H.F., who at first "resolves to go" but within paragraphs is again questioning his decision. Leaving, he thinks, could be seen as "flying from God" (it also represents a flight from his business, from the rule of law, and from the community), yet staying seems perilous as he watches the city empty out.

H.F. attempts to resolve his ambivalence by ambivalently engaging the cognitive tools available to him. First, he turns to a sort of accountancy as he "stated the Arguments with which my Brother had press'd me . . . and set against them the strong Impressions which I had on my Mind for staying" (14–15), impressions that are both spiritual and (adding a pragmatic and possibly humorous note) economic, that is, "the Preservation of my Effects" (15). We can visualize this playing out in columns, a device Defoe had recently used in *Robinson Crusoe.* But weighing heavy in the balance is a "secret satisfaction" that God will keep H.F. safe. Eventually, he turns to "bibliomancy," treating the Bible as the law and landing on the ninety-first Psalm, where he reads that God will "deliver thee . . . from the noisome pestilence . . . no evil befall thee, neither shall any plague come nigh" (15). Finally resolved to stay, H.F. goes to bed, only to wake too ill to go – though not with the plague. He is sick for three days, long enough to miss departing with his brother, a circumstance he declines to interpret from a spiritual perspective. We might so interpret it, however: Jesus rose after three days, and Jonah ascended from the whale after three days. While H.F. seems to have held the possibility of leaving London in reserve, his body has at least temporarily resolved his ambivalence: In staying he obeys God's law but he also obeys the London plague regulations.

At this point, we are only fifteen pages into a two-hundred-page narrative that could be expected to have adopted the formal structures of pandemic narratives that we have now become accustomed to: a gradual buildup of fear, the breakdown of communal and governmental regulatory services, then a slow return to a new normal as the population adjusts.[37] But the structure here is not so much that of the plague cresting followed by a return to normality as one of interlocking interpolated narratives, embedded within each other. I have dwelled on the opening pages because they set the terms for the rest of the narrative, demonstrating Defoe's commitment to ambivalence as a response to crisis situations. This narrative decision allows H.F. to become a consummate observer, poised between and above but rarely playing a major role in the action. Defoe makes of him an independent agent, seemingly without attachments, family, servants, employees, even pets. He moves around London freely, ruled equally by impulses, conscience, spiritual beliefs, and worldly concerns as he observes his own and others' behaviors. In doing so, he exemplifies the current scholarly construction of ambivalence as positive in that the experimentation and flexibility it fosters allows people to explore their environments and create new understandings of them. Along these lines, H.F. seems almost to rely on ambivalence to construct a protective balance between isolation and interaction and to provide him with the material he needs to create *Plague Year,* giving him a sense of purpose even while he is surrounded by the chaos of plague life.

Once established, ambivalence is expressed not so much through expressions of interiority as through H.F.'s and other characters' contradictory behaviors and movements. Knowing that he should remain isolated, H.F. repeatedly goes out, resolves "to go out no more" (65), is unable to control himself, and allows his impatience to overcome his restraint. Meanwhile, on a meta level, embedded narratives and inset stories jostle for attention as Defoe jumps from one story to another and back and forth through time, creating a sense that the text, like the human bodies depicted within it, cannot commit to a specific course of action. To reinforce the point, the first of these embedded narratives is a false start, for H.F. seems unable to sustain linearity. He begins to tell the story of the "two brothers and their kinsman" who escape London in order to try to find safety in the countryside (51). But he suddenly drops this narrative for almost fifty pages, only to take it up again much later. In the story, three brothers band together, determined to seek a contagion-free zone outside London.[38] But after many adventures in which they form and join small, isolated communities to receive and give help, they despair of escaping the plague and,

[37] Stephanie Boluk and Wylie Lenz, "Infection, Media, and Capitalism: From Early Modern Plagues to Postmodern Zombies," *Journal for Early Modern Cultural Studies* 10, no. 2 (Fall/Winter 2010): 126–47, at 127.

[38] See Everett Zimmerman, "H.F.'s Meditations: *A Journal of the Plague Year,*" in Defoe, *Journal of the Plague Year,* 285–95, for a discussion of the religious implications of this interpolated tale.

in a disappointing and under-discussed conclusion, return to London. Although Defoe claims that "Their Story has a Moral in every Part of it" (100), in the end, it seems to have no moral other than that these are desperate times that refuse to be reduced to one unequivocal emotional response.

The brothers' story, of course, is important for an understanding of how ambivalent attachment motivates disparate efforts to isolate and to form community because during the course of their travels, the three men make repeated efforts to form socio-legal contracts with each other and with those they meet.[39] But here I want to focus on Defoe's use of the story to create a particular structure. For the lengthy gap between the beginning and end of the tale operates as a sort of narrowing funnel leading to the most embedded inset story in *Plague Year*, H.F.'s much-discussed venture into trauma tourism, or what H.F. characterizes as a visit to the "great Pit." This episode showcases the embodied and simultaneously emotive nature of ambivalence as H.F. ricochets between desiring liberty from the law and affirming his commitment to it. It is "curiosity" that drives H.F. to visit "the Pit," a hole in the ground where the bodies of over four hundred of the dead have been tossed in lieu of a proper burial (53). H.F. has visited already, but only during the day when there is nothing to be seen but dirt. Now in a brutally expressed admission, he decides to go at night so he can "see some of them thrown in" (53). Aware of but ignoring the illegality of his acts, H.F. is careful to point out that "there was a strict Order to prevent People coming to those Pits" (53), an order made even more necessary because the dying had taken to throwing themselves in so as to "bury themselves." H.F. seems both drawn to the pit and yet hesitant to approach it. He offers the excursion as one of the few times he risks his safety, saying that it is impossible to "resist [his] Curiosity" (52). And while the pits are dangerous, this is, of course, only one of the many times H.F. has risked his own safety. Once he is there, a church sexton – who himself cannot make up his mind – almost persuades H.F. to give up the effort but also tells him that he should proceed: "'Tis a speaking Sight . . . and has a Voice with it, and a loud one, to call us all to Repentance" (54). Despite or maybe because of this advice, H.F. again falters and stands "wavering" (54), as if on the threshold between life and death. Yet when he notices a "Dead Cart" approaching, he can "no longer resist [his] Desire" (54). We have here, as Giorgio Agamben has said, the modern subject, who

[39] For a nuanced discussion of this issue, see Peter DeGabriele, "Intimacy, Survival, and Resistance: Daniel Defoe's *A Journal of the Plague Year*," *ELH* 77, no. 1 (Spring 2010): 1–23.

"exists on the threshold that belongs neither to the world of the living nor to the world of the dead: he is a living dead man."[40] Following this, Defoe again departs from linear narrative to tell yet another nested story of a man "in great Agony" (54) who sees his family dead in the pit. After a bit of exposition, H.F. returns to his own story, describing the pit as "full of Terror" as he watches "sixteen or seventeen" bodies being disposed of (55). But we are not done. He leaves, sees another Dead Cart, almost returns, thinks better of it, and goes home, thinking of "the Risque I had run" and "believing I had gotten no Injury" (56). By now it is one o'clock in the morning and yet H.F. decides to go out again to check on the man "in great agony," comforting him, eventually fighting off some tavern hecklers, and then engaging with his own conscience as he vacillates between rage and forgiveness.

I want to return here to two points raised by this recounting. I will start with H.F.'s seemingly offhand comment about those who "bury themselves," committing what constituted "self-murder" (the word "suicide" was not yet in common use) rather than waiting for the plague to take them, a key moment in any reading of the value of ambivalence.[41] It is notable that H.F. expresses both sympathy for and horror at those so afflicted, an atypical reaction during a period when some people reviled the victims of suicide as traitors to the state while others mocked them as fools or effeminate or both.[42] Defoe seems to have been ambivalent in his attitude toward suicide. In his journalism, he was not above poking fun at those who manipulated the idea of suicide for their own ends.[43] In this regard, he represents suicide as an undesirable escape hatch from the responsibilities that accompany legal subjectivity. As Eric Parisot has documented, suicide often evoked a critique rooted in "discrediting the

40 Giorgio Agamben, *Homo Sacer: Sovereign Power and Bare Life*, trans. Daniel Heller-Roazen (Stanford, CA: Stanford University Press, 1998), 99.

41 Prior to the 1650s, the word "suicide" was not in use. Instead, terms like "self-murder," "self-killing," and "self-slaughter" were common. See Mark Robson, "General Introduction," in *The History of Suicide in England, 1650–1850*, ed. Mark Robson, vol. 1 (London: Pickering and Chatto, 2012), vii–xxvi, at xii–xiii.

42 Eric Parisot, "Performing Selves: Communicating Authentic Humanity," in *Passions, Sympathy and Print Culture: Public Opinion and Emotional Authenticity in Eighteenth-Century Britain*, ed. Heather Kerr, David Lemmings, and Robert Phiddian (Houndmills: Palgrave Macmillan, 2016), 183–202, at 197; Kelly McQuire, *Dying to Be English: Suicide Narratives and National Identity, 1721–1814* (London: Pickering and Chatto, 2012), 11.

43 Maximillian E. Novak, "Defoe and the Disordered City," *PMLA* 92, no. 2 (March 1977): 241–52, at 247. See also Michael MacDonald, "Suicide and the Rise of the Popular Press in England," *Representations* 22 (Spring 1988): 36–55.

authenticity of suicidal emotions."[44] While to our contemporary eyes, suicide may seem an excusable though tragic response to alienation, depression, social conditions, neurological disorders, or despair, in Defoe's time, suicide was a highly overdetermined act, one in which a legal subject who owed his life, labor, and loyalty to God and the crown chose instead to exercise sovereignty over his own body.[45] Those who committed suicide, for whatever reasons, were thought to have rejected the rule of law, the larger community, and their debt to the state in favor of the right to autonomy. The law thus exerted severe penalties on the living body should the attempt fail and on the corpse of the deceased in successful cases, in both instances returning the suicidal person or their body back into, as Kelly McGuire puts it, "the biopolitical fold."[46] H.F., of course, does not commit suicide. But by giving in to his urge to see the pit, by "wavering" on the threshold, he has placed himself on a continuum with others who commit "self-murder," and thus for these moments he positions himself on the threshold of a commitment to one of the most extreme forms of individualism, one that puts the subject, if not their body, beyond the reach of the law's sovereignty. In this context, suicide in *Plague Year* is more than an illegal act. Suicide represents a final decision on the side of liberty and ends the obligations of the subject to the state. But it also ends the life of the victim and removes all their choices, providing a sort of certainty that marks the end of a life story. Ambivalence meanwhile preserves lives as it does H.F.'s life. He teeters but he does not descend.

If suicide defines one end of the liberty–legality continuum, the other end could be defined as full capitulation to the law, a deadly option given the deaths that occurred when citizens were confined to their homes. In *Plague Year*, though, absolute obedience gives way to what law actually represents, our agreement to act together as a community. While the novel is full of moments that reject legality, perpetrated not least by H.F., it is also full of communal moments as H.F., true to his ambivalence, both rejects the need to adhere to community standards and at times becomes their advocate. This is apparent in H.F.'s reaction to the "man in great

[44] Parisot, "Performing Selves," 197.

[45] Attempted suicide is still considered a crime in some jurisdictions in the United States, although it is seldom prosecuted. Suicide was decriminalized in the United Kingdom in 1961. See Helen Y. Chang, "A Brief History of Anglo-Western Suicide: From Legal Wrong to Civil Right," *Southern University Law Review* 46, no. 1 (2018): 150–94.

[46] McGuire, *Dying to Be English*, 3.

agony" who comes to the pit not as a trauma tourist but as a mourning husband and father, "oppress'd with a dreadful Weight of Grief . . . in an Agony and excess of Sorrow" (54). H.F. returns to the scene in the early morning hours because of his concern for the man in "great Agony" and finds himself in the position of a representative of order and civility in contrast to the drunken "dreadful Set of Fellows" (56) who have turned on the bereaved father and are taunting him "with want of Courage to leap into the great Pit and go to Heaven" (57). In an uncharacteristic move, H.F. abandons his position as observer and stands up to the "hellish abominable raillery" of these men who "were not afraid to blaspheme God . . . and even [laugh] at the Word Judgment" (57). The scene is followed by a lengthy meditation on God, the value of the church, and the importance of communities gathering for religious services, all meant to represent the common good, an odd meditation for H.F. given his detachment from others but one that demonstrates his ambivalence. A similar impulse drives H.F. toward God, where God represents the law and following the rule of law represents acquiescence to community values. In other examples, H.F.'s enthusiastic inclusion of statistics gathered by the authorities repeatedly reminds the reader of the law's omnipresence; stories of heroic doctors and nurses, of watchmen attempting to enforce quarantine, of the boatman feeding his family while protecting himself so he can continue to serve, all remind us of the fact that humans have equal and competing emotional drives that position us between the desire for liberty and the need for communal solidarity. In the Lockean tradition and as Kennedy and others have asserted, it is the community that protects the liberty we desire.

I have dwelled on these contradictory episodes at length because they consolidate many of the issues I have raised here: H.F. embodies ambivalence, in part because he cannot make decisions, struggles with his conscience, and comes and goes in a frantic display of indecision, but also because he is a walking contradiction, both outside observer and concerned interventionist, both seemingly immune to the plague and yet obsessed with it, both rejecting legality and representing it. Standing on the threshold of a suicidal act depolarizes suicide; shifting from lawful to unlawful behaviors and back again depolarizes the law–chaos dichotomy. The effect is multiplied by the many other characters who play supporting if not fully articulated roles: they are "the walking dead" of 1660s London, either about to be infected or already infected and contagious without showing symptoms as they wander about London infecting others and engaging if not in suicide, in the suicidal act of courting death. H.F.

himself is dead by the time the reading public encounters Defoe's narrative in 1722 (he is the "talking dead"): a point Defoe makes when he mentions H.F.'s grave in a footnote inserted in the middle of a discussion of burial grounds as if he has forgotten that H.F. is currently narrating *Plague Year* (181). Burrowing down through H.F.'s introspection, through the structural funnel represented by his inset story involving the brothers and into the depths of the narrative represented by the visit to the burial pit, suggests the value of ambivalence as sustained uncertainty, as the emotional tool that resists the destructive force of a state of absolute liberty while also resisting absolute subjugation to legality.

Conclusion: The Value of Sustained Ambivalence

The end of *Plague Year* is, as David Brooks notes, "a confused movement between two opposite points of view."[47] As if to underscore the value of ambivalence in the last moments of the faction, H.F. shifts back and forth uneasily between suggesting that God has finally relented and ended the plague and insisting that "no Account could be given" (191) for its end. Attributing London's recovery to God, of course, recognizes the power of an authority higher than but related to legality, while "no Account" suggests a world in which chaos cannot be managed through the imposition of order. Defoe thus holds the fundamental contradiction in tension in that both his protagonist and the other characters vacillate between the drive toward individual liberty and that toward community with its full embrace of legal subjectivity. That Defoe manages to place these two emotional impulses in tension with each other also makes of *Plague Year* an object lesson, a reminder that at the very moment when pandemics require us to limit spread contagion by self-isolating we also need to work together, to see ourselves as part of a larger community as we mutually agree on restrictive measures. This need for physical isolation directly conflicts not only with the pragmatic need for community but also with the *emotional* connections that signify community to our bodies. The fundamental contradiction is thus both embodied and in Defoe *symbolically encapsulated* in what might be called the pandemic condition. At the very moment when his protagonist desires to function as a free and self-reliant individual, he also needs to function as part of the larger community. What Defoe shows, then, is the value of suspending this clash of needs and loyalties in a state of sustained ambivalence, and thus the value of ambivalence as a survival emotion.

[47] Brooks, "Daniel Defoe," 173.

CHAPTER 4

The Court of Justice and the Court of Conscience
Legal Ethics in Tom Jones

Suzanna Geiser

From the unethical judges in *Joseph Andrews* (1742) and *Jonathan Wild* (1743) to the unskilled and often unprincipled lawyers and magistrates in *Tom Jones* (1749) to the corrupted prison officials in *Amelia* (1751), flawed legal characters abound in Henry Fielding's novels. Critics often attribute these characters and their stories to Fielding's own professional relationship to and interest in the law.[1] Called to the Bar in 1740 and appointed to the magistracy in 1748, Fielding was practicing law and adjudicating cases at the same time as he was creating legal worlds in his fiction and offering legal commentary in his scholarly and journalistic endeavors.[2] During this period, Fielding was also engaged with moral philosophy – in particular, classical and contemporary theories about human character and moral judgment. As Michael McKeon has demonstrated, Fielding's writing pursues both "questions of truth" and "questions of virtue," the former concerned with "how to tell the truth in narrative" and the latter with how to determine the "internal, moral state" of individuals.[3] In 1743, for example, Fielding published "An Essay on the Knowledge of the

[1] See Lance Bertelsen, *Henry Fielding at Work: Magistrate, Businessman, Writer* (New York: Palgrave, 2000); Ronald Paulson, *The Life of Henry Fielding: A Critical Biography* (Oxford: Blackwell, 2000); Frances L. Alfandary, "An Odd Sort of Author: Henry Fielding, Writer and Magistrate," *Columbia Library Columns* 43, no. 3 (1994): 26–37; Hugh Armory, "Magistrate or Censor? The Problem of Authority in Fielding's Later Writings," *Studies in English Literature, 1500–1900* 12, no. 3 (1972): 503–18; Pat Rogers, "Fielding on Society, Crime, and the Law," in *The Cambridge Companion to Henry Fielding*, ed. Claude Rawson (Cambridge: Cambridge University Press, 2007), 137–52; Yoichi Kanecko, "Law and Evidence in *Joseph Andrews*," *Poetica: An International Journal of Linguistic-Literary Studies* 69 (2008): 41–69; and John C. Stephens, Jr., "The Verge of the Court and Arrest for Debt in Fielding's *Amelia*," *Modern Language Notes* 63, no. 2 (1948): 104–09.

[2] Fielding published a number of legal pamphlets and treatises related to crime during his writing career, including *The Charge to the Grand Jury* (1745), *An Enquiry into the Causes of the Late Increase of Robbers* (1751), and *A Clear State of the Case of Elizabeth Canning* (1753). For a discussion of the connections between Fielding's journalism, scholarship, and work in the law, see Paulson, *The Life of Henry Fielding*, 98–135, 261–328.

[3] Michael McKeon, "Generic Transformation and Social Change: Rethinking the Rise of the Novel," *Cultural Critique* 1, no. 1 (Autumn 1985): 159–81, at 161, 180–81.

Characters of Men," which Roger Maioli aptly describes as an empiricist "treatise in moral epistemology."[4] The essay communicates Fielding's observations about the unscrupulous contingent of society and offers a methodology for knowing the true nature of any human character.[5] The essay also suggests Fielding's concerns about the state of human ethics – concerns that permeate his novels in the form of characters who occupy liminal ethical spaces. Thus, Fielding's errant legal characters and their stories are traceable not only to the author's participation in the law but also to his experience as a social and ethical being.

Fielding's investment in the idiosyncrasies of law and ethics is perhaps most apparent in *Tom Jones*, the rich satire that Fielding published after his transition from barrister to magistrate. Fielding scholars have recognized that *Tom Jones* interacts with eighteenth-century laws and legal doctrines, particularly those associated with property, commerce, and marriage, in ways that can help us understand the complexities of the novel form's position as property under the law and its relationship to the credit economy, as well as "the law's failure to punish moral outrage."[6] Scholars have also explored how the novel employs legal procedure, especially the criminal trial, to comment on problems of human judgment and understanding as well as criminal justice.[7] This interest in morality is further evident in the scholarship devoted to examining the range of ethical philosophies that govern the universe of *Tom Jones*, with some scholars emphasizing religious ethics, especially Christian Humanism, and other

4 Roger Maioli, "Empiricism and Henry Fielding's Theory of Fiction," *Eighteenth-Century Fiction* 27, no. 2 (Winter 2014–15): 201–28, at 206, 207.

5 See Henry Fielding, "An Essay on the Knowledge of the Characters of Men," in *Miscellanies by Henry Fielding, Esq.*, ed. Henry Knight Miller, 2 vols., The Wesleyan Edition of the Works of Henry Fielding (Oxford: Clarendon Press, 1972), 1:153–78.

6 Simon Stern, "*Tom Jones* and the Economies of Copyright," *Eighteenth-Century Fiction* 9, no. 4 (July 1997): 429–46; Martin A. Kayman, "The 'New Sort of Specialty' and the 'New Province of Writing': Bank Notes, Fiction, and the Law in *Tom Jones*," *ELH* 68, no. 3 (Fall 2001): 633–53; and William G. Sayres, "A Loophole in the Law: The Case of Black George and the Purse in *Tom Jones*," *Journal of English and Germanic Philology* 94, no. 2 (April 1995): 207–19, at 208.

7 See John Allen Stevenson, *The Real History of Tom Jones* (Palgrave Macmillan, 2005), 9, 103–04; John E. Loftis, "Trials and the Shaping of Identity in *Tom Jones*," *Studies in the Novel* 34, no. 1 (Spring 2002): 1–20; Alexander Welsh, *Strong Representations: Narrative and Circumstantial Evidence in England* (Baltimore: Johns Hopkins University Press, 1992), 44–76; and Raymond Stephanson, "Fielding's 'Courts': The Legal Paradigm in *Tom Jones*," *English Studies in Canada* 14, no. 2 (June 1988): 152–69. For a more sweeping discussion of representations of the law and legal actors in the eighteenth-century novel, see David Punter, "Fictional Representation of the Law in the Eighteenth Century," *Eighteenth-Century Studies* 16, no. 1 (Fall 1982): 47–74. While Punter addresses Fielding's representations of the magistrate and the attorney in *Tom Jones*, he does not discuss what those representations suggest about the state of legal ethics in the period.

scholars underscoring Aristotelian ethics and Mandevillian egoism.[8] Together, this scholarship offers insight, first, into how the law operated in the mid eighteenth century and shaped the novel and its publication, and second, into Fielding's personal view of ethics and its impact on individual characters and plots. What this scholarship does not do – and what this chapter seeks to accomplish – is examine how the legal plots and characters of *Tom Jones* comment on eighteenth-century law as a profession and an ethical system.

This chapter also seeks to show how *Tom Jones* can be useful to critical applications of and responses to twenty-first-century legal ethics. Law-and-literature scholars have long argued that representations of law in literature can change the ways in which law students, academics, lawyers, and judges conceptualize and approach the law. As a result, scholars have advocated a pedagogical purpose in approaching fiction as a legal artifact, a historical – or cultural – representation of the ethical challenges inherent in legal practice and judgment. For example, Richard Weisberg argues that literature can both teach lawyers about the values and virtues needed to maintain and practice legal justice and offer humanist solutions to contemporary ethical issues within the profession.[9] Similarly, James Boyd White, the widely recognized founder of the law-and-literature movement, maintains that "the habitual reading of literature" teaches one how to read for power, how to judge uses and abuses of power, how to understand the self in relation to power, and how to employ positions of power

[8] See Martin C. Battestin, "Fielding's Definition of Wisdom: Some Functions of Ambiguity and Emblem in *Tom Jones*," *ELH* 35, no. 2 (1968): 188–217; Gerald Butler, "Making Fielding's Novels Speak for Law and Order," in *Ideology and Form in Eighteenth-Century Literature*, ed. David H. Richter (Lubbock: Texas Tech University Press, 1999), 75–88; Carol Stewart, *The Eighteenth-Century Novel and the Secularization of Ethics* (Farnham: Ashgate, 2010), 2, 33–70; David Diamond, "Secular Fielding," *ELH* 85, no. 3 (Fall 2018): 691–714; Eileen Jacques, "Fielding's *Tom Jones* and the *Nicomachean Ethics*," *English Language Notes* 30 (1992): 20–32; Laura F. Hodges, "Aristotle's *Nicomachean Ethics* and *Tom Jones*," *Philological Quarterly* 63, no. 2 (Spring 1984): 223–38; Frederick Ribble, "Aristotle and the 'Prudence' Theme of *Tom Jones*," *Eighteenth-Century Studies* 15, no. 1 (Autumn 1981): 26–47; and Andrew Benjamin Bricker, "Fielding after Mandeville: Virtue, Self-Interest, and the Foundation of 'Good Nature,'" *Eighteenth-Century Fiction* 30, no. 1 (Fall 2017): 65–87.

[9] See Richard Weisberg, "What Remains 'Real' about the Law and Literature Movement?," *Journal of Legal Education* 66, no. 1 (Autumn 2016): 37–43; and Richard Weisberg, "Coming of Age Some More: 'Law and Literature' beyond the Cradle," *Nova Law Review* 13 (1988–89): 107–24. In "Coming of Age," Weisberg posits that literature is unrivaled in its ability to teach lawyers about "sense and sensibility," about the values, virtues, ethics, and empathy needed to maintain and practice legal justice (110, 122–24). In "What Remains," he maintains that literature can help us understand the trajectory of legal injustice as well as locate "a pathway to a sound and fair outcome" (42–43).

responsibly.[10] Such reading challenges the legal practitioner to understand justice as "ethical and relational," to become more attentive "to opposing claims and to the experiences of opposing parties," to open themself up "to new formulations [and] new voices," and to be more thoughtful in composing "judicial or legal opinion[s]."[11] Moreover, Paul Heald has argued for "Law and Literature as Ethical Discourse," a dialectic approach that rests on "the assumption that [just as] literature can transform human beings," it can likewise change judicial decision-making and, presumably, strengthen professional ethical standards.[12]

Taking *Tom Jones* as its historical-legal object, this chapter aims to engage in interdisciplinary ethical discourse of the sort proposed by Heald and imagined by Weisberg and White. To provide context for Fielding's fictional intervention in his legal world, the chapter begins by offering an overview of the educational requirements and ethical responsibilities of the legal positions featured in *Tom Jones*, specifically the magistrate (or the justice of the peace) and the attorney. It also outlines three ethical systems that informed the law in the mid eighteenth century: duty-based ethics (later known as deontological ethics), consequentialism, and virtue ethics. The chapter then examines the legal characters and plots of *Tom Jones* in the context of this legal-ethical discourse. The chapter suggests that Fielding offers a rather cynical view of the legal profession; he shows that the law and its actors are, in many respects, undisciplined and uninformed, arbitrary and capricious, and unethical and unjust. Yet Fielding also implicitly offers a solution to the law's incompetence: He reaches toward a model of professional ethics that cultivates innate virtue while also requiring adherence to encoded duty and obligation, a hybrid system that unites the court of justice, a formal, often absolutist, juridical forum, with the court of conscience, a more flexible space that privileges subjectivity in moral judgment.

The Eighteenth-Century Magistrate and Attorney

The law in eighteenth-century England was not yet a formally organized, self-regulating institution. Legal historian Robert W. Gordon describes it as a "profession" only in the sense in which, like other "learned

[10] James Boyd White, "Law and Literature: 'No Manifesto,'" *Mercer Law Review* 39 (Spring 1987): 739–51, at 747–51.

[11] White, "Law and Literature," 751.

[12] Paul J. Heald, "The Death of Law and Literature: An Optimistic Eulogy," *Comparatist* 33 (May 2009): 20–28, at 25.

professions," it was an employment "of special dignity linked with university education, gentlemanly social status, some degree of leisure and discretion, and exemplary character."[13] In fact, it was not until the nineteenth century that the law could be defined as an occupation that "regulates itself through systematic, required training and collegial discipline; that has a base in technical, specialized knowledge; and that has a service rather than profit orientation enshrined in [a] code of ethics."[14] Thus, when Fielding was writing *Tom Jones*, the law's ethical expectations were relatively inchoate, and, as we shall see, a significant number of its jurists and practitioners were relative amateurs, seemingly ill-equipped for their roles in the justice system.

One of the central legal offices in the eighteenth century was that of the justice of the peace, or the magistracy, which was established in the Middle Ages. It was a local appointment that, by the fourteenth century, conferred authority over a range of criminal and administrative cases within the jurisdictional boundaries of the magistrate's county of residence.[15] Because the magistracy was an unpaid post, it was often occupied by men of "high status and independent means" – that is, men of the landed classes.[16] Its members were not required to have formal education or training in the law. Indeed, rather than being informed by exposure to a rich and rigorous professional curriculum, the magistrate's judgment was often guided either by the advice of law clerks and fellow magistrates or by the contents of increasingly voluminous legal texts.[17] His judgment was also, it appears, influenced by his own inclination. Peter King explains that most magistrates in the period had "a very flexible attitude to what might be broadly called the rule of law," while Norma Landau writes, "[magistrates] did what they did because they wanted to do it and thought they should do it."[18] With such unchecked power came, from time to time, unjust outcomes. Perhaps the most egregious abuse of the office was the tendency of some magistrates to use their summary conviction powers to

[13] Robert W. Gordon, "Professionalisms Old and New, Good and Bad," *Legal Ethics* 8, no. 1 (2005): 23–34, at 25–26.

[14] Paul Starr, *The Social Transformation of American Medicine* (New York: Basic Books, 1982), 15; Gordon, "Professionalisms," 26. I follow Gordon here in adapting Starr's definition of professionalism for the legal context.

[15] Norma Landau, *The Justices of the Peace, 1679–1760* (Berkeley: University of California Press, 1984), 6; Peter King, *Crime, Justice, and Discretion in England, 1740–1820* (Oxford: Oxford University Press, 2000), 82.

[16] King, *Crime, Justice, and Discretion*, 82.

[17] Peter King, *Crime and Law in England, 1750–1840: Remaking Justice from the Margins* (Cambridge: Cambridge University Press, 2006), 26.

[18] King, *Crime and Law*, 55; Landau, *Justices of the Peace*, 2.

punish the poor and the laboring classes for behavior that, though a violation of elitist norms or values, was not strictly illegal.[19]

While processes for challenging a magistrate's decision-making existed in Fielding's time, they were underutilized and relatively ineffective. Appeals of magistrates' judgments were rare, as were charges of judicial misconduct. Procedural requirements, costs, and beliefs about judicial autonomy and integrity made pursuing appellate review unfeasible for most lay persons.[20] In addition, staffing concerns and perceptions of the magistrate as a judicial ideal made commencing misconduct proceedings for failure to apply the law correctly or to follow established legal procedures distasteful to the magistrate's judicial and political superiors. Apparently, the Court of King's Bench and Parliament worried that disciplining or contradicting the magistracy would lead to resignations from and rejections of the office by current and future holders as well as to distrust of the system by the citizenry.[21] Ultimately, the government wanted to avoid "condemn[ing] the gentlemen who volunteered to rule England under law."[22]

The period's two branches of legal practitioners, the upper and the lower, also sparked concerns over competence and ethics. Members of the upper branch, or barristers, were often part of the social elite, though increasingly sons of bourgeois and professional origins were gaining admittance to one of the four educational facilities – together, the Inns of Court – that prepared this branch.[23] While a prospective barrister was required to attend an Inn in order to be admitted to the Bar, the relative

[19] King, *Crime and Law*, 31. King provides a list of the types of cases subject to summary judgment in the eighteenth century: "[d]isputes about assaults, about property ownership, about the non-payment of wages or relief, about the behaviour of servants or of the poor, about the settlement of bastardy laws, and about such diverse issues as alehouse regulations, friendly society procedures, turnpike laws, or the swearing of oaths." *Crime, Justice, and Discretion*, 84. For more on the magistrate's use of his summary conviction powers against the poor and laboring, see Landau, *Justices of the Peace*, 23–27.

[20] Landau, *Justices of the Peace*, 7–8, 346–52; King, *Crime and Law*, 31–35. Landau and King demonstrate that the efficacy of the most common form of appellate review by the King's Bench, *certiorari* or an appeal of the judgment, was undercut by strict limitations on the corpus of legal issues subject to reconsideration, by relaxed standards on what constituted a comprehensive written record of prior proceedings, and by statutory restrictions arising out of Parliament's reluctance to interfere with the magistrate class's autonomy. Cost was, of course, another obstacle to bringing an appeal.

[21] See King, *Crime and Law*, 33; Landau, *Justices of the Peace*, 333–62.

[22] Landau, *Justices of the Peace*, 356. For a detailed overview of consistencies and changes in the supervision of the magistracy over the course of the eighteenth century, see Landau, *Justices of the Peace*, 333–62.

[23] David Lemmings, *Gentlemen and Barristers: The Inns of Court and the English Bar, 1680–1730* (Oxford: Clarendon Press, 1990), 13, 8–17.

informality and limited educational resources of the academy meant that he could emerge with only a perfunctory understanding of the law and legal processes.[24] David Lemmings explains that the most a student had to do in order to appear before the Bar was eat a "set number of dinners," stay enrolled for the requisite number of terms, and complete, or pay someone to complete, his exercises. The students who met these prerequisites often entered the profession as litigators and practiced with a significant degree of autonomy.[25] Although their conduct was "inform[ed] and constrain[ed]" by an established "complex of customs, working habits, role models, and ideologies," it was not often subject to formal supervision.[26] Indeed, the law found no reason to institute strict controls over the upper branch because it was populated by and designed "for men who were the rulers rather than the ruled."[27]

Notwithstanding the lack of professional oversight, the barrister was expected to aspire to a professional model. He was distinguished from the members of the lower branch by his advanced advocacy and counseling skills, his privilege to plead in the royal courts, and his prestigious reputation, which brought him wealthy clients. According to Lemmings, the ideal barrister used the "ennobling virtues" of honesty, disinterest, and independence "to conduce to the achievement of justice and defeat of evil."[28] Yet, even with this paragon of legal professionalism to emulate, the real-life barrister struggled to maintain a polished and principled ethos. Lemmings explains that members of the Bar were often accused of overstaffing cases, overcharging clients, and in general "deliberately pervert[ing] the law for their own ends."[29] They were also, it seems, resistant to common-law norms of justice; rather than focus on "justice as a public good," these men tended to fixate on maintaining their elite status.[30]

[24] For a discussion of contemporary criticism of Fielding's performance at the Bar, see Frederick G. Ribble, "Henry Fielding at the Bar: A Reappraisal," *Studies in Philology* 110, no. 4 (Fall 2013): 903–13.

[25] David Lemmings, *Professors of the Law: Barristers and English Legal Culture in the Eighteenth Century* (Oxford: Oxford University Press, 2000), 143, 143–44; see also Penelope Corfield, *Power and the Professions in Britain 1700–1850* (London: Routledge, 1995), 73.

[26] Lemmings, *Professors of the Law*, 7. For a discussion of the ways in which the judiciary attempted to exercise supervisory power over both branches of practitioners, see Rachel Ellenberger, "'Doubly Damned Attornies': Lessons on Professional Regulation from Eighteenth-Century England," *Georgetown Journal of Legal Ethics* 32 (2019): 577–96, at 591–95.

[27] C. W. Brooks, *Pettyfoggers and Vipers of the Commonwealth: The "Lower Branch" of the Legal Profession in Early Modern England* (Cambridge: Cambridge University Press, 1986), 268.

[28] Lemmings, *Professors of the Law*, 43, 17, and 25–43 generally.

[29] Lemmings, *Professors of the Law*, 19–20.

[30] Lemmings, *Professors of the Law*, 301, 293–309.

Accusations of unethical behavior were particularly strong against members of the lower branch, which was subdivided into attorneys and solicitors. Men belonging to this class were educated through apprenticeships with "enrolled lawyer[s]" and performed primarily transactional and pre-litigation work.[31] Lemmings observes that while "anti-lawyerism was hardly exceptional," attorneys bore the brunt of the social ire as they were the ones who dealt with clients directly and who "presented the final bill."[32] Yet their perceived shortcomings were not merely conjecture; the group also had issues with licensure and oversight. While all attorneys and solicitors, beginning in 1730, were required to complete an enrollment process in which they were examined by a judge and undertook an oath to "Practice . . . according to the best of [their] Knowledge and Ability," the examination itself was not particularly rigorous and the entrance requirements were not consistently enforced. In fact, the "scrutiny" given to those who appeared before the licensing judge was often "casual," and thousands of applicants avoided scrutiny altogether.[33]

The poor reputation of attorneys and solicitors led, in 1739, to the formation of the Society of Gentlemen Practisers in the Courts of Law and Equity, a voluntary association comprised of the two sub-branches. The society "accepted the need for professional monitoring," working to expel "improperly admitted" attorneys from the rolls, prosecuting malpractice, and "lobb[ying] Parliament on a wide range of legal issues."[34] The society also invested in knowledge and skills development by meeting to moot hypothetical cases that addressed both substantive and procedural legal issues.[35] Nevertheless, the society's influence was limited. Unlike the regulatory Bar associations of today, the society was not vested with the power to define and enforce educational standards and rules of professional conduct. As was the case with magistrates and barristers, attorneys and solicitors were commonly left to fend for their too often incompetent, or unqualified, selves.[36]

Thus, the legal profession in the middle of the eighteenth century was marked by problems with education, operation, and regulation, resulting

[31] Corfield, *Power and the Professions*, 76, 73; Lemmings, *Professors of the Law*, 25–29. Attorneys generally practiced in the courts of law, while solicitors practiced in the courts of equity. See Henry Horwitz and Lloyd Bonfield, "The 'Lower Branches' of the Legal Profession: A London Society of Attorneys and Solicitors of the 1730s and Its 'Moots,'" *Cambridge Law Journal* 49, no. 3 (1990): 461–90, at 462.

[32] Lemmings, *Professors of the Law*, 15.

[33] Corfield, *Power and the Professions*, 76–77.

[34] Corfield, *Power and the Professions*, 80–81; Ellenberger, "'Doubly Damned,'" 588–91.

[35] Horwitz and Bonfield, "The 'Lower Branches,'" 469–79.

[36] See Corfield, *Power and the Professions*, 76–77, 80–84.

in public disdain and skepticism. It is no wonder that Samuel Johnson, having met a man he instantly disliked, remarked that while "he did not care to speak ill of any man behind his back, . . . he believed the gentleman was an ATTORNEY."[37]

Mid-Century Ethical Theories

Provided with a limited education and subject to little institutional guidance or authority, legal actors in the eighteenth century would have had to prescribe, in some measure, the ethical boundaries of their own practice by drawing on the moral thought embedded in their socio-cultural consciousness. As legal scholars Donald Nicholson and Julian Webb observe, when lawyers "resolve moral dilemmas [that are] not governed by [professional] norms, they do so in terms of ethical ideas that are generally at large in society."[38] In other words, they draw upon theories circulating, often inconspicuously, in their religious or secular communities. Three major systems of ethics circulated, in either nascent or full form, in the early to mid eighteenth century: deontological, consequentialist, and virtue ethics. These systems likely informed the behavior of the era's magistrates and attorneys.

Deontological and consequentialist ethics are generally understood to stand in opposition to one another. Deontological ethics defines ethical responsibilities according to the rights and duties, or rules and principles, that derive from the "supposed intrinsic qualities" of social behaviors, while consequentialist philosophy defines ethical behavior according to "the total amount of good or bad" that behavior produces.[39] In other words, a person operating under a deontological scheme is subject to moral duties that are "*a priori* and self-evident" and "knowable by all rational persons," whereas an individual operating under a consequentialist scheme is guided by the desire to increase their own "self-interest, desires, and sense of happiness" (egoism) or to maximize "social welfare" (utilitarianism).[40] Simply put, deontology requires a person to perform an extant duty even if it is not in their best interests or in the interests of

[37] James Boswell, *Life of Johnson*, ed. George Birbeck Hill, 6 vols. (Oxford: Clarendon Press, 1887), 2:126.

[38] Donald Nicholson and Julian Webb, *Professional Legal Ethics: Critical Interrogations* (Oxford: Oxford University Press, 1999), 10.

[39] Nicholson and Webb, *Professional Legal Ethics*, 13.

[40] Nicholson and Webb, *Professional Legal Ethics*, 14, 22, 24.

society, and consequentialism necessitates consideration of the effects of a decision or action on oneself or others.[41]

Deontology and the utilitarian form of consequentialism are often associated with philosophical thought produced after 1750; yet both systems are connected to seventeenth-century and early eighteenth-century moral philosophy. For example, natural law theorists such as Hugo Grotius (1583–1645), Samuel von Pufendorf (1632–94), Gottfried Wilhelm Leibniz (1646–1716), and Christian Wolff (1679–1754) influenced the work of Immanuel Kant (1724–1804), who is considered the father of deontology.[42] For these philosophers, the rights, duties, and obligations governing human behavior are located in natural law, which is "backed by the will of God."[43] Moreover, the Anglican utilitarianism of philosophers such as Anthony Ashley Cooper, Third Earl of Shaftesbury (1671–1713) and John Gay (1699–1745) anticipated the secular utilitarianism of Jeremy Bentham (1748–1832) and John Stuart Mill (1806–73).[44] This spiritual form of utilitarianism holds that individual duty is inextricably linked to what is "owe[d] to others and to God"; moral action is that which "promote [s] the happiness of others."[45] In contrast to the foregoing philosophies, the egoist form of consequentialism – the notion that human conduct is motivated by self-interest – was already embedded in mid-century moral thought as a result of the work of such theorists as Thomas Hobbes (1588–1679) and Bernard Mandeville (1670–1733).[46]

A third philosophy that circulated in the first half of the eighteenth century is associated with the Greek tradition. Virtue ethics derives from Aristotle's conception of the "good life" as one that is lived by individuals vested with "moral virtues."[47] Under this ethical system, one's moral agency derives, not from a set of prescriptive rules for behavior, but from

[41] See Nicholson and Webb, *Professional Legal Ethics*, 14.

[42] J. B. Schneewind, "Kant and Natural Law Ethics," *Ethics* 104, no. 1 (1993): 53–74.

[43] Schneewind, "Kant and Natural Law Ethics," 56.

[44] See Colin Heydt, *Moral Philosophy in Eighteenth-Century Britain* (Cambridge: Cambridge University Press, 2018), 144. On Shaftesbury's utilitarianism, see Lisa Hill and Eden Blazejak, *Stoicism and the Western Political Tradition* (Gateway East, Singapore: Palgrave Macmillan, 2021), 124–30. On John Gay's contribution to modern utilitarianism, see Getty L. Lustila, "John Gay and the Birth of Utilitarianism," *Utilitas* 30, no. 1 (March 2018): 86–106. For a compelling history of the origins of consequentialism, and eventually utilitarianism, in seventeenth-century theological thought, see Ryan Darr, *The Best Effect: Theology and the Origins of Consequentialism* (Chicago: University of Chicago Press, 2023).

[45] Heydt, *Moral Philosophy*, 145–46. Heydt considers Shaftesbury a virtue theorist, rather than an Anglican utilitarian (48–54); however, Hill and Blazejak's description of Shaftesbury's philosophy places him squarely within Heydt's definition of the latter.

[46] See Heydt, *Moral Philosophy*, 144; and Bricker, "Fielding after Mandeville."

[47] Nicholson and Webb, *Professional Legal Ethics*, 31–32.

an internal compass that distinguishes right from wrong, or good from evil. The focus, therefore, is "on being, rather than doing."[48] Virtue ethics is thought, more than deontological or consequentialist ethics, to "equip individuals with the moral tools necessary to resolve . . . moral problems"; yet it recognizes that "even the highly virtuous may at times commit individual immoral acts or have ongoing minor vices."[49] Although virtue ethics was on the wane in the eighteenth century, it remained a part of the period's ethical discourse. Students at Oxford, for example, studied Aristotle's work at least until mid century, and renowned philosophers such as David Hume elevated virtue within their versions of moral goodness.[50]

Fielding's education, reading, and writing suggest more than a passing familiarity with these ethical theories. Fielding's early education at Eton focused on the classics and would have included instruction in Aristotle, while his legal studies at the University of Leiden would have put him in contact with the work of Grotius, a celebrated alumnus of and former teacher at the university. Both learning experiences also would have included the study of Pufendorf, another distinguished alumnus of Leiden whose ethics dominated instruction in moral philosophy in the English undergraduate curriculum.[51] In addition, Fielding's library contained a variety of texts by Greek and Latin authors, including at least three editions by and eleven commentaries on the works of Aristotle – the collection's highest number for any classical author – and his writing includes numerous allusions to Aristotle, Shaftesbury, Hobbes, and Mandeville.[52] Fielding's knowledge of classical and Enlightenment moral philosophy informs *Tom Jones*'s preoccupation not only with human nature's intricacies but also with matters of professional legal ethics.

Fielding's Legal Professionals

In *Tom Jones*, Fielding introduces the reader to two courts that pass judgment on the guilt and innocence, or immorality and morality, of human behavior. The court of justice is formalist and absolutist; it does

48 Nicholson and Webb, *Professional Legal Ethics*, 29–30.
49 Nicholson and Webb, *Professional Legal Ethics*, 30–31.
50 See Heydt, *Moral Philosophy*, 8; and Christine Swanton, *The Virtue Ethics of Hume and Nietzsche* (Malden, MA: Wiley Blackwell, 2015).
51 See Paulson, *The Life of Henry Fielding*, 8, 20; and Heydt, *Moral Philosophy*, 2.
52 On Fielding's collection of Aristotle's works, see Nancy A. Mace, "Henry Fielding's Classical Learning," *Modern Philology* 88, no. 3 (February 1991): 243–60, at 244–46.

not deviate from the law or legal precedent, and it is "indifferent" to the inequities of those who appear before it.[53] The court of conscience, on the other hand, is (or should be) equitable and empathetic; it considers the circumstances surrounding bad behavior as well as the inherent fairness of a particular judgment. Although neither court receives much explicit attention in the novel – the courts, including their differences and functions, are mentioned in passing – they are prominent symbols of the nature and limits of human judgment.[54] They are also the notional spaces into which Fielding invites his reader to pass judgment on and resolve the ethical dilemmas faced by social institutions and their actors. Unsurprisingly, the law and its undereducated, under-regulated magistrates and attorneys figure prominently in these notional spaces. At the intersections of court and character, readers are guided to a possible resolution for the law's professional failings. Read in the context of the era's moral philosophy, the novel encourages the reader-judge to consider the ethical viability of a professional system that not only relies on duty, obligation, and social consciousness to direct behavior but also recognizes the importance of developing a professional moral character prepared to follow and critically assess the law's directives.

Fielding sets up the law's "professionalism problem" through the narrator's unabashedly biting commentary on the eighteenth-century magistrate. In an intercalary chapter entitled "A Crust for the Critics," the narrator equates the theater critic (who is often a disgruntled lawyer) with the justice of the peace. Both "pronounce [and] execute their own judgment" and both "condemn[] without mercy" (492). Later, in a narrative chapter, the narrator uses the heroine Sophia Western's fear of her father to comment on "a common fault of a justice of peace": he is "apt to conclude hastily from every slight circumstance, without examining the evidence on both sides" (528). In these similitudes, the magistrate emerges as a

[53] Henry Fielding, *Tom Jones*, ed. John Bender and Simon Stern (1749; Oxford: Oxford University Press, 1996), 803. Hereafter cited parenthetically in the text.

[54] The first reference is one of comparison: The narrator observes that the excuse of intoxication for criminal behavior is allowed in the court of conscience but prohibited in the court of justice, and he concludes that "there is more of policy than justice" in criminal laws that increase punishment for drunkenness (223). The next reference to the court of conscience appears in the title to book VI, chapter 13—"a knotty point in the court of conscience"—and anticipates Black George's internal debate over whether to return Tom's purse (275–79). The next reference to the court of justice occurs during a conversation between Tom and his friend Nightingale when Tom is in prison for mortally wounding Mr. Fitzpatrick in a duel. Nightingale voices his concern that the "indifferent court of justice" will not be persuaded by Tom's claim of self-defense (803); as it turns out, Fitzpatrick survived and the charges against Tom are dropped.

merciless and injudicious legal vigilante, a figure at odds with the traditional concept of justice as fairness, a figure in need of professionalization.

Fielding represents the prototypical magistrate in the figure of Squire Western, whose court teeters on the verge of becoming a court of injustice. The reader observes Western in his role as magistrate when his sister, Mrs. Western, seeks to prosecute a family servant, Honour, for incivility – in particular, for implying that Mrs. Western is not as attractive as her niece, Sophia. The narrator informs us that "no sooner" had the squire "heard of [Honour] having abused his sister than he swore twenty oaths he would send her to Bridewell" (311), a prison for the "idle and disorderly."[55] Honour is not afforded the benefit of a trial; rather, Western convicts and sentences her by summary judgment. Fortunately, Honour's legal victimization is short-lived. While Bridewell may be, as Mrs. Western posits, a common punishment for servants who "affront[] their masters," it is not an entirely legal one (312).[56] Western's clerk, who (unlike the squire) has "some understanding in the law of [the] realm," explains that Western "would exceed his authority by committing the girl to Bridewell" because "ill breeding" does not provide grounds for commitment (312). As Western is already the subject of complaints to the King's Bench, he capitulates and commutes Honour's sentence. She is, in the end, merely "turned away" (313).

Although the squire's final judgment is legally sound, the ethical grounds on which it is founded are as morally dubious as those that sustain his initial ruling. Western is driven to punish Honour by an interest in protecting the deferential social conventions to which he and his family are used and from which they reap a benefit, and he is induced to retract the Bridewell sentence by an interest in avoiding the personal consequences of performing another breach of his legal duty. In other words, his judgment is not motivated by an ethical responsibility to uphold the law; rather, it is encouraged by the well-established principle that the upper classes hold moral authority over the lower classes and by the egoist principle that equates justice with self-interest. Fielding's decision to attach such motivations to a character who is irascible and arbitrary suggests that Western's function is to expose as illusory the sentiment that a judge's birth connotes his elevated moral worth and, therefore, serves as a safeguard against

[55] Joanna Innes, "Prisons for the Poor: English Bridewells, 1555–1800," in *Labour, Law, and Crime: An Historical Perspective*, ed. Francis G. Snyder and Douglas Hay (London: Tavistock, 1987), 42–122, at 95.

[56] Innes provides support for Mrs. Western's assessment, writing that Bridewell was a disciplinary measure of "choleric" employers. "Prisons for the Poor," 106.

injudicious decision-making. If Western is to run a legitimate court of justice, his privilege and passions need to be checked by externally imposed duties and obligations.

Fielding continues his critical representation of the eighteenth-century magistrate, and the court over which he presides, in the figure of Tom Jones's adopted father, Squire Allworthy. As scholars have noted, although initially positioned as the judicial ideal – as a moral anomaly in his profession – Allworthy ultimately demonstrates the fallibility of human judgment.[57] Early in the novel, the narrator describes Allworthy as "an agreeable person [with] a sound constitution, a solid understanding, and a benevolent heart" (31). Allworthy enacts these descriptors in his treatment of Jenny Jones after she confesses to having a baby out of wedlock and then abandoning him to Allworthy's care. Although Allworthy commences Jenny's informal hearing by reminding the young woman of his "power, as a magistrate, to punish [her] very rigorously for what [she] ha[s] done," he quickly assures her that he will "act in a milder manner with [her]" (44).[58] Drawing on the maxim that "no private resentment should ever influence a magistrate," Allworthy informs Jenny that, rather than assuming she acted with criminal intent in relinquishing her parental duties, he will interpret her action as a consequence of "natural [parental] affection" (44). She, therefore, escapes internment at a "house of correction" (51); instead, her punishment amounts to a tedious lecture on chastity and repentance. By the end of the episode, Jenny's case has been settled in the court of conscience, where the magistrate's internal virtue – his natural moral inclination to "temper[] justice with mercy" (52) – prevails over both egoist principles and legal norms. Justice is achieved through deliberate and empathetic, as opposed to mechanical and formalist, decision-making.

Yet Allworthy does not sustain this compassionate approach to legal judgment. In the second trial over which he presides, Allworthy is rigid

[57] See John Preston, "*Tom Jones* and the 'Pursuit of True Judgment,'" *ELH* 33, no. 2 (1966): 315–26, at 321–23; Stephanson, "Fielding's 'Courts,'" 156–59; Leland E. Warren, "Fielding's Problem and Ours: Allworthy and Authority in *Tom Jones*," *Essays in Literature* 5 (1978): 15–25; and Welsh, *Strong Representations*, 44–76. In a departure from this reading, Eric Rothstein argues that the magisterial Allworthy serves as Fielding's foil. According to Rothstein, it is through Allworthy's failure to properly understand and apply the law that "Fielding . . . legitimizes his own law-making, his de jure as well as de facto authority." "Virtues of Authority in *Tom Jones*," *Eighteenth Century: Theory and Interpretation* 28, no. 2 (1987): 99–126, at 107.

[58] Although Bender and Stern point out that the judgments of two justices of the peace were required to imprison the mother of an illegitimate child, the practice of committing an unwed mother was not unheard of in the period. See Fielding, *Tom Jones*, 875n44; Innes, "Prisons for the Poor," 106.

and uncompromising to the point of allowing the censorious aspects of his conscience to interfere with established legal procedure. The result is the summary conviction of an innocent man. The trial involves the community's schoolmaster, Mr. Partridge, who has been accused of adultery and bastardy. At the outset of the proceedings, the narrator re-attests to Allworthy's inherent goodness and remarkable capacity for contemplative moral and legal judgment. Nevertheless, as the scene unfolds, Allworthy's behavior deviates from this assessment. He disregards Partridge's "vehement protestations of his innocence" (85) in favor of the false – and inadmissible – testimony of Partridge's wife (86–87).[59] This testimony includes Partridge's coerced confession to the offenses – Partridge confessed only after Mrs. Partridge verbally and physically attacked him – as well as Mrs. Partridge's specious "bodily oath" that she witnessed Partridge's affair (86). Allworthy also reneges on his promise to "defer his final determination" until the other *legitimate* eyewitness (Partridge's alleged paramour) can be found; rather, he convinces himself that the additional testimony from a known "slut" would either lack credibility or support Partridge's guilt (87). Allworthy's swift and unsympathetic decision to deprive Partridge of his living and exile him from the community draws the ire of the public, who condemn Allworthy's "rigour," "severity," and "cruelty" (89).

It is not just the public that demonstrates dissatisfaction with Allworthy's use of his judicial office. Although the narrator assures readers that "the evidence was more than sufficient to convict [Partridge]" (88), his attention to Allworthy's failure both to scrutinize Mrs. Partridge's testimony and to require evidence secured through proper lines of inquiry lays bare the magistrate's shortcomings. Allworthy's capacity for thoughtful deliberative judgment has been displaced by his inclination for moralistic censure. Allworthy no longer represents the narrator's "man of candour and of true understanding [who] is never hasty to condemn" (286); he now epitomizes a man of self-righteous piety who will "condemn a character as a bad one, because it is not perfectly a good one" (454). With this complication of moral character, the court of conscience falters. Subject to a version of virtue ethics that has no regard for institutional rules or communal values, the court cannot produce a legitimate outcome.

Fielding's final depiction of Allworthy as magistrate raises further doubts about the efficacy of virtue ethics in the eighteenth-century courtroom. The case at issue centers on Molly Seagrim, a poor, pregnant servant

[59] As the narrator notes, Mrs. Partridge's testimony is inadmissible because the law prohibited a wife from testifying against her husband (86).

accused of assault. When Molly appears before Allworthy on the charge, he questions her, not about the acts of violence she allegedly perpetrated against another community member, but about her pregnancy. When she "pertinaciously refuse[s]" to name her child's father, Allworthy summarily sentences her to Bridewell (162). His decision is one over which the narrator seems to express ambivalence. The narrator declares:

> A lawyer may, perhaps, think Mr. Allworthy exceeded his authority a little in this instance. And, to say the truth, I question, as here was no regular information before him, whether his conduct was strictly regular. However, as his intention was truly upright, he ought to be excused *in foro conscientae*; since so many acts are daily committed by magistrates who have not this excuse to plead for themselves. (165)

While the last part of this comment serves to exculpate Allworthy from a potential charge of abuse of power, the first part underscores Allworthy's inability to judge fairly and squarely in both the court of justice and the court of conscience. As in Partridge's case, Allworthy's legal judgment is unsound because it is uninformed and unauthorized – Allworthy heard no evidence about the alleged assault, and he did not consult with a second magistrate about the Bridewell sentence, as was required in cases of extramarital pregnancy – and his moral judgment is flawed because it is based on a version of morality that refuses to accommodate the unchaste and undisciplined soul. Allworthy's conception of virtue is so hostile to female immodesty that it eclipses any sympathies he might have had for Molly's situation and, ultimately, obstructs the path to justice.

Fielding's portrayal of Molly's trial also sets up a contest between virtue ethics and utilitarian ethics. Allworthy's decision to sentence Molly to Bridewell, as Squire Western initially sentenced Honour, is motivated by the period's common, but misguided, *a priori* assumption that the way "to effect significant social change" in regard to the economic and moral plight of the poor and laboring classes is to commit them to workhouse prisons.[60] Yet, as the narrator observes, what Allworthy sees as an ethical obligation born out of a rational existential rule is not conducive to the social good: While Bridewell may teach "respect and deference to [one's] superiors," it "rarely" offers "any other good lesson" nor does it operate to "improve" the "morals" of its inhabitants (165). Allworthy's inability to discern the reformative failures of houses of correction further demonstrates the problem of relying on ethical rules that are not accountable to the common

[60] Innes, "Prisons for the Poor," 101.

good. For the law to behave ethically, it must consistently examine the social impact of its judgments.

The ethical conundrums confronted by Fielding's fictional magistrates are also encountered by his attorneys. Like the magistrate class, this group of legal actors struggles to find its ethical footing. While the group includes virtue-motivated individuals who have committed "a thousand good and charitable acts" (828), it is also, as Fielding emphasizes in a note to the text, comprised of entirely self-interested individuals, such as the attorney who practices deception in court and "oppress[es] the poor" to "bring money into [his] pockets" (828, note 1). This latter type makes an appearance in the middle of the narrative. Identified by the narrator as "a most vile pettifogger, without sense or knowledge of any kind," and classed among the "sort of supernumeraries in the profession, who are the hackneys of attorneys," this "fellow" is manipulative and obsequious (374). He is so devoid of virtue that he is not particularly threatening to those imbued with reason and rationality; his "outward appearance and behaviour" expose his character, and his "conversation" renders his company "detestable to men of any sense" (374–75). Nonetheless, his very existence suggests the need for stricter standards in education, licensure, and regulation, including perhaps for a professional body similar to the Society of Gentlemen Practisers but with the full authority to define and enforce professional standards and principles.

Yet it is not just the pettifogger who performs a critical ethical function in the text. Fielding's conception of another category of attorney also demands legal-ethical attention. This type, embodied in the Allworthy family attorney, Mr. Dowling, is a composite of virtue and vice. When acting outside his professional capacity, he is sympathetic to injustices experienced by his fellow man. In fact, when Tom Jones relates his difficult history – his disinheritance by Allworthy, his exile from Paradise Hall, and his unrequited love for Sophia – Dowling is "greatly affected" (574). This response prompts the narrator to observe that Dowling "had not divested himself of humanity by being an attorney," and it generates a narratorial digression on the connection between one's character and one's profession:

> [N]othing is more unjust than to carry our prejudices against a profession into private life, and to borrow our idea of a man from our opinion of his calling. Habit, it is true, lessens the horror of those actions which the profession makes necessary, and consequently habitual; but in all other instances, nature works in men of all professions alike. ... [A]n attorney may feel all the miseries and distresses of his fellow creatures provided he happens not to be concerned against them. (574)

Here, the narrator suggests that the adversarial nature of the legal profession itself, rather than the character of its members, bears responsibility for the group's unethical behaviors at law. It is the law, even more than the lawyer, that needs moral rehabilitation.

Yet the narrator's assessment of this apparent dichotomy becomes muddled at the end of the novel when Dowling is summoned by Allworthy to account for his unscrupulous professional conduct. During the encounter, Allworthy learns that Dowling, acting at the behest of Allworthy's nephew, Blifil, has tampered with potential witnesses in Tom's forthcoming murder trial; he also discovers that Dowling, again acting at the direction of Blifil, failed to inform Allworthy of Tom's true parentage, as he had been instructed to do by his client, Blifil's mother, before her death years earlier. Dowling defends his actions to Allworthy by referring to his professional duty. He claims that he did not act of his "own accord" but was merely following "Mr. Blifil's instructions"; he was trying to "oblige" Allworthy and protect the family (839–40). While Dowling's respect for the attorney–client relationship may have influenced his behavior, the narrator clarifies that his primary motivation was the "promises which Blifil had made to [him]"; Dowling confessed only because he realized that "Blifil would not be able to keep [those promises]" (840). Thus, Dowling's unscrupulousness is neither required nor induced by his profession; it is, rather, a product of his desire to realize, in whatever way possible, his own version of the good life. Once again, the ethics of egoism conflict with and seem to exclude virtue ethics, and we are left with a sense that the two cannot coexist in a professional ethical system.

The failure of individual ethics to uphold justice in *Tom Jones* is a subtle rallying cry for reform – for the increased professionalization, through education and discipline, of the law and its actors. The novel's magistrates and attorneys demonstrate the ethical pitfalls imbued in any social system that relies on intelligent human judgment to establish its legitimacy. Through them, Fielding challenges traditional assumptions about the relationship between one's position in the social hierarchy and one's fitness for legal service. It is no longer birth or social rank that signals morality and ethics; rather, the best indicator of these attributes is what David Paxman terms "real goodness, or good nature," a virtuous way of being that is either "inbred and independent of circumstance" or developed through external "forms and principles."[61]

[61] David Paxman, "*Tom Jones* and the Paradox of Moral Purpose," *Eighteenth-Century Novel* 2 (2002): 113–35, at 114, 133. Paxman argues that Fielding so "convincingly . . . demonstrates the power of [innate] good nature" to enact "moral purpose" that he seems to elide the need for "novels or

Yet Fielding also implies that a good nature does not guarantee professional integrity or ensure fair and just treatment under the law. Indeed, his juridical characters demonstrate that even those gifted with an innate sense of virtue are vulnerable to values, mores, and pressures – to egoist desires and irrational beliefs – that conflict with the law's natural, preeminent design. Thus, ethicality begotten through good nature, whether intrinsic or cultivated, is always in need of protection, direction, and refinement, all of which can be achieved through a set of socially conscious, prescriptive, and binding rules and regulations. In the model that Fielding reaches toward, virtue ethics and the court of conscience become partners with deontological ethics, utilitarianism, and the court of justice such that legal actors are encouraged to nurture and exercise their inner goodness while remaining subject to and accountable for knowing and following the law and its professional standards.

Although the novel does not offer a detailed framework for developing and enacting this model of cooperative ethics, it does propose a few foundational principles from which a preliminary sketch might emerge. First, unadulterated egoism is incapable of meeting the law's fundamental goals of preserving integrity and effecting justice. In order to avoid claims of illegitimacy and abuse, Fielding suggests that the profession must institute a rigorous course of study and adopt standards that limit a self-interested approach to practicing or adjudicating the law. Second, virtue ethics are shaped by diverse individual and community values, some of which conflict with or obscure both legal norms and rational approaches to social welfare.[62] Thus, any professional education devoted to how one should *be* must include strategies to build self-awareness and social awareness. Third, deontological principles, which abound in legal culture in the form of statutes and case law and, beginning in the nineteenth century, in codified ethical rules, are not always already rational. While framing them as such can have a legitimizing effect on the law, it can also have the opposite impact, particularly when the social consequences of the behaviors that arise out of these duties and obligations – their utilitarian effects – are undervalued or ignored.[63] As society changes so too does its conception of what is just, right, and rational. To account for historical transformations like those experienced during the Enlightenment, the profession

treatises about it" or for "deliberate instructions in [moral] duty" (117). Yet Fielding does not always present good nature as inherent or steadfast; rather, he often represents the quality as in need of development and guidance.

62 For a discussion of this conflict as it relates to the contemporary legal context, see Nicholson and Webb, *Professional Legal Ethics*, 32–33.

63 See Nicholson and Webb, *Professional Legal Ethics*, 16, 50.

must consistently reassess which of its rules are logical, reasoned, and morally just, and it must promote dialectic exchange about the law's moral achievements and its moral failures.

The foregoing principles are as important today as they were in Fielding's lifetime. Twenty-first-century society is as much invested in questions of truth and virtue as was Enlightenment society, and today's legal institutions are as much plagued by questions of fairness and equity as were their eighteenth-century counterparts. From politics in judicial decision-making, to the role of *stare decisis* in legal interpretation, to diversity and equity in legal practice, contemporary law is an intensely contested site. This is true even though attorneys and judges have received comprehensive and rigorous educations and have been subject to ethical codes for well over a century. Pre-professional legal plotlines such as those in *Tom Jones* prompt the reader to consider this apparent disconnect: Why does the law continue to be perceived as unethical when it has heavily invested in legal education and achieved ethically grounded self-regulation? Perhaps, legal morality is seemingly compromised because it is, or appears to be, uncompromising – too resistant to change, too dismissive of diverse perspectives, or too averse to facilitating hard conversations about its past and its future. Whatever the reason, Fielding's novel shines a spotlight on a troubling pattern of historical stasis in perceptions of the law as a profession and invites us to reexamine how we conceptualize the ethical structures that have come to define legal culture.

CHAPTER 5

"A Higher Tribunal"

Equity, Law, and the Family in Sir Charles Grandison

Melissa J. Ganz

"Shall we do nothing but *legal* justice?" the eponymous hero of Samuel Richardson's *The History of Sir Charles Grandison* (1753–54) asks his sisters early in the novel.[1] Although their dissolute father has died without making a will, Sir Charles declares that their father's longtime mistress, Mrs. Oldham, should keep the 1,200 pounds she saved during her partner's life. Having just returned from a lengthy stay on the Continent, Sir Charles further advises that if Mrs. Oldham or his sisters can tell him anything their father "intended or inclined to do [for] any one of his people, that intention [Sir Charles] will . . . execute with as much exactness, as if [their father] had made a will, and it was part of it" (1:397). Without being apprised of any such intentions, Sir Charles gives 10,000 pounds to each of his sisters, performing "an article of the Will" that he makes in his mind for his father (1:408); he tells his sisters to look upon him as "executor of a will, that *ought* to have been made, and perhaps *would* [have], had time been given" (1:409). Sir Charles likewise alters the will of his friend Mr. Danby and gives part of his own bequest to Danby's niece and nephews. So, too, does Sir Charles enable his ward, Emily Jervois, to give an annuity to her mother for the latter's "sole and separate use," "as from" Mrs. O-Hara's second husband (2:820, 2:821). Late in the novel, Sir Charles also declares that Emily's mother must be consulted in the matter of Emily's marriage. In these and other instances, Sir Charles relies upon and extends emerging principles of equity to rectify injustices enshrined in and fostered by English common and statutory law.

Scholars have examined Richardson's treatment of law in *Pamela; or, Virtue Rewarded* (1740) and *Clarissa, or The History of a Young Lady*

[1] Samuel Richardson, *The History of Sir Charles Grandison*, ed. E. Derek Taylor, Melvyn New, and Elizabeth Kraft, 4 vols. (1753–54; Cambridge: Cambridge University Press, 2022), 1:397. Hereafter cited parenthetically in the text by volume and page number.

(1747–48), but the legal questions raised by his final novel have received less attention. Where critics such as Thomas Keymer, Erin Mackie, and Beth Swan contend that *Clarissa* presents English law as irredeemably corrupt, Allison Cardon and John P. Zomchick argue that in his first two novels, Richardson substitutes poetic justice for legal justice. In doing so, they suggest, he anticipates remedies that the law does not yet provide.[2] Lois A. Chaber, by contrast, argues that in *Grandison*, Richardson looks to divine justice for relief; in her reading, Sir Charles "serves as a kind of providence surrogate."[3] Lisa O'Connell, for her part, proposes that Sir Charles "embodies a synthesis of divine law, secular authority and human sympathy."[4] In her view, Richardson imagines "an alternative conception of natural law which casts Sir Charles as an Anglican landed gentleman doing the paternalist state's work from a position of independence outside the state itself."[5]

In this chapter, I build upon these readings but propose that Richardson looks instead to equity to rectify legal wrongs. As conceived by Greek and Roman philosophers and formalized in England in a separate set of courts, equity served to rectify injustices arising from the application of general laws. Based upon a consideration of the circumstances of each case and the demands of natural justice, English equity courts offered remedies that the common-law courts either could not or would not provide.[6] Law-and-literature scholars have long viewed literature, especially fiction, as enacting a form of equitable justice. Martha C. Nussbaum, for example, suggests that in its "formal commitment to following complex life histories" and its

[2] See Tom [Thomas] Keymer, *Richardson's "Clarissa" and the Eighteenth-Century Reader* (Cambridge: Cambridge University Press, 1992), 218–39; Erin Mackie, *Rakes, Highwaymen, and Pirates: The Making of the Modern Gentleman in the Eighteenth Century* (Baltimore: Johns Hopkins University Press, 2009), 59–70; Beth Swan, "Clarissa Harlowe, Pleasant Rawlins, and Eighteenth-Century Discourses of Law," *Eighteenth-Century Novel* 1 (2001): 71–93; Allison Cardon, "Pamela's Complaint: Injury, Rights, and the Politics of Story," *Novel: A Forum on Fiction* 54, no. 1 (May 2021): 65–84; and John P. Zomchick, *Family and the Law in Eighteenth-Century Fiction: The Public Conscience in the Private Sphere* (Cambridge: Cambridge University Press, 1993), 81–104. Sandra Macpherson, by contrast, argues that "the poetry of Richardson's justice is one and the same as the formalism of the law." *Harm's Way: Tragic Responsibility and the Novel Form* (Baltimore: Johns Hopkins University Press, 2010), 94.

[3] Lois A. Chaber, "'Sufficient to the Day': Anxiety in *Sir Charles Grandison*," *Eighteenth-Century Fiction* 1, no. 4 (July 1989): 281–304, at 285.

[4] Lisa O'Connell, *The Origins of the English Marriage Plot: Literature, Politics and Religion in the Eighteenth Century* (Cambridge: Cambridge University Press, 2019), 115.

[5] O'Connell, *Origins of the English Marriage Plot*, 116.

[6] For overviews of equity and its place in the English legal system, see Sir John Baker, *An Introduction to English Legal History*, 5th ed. (Oxford: Oxford University Press, 2019), 105–25; Mark Fortier, *The Culture of Equity in Early Modern England* (Aldershot: Ashgate, 2005); and Dennis R. Klinck, *Conscience, Equity and the Court of Chancery in Early Modern England* (Farnham: Ashgate, 2010).

attention to "the minute details of motive and intention and their social formation," realist novels put readers in contact with "two features of the equitable: its attention to particularity and its capacity for sympathetic understanding."[7] Yet scholars have largely overlooked the significance of equity for eighteenth-century fiction.[8] Nussbaum's insights, I suggest, are especially relevant to the epistolary novel developed by Richardson. Pursuing these insights helps us better understand the many of scenes of adjudication in Richardson's fiction while shedding light on questions concerning the relationship between law and equity that remain of interest to this day.

In *Grandison*, I argue, Richardson not only affirms the value of equity as the basis for judgment in the Court of Chancery in the mid eighteenth century but also shows the importance of applying equitable principles to everyday life. In doing so, he responds to critics' concerns about the subjective nature of equitable judgment as well as the extension of equitable principles to the family. Sir Charles serves as the primary embodiment of equity in the novel, but Harriet Byron (later Lady Grandison) supports and extends his ethical sensibility. Through their interventions in a range of domestic disputes, the novel exposes and critiques the ways in which the common and statutory laws disempower women and minor children.

[7] Martha C. Nussbaum, "Equity and Mercy," *Philosophy and Public Affairs* 22, no. 2 (Spring 1993): 83–125, at 105; see also Martha C. Nussbaum, *Poetic Justice: The Literary Imagination and Public Life* (Boston: Beacon Press, 1995).

[8] Margot C. Finn briefly but helpfully discusses Richardson's reliance upon equitable principles in *Pamela*, arguing that "the justice of strict contracts" in the novel is "situated within a wider network of exchange activities in which social and moral calculations continuously undercut purely legalistic thinking." *The Character of Credit: Personal Debt in English Culture, 1740–1914* (Cambridge: Cambridge University Press, 2003), 33. In a similar vein, Cheryl Nixon suggests that eighteenth-century novels created a "popular juridical imagination" that looked to "forms of justice, equity, and morality that operate[d] outside of legal forms and structure." "Gender, Law, and the Birth of Bourgeois Civil Society," in *Law and Literature*, ed. Kieran Dolin (Cambridge: Cambridge University Press, 2018), 124–41, at 127, 130. Most studies of equity in literature, however, focus on either the early modern period or the nineteenth century. See, e.g., Fortier, *Culture of Equity in Early Modern England*, 107–36; Andrew J. Majeske, *Equity in English Renaissance Literature: Thomas More and Edmund Spenser* (New York: Routledge, 2006); Elliott Visconsi, *Lines of Equity: Literature and the Origins of Law in Later Stuart England* (Ithaca, NY: Cornell University Press, 2008); Gary Watt, *Equity Stirring: The Story of Justice beyond Law* (Oxford: Hart, 2009); Simon Petch, "Law, Equity, and Conscience in Victorian England," *Victorian Literature and Culture* 25, no. 1 (1997): 123–39; and Sarah Winter, "Scottish Enlightenment Concepts of Equity in the Nineteenth-Century British Novel," in *The Scottish Enlightenment and Literary Culture*, ed. Ralph McLean, Ronnie Young, and Kenneth Simpson (Lewisburg, PA: Bucknell University Press, 2016), 245–68. Mark Fortier claims that the Restoration and eighteenth century "are [not] particularly rich grounds for equity in literature." "Rarely," he suggests, "is there exploration or questioning of equity in any complex or sophisticated sense." *The Culture of Equity in Restoration and Eighteenth-Century Britain and America* (Farnham: Ashgate, 2015), 21.

The central principle underlying Richardson's equitable jurisprudence is impartiality. Sir Charles's and Harriet's ability to assume other perspectives allows them to mediate conflicts and rectify injustices without imposing arbitrary or subjective judgments. Richardson's commitment to equity at once draws from and shapes his experiments with epistolary form: By presenting competing accounts of the conflicts, he prompts readers to examine the disputes from multiple points of view. After serving for many years as the printer for the House of Commons and observing the workings of the law, this chapter suggests, Richardson comes to perceive both the value and the limits of legal justice. In his final novel, he uses the resources of fiction to intervene in controversies about the nature and value of equity while contesting the patriarchal underpinning of English marriage and property laws.

Equity in England, ca. 1300–1800

Before we turn to Richardson's novel, we need to take a closer look at the origins and development of equity. Equity emerged in England in the fourteenth century as a court of conscience to remedy the deficiencies of the common law. When the law courts gave harsh or unsatisfactory judgments, disappointed parties sought redress from the king and his Privy Council. The latter typically referred such matters to the chancellor, who was empowered to mitigate or modify judgments on the king's behalf. Over time, the prerogative courts, especially the Court of Chancery, assumed jurisdiction over these cases, an authority they retained until the Judicature Acts of 1873 and 1875 fused the two systems of law and equity.[9] The nature and scope of Chancery's jurisdiction, however, sparked heated debates in the seventeenth and eighteenth centuries. Controversies emerged over the discretion exercised by chancellors as well as the substance of the court's holdings, including its holdings in cases concerning marriage and property.

Equity took on a number of meanings in early modern England. The word, derived from the Latin *aequitas*, connoted fairness, evenness, and impartiality. Some thinkers also emphasized the Stoic notion of

[9] On Chancery's origins and development, see Baker, *Introduction to English Legal History*, 105–14; W. H. Bryson, introduction to *Cases concerning Equity and the Courts of Equity 1550–1660*, ed. W. H. Bryson, 2 vols. (London: Selden Society, 2001), 1:xviii–lii; and Klinck, *Conscience, Equity and the Court of Chancery*. On the Judicature Acts, see Baker, *Introduction to English Legal History*, 122–23; and Michael Lobban, "Preparing for Fusion: Reforming the Nineteenth-Century Court of Chancery, Part II," *Law and History Review* 22, no. 3 (Autumn 2004): 565–99.

equanimity, while others highlighted the connections between equity and mercy as exemplified by Christ's grace.[10] But early modern jurists were especially attracted to Aristotle's conception of equity as "a correction of law where it is defective owing to its universality."[11] As legislators could not anticipate every possible situation that might arise, Aristotle explained in *The Nicomachean Ethics*, following the strict letter of the law would lead to unjust outcomes in some cases. It was thus necessary to take into account the circumstances of each case. Aristotle expanded upon this idea in *The Art of Rhetoric*, explaining that it was equitable to look to an agent's intentions rather than his words and "[t]o try to grasp the whole picture rather than some detail or other."[12] It was equitable, too, "[t]o make allowances for human failings" and "[t]o prefer arbitration to trial."[13] Overall, Aristotle insisted, equity required flexibility and mercy; "the equitable man" was one who was "no stickler for his rights in a bad sense but tend[ed] to take less than his share though he ha[d] the law on his side."[14] These ideas became central to the accounts offered by jurists including Christopher Saint German, Edmund Plowden, and William Lambarde in the sixteenth century.[15]

These ideas also shaped practices in the Court of Chancery. As England's chief equity court, Chancery handled a range of matters, with a particular emphasis on disputes involving property and contracts. Unlike common-law judges, chancellors decided questions of both law and fact, combining the roles of judge and jury. The process was slow and the judgments were highly discretionary: The chancellor and his deputies issued verdicts after carefully considering written submissions by all affected parties in each case.[16]

Chancery's jurisdiction became the subject of considerable dispute in the early seventeenth century as its caseload increased and chancellors

[10] See Fortier, *Culture of Equity in Early Modern England*, 1–4, 29–57; Mark Fortier, "Literature and Equity in Early Modern England," in Dolin, *Law and Literature*, 109–23, at 109–10.

[11] Aristotle, *The Nicomachean Ethics*, trans. David Ross, ed. Lesley Brown (Oxford: Oxford University Press, 2009), 99.

[12] Aristotle, *The Art of Rhetoric*, trans. Robin Waterfield (Oxford: Oxford University Press, 2018), 52.

[13] Aristotle, *Art of Rhetoric*, 52.

[14] Aristotle, *Nicomachean Ethics*, 99. For discussions of Aristotle's conception of equity, see Kathy Eden, *Poetic and Legal Fiction in the Aristotelian Tradition* (Princeton, NJ: Princeton University Press, 1986), 41–49; and Nussbaum, "Equity and Mercy," 92–96.

[15] See Fortier, *Culture of Equity in Early Modern England*, 59–76.

[16] See Baker, *Introduction to English Legal History*, 112–16. England's equity courts included the courts of Star Chamber and Wards, which were abolished in the seventeenth century, and the equity side of the Exchequer. See David Lemmings, *Professors of the Law: Barristers and English Legal Culture in the Eighteenth Century* (Oxford: Oxford University Press, 2000), 31–32.

began issuing judgments that conflicted with those of the common-law courts. Sir Edward Coke, Chief Justice of the King's Bench, objected to the idea that a court of equity could give relief contrary to or after the judgment of a common-law court. In Coke's view, such practices eroded the law's predictability and stability. The dispute came to a head in *The Earl of Oxford's Case* (1615) and was soon after referred to James I, who issued a royal decree in favor of his chancellor, Lord Ellesmere, affirming Chancery's status as the highest court in England. The decision fueled critics' concerns.[17] In his posthumously published *Table-Talk* (1689), the jurist John Selden declared equity to be a "Roguish thing": "[F]or Law we have a measure, [and] know what to trust to," he explained. "Equity," by contrast, "is according to the Conscience of him that is Chancellor, and as that is larger or narrower, so is Equity."[18]

Conflicts continued in spite of efforts to rein in chancellors' discretion. Lord Francis Bacon, who succeeded Lord Ellesmere in 1618, reduced the practice of the Chancery Court to a more regular system, and subsequent chancellors developed rules that were in many respects as clear as those of the common law. The reporting and publishing of Chancery cases, which began in 1660, aided this effort. As Sir John Baker explains, the practice of "giving reasons for decisions, with a view to their being reported, … complete[d] the reduction of equity to a system of general principles."[19] However, the publication process was slow and uneven, with cases appearing years or even decades after they were decided.[20] Although the rulings of the Chancery Court came to be more predictable by the early eighteenth century, concerns remained about the nature and scope of its jurisdiction.

Richard Francis sought to alleviate these fears in *Maxims of Equity* (1727). "[W]here Conscience is to direct the Judge," he explained, "[the Equity] Court cannot with any Propriety of Sense or Speech, be said to be arbitrary": "The Judge knows and is sensible, that he sits there, not to

[17] See Baker, *Introduction to English Legal History*, 116–18; Fortier, *Culture of Equity in Early Modern England*, 76–81; and David Ibbetson, "*The Earl of Oxford's Case* (1615)," in *Landmark Cases in Equity*, ed. Charles Mitchell (Oxford: Hart, 2012), 1–32.

[18] John Selden, *Table-Talk: Being the Discourses of John Selden Esq.* (London: E. Smith, 1689), 18.

[19] Baker, *Introduction to English Legal History*, 119. On Bacon's efforts as chancellor, see Klinck, *Conscience, Equity and the Court of Chancery*, 168–72.

[20] The landmark *Earl of Oxford's Case* did not appear in print until 1716. Only twenty-three collections of Chancery reports were published in the eighteenth century; annual publication did not begin until the nineteenth century. See Fortier, *Culture of Equity in Restoration and Eighteenth-Century Britain and America*, 17; and Nixon, "Gender, Law, and the Birth of Bourgeois Civil Society," 138.

Dictate according to his Will and Pleasure, but to be guided by that infallible Monitor within his own Breast."[21] Although the court "will not adhere to its own most established Rules, if the least Injustice arises from thence," he continued, ". . . it cannot from thence be infer'd that it is governed by no Rules at all."[22] Francis distilled equity into fourteen principles, such as "Equality is Equity," "Equity prevents Mischief," and "He that will have Equity Done to him, must Do it to the same Person."[23] Such principles, in Francis's view, provided guidance while leaving room for fair and flexible judgments.

William Blackstone also sought to alleviate concerns about the practice of the Chancery Court. Unlike Francis, however, he denied equity's Aristotelian foundation. In the third volume of his *Commentaries on the Laws of England* (1768), Blackstone identified several misconceptions about equity, including the idea that "equity determines according to the spirit of the rule, and not according to the strictness of the letter."[24] So, too, did Blackstone dispute the idea that "a court of equity is not bound by rules or precedents, but acts from the opinion of the judge, founded on the circumstances of every particular case."[25] "[I]f a court of equity in England did really act" as some writers suggested it did, he concluded, "it would rise above all law, either common or statute, and be a most arbitrary legislator in every particular case."[26] Such misunderstandings were fostered by jurists such as Coke, Selden, and "even the great Bacon himself," Blackstone explained, but that was "in the infancy" of equity.[27] As he saw it, the courts of equity and common law were founded on the same principles of justice, though their forms and modes of proceedings differed. Neither court could "vary men's wills or agreements," he reminded, "or (in other

[21] Richard Francis, "To the Reader," in *Maxims of Equity, Collected from, and Proved by Cases, Out of the Books of the Best Authority, in the High Court of Chancery* (London: E. and R. Nutt, and R. Gosling, 1727), [i–v], at [ii].

[22] Francis, "To the Reader," [iii].

[23] Francis, *Maxims of Equity*, 1–5, 9–18, 30–35.

[24] William Blackstone, *Commentaries on the Laws of England*, ed. Wilfrid Prest, bk. 3, *Of Private Wrongs*, ed. Thomas P. Gallanis (1768; Oxford: Oxford University Press, 2016), 283. On Blackstone's view of equity, see David Lieberman, *The Province of Legislation Determined: Legal Theory in Eighteenth-Century Britain* (Cambridge: Cambridge University Press, 1989), 83–87, 171–72.

[25] Blackstone, *Commentaries*, 3:284.

[26] Blackstone, *Commentaries*, 3:284. In the first volume of his treatise, Blackstone acknowledged the potential conflicts between the courts, concluding that "law, without equity, tho' hard and disagreeable, is much more desirable for the public good, than equity without law; which would make every judge a legislator, and introduce most infinite confusion." *Commentaries on the Laws of England*, ed. Wilfrid Prest, bk. 1, *Of the Rights of Persons*, ed. David Lemmings (1765; Oxford: Oxford University Press, 2016), 47.

[27] Blackstone, *Commentaries*, 3:284–85.

words) make wills or agreements for them. . . . Both courts will equitably construe, but neither pretends to control or change, a lawful stipulation or engagement."[28] In short, Blackstone insisted, both common-law courts and equity courts had limits that constrained judges' discretion. These claims were largely supported by the practices of Philip Yorke, Lord Chancellor Hardwicke, who presided over the court from 1736 to 1756 and who worked to regularize its rules. But jurists would continue to debate the nature and scope of Chancery's jurisdiction and the relationship between law and equity well into the nineteenth century.[29]

Many of the principles that Chancery developed also sparked controversy in this period. The court dealt with a number of issues, but it had particular jurisdiction over trusts, and it contributed significantly to the development of the area we now know as family law. Its rulings in these areas worked to chip away at legal principles that disempowered women and minor children. According to the common-law doctrine of "coverture," or marital unity, a wife's legal identity was subsumed by and incorporated into that of her husband. As a result, women could not own property or enter into contracts during marriage.[30] In the late seventeenth century, Chancery began formulating rules that enabled wives to retain ownership and control of their property and to form contracts on their own behalf.[31] These judgments were limited in practice, however. As Susan Staves has shown, equitable innovations such as the trust were of use only to women of the propertied classes, and by the end of the century, when judges realized the full implications of these developments, they retreated from them and reimposed "deeper patriarchal structures."[32] As the chancellor was "the general and supreme guardian of all infants," the court also handled custody disputes and guardianships and intervened in certain cases arising under the 1753 Clandestine Marriages Act. There

[28] Blackstone, *Commentaries*, 3:286.

[29] On Lord Hardwicke's regularization of Chancery practices, see Lieberman, *Province of Legislation*, 81–82. On the nineteenth-century debates, see Michael Lobban, "Preparing for Fusion: Reforming the Nineteenth-Century Court of Chancery, Part I," *Law and History Review* 22, no. 2 (Summer 2004): 389–427; and Lobban, "Preparing for Fusion, Part II." On debates about equity's place in common-law systems since the nineteenth century, see John C. P. Goldberg, Henry E. Smith, and P. G. Turner, eds., *Equity and Law: Fusion and Fission* (Cambridge: Cambridge University Press, 2019).

[30] See Baker, *Introduction to English Legal History*, 522–23; and Blackstone, *Commentaries*, 1:284–87.

[31] See Baker, *Introduction to English Legal History*, 524–25; and Susan Staves, *Married Women's Separate Property in England, 1660–1833* (Cambridge, MA: Harvard University Press, 1990).

[32] See Staves, *Married Women's Separate Property*, 4, 221–30. On equity's mixed legacy for women, see also Eileen Spring, *Law, Land, and Family: Aristocratic Inheritance in England, 1300 to 1800* (Chapel Hill: University of North Carolina Press, 1993), 112–22, 184–85.

were limits to the justice that Chancery meted out in these areas, too: The court accorded fathers and guardians priority over mothers in custody disputes, and it had limited authority to intervene in conflicts related to minors' matches.[33] Overall, Chancery responded in uneven ways to the patriarchal principles underlying England's marriage and property laws. In spite of critics' concerns about the seemingly subjective nature of Chancery's judgments, the court did not effect significant changes to the law in these areas.

Equitable Judgment in *Grandison*

Richardson showed a keen interest in and knowledge of England's legal system. His appointment as the first official printer for the House of Commons in 1733 and as the exclusive printer of the *Journal* of the House of Commons in 1742 exposed him to a wide range of legal disputes.[34] As Keith Maslen has shown, in addition to twenty-eight retrospective volumes of the *Journal*, Richardson printed over 1,000 private bills, including bills dissolving marriages, settling estates, arranging guardianships, and establishing marriage settlements.[35] Richardson also printed bills related to the regulation of trials and the qualifications and powers of justices of the peace, themselves appointed by the Lord Chancellor.[36] Perhaps most famously, Richardson printed 900 copies of Lord Hardwicke's 1753 bill "for the better preventing of clandestine marriages," which provided the basis for the Marriage Act.[37] In 1760 Richardson would purchase half the patent for English law printing and would publish new editions of Saint German's *Doctor and Student* (1761) and Plowden's *Commentaries* (1761), which contained influential discussions of law and equity.[38] Yet long before then, he printed works like Jean Domat's *The Civil Law in Its Natural Order* (1737) and Thomas Salmon and Sollom Emlyn's *Complete Collection of State Trials*

[33] See Blackstone, *Commentaries*, 1:281–82, 1:299–300; and "An Act for the Better Preventing of Clandestine Marriages," 26 Geo. II c. 33, in *The Statutes at Large*, ed. Danby Pickering, vol. 21 (Cambridge: Joseph Bentham, 1766), 124–30, at 127–28.

[34] See Keith Maslen, *Samuel Richardson of London, Printer: A Study of His Printing Based on Ornament Use and Business Accounts* (Dunedin: University of Otago, 2001), 22–25.

[35] See Maslen, *Samuel Richardson*, 18–20, 296–98.

[36] See Maslen, *Samuel Richardson*, 273, 275–76, 288; and Norma Landau, *The Justices of the Peace, 1679–1760* (Berkeley: University of California Press, 1984), 14.

[37] See Maslen, *Samuel Richardson*, 288.

[38] See Maslen, *Samuel Richardson*, 42–43, 117, 135. On Saint German and Plowden, see Fortier, *Culture of Equity in Early Modern England*, 59–67.

(1730, 1742).[39] In 1740, moreover, he edited, adapted, and printed Roger L'Estrange's *Aesop's Fables: With Instructive Morals and Reflections* (1692), which – as Mark Fortier has shown – presented foundational principles of equity.[40]

Richardson's interest in the nature and limits of legal justice informs all his novels. In *Pamela*, the unscrupulous Mr. B., who is himself an MP and a justice of the peace, subjects the heroine to numerous "trials" before reforming and marrying her, while in *Clarissa* the libertine Robert Lovelace imagines himself introducing bills in Parliament even as he declares his own actions to be "above all law."[41] Richardson offers a glimpse of equitable justice in Mr. B.'s response to Pamela's suffering (after Mr. B. reads her account and views his actions through her eyes) as well as in the interventions of Lovelace's friend John Belford, who aids Clarissa after Lovelace rapes her. In *Grandison*, though, Richardson offers his most sustained meditation on the value of equitable remedies for legal wrongs. The novel responds at once to long-standing concerns about Chancery's reliance upon the individual conscience as the basis for judgment and to more recent debates about England's marriage and property laws. In *Grandison*, I suggest, Richardson draws upon and imaginatively extends the era's equity jurisprudence to contest the patriarchal underpinning of English family law. At a time when jurists applauded Chancery's move away from equity's Aristotelian foundation toward a system of general principles, Richardson shows that it is possible to rectify harsh laws without substituting arbitrary rulings in their place. Richardson offers a portrait of the ideal judge in his eponymous hero, who possesses an exceptional ability to adopt other points of view and who consistently issues judgments in others' favor even when those judgments run counter to his own interests. Sir Charles's selflessness is matched by that of Harriet Byron, whom Sir Charles rescues from abduction by a libertine early in the novel and eventually marries. Like Sir Charles, Harriet adopts an impartial stance when mediating disputes;

[39] See Maslen, *Samuel Richardson*, 81, 136–37.

[40] See Fortier, *Culture of Equity in Restoration and Eighteenth-Century Britain and America*, 53–61; Samuel Richardson, *Aesop's Fables: With Instructive Morals and Reflections* (York: T. Wilson and R. Spence, 1740). Richardson issued another edition of *Aesop's Fables* in 1753. In addition, he published Seneca's *Select Epistles on Several Moral Subjects* (1739) and *A Supplement to Seneca's Morals, as Abstracted by Sir Roger L'Estrange* (1740), the latter of which contained Seneca's own thinking about equity. On Richardson's printing, see Maslen, *Samuel Richardson*, 56–57, 137–38. On Seneca, see Nussbaum, "Equity and Mercy," 97–105.

[41] See Samuel Richardson, *Pamela; or, Virtue Rewarded*, ed. Thomas Keymer and Alice Wakely (1740; Oxford: Oxford University Press, 2008), 198, 230; Samuel Richardson, *Clarissa, or The History of a Young Lady*, ed. Angus Ross (1747–48; London: Penguin, 1985), 419, 873–74.

also like Sir Charles, she prioritizes mercy and forgiveness over strict legal justice. Richardson's epistolary technique reinforces this point; the novel's multiple and overlapping exchanges of letters prompt readers to consider opposing perspectives and to cultivate the practice of equitable judgment. Through his portraits of Sir Charles and Harriet and his experiments with epistolary form, Richardson affirms the value of the individual conscience as the basis for decisions in the Court of Chancery while underscoring the need to incorporate fair and flexible judgments into everyday life.

Sir Charles studies law during his time on the Continent, but he goes well beyond the requirements of legal justice. "The Laws were not made so much for the direction of good men, as to circumscribe the bad," he advises his Italian friend Jeronymo della Porretta. "Men are to approve themselves at a higher tribunal than at that of men" (2:646). Sir Charles routinely holds himself to this standard; he "judges of every-thing, according to the rules of right and prudence" (3:1520), as his mentor Dr. Bartlett observes. Grandison puts his ethical principles into action when, at the age of twenty-five, he returns to England and begins to rectify his late father's dissolute ways. We learn of Sir Charles's behavior through his sister Charlotte's account, which Harriet relates in a letter to her cousin Lucy Selby. First, Sir Charles considers the case of his father's housekeeper and mistress, Mrs. Oldham, who has been "living in a kind of wife-like state" at Sir Thomas's Essex seat for many years (1:375). After Sir Thomas's unexpected illness and death, Grandison's cousin Everard throws Mrs. Oldham out of the house, allowing her to take just one set of clothes in addition to what she is wearing. When she weeps and complains of his harsh treatment, Everard refers her to his absent cousin "for still more rigorous justice" (1:381). Charlotte and her sister, Caroline, likewise deny Mrs. Oldham's appeals, rebuking the woman for living a shameful life. To their surprise, however, when Sir Charles arrives he treats her with kindness and respect. Through his response, the novel shows the need to exceed the requirements of legal justice in this case. Although his father did not leave a will, Sir Charles considers the circumstances of Mrs. Oldham's relationship with his father and the latter's apparent intentions. Citing his father's praise of Mrs. Oldham in his letters as well as Mrs. Oldham's penitent behavior, Sir Charles permits her to take all the money, notes, and securities she has saved in addition to the presents she received from Sir Thomas. If his father had made a will, he tells her, "would [the presents] not have been yours?" (1:397). At this point, Sir Charles reminds his sisters of the need to do more than "*legal* justice," declaring that "The Law was not made for a man of conscience" (1:397).

In this episode, Richardson shows the importance of applying equitable principles to inheritance disputes. Mrs. Oldham has no formal, legal claim upon Sir Thomas, and even Chancery, as we have seen, would not grant relief in such cases. (Equity would not alter or "make wills" for men, as Blackstone emphasized.) In permitting Mrs. Oldham to keep the money and gifts she received from her partner, Sir Charles effectively honors an implicit contract between unmarried cohabitants – a contract that the common-law courts would not recognize until the late twentieth century.[42] But it is unjust to leave Mrs. Oldham without any property given her genuine devotion to Sir Thomas and the latter's feelings for her, Sir Charles suggests. In issuing this verdict, Sir Charles relies upon his own sense of justice as well as his ability to consider all perspectives in the case. "No one can judge of another, that cannot be that very other in imagination, when he takes the judgment-seat" (1:390), he explains, articulating a principle that Adam Smith would develop in *The Theory of Moral Sentiments* (1759).[43] Richardson's narrative technique reinforces this point. Harriet emphasizes the extenuating circumstances of the case when she first mentions Mrs. Oldham, and she goes on to express pity for Sir Thomas's mistress as well as surprise and dismay at Caroline's and Charlotte's ungenerous behavior. ("Dear ladies!" she observes, "they forgot, at that moment, that *mercy* and *justice* are sister-graces, and cannot be separated in a virtuous bosom" [1:389]). Not only has Mrs. Oldham borne Sir Thomas two sons, but many people call her "Lady Grandison," and her birth, education, and good sense, Harriet observes, would have given her a claim to this title (1:388). Through Sir Charles's generous treatment of Mrs. Oldham and Harriet's praise of Sir Charles's actions, Richardson invites readers to consider Mrs. Oldham's perspective while underscoring that the circumstances justify an expansive interpretation of property rights in this case.

The novel further holds up an equitable model of justice through Sir Charles's treatment of his sisters. Critics such as Jeremy W. Webster argue that the novel "participates in the reformulation of patriarchal tactics of

[42] See Rebecca Probert, *The Changing Legal Regulation of Cohabitation: From Fornicators to Family, 1600–2010* (Cambridge: Cambridge University Press, 2012), 207–14. Chancery courts began to recognize *explicit* contracts between unmarried cohabitants in the late seventeenth century, except in cases where the woman was shown to have had an "immodest" character prior to the relationship (Probert, *Changing Legal Regulation of Cohabitation*, 43–51).

[43] See Adam Smith, *The Theory of Moral Sentiments*, ed. Knud Haakonssen (1759; Cambridge: Cambridge University Press, 2004), 11–13.

control."[44] In this view, the novel critiques traditional patriarchal authority only to reestablish it on sentimental grounds. Rebecca Anne Barr, for her part, contends that *Grandison* is a "novel of totalitarian morality" that "offers no *genuine* options to its characters" and that "veils the threat of coercion made possible by the constant surveillance of subjects."[45] In this novel, however, Richardson offers significant challenges to men's legal and moral authority. After Sir Charles resolves the dispute surrounding Mrs. Oldham's inheritance, he asks his sisters about their own situations, exchanges that Charlotte relates to Harriet and that Harriet again recounts to her cousin. Sir Charles learns that Caroline also suffered from their father's dissipation: Sir Thomas refused to consent to her marriage to the upstanding Lord L. because he wished to keep all his property for himself and his son. After inquiring into his sister's desires, Sir Charles promptly gives his consent to Caroline's marriage and provides both Caroline and Charlotte with bequests of 10,000 pounds. When Charlotte later tells him, in Harriet's presence, that his goodness is "without example," he responds, "Not so, I hope. My sisters had an *equitable*, if not a *legal* right to what has been done":

> I found, on looking into my affairs, that, by a moderate calculation of the family-circumstances, no man should think of addressing a daughter of Sir Thomas Grandison, without supposing himself intitled, either by his merits or fortune, to expect 10,000 *l.* with her – And this, even allowing to the Son the customary preferences given to men as men; tho' given for the sake of pride, perhaps, rather than natural justice. For does not tyrant custom make a daughter change *her* name in marriage, and give to a son, for the sake of *name* only, the estate of the common ancestor of both? (1:424–25)

In this passage, Sir Charles at once invokes and contests the patriarchal logic of the common law. The law, as we have seen, considered a wife's identity to be subsumed by that of her spouse; she lost both her surname

44 Jeremy W. Webster, "Sentimentalizing Patriarchy: Patriarchal Anxiety and Filial Obligation in *Sir Charles Grandison*," *Eighteenth-Century Fiction* 17, no. 3 (April 2005): 425–42, at 430. For a similar view, see Caroline Gonda, *Reading Daughters' Fictions, 1709–1834: Novels and Society from Manley to Edgeworth* (Cambridge: Cambridge University Press, 1996), 93–104.

45 Rebecca Anne Barr, "Richardson's *Sir Charles Grandison* and the Symptoms of Subjectivity," *Eighteenth Century: Theory and Interpretation* 51, no. 4 (Winter 2010): 391–411, at 393, 400, 401. Sarah Raff, by contrast, suggests that the care and protection that Sir Charles shows to his literal and figurative wards serve as a model for Richardson's relationship with his readers. See "Ghosts of the Guardian in *Sir Charles Grandison* and *Bleak House*," in *The Afterlives of Eighteenth-Century Fiction*, ed. Daniel Cook and Nicholas Seager (Cambridge: Cambridge University Press, 2015), 91–110. Bonnie Latimer underscores the novel's fundamental ambivalence about women's free choice and consent to marriage. See *Making Gender, Culture, and the Self in the Fiction of Samuel Richardson: The Novel Individual* (Farnham: Ashgate, 2013), 153–90.

and her property upon marriage. According to the rules of primogeniture, the eldest legitimately born son also inherited the entirety of his father's estate.[46] In the seventeenth century, the courts of equity began chipping away at the principle of spousal unity. But the courts offered no remedy for daughters with selfish fathers like Sir Thomas. In presenting each of his sisters with 10,000 pounds, Sir Charles again goes further than Chancery did to rectify the injustices of the common law, acting as executor of a will that he feels *ought* to have been made – "the supposed will," he tells his sisters, "of either of [their] parents, [if] either had survived the other" (1:409). Although Sir Charles's decision works against his own interests, it effects what he calls "natural justice." There are, of course, limits to Sir Charles's generosity: The money he gives his sisters will become the property of their husbands, and Sir Charles seems just as concerned with the claims of his prospective brothers-in-law as with his sisters' own rights. (In speaking of the men's "intitle[ment]" to a minimum dowry "with" their brides, Sir Charles conceives of marriage as an exchange between men.) But the episode nonetheless challenges the common law's dispossession of daughters while highlighting women's loss of legal personhood in marriage. There is no reason other than "tyrant custom" why Sir Charles's sisters should not receive an inheritance, Richardson suggests. Harriet's recognition of the injustice of her own position as a dispossessed orphan – similar in many respects to that of the Grandison sisters – underscores this point. While Lord L. assumes ownership of Caroline's portion after they marry, moreover, he shares all his property with her. Lady L. later explains that she and Lord L. have "one purse" and "one interest" (2:861); Lord L. gives her a key to the drawer where he keeps the money, and she takes whatever she needs, within reason, just as he does – an arrangement that Harriet endorses. Through Charlotte's account of her brother's generous behavior and Caroline's description of her and Lord L.'s equitable arrangement, the novel contests the common law's privileging of sons over daughters as well as its erasure of wives' property and personhood.

Sir Charles shows a similar selflessness when he revises the will of his late friend Danby. Unlike Sir Thomas, Danby records his intentions regarding the eventual distribution of his property. But he uses his will as an instrument of revenge: He all but disinherits his niece and nephews because their father hired an assassin to take his life, which Sir Charles fortuitously saved.

[46] See Baker, *Introduction to English Legal History*, 287–88; and William Blackstone, *Commentaries on the Laws of England*, ed. Wilfrid Prest, bk. 2, *Of the Rights of Things*, ed. Simon Stern (1766; Oxford: Oxford University Press, 2016), 140, 143–45.

Although the children are innocent, Danby gives his young relations just 1,000 pounds each and names Sir Charles executor and residuary legatee. Leah Price contends that it makes sense for Richardson "to give wills the prominence usually reserved for marriage articles" in this "self-consciously masculine novel" because "executorship legalizes men's relationships with other men as marriage does men's relationships with women."[47] Yet in this case, as in those of Mrs. Oldham and the Grandison sisters, Richardson's interest in wills signals a broader concern with women's and children's dispossession. Upon learning of his friend's death, Sir Charles immediately goes about rectifying the injustice. He recounts these efforts in a series of letters to Dr. Bartlett, who shares them with Harriet. After summoning Danby's relations and inquiring into their situations, Sir Charles decides to give them each an additional 5,000 pounds, and he expresses his willingness to supplement this amount if it does not answer their purposes. The admiration of the attorney who is present underscores the virtue of this behavior, as do the responses of the Danby children. Danby's relations are so deeply affected by Sir Charles's generosity that they weep with joy; the brothers declare that they are inspired by his example. Sir Charles tells them to consider the gifts "not as the reward of any particular merits in [them]-selves, but as [their] debt to that Providence, which makes it a principal part of [their] religion, To do good to [their] fellow-creatures." "In a word," he explains, "let me enjoin you, in all your transactions, to *remember mercy* as well as *justice*" (1:485). Shortly afterward, Sir Charles conflates the two terms, explaining to Dr. Bartlett that he has "done nothing but mere justice" (1:485).

In Sir Charles's treatment of Danby's relations, Richardson underscores the Christian foundations of equity. When Charlotte praises her brother for his liberality, he replies, "Any-body may [act this way] . . . , who will be guided by the well-known rule of *Doing to others, as you would they should do unto you*" (1:589). This precept stems from the teachings of Sir Charles's mother. As he explains to Harriet's abductor, the vindictive libertine Sir Hargrave Pollexfen, earlier in the novel, his mother instilled in him "notions of moral rectitude, and the first principles of Christianity"; she repeatedly read lectures to him on "the law of kindness, benevolence, and forgiveness of injuries" (1:277). These lessons prompt Sir Charles not only to pardon Sir Hargrave (who challenges him to a duel) but also to subvert Danby's attempted vengeance even though it means depriving

[47] Leah Price, "*Sir Charles Grandison* and the Executor's Hand," *Eighteenth-Century Fiction* 8, no. 3 (April 1996): 329–42, at 335.

himself of his own rights under the law. In making and amending wills to benefit his father's mistress, his disinherited sisters, and his friend's niece and nephews, Sir Charles goes further even than Chancery did to rectify injustices enabled and perpetuated by the common law. His judgments, though, are far from arbitrary: In each case, he is guided by the Golden Rule as well as a desire to counteract men's selfish and vindictive behavior. Sir Charles's judgments are aided by his ability to transcend his own perspective and to consider other points of view, a practice that Richardson reinforces through his epistolary method.

Richardson is less willing, however, to apply equitable principles to custody disputes than to property disputes. Approximately one year after Sir Charles returns to England, his ward's mother, the newly remarried Mrs. O-Hara, informs him that she wishes to undertake the care of her daughter. When Sir Charles denies her request, Mrs. O-Hara and her husband, Major O-Hara, go to Lord L.'s residence, where Emily is staying, and demand to see her. (Charlotte is present during the exchange and later recounts the incident to Harriet, who relates it in a letter to her cousin.) When Lord L. explains that Emily is "very happy" in Sir Charles's "protection," Mrs. O-Hara replies that "no father can give away the authority a mother has, as well as himself, over her child" (1:516). Mrs. O-Hara threatens to bring a Chancery suit to assert her rights. The Major echoes her claim, expressing his hope that "no father's will, no guardian's power, is to set aside the natural authority which a mother has over her child" (1:517). The argument that Mrs. O-Hara and the Major put forward, though, would not begin to be accepted in English law until the end of the nineteenth century. As Blackstone explained, "a mother, as such, [was] entitled to no power, but only to reverence and respect"; a father, by contrast, had "legal power . . . over the persons of his children" until they reached the age of twenty-one. Although the Chancery Court regulated and supervised guardianships, including those established by fathers' deeds and wills, it privileged the authority of legally appointed guardians over that of mothers.[48] The novel suggests that this is as is

[48] Blackstone, *Commentaries*, 1:292. On Chancery's power to regulate testamentary guardianships and mothers' limited rights in this period, see Sarah Abramowicz, "English Child Custody Law, 1660–1839: The Origins of Judicial Intervention in Parental Custody," *Columbia Law Review* 99, no. 5 (June 1999): 1344–91. The 1839 Custody of Infants Act granted mothers the right to petition for the custody of children under the age of seven; the 1886 Custody of Infants Act raised the age to twenty-one and gave mothers and fathers equal rights to appoint testamentary guardians. A 1925 statute further chipped away at fathers' authority. But mothers would not gain equal custody rights until 1973. See Mary Lyndon Shanley, *Feminism, Marriage, and the Law in Victorian*

should be and that judicial interference is not warranted in this case. As Emily realizes, her mercenary mother wants to obtain custody so that she can marry Emily to a wealthy suitor; unlike Emily's exemplary guardian, Mrs. O-Hara does not have her daughter's best interests in mind. Richardson reinforces this point by distancing readers from Mrs. O-Hara's perspective while aligning readers with that of Harriet, who expresses pity for Emily and horror at the O-Haras' greed and violence. Although Richardson imaginatively extends the reach of equity in his treatment of Mrs. Oldham, the Grandison sisters, and the Danby children, he is unwilling to do so in this case.

Yet while the novel rejects Mrs. O-Hara's claim to the custody of her daughter, it contests the idea of stripping mothers of all authority over and connections to their children. Several weeks later, Sir Charles facilitates Emily's reconciliation with her mother and stepfather. After inviting Emily to congratulate the couple on their marriage, he gives the Major, in Emily's name, an additional 100 pounds per year for his and his wife's "mutual use" (2:820). Also in Emily's name, Sir Charles gives Mrs. O-Hara another 100 pounds per year for pin money, "as from" the Major, for Mrs. O-Hara's "sole and separate use" (2:821). Sir Charles thus reverses the usual line of inheritance, enabling the transfer of property from daughter to mother, while shoring up Mrs. O-Hara's own agency vis-à-vis her spouse. Emily and Mrs. O-Hara are deeply moved by his proposal, as is Harriet, who weeps while relating the incident. Mrs. O-Hara and her husband apologize for their behavior; the former is overcome with remorse, while the latter declares that he acted like a "wretch" the last time he saw them (2:821). Later on, Sir Charles insists that Emily obtain her mother's consent before she relocates to Northamptonshire to reside with Harriet's relatives. And at the end of the novel, Sir Charles declares that his friend Sir Edward Beauchamp must obtain Mrs. O-Hara's consent in addition to his own and that of Harriet before proposing to Emily. The Marriage Act – which received royal assent on June 7, 1753 after heated debates in the Commons, five months before Richardson began publishing his novel – did not require minors to seek their mothers' consent; fathers and guardians retained absolute authority over children's marriages.[49] In Sir Charles's treatment of Mrs. O-Hara, the novel imaginatively extends

England (Princeton, NJ: Princeton University Press, 1989), 131–55; and Stephen Cretney, *Family Law in the Twentieth Century: A History* (Oxford: Oxford University Press, 2003), 566–76.

49 See "Act for the Better Preventing," sec. 11. On the debates leading up to the passage of the act, see R. B. Outhwaite, *Clandestine Marriage in England, 1500–1850* (London: Hambledon Press, 1995), 78–84; and "Debate in the Commons on the Clandestine Marriage Bill," in *The Parliamentary*

mothers' authority while endorsing equitable innovations that shore up wives' agency.

Through Sir Charles's exchanges with his would-be fiancée, Clementina della Porretta, the novel further extends equitable principles to the negotiation of marriage. Even in Italy, amid Catholics who revile his Protestant faith, Sir Charles shows a keen understanding of and tolerance for perspectives that differ from his own. Sir Charles demonstrates this capacity in his dealings with Clementina and her family. A devout Catholic, Clementina experiences an agonizing conflict between her religious convictions and her love for Sir Charles. Eventually, she resolves to repress her love and tells her suitor that he must no longer pursue her. But, in a surprising turn of events, her proud relatives, who initially opposed the match, now insist that she marry him. After reading a letter from Clementina imploring him to withdraw his suit, Sir Charles pledges to support her wishes even though they run counter to his own. He does so after imaginatively placing himself in her position and assuming the role of her advocate. As he explains to her parents,

> I could not so much as *seem* to give way to [her arguments], had I not been accustomed, when I was to judge of another's actions, to suppose myself that very person: Hence have I often thought myself obliged to give judgment against my own wishes; though, on resuming MYSELF, I have not found reason to disapprove of my first expectation. (2:1121)

In this passage, Richardson models the ethical and epistemological shifts that enable Sir Charles to comply with Clementina's request. Sir Charles is able to reevaluate his relationship with Clementina because he temporarily views it from her perspective. As further "*proof* of [his] disinterestedness" (2:1122), he proceeds to adopt the perspective of Clementina's parents. Upon finally "resuming [HIM]SELF," he advises the Porrettas to give their daughter "full time to consider and *re*-consider the case" (2:1122). Again, he issues a verdict against his own wishes, countering the coercion enabled by the law. The Marriage Act permitted minors to appeal to the Lord Chancellor if their guardians or mothers unreasonably withheld their consent to a match but, as critics noted, the act provided no such relief against the wishes of fathers.[50] Sir Charles recognizes the importance of

History of England, from the Earliest Period to the Year 1803, comp. William Cobbett and T. C. Hansard, 36 vols. (London: T. C. Hansard, 1813), 15:1–84.

50 See "Act for the Better Preventing," sec. 12; "Debate in the Commons," 16, 40, 59, 61; and *Reflections on the Marriage Act; with Some Hints for a New Law: Humbly Offered to the Consideration of Parliament* (London: G. Woodfall, 1764), 34.

obtaining Clementina's full, free, and explicit consent to their union, and he acts to shore up her will. Richardson's epistolary technique reinforces this point. By presenting Clementina's letter as well as Sir Charles's accounts of his exchanges with both Clementina and her relatives, Richardson prompts readers to view the conflict from multiple perspectives. At the same time, the novel underscores the importance of heeding women's voices and choices. In doing so, Richardson invites would-be suitors to consider women's own wishes while encouraging fathers and guardians to rethink their attempts to force daughters into unwanted unions.

Richardson recognizes, though, that not all suitors will be able to act as selflessly and impartially as Sir Charles does. Through Sir Charles's intervention in Clementina's exchanges with her parents concerning her prospective marriage to Count Belvedere, the novel shows the importance of involving neutral third parties in disputes over nuptial negotiations. After Sir Charles withdraws his suit, Clementina's relatives become determined to marry her to the wealthy Count. Clementina, however, insists upon taking the veil. Eventually, she flees to England, where she seeks out Sir Charles and implores him to mediate the conflict. In his capacity now as "judge" (3:1564), he again impresses upon her relatives the need to respect her will. Although Sir Charles and Charlotte (now Lady G.) underscore the value of marriage for women, the novel emphasizes that the decision whether to marry the Count must be Clementina's. Through Sir Charles's intervention, Richardson contests the patriarchal principle inscribed in Hardwicke's act and shows the need for impartial mediation to prevent fathers and guardians from exerting undue influence in the matter of marriage.[51]

Equitable interventions in familial disputes, however, are not limited to men in the novel. Like Sir Charles, Harriet possesses the ability to adopt others' perspectives and to mete out fair and flexible judgments. Through Harriet's mediation of the conflicts between Lady G. and Lord G., the novel further challenges the patriarchal underpinning of the common law while showing the importance of applying equitable principles to everyday life. The lively, liberty-loving Charlotte reluctantly agrees to marry Lord G. before her brother returns to Italy; as Lord G. leads her to the altar, she informs her doting partner that she expects to have "all [her] way" (2:852)

[51] For an extended discussion of the novel's engagement with the debates surrounding the Marriage Act, see Melissa J. Ganz, *Public Vows: Fictions of Marriage in the English Enlightenment* (Charlottesville: University of Virginia Press, 2019), 94–111.

after they wed. Less than a week later, when her husband comes to kiss her and ask her to join him for breakfast with Harriet the next day, she rebukes him for invading her privacy and taking "odious freedoms" with her. She is determined, as she tells Harriet, not to permit him "to make a shew of his bride, as his property" (2:911). The dispute escalates over the course of the day; the next morning, Lady G. sends a note to Harriet signed "Charlotte Grandison," declaring her resolution to be "unmarried" (2:910). When Harriet arrives, Lord G. asks her to mediate the dispute; Lady G. agrees that Harriet "had best be Lady Chancellor" (2:918). Women, of course, were excluded from serving in an official legal or judicial capacity in this period, but Richardson shows that they stand to play a crucial role in the resolution of domestic disputes. In her role as mediator, Harriet applies equitable principles, declaring that Lady G. must acknowledge that she is at fault and promise to change her behavior, while Lord G. must forgive his wife and pledge that he will attempt to distinguish between her "good and [her] ill-nature" (2:918). Harriet, in short, prompts her friends carefully to consider each other's feelings and perspectives and to show each other mercy.

Nearly two months later, when Lord G. arranges for himself and his wife to move to a spacious new residence in Grosvenor Square, Lady G. again condemns her husband's actions. "Does he not, by this step, make me his chattels, a piece of furniture only, to be removed as any other piece of furniture, or picture, or cabinet, at his pleasure?" she asks Harriet (2:1023). Harriet recognizes that her friend's fears are unreasonable and helps Lady G. view her husband's actions in a different light. Lady G.'s Aunt Eleanor, Dr. Bartlett, Emily, and Lord and Lady L. similarly rebuke her for carrying her jests too far. Eventually their reprimands produce an important change: Lady G. comes to respect her spouse, and he, in turn, shows himself to be, as Harriet puts it, "a manly, sensible man" (3:1639). Through Lady G. and Harriet's exchanges, Richardson calls attention to wives' loss of legal personhood in marriage even as he shows that Charlotte's fears of her husband are not warranted in this case. At the same time, Richardson underscores the value of mediation in promoting compromise and reconciliation between spouses.

Through Harriet's union with Sir Charles, Richardson develops his critique of the legal inequalities underpinning marriage while affirming the importance of applying equitable principles to conjugal life. Jerry C. Beasley claims that the novel endorses the traditional, patriarchal conception of marriage. In his view, Harriet's "submission to her … husband – her loss of voice, independence, separate identity – is progressive, complete and fully apparent."[52] Yet, far from losing her identity when she marries, Harriet gains power and authority. Sir Charles looks to his wife as his trusted counselor. "My dearest Life, you must advise me. I will not take any important step, whether relative to myself or friends," he tells Harriet, "but by your advice, and, if you please, Dr. Bartlett's. . . . Yours and his, will establish my judgment in every case" (3:1569). True to his word, when Sir Charles receives news that Clementina has fled to England, he consults Harriet, who advises her husband and gives her own view of the case. With the exception of five letters written by Sir Charles, Harriet recounts all the incidents involving his mediation between Clementina and her parents, affirming his efforts to shore up Clementina's will. At the same time that Harriet's letters highlight the need for greater checks on fathers' and guardians' authority, they subvert women's loss of agency and personhood during coverture.

Harriet's union with Sir Charles contests the legal fiction of marital unity in other ways, as well. In addition to advising Sir Charles on Clementina's dispute with her parents, Harriet assumes the role of Emily's "co-guardian" (3:1496). In this capacity, she offers advice to her husband and her young friend about Sir Edward's prospective suit. When the repentant Sir Hargrave leaves Harriet a large legacy in his will, moreover, Sir Charles declares that he will "not interfere, . . . not so much as by his advice, in the disposal" of her property (3:1693). Sir Charles here goes beyond the equitable arrangement provided by Lord L., who gives his wife equal access to all his money. Through Harriet's inheritance, the novel affirms the importance of wives' ownership of separate property while contesting the disabilities associated with coverture. The form of the novel itself evokes Harriet's agency: Although she temporarily gives up her pen during and after her wedding, Harriet quickly resumes her writing. Through her account of her married life and Sir Hargrave's bequest, Richardson exposes and challenges women's loss of property and personhood under the law.

Conclusion

In *Grandison*, as we have seen, Richardson looks not to common law or statutory law but to equity to reform familial life. Through Sir Charles's actions as a son, brother, friend, guardian, suitor, and husband, as well as

[52] Jerry C. Beasley, "Richardson's Girls: The Daughters of Patriarchy in *Pamela*, *Clarissa* and *Sir Charles Grandison*," in *New Essays on Samuel Richardson*, ed. Albert J. Rivero (New York: St. Martin's Press, 1996), 35–52, at 46.

Harriet's interventions in the disputes between her friends, the novel endorses and imaginatively extends the principles being developed in the Court of Chancery. Specifically, Richardson challenges the common law's refusal to give property rights to daughters and long-term cohabitants as well as its erasure of wives' property and personhood. At the same time, he seeks to shore up women's agency in the negotiation of marriage, challenging the authority accorded to fathers and guardians under the Marriage Act. There are, of course, limits to Richardson's equitable imagination. Richardson is unwilling to challenge a father's right to provide for the guardianship of his minor children after his death, and he is reluctant to countenance a life for women outside marriage. But the novel nonetheless exposes and undermines the patriarchal foundations of English marriage and property law. At the same time, Richardson responds to the concerns of equity's critics, affirming the possibility of rectifying legal wrongs through individualized inquiries without substituting arbitrary and subjective rulings in their place. Richardson's experiments with epistolary form are central to his critique. By presenting competing accounts of the conflicts, the novel incessantly invites readers to consider opposing perspectives. During a period when critics questioned chancellors' reliance upon their conscience as the basis for judgment and Chancery increasingly distilled equity into a set of general rules and principles, Richardson uses the resources of epistolary fiction to show the value of discretionary justice while prompting readers to cultivate their own capacities for fair and flexible judgment.

In *Grandison*, though, Richardson does not simply endorse equitable alternatives to the law. The novel also anticipates legal reforms. Toward the end of the text, Sir Charles reveals to Lady G. and Lord G. that he has considered becoming a justice of the peace and that "nothing but the engagements [their] . . . guests [the Porrettas] have given [him], would have prevented [him] from acting in [that] useful character" (3:1667). Although the spirited Lady G. initially jests with her brother about taking up "the appeals of scolding wives, forsaken damsels, and witches presumptive" (3:1667), she quickly joins her husband in applauding Sir Charles's willingness to serve the larger community. In this discussion, related by Sir Charles's admiring sister, the novel anticipates the fusion of law and equity, highlighting the need for judges who can bring flexibility, compassion, and mercy to the common law. Through his depictions of Sir Charles's and Harriet's exemplary consciences and his suggestion of Sir Charles's future contributions to the English judiciary, as well as his experiments with epistolary form, Richardson seeks to strengthen the ethical underpinning of both legal justice and everyday life.

CHAPTER 6

Mansfield, Burrow, and the Reformulation of the Legal Decision

Simon Stern

Research on the history of precedential reasoning in law has focused mainly on questions concerning precedents' role in grounding an argument. These questions include judicial attitudes about the need to justify a proposition by citing a case for it; the extent to which the courts have declared themselves committed to *stare decisis* such that an earlier judgment may control the case at hand or may leave room for maneuver; and the quality and frequency of case reporting such that it reliably serves to make decisions available to lawyers and judges.[1] The discussion that follows will give some attention to the last of these considerations, but will also focus on a different and less frequently examined issue: the rhetorical techniques that judges adopt when crafting decisions, and the structures they use, to clothe their decisions with the power of precedential force.

Lord Mansfield, Chief Justice of the King's Bench from 1756 to 1788, used a range of these techniques to mark out certain decisions (and rulings within them) as precedential, and to set aside older cases as incorrect or

[1] On judges' attitudes about the need for precedents in forensic arguments, see Ian Williams, "Early Modern Judges and the Practice of Precedent," in *Judges and Judging in the History of the Common Law and Civil Law: From Antiquity to Modern Times*, ed. Paul Brand and Joshua Getzler (Cambridge: Cambridge University Press, 2012), 51–66. Legal philosophers have devoted a great deal of attention to the binding force of precedent; the most useful historical discussions appear in Neil Duxbury, *The Nature and Authority of Precedent* (Cambridge: Cambridge University Press, 2008); and Rupert Cross and J. W. Harris, *Precedent in English Law*, 4th ed. (Oxford: Clarendon Press, 1991). On the history of case reporting, see John W. Wallace, *The Reporters*, 4th ed. (Boston: Soule and Bugbee, 1882); W. S. Holdsworth, *A History of English Law*, 6th ed., 12 vols. (London: Methuen, 1938), 12:102–62; James Oldham, "The Indispensability of Manuscript Case Notes to Eighteenth-Century Barristers and Judges," in *Making Legal History: Approaches and Methodologies*, ed. Anthony Musson and Chantal Stebbings (Cambridge: Cambridge University Press, 2012), 30–52. Literary scholars have explored these questions in a different register, asking how the invocation of precedent bears on legal forms of narrative. See Ayelet Ben-Yishai, *Common Precedents: The Presentness of the Past in Victorian Law and Fiction* (New York: Oxford University Press, 2013); Andrew Benjamin Bricker, "Is Narrative Essential to the Law? Precedent, Case Law and Judicial Emplotment," *Law, Culture and the Humanities* 15 (2019): 319–31.

misreported. Mansfield was more explicit and self-conscious than most of his contemporaries in his efforts to signal that he had reviewed the jurisprudence in a given area and meant to introduce a change that would govern future cases. In this endeavor he was aided by James Burrow, whose published case reports used various formal and typographical features that complemented Mansfield's efforts, drawing the reader's attention to the holding and identifying significant legal points by setting them off visually. Burrow was the first of the four reporters who covered Mansfield's decisions, and the others (Capel Lofft, Henry Cowper, and Sylvester Douglas) largely followed Burrow's model, adopting his use of headnotes but only rarely using typography and page layout to distinguish significant aspects of the judgment.[2]

Burrow already had extensive legal experience by the time he began reporting Mansfield's decisions in 1756. He was appointed Master of the Crown Office in 1723 and was called to the Bar in 1724. He was also a member of the Royal Society, an affiliation that probably influenced his ideas about the generic features of case reports (as discussed further below). By contrast with earlier law reporters, Burrow adopted a format that anticipates the reader's use of the reports. The introduction of the headnote is perhaps the most prominent example of Burrow's efforts to enhance the reports' utility. Earlier reporters had occasionally included some prefatory information, but Burrow routinely capped the report of each case with a short summation, giving the substance of the dispute and the central issue.[3] We do not know the details of the working relationship between reporter and judge, but scholars have suggested that Mansfield may have supervised Burrow's work, even extending to his selection of cases and the form of his reports.[4]

[2] The first two volumes of Burrow's reports appeared in 1766, and the next three appeared successively in 1771, 1776, and 1781, ending with decisions from 1772. Lofft's reports, in one volume, appeared in 1776 (covering 1772–74). Cowper published two volumes in 1783 (covering 1774–78). Douglas published a large volume (divided into two in later editions) in 1783 (covering 1778–81); two more volumes of his reports, going up to 1785, appeared in 1813.

[3] Percy H. Winfield, *The Chief Sources of English Legal History* (Cambridge, MA: Harvard University Press, 1925), 190; C. G. Moran, *The Heralds of the Law* (London: Stevens, 1948), 136.

[4] Moran, *Heralds of the Law*, 136–37. According to an article published some forty years after Burrow's death, "it is said that [Burrow] ... regularly submitted his own manuscript to Lord Mansfield for approval and correction before it went to the press." "Life of Lord Hardwicke," *Law Magazine* (London) 3 (1830): 72–118, at 97. The source for this claim has not been traced, but other discussions of Burrow (including Moran's) appear to accept it.

There is some disagreement as to whether Burrow had planned, from the outset, to publish his reports, but a contemporaneous note indicates that when he started, in 1756, he announced his intention to publish them. While in law practice, Sir John Eardley Wilmot took notes of legal disputes, and "continued after he was raised to the Bench [in 1755]," but ceased in 1756. According

It might seem obvious that every decision has the potential to become a precedent, because to question that possibility is, in effect, to question the very foundations of a system built on precedent-based reasoning. But it is one thing to say that a case may stand as a precedent for some proposition, and another thing to say that the case offers itself up as doing so, self-consciously advertising its future utility. Even a deliberate effort to create a precedent may fail for any number of reasons, but the deliberate effort at least seeks to facilitate the decision's adoption and application in future cases, whereas the opinion that simply reasons its way through, without inviting that use or marking any particular point as having carrying power, leaves its future application more uncertain. The deliberately marked decision is, we might say, self-indexing. Together, Mansfield's decisions and Burrow's reports often do some of the work achieved by the indexes, compendia, treatises, and abridgments available to eighteenth-century lawyers, while also anticipating some of the more granular distinctions that would be presented by services such as the West Key System (first called the West Digest System when created in 1848).[5]

A judge's deliberate effort to create a precedent manifests a distinctive conception of the judicial role – a conception that carries with it a raft of assumptions about the law's role in guiding behavior, the public's access to judicial decisions, and judges' ability to understand and anticipate the typical person's response (such that the proposed solution can be expected to achieve its goal). Once this conception became influential, it worked a significant change across the domains of the common law, establishing various conventions that today we take for granted as elements of judicial writing. To approach legal problems in this anticipatory way requires the judge not only to mark out the decision's salient contributions, in order to assist readers in finding and applying them, but also to think through their possible applications, and accordingly to take care in fashioning the

to "an indorsement in his Note-book in his own hand in Michaelmas 1756," Wilmot wrote, "When I was proceeding to transcribe the rest of my Notes, I heard of Mr. Burrow's intending to publish from the time of Lord Mansfield's coming into Court, and therefore stopped." *Memoirs of the Life of the Right Honourable Sir John Eardley Wilmot* (London: Cadell, 1802), 14. Burrow's reports begin with the Michaelmas Term of 1756 (October to December). If, as he claimed in the preface to the first volume of his reports, "these Papers ... were intended for [his] own private use, and not for public Inspection," he evidently changed his mind quickly. *Reports of Cases Adjudged in the Court of King's Bench, since the Death of Lord Raymond; in Four Parts, Distributed According to the Times of His Four Successors, Lord Hardwicke, Sir William Lee, Sir Dudley Ryder, and Lord Mansfield*, 2 vols. (London: Worrall, 1766), 1:i.

[5] On the development and intellectual context of the West system, see Joseph A. Custer, "The Truthiness of Thinkable Thoughts versus the Facts of Empirical Research," *Law Library Journal* 102 (2010): 251–68.

doctrine or rationale so as to avoid creating new problems. That requirement, in turn, requires judges to spend more time explaining and justifying the doctrine, so that when unanticipated circumstances arise, and the doctrine as set out does not clearly apply, the justification can help to guide any new modification.

Together, these ideas about how precedents work, how to facilitate their use, and the mentality that informs their creation point to a broad and significant change in attitudes about the judge's work. The result constitutes one of the most important developments in legal thought during the nineteenth century, the idea that "thinking like a lawyer" (and like a judge) involves thinking ahead, mapping out possible results, and managing them. This view brings with it a range of tools and concepts that are omnipresent in modern writing and argumentation, but that were only nascent, if visible at all, during the eighteenth century. Some examples include Oliver Wendell Holmes, Jr.'s "bad man" and the measures required to frustrate him; the specification of incentives and disincentives and the figures of the rational actor and the reasonable person who can be counted on to respond to those stimuli; and the demand for certainty, which yields a preference for clear rules as having even more value than correct outcomes.[6] My aim in this discussion is not to credit Mansfield as the originator of the legal mentality associated with all these habits (many of which he could not have anticipated) but to show how his ideas about the form of the judicial opinion helped to move the law in this direction.

Redesigning the Decision

The effort to invest a decision with precedential force has both rhetorical and formal aspects. Rhetorical techniques for highlighting a proposition or holding, to signal its eligibility for adoption by future courts, were not new in Mansfield's era, although he was unusually attentive to this opportunity.[7] Formal techniques for enhancing a decision's precedential use, such as

[6] Mansfield addressed this last point in *Vallejo v. Wheeler*, (1774) 1 Cowp. 143, 153: "In all mercantile transactions the great object should be certainty: and therefore, it is of more consequence that a rule should be certain, than whether the rule is established one way or the other." An oft-quoted modern variant comes from a dissent by Justice Louis Brandeis: "It is usually more important that a rule of law be settled than that it be settled right." *Di Santo v. Pennsylvania*, 273 US 34, 42 (1927). Burrow, echoing this theme, wrote in the preface to his *Reports* that when a court agrees unanimously "the direct point determined becomes a RULE for ever, and establishes *certainty*, the mother of security and peace." *Reports*, 1:v.

[7] On this point more generally, see Austin Sarat, ed., *Rhetorical Processes and Legal Judgments: How Language and Arguments Shape Struggles for Rights and Power* (Cambridge: Cambridge University Press, 2016), and particularly Bernadette Meyler's essay, "The Rhetoric of Precedent," 83–99.

experiments with the sequencing of paragraphs and their placement on the printed page, on the other hand, were largely absent before the later eighteenth century. Mansfield was a vital innovator in the development of these techniques, as was Burrow, whom the historian W. S. Holdsworth describes as "the connecting-link between the reporters of the old school who wrote their reports primarily for their own use and the reporters of the new school who wrote their reports primarily for publication."[8] These formal methods would, in time, grow to be so conventional as to become taken for granted, which helps to explain why modern legal scholarship has rarely looked into their origins.[9] Whereas in Mansfield's era, few decisions evinced any particular effort to render themselves open to future use, over the last century it has become conventional for judges to anticipate such use. At the same time, law reporting services have continued to develop enhanced methods of festooning the results with the paraphernalia of classificatory and indexical devices to facilitate the decisions' findability and reuse.[10]

One of the most obvious differences between modern judicial decisions and those of the earlier eighteenth century involves the formal delineation of the elements that make up the judge's analysis, beginning with the distinction between the facts and the law. Modern decisions usually mark out these elements as separate, beginning with a clearly marked recitation of the facts, and typically then turning to some settled legal principles that bear on the dispute before applying them to the case at hand. Decisions may depart from this pattern in various respects, but the insistence on starting with the facts and then moving on to the law is a near-universal reflex, so widely observed in common-law decision-writing that it would now seem peculiar to do anything else.

One need only call attention to this practice, however, to see how inconsistently observed it was before Mansfield's time. Through the mid eighteenth century, printed law reports often presented the facts so elliptically as to render that information nearly inaccessible. There was no general expectation that a judgment must set out the facts before turning to legal issues. Because of the erratic quality of reporting before the later

8 Holdsworth, *History of English Law*, 12:116.

9 A related development involves the use of sections and subsections within the judgment's legal analysis; see B. Rudolph Delson, "Typography in the U.S. Reports and Supreme Court Voting Protocols," *New York University Law Review* 76, no. 4 (October 2001): 1203–32.

10 These developments have spawned a proliferating literature on the efficacy of various techniques for coding and indexing judicial decisions, but less work on the epistemology they promote. For helpful treatments, see Daniel Dabney, "The Universe of Thinking Thoughts: Literary Warrant and West's Key Number System," *Law Library Journal* 99 (2007): 229–47; Michael A. Livermore et al., "Law Search in the Age of the Algorithm," *Michigan State Law Review* (2020): 1183–239.

eighteenth century, it is hard to be confident that the existing text of an earlier judicial decision corresponds to the judge's work, but the almost complete absence of any such pattern before Mansfield's era suggests that judges rarely adopted it. It was conventional, at that time, to include the arguments of the counsel as part of the report, and most of what can be gleaned of the facts emerges from this material, which appears before the judgment and sometimes occupies more space than the judicial decision. (One of the long-term effects of Burrow's innovations would be the excision of the lawyers' arguments from the reports in the later nineteenth century.) As Holdsworth observes, up to Burrow's time, reporters were writing "primarily for their own use," and they were often more concerned with issues related to doctrine or pleading than with the facts.

Burrow's reports of the judgments in the King's Bench, first published in 1766 (in two volumes covering decisions from 1756 to 1761), introduced a series of important changes. He announced, in the introduction to the first volume, that besides striving for accuracy in recording the operative principles in the cases, his book's "Merit consists in the Correctness of the *States* of the Cases" – that is, in presenting the facts.[11] He omitted "all cases where the questions turned upon facts and evidence only" – cases that decided no significant legal issues.[12] As mentioned above, he also took care to preface each case with a short headnote identifying the main issue in dispute. The first case in his first volume offers a good example. The question in *Raynard v. Chace* (1756) was whether the defendant, a partner in a brewery, did not have to complete a statutorily required apprenticeship so long as the other partner had done so.[13] Figure 6.1, taken from the report, illustrates the value of the headnote more effectively than an extended quotation could do.

The language is Burrow's, not the court's. He mentions the relevant statute, the nature of the dispute, and the parties' litigating positions, and ends by specifying the issue in contention. Even for readers who find some aspects of the description opaque, it will be evident that the headnote clarifies the case's significance and legal context.

John Wallace, in the most comprehensive review of the nominate reporters and their reputations and achievements, gives Burrow a place of pride, calling him the first "to have perceived . . . that every report, in

[11] Burrow, *Reports*, 1:viii. Since Burrow had originally planned to publish his reports in four parts (one for each of the judges listed on the title page), the first two volumes, devoted to Mansfield, were labeled "Part the Fourth" in the 1766 edition. However, he removed this from the subtitle of later editions because he never published the other three parts (covering Hardwicke, Lee, and Ryder).

[12] Burrow, *Reports*, 1:ix.

[13] *Raynard v. Chace*, (1756) 1 Burr. 2.

Raynard *verſus* Chace.

THIS was an Action of Debt for a Penalty on 5 *Eliz. c.* 4. for exerciſing the *Trade of a* BREWER, without having ſerved an Apprenticeſhip. In the Declaration there were two Counts. To the former " *nil debet*" was pleaded: And there was a general Verdict for the Defendant; (*viz.* " That " the Defendant does not owe, *&c.*") But on the 2d Count there was a Special Verdict: Which was to the following Effect; *viz.* that the Defendant *Chaſe* and one *Coxe*, were, and have been, during all the Time charged in this Count, Partners in the Trade; and that the Trade was carried on, and had been for 4 Years carried on, in their *joint* Names; that *Coxe* did ſerve an Apprenticeſhip, *&c.* but *Chaſe* never did; and that COXE *is a working Brewer*, and was paid a Salary for his Labour; which Salary was always deducted, and allowed to him, *previous* to a Diviſion of the Profits; and the Entries at the Exciſe-office were in their *joint* Names: But that the Defendant *John Chaſe* NEVER *exerciſed the Trade* HIMSELF; (which was wholly managed and carried on by *Coxe*;) but *only ſhared the Profits*, and *ſtood the Riſques* of the Partnerſhip. And they find it to be a Trade within 5 *Eliz. c.* 4.

Queſtion, on 5 *Eliz. c.* 4. § 31. " Whether the Defendant *John* " *Chaſe* is within the Act, upon this ſpecial Finding".

Figure 6.1 Headnote for *Raynard v. Chace* (1756) in Burrow, *Reports*, 1:2–3.

the form in which comes out . . . should be preceded by a Statement of the Case . . . in a form separated from the opinion of the court."[14] Wallace adds:

> The Reports of Burrow, therefore, give us in each suit three divisions: 1st. The case or statement of the facts . . . 2d. Arguments of counsel on that case. 3d. The opinion or judgment of the court upon it; – each of the parts being separate and pure, the statement or "case" being pure fact, the argument of counsel [being] argument merely, the opinion of the court [being] opinion simply on the case, with answer, perhaps, more or less full to the argument decided against, and an announcement of the judgment.[15]

[14] Wallace, *Reporters*, 447. [15] Wallace, *Reporters*, 448.

Wallace continues in this vein, but his basic point is clear: He credits Burrow with recognizing the importance of dividing the report into sections, providing the facts in a clear and succinct manner at the outset, and ensuring that the lawyers' contentions are separated from the decision, so that readers may readily orient themselves and understand the use of each section. The lawyers' arguments may serve as useful illustrations of advocacy, and are followed by the opinion, with its authoritative statement of the doctrine. Wallace considered the headnotes particularly valuable, observing that even if Burrow "presented no report of argument at the bar at all, nor of any other part of the opinion than the judgment, we should have, in a majority of cases, an intelligible report."[16] Wallace does not, however, mention the typographical means that Burrow used to segment and highlight significant points within the judgment – his use of spacing, italics, and small capitals – which also played an important role in his reports.

Mansfield was similarly concerned with the cases' pedagogical value and their ability to serve a precedential function, and he used both rhetorical and formal strategies to highlight this function. In an early decision, *Bright v. Eynon* (1757), Burrow records Mansfield as stating that he "did not choose, in any Cause tried before him, to conclude the Matter by a short Report, 'that He was satisfied, or dissatisfied, with the Verdict.' He would state the Case particularly to the Court, and reserve declaring his Opinion … till he had heard the Counsel on both Sides."[17] In a number of cases, Mansfield made a point of starting by specifying the essential issues and the decision's effect, for students sitting in the courtroom. In *R. v. Peters* (1758), before delivering his judgment Mansfield asked one of the lawyers

> to state the Case, for the Sake of the Students: (For He took this opportunity of observing and declaring "that nothing *misleads* so much as reporting the Determination of Courts of Justice, without having a sufficient and correct state of the case;" which, He said, was only an *ignis fatuus*, leading People into *Error* and *Mistake*.)[18]

Insisting on the importance of the case's factual setting, Mansfield offers a more general warning about the dangers of incomplete reports.[19] Burrow, in rendering this warning, further underscores the point with a manicule in

[16] Wallace, *Reporters*, 448. Similarly, Van Vechten Veeder observes that "Burrow's reports … mark an epoch in law reporting. … Burrow was the first reporter to appreciate the advantage of prefixing to the report of each case a statement of the facts and issues separate from the opinion of the court." "The English Reports, 1292–1865," *Harvard Law Review* 15 (1901): 1–25, at 21.

[17] *Bright v. Eynon*, (1757) 1 Burr. 390, 390–91.

[18] *R. v. Peters*, (1758) 1 Burr. 568, 571.

[19] This would be a frequent complaint in his judgments, which some have regarded as a strategic means of eliminating contrary authority. For instance, in *Millar v. Race*, (1758) 1 Burr. 452, 457,

And now Lord *Manſfield* delivered the Opinion of the Court; having firſt deſired Mr. *Huſſey* to ſtate the Caſe, for the Sake of the Students: (For He took this Opportunity of obſerving and declaring "that Nothing *miſleads* ſo much as reporting the Determination of "Courts of Juſtice, without having a ſufficient and *correct State of* "*the Caſe*;" which, He ſaid, was only an *ignis fatuus*, leading People into an *Error* and *Miſtake*.)

Here, the *Queſtion*, upon the *true* State of the Caſe, (which *V. ante*, *p.* 568.) appears to be "Whether an INFERIOR *Court* has "POWER *to* SET ASIDE *a* REGULAR INTERLOCUTORY *Judg-* "*ment*, *in* ORDER *to let in the Trial of the* MERITS."

Figure 6.2 *R. v. Peters* (1758) in Burrow, *Reports*, 1:571.

the left margin (Figure 6.2). With this preliminary observation out of the way, Mansfield then commences the judgment by moving directly to the basic point in contention: "Here, the *Question*, upon the *true* State of the Case, (which *V[ide] ante*, *p.* 568.) appears to be 'Whether an INFERIOR *Court* has POWER *to* SET ASIDE *a* REGULAR INTERLOCUTORY *Judgment*, *in* ORDER *to let in the Trial of the* MERITS." Again, Burrow uses typography to draw the reader's attention to this issue and to indicate its central importance: It stands in its own paragraph, with a parenthetical cross-reference to the first page of the case, and with italics and large and small capital letters to make the issue inescapable to the eye traveling across the page (Figure 6.2).[20]

In various later decisions, Mansfield similarly insisted on rehearsing the facts "for the sake of the students" before addressing the issues in earnest.[21]

which set an important precedent concerning the status of banknotes as a form of property (rather than merely evidence of a debt), Mansfield remarked, "'Tis pity that Reporters sometimes catch at quaint Expressions that may happen to be dropped at the Bar or Bench; and mistake their Meaning." This line has been widely reprinted in various dictionaries of legal quotations and compilations of legal sayings. Wallace, noting Mansfield's tendency to disparage reporters when challenging the validity of an earlier case, observed that when "a judge is combating an authority, ... his mind may have been somewhat warped by the interest of his argument. Pressed by an authority, it is found safer to discredit a reporter than to depart from a precedent. Mansfield was quite unscrupulous in this way." *Reporters*, 30.

20 This example offers yet another reminder of the differences between the nominate reports as they originally appeared, and the text as reprinted in *The English Reports* (Edinburgh: Green, 1900–32). Useful as this compilation is, *The English Reports* excises all manner of typographical idiosyncrasy – in this case including the italics and the large and small capitals.

21 See, e.g., *Wilson v. Mackreth*, (1766) 3 Burr. 1824, 1826: "Lord Mansfield said, There wants Nothing to answer the Objection, but to state the Case; Which I will do, for the Sake of the Students"; *Lee v. Gansell*, (1774) Lofft 374, 381: "I will state the Case ... I speak for the Sake of the

Morgan v. Jones (1773) offers an especially useful illustration. The case involved a complicated property dispute. Mansfield first sets out the relevant facts, and adds, "For the sake of the *bar* and *students*, I cite so much of the case."[22] He then proceeds to state, and to answer conditionally, the central question: "Whether the limitation, as to all the lands under the settlement, is not void? If it is, the daughter is entitled, as the reversion was in [her father] in fee."[23] Rather than allowing the issue to drift slowly into visibility, as so many of his contemporaries would do, Mansfield frames it along with the facts at the outset, adopting much the same procedure that Burrow did in his headnotes.

Mansfield would also make a point of stating the facts as a way of clarifying the future circumstances in which a holding might apply. For instance, *Ringsted v. Lady Lanesborough* (1783) sounds very much like a modern decision in which the judges take pains to cabin the precedential value of the case. Mansfield begins by rehearsing the allegations in the pleadings, remarking, "I state the pleadings, because the opinion we give will turn on all the circumstances of the case taken together; and what I say will only apply to a case situated exactly like the present."[24]

Again, with an eye to the judgment's precedential use, Mansfield would often make a point of eliminating confusion and error – not simply distinguishing earlier cases or questioning their validity, but deliberately and explicitly clearing them away with the air of a judicial roustabout, to give his solution a more prominent status. For instance, in *Abrahams v. Bunn* (1768), when explaining why a borrower may be a witness in a case alleging that a loan was usurious, Mansfield rebuts the reasons given for prohibiting such testimony in the only prior case that addressed the issue directly, and he adds, "All the other cases are loose notes of sayings, . . . general assertions, general inferences, without particulars, without argument, without consideration, without any state of pleadings or facts." Next, emphasizing the precedential status of the judgment to follow, he remarks, "This question having now come before the Court, it is necessary to consider it with accuracy and precision."[25] Unlike the earlier judges, with their general and unjustified "sayings," he would provide a rationale and ensure that all readers could see that he was doing so. Similarly, in *Heylyn v. Adamson* (1758), on the steps required to collect

Students and those who attend"; *Hurst v. Earl of Winchelsea*, (1759) 2 Keny. 442, 462: "for the sake of the students, I will just break [i.e., introduce] the case."

[22] *Morgan v. Jones*, (1773) Lofft 160, 176. [23] *Morgan*, Lofft at 176.

[24] *Ringstead v. Lady Lanesborough*, (1783) 3 Dougl. 197, 202.

[25] *Abrahams v. Bunn*, (1768) 4 Burr. 2251, 2253.

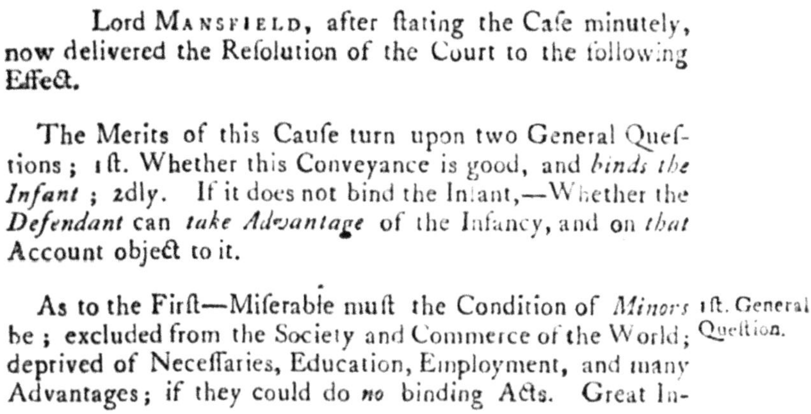

Lord Mansfield, after ſtating the Caſe minutely, now delivered the Reſolution of the Court to the following Effect.

The Merits of this Cauſe turn upon two General Queſtions; 1ſt. Whether this Conveyance is good, and *binds the Infant*; 2dly. If it does not bind the Infant,—Whether the *Defendant* can *take Advantage* of the Infancy, and on *that* Account object to it.

As to the Firſt—Miſerable muſt the Condition of *Minors* be; excluded from the Society and Commerce of the World; deprived of Neceſſaries, Education, Employment, and many Advantages; if they could do *no* binding Acts. Great In- 1ſt. General Queſtion.

Figure 6.3 *Zouch v. Parsons* (1765) in Burrow, *Reports*, 3:1801.

on a bill of exchange, Mansfield begins by questioning whether "there had really been such a variety of opinions upon this question," as the lawyers on both sides had contended, and he continues, "But however that may be, It must now be determined upon the Nature of the Transaction, General Convenience, and the Authority of deliberate Resolutions *in Court*."[26] That is, Mansfield sets out in broad strokes the policy rationales that will drive his analysis (openly stating that such concerns as "General Convenience" must be taken into account), and he also presents the result as a careful reflection that does not simply decide the matter at hand but also applies to future cases.

In many instances, Mansfield's lucid and enumerative mode of analysis and Burrow's efforts to capture it combine to produce a judgment that appears distinctively methodical and well structured, in a way that anticipates the analytical style of modern judicial opinions. For instance, Mansfield's judgment in *Zouch v. Parsons* (1765) (Figure 6.3) begins with a standalone paragraph that states, "The Merits of this Cause turn upon two General Questions; 1st. Whether this Conveyance is good, and *binds the Infant*; 2dly. If it does not bind the Infant, – Whether the *Defendant* can *take Advantage* of the Infancy, and on *that* Account object to it."[27] Having succinctly identified these two issues at the start, Mansfield proceeds immediately to the conveyance: "As to the First . . . ." In the following pages he reviews several rules and their application to the case at hand, and concludes

[26] *Heylyn v. Adamson*, (1758) 2 Burr. 669, 674.

[27] *Zouch v. Parsons*, (1765) 3 Burr. 1794, 1801.

this section by stating, "We are All of Opinion; 'That this Conveyance *binds the Infant*.'"[28] He starts the next part by repeating the second question (for which Burrow supplies a marginal gloss, "2d General Question"), and then breaks the answer into two sub-points, again enumerated and investigated in turn.[29] Burrow's marginal glosses complement the effect of his headnotes, and of Mansfield's systematic and orderly analytical style, to produce a judgment in which any significant point can easily be found and adopted by a lawyer making a related argument.

Hamilton v. Mendes (1761) offers another useful illustration of this effect. Determining how to assess the amount of insurance due to the owner of an abandoned vessel, Mansfield starts by noting that "the Counsel for the Plaintiff insisted on the four following Points,"[30] which appear in the four following paragraphs in Burrow's rendering, and which Mansfield then addresses in order on the following pages (Figure 6.4). Yet another example appears in Mansfield's opinion in *Johnson v. Smith* (1760) (Figure 6.5), which begins by observing, "This Demurrer can only be supported upon one of these two Grounds; either (1st.) That the *Fact averred is not relevant;* Or (2dly.) Supposing it relevant, That *Proof cannot be received*, to *shew* the Truth."[31] Again, in *Campbell v. Hall* (1774), Mansfield begins by observing, "A great deal has been said and authorities cited – relative to propositions in which both sides exactly agree, or which are too clear to be denied. The stating of these will lead us to the solution of the first point."[32] What follow are six enumerated short paragraphs, some consisting only of one sentence, setting out facts and propositions to establish collectively the nature of the crown's authority over Granada at the time when the dispute arose.

Mansfield was not unique in adopting this deliberate method of specifying the issues and using his list to structure the following discussion, but he relied on this format repeatedly, and Burrow (and the reporters who followed him) used the same method in rendering the analysis on the page. The result is a long series of decisions that are presented with an unusual degree of organizational clarity as compared to other judgments in this era. Burrow's visual presentation highlights the analytical force of Mansfield's rhetoric, helping to underscore the judgments' precision and promoting their use as precedents.

Mansfield's methods of signaling his decisions' precedential significance reinforce his well-known tendency to update the law on policy grounds.

[28] *Zouch*, 3 Burr. at 1804. [29] *Zouch*, 3 Burr. at 1804.
[30] *Hamilton v. Mendes*, (1761) 2 Burr. 1198, 1208. [31] *Johnson v. Smith*, (1760) 2 Burr. 950, 959.
[32] *Campbell v. Hall*, (1774) Lofft 655, 741.

Lord MANSFIELD now delivered the Reſolution of the Court; having firſt ſtated the Caſe, as ſettled at *Niſi Prius.*

The Plaintiff has averred in his Declaration, as the Baſis of his Demand for a *total* Loſs, " that by the Capture the Ship became " wholly loſt *to Him.*"

The General Queſtion is, Whether the Plaintiff, who at the Time of his Action brought, at the Time of his Offer to abandon, and at the Time he was firſt apprized of any Accident having happened, had only, in Truth, ſuſtained an Average-Loſs, ought to recover for a *Total* One.

In Support of the Affirmative, the Counſel for the Plaintiff inſiſted upon the four following Points;

1ſt. That by this Capture, the *Property was changed*, and therefore the Loſs total for ever.

2dly. If the Property was not changed, yet the Capture was a *total* Loſs.

3dly. That when the Ship was brought into *Plymouth*, particularly *on the 26th of June*, the Recovery was not ſuch as, in Truth, *changed* the Totality of the Loſs into an Average.

4thly. Suppoſing it did, yet, the Loſs having *once* been total, a Right *veſted* in the Inſured to recover the Whole upon abandoning; which Right could never afterwards be *diveſted or taken from him* by any ſubſequent Event.

1ſt Point. As to the *firſt Point*—IF the Change of Property was at all material *as between the Inſurer and Inſured*, it would not be applicable to the preſent Caſe; Becauſe by the marine Law received and practiſed

Figure 6.4 *Hamilton v. Mendes* (1761) in Burrow, *Reports*, 2:1208.

His efforts to modernize the commercial law have received a considerable amount of attention from legal historians, particularly James Oldham.[33] It bears mentioning, however, that in fashioning new rules and seeking to endow them with precedential force, Mansfield also reflected self-consciously on this practice and its rationale. For instance, in *Barclay*

[33] James Oldham, *The Mansfield Manuscripts and the Growth of English Law in the Eighteenth Century*, 2 vols. (Chapel Hill: University of North Carolina Press, 1992).

Lord Mansfield now delivered the ſolemn Reſolution of the Court; (having firſt ſtated the Pleadings very particularly; in which, he ſaid a great Part of the Argument conſiſted.)

This Demurrer can only be ſupported upon one of theſe two Grounds; either (1ſt.) That the *Fact averred is not relevant*; Or (2dly.) Suppoſing it relevant, That *Proof cannot be received*, to *ſhew* the Truth.

The firſt depends upon the Conſtruction of the Statute of Limitations * 21 *Jac.* 1. *c.* 16. * Sect. 3.

Figure 6.5 *Johnson v. Smith* (1760) in Burrow, *Reports*, 2:959.

v. Gana (1784), he ruled that the owner of a ship was liable for the value of goods stolen while the vessel was waiting to depart, because the ship resembled a "common carrier." Mansfield acknowledged that the decision entailed a change in the law, but said that the result would soon become integrated into regular practice. "At first the rule appears to be hard, but it is settled on principles of policy, and when once established, every man contracts with reference to it, and there is no hardship at all."[34]

Nor did Mansfield regard this view as merely a hopeful or theoretical view of the doctrine's uptake. In a 1778 case, ruling that the Post Office was not liable for the value of a banknote which its employee had stolen from a letter, Mansfield cited an earlier decision holding that the Postmaster General was not responsible for losses "by … fault of his servant." "The bar have taken notice of it as a judgment, the parliament and the people have taken notice of it; every man who has sent a letter since has taken notice of it. The mail has been robbed a hundred times since and no action whatever has been brought." Instead, he explained, people found workarounds, by "cut[ting] their bills and notes into two or three parts and send[ing] them at different times."[35] Mansfield's policy-based rulings were based on what he took to be empirical evidence that people understand and guide their behavior according to the law. In fact, these statements are among the earliest by a common-law judge to speak directly to the grounds for believing that law is an effective means of inducing behavioral change, and they hint at the distinctive view of the

[34] *Barclay v. Gana*, (1784) 3 Dougl. 389, 391.
[35] *Whitfield v. Le Despencer*, (1778) 2 Cowp. 754, 766.

judicial role that assumes a rational actor to be the subject of its directives. That view places burdens on the judge as well as the public. The ruling's presumed efficacy depends on the same logic that guides Mansfield's rhetorical practices: To justify the belief that a new rule will be adopted and will not result in any hardship, the judge must strive to communicate it clearly to those whom it governs.

Among the reasons that might prompt a judge to write in this format, a self-conscious concern with precedential value stands out as one of the most salient. Someone who wants to help others (judges and lawyers) in isolating the features that help to establish the case's significance will have reason to make the facts clear (to show when the case at hand applies directly to another dispute), and to make it easy to find not only the application of the law to the facts at hand, but also the justification and explanation of the legal principles, so they may be easily extracted and transposed. This is a point related to ease of finding (which Burrow assisted, by his use of typography and paragraphing), ease of comprehension (the progression is segmented so that if questions arise about the rationale, the reader can identify the step at which each point emerges), and ease of application (the doctrine is formulated in a way that facilitates its transposition). Finally, by requiring himself to devote a distinctive section to the articulation, development, and justification of principles, Mansfield adopted a form that by its very nature reminded him of the need to clarify and rationalize, rather than answering with a short and elliptical assertion (such as the mere statement that he was "satisfied," which he eschewed in *Bright v. Eynon*).

An especially vivid illustration of this approach appears in *Carter v. Boehm* (1766), a landmark insurance decision in which the defendant sought to avoid paying out on an insurance policy, contending that the plaintiff had concealed material information relating to the risk at the heart of the policy.[36] Mansfield rejected this argument, holding that some of the supposedly concealed details were readily available to the defendant, and others were so speculative that the plaintiff had no obligation to disclose them. Mansfield's judgment begins by methodically articulating the structure of the analysis to follow:

> 1st. It may be proper to say something, in general, of *Concealments which* [*void*] *a policy.*
> 2dly. To state particularly the Case *now* under consideration.

[36] *Carter v. Boehm*, (1766) 3 Burr. 1905.

> 3dly. To examine whether the [trial] *Verdict*, which finds this Policy good, although the Particulars objected [to] were not mentioned, is *well founded*.[37]

Mansfield then proceeds to do just that. He opens with a series of reflections on the disclosures required of parties entering into an insurance contract, explaining how the obligation of good faith applies to both parties. Next he explains the kind of general knowledge that both parties are assumed to have (such that no express disclosure is required), the kind of speculative views ("mere *general Speculation*") that either party might have (which also need not be disclosed), and the kind of privately known and material information that a party must disclose. Mansfield then recites with care the facts of the case at hand, and the legal proceedings that ensued, with particular attention to the evidence at trial that the insurer emphasized. The next stage (marked "3dly" in his opening outline) occupies about half of the judgment's text. In this part, Mansfield scrutinizes the insurer's evidence and subjects each item to the scheme set out in the first section (general knowledge, speculation, private and material information), and concludes that none of the evidence belongs in the last category. He ends, very briefly, with the general lesson that "every Rule of law" is subject to the constraint that "it should never be . . . used . . . to protect or be a Means of Fraud."[38]

Mansfield does not start with a recitation of the facts. Yet the judgment does devote a significant amount of attention to the facts, in a way that was unusual at the time. In his treatment of "the Case now under Consideration," Mansfield goes into highly circumstantial detail about the insurance policy and the events giving rise to the dispute.[39] In addition, the judgment's overall structure bears striking similarities to the "issue/rule/application/conclusion" format that figures so prominently in the modern legal-writing course. The decision thus models, in its general approach and at each step, a style of methodical analysis that appears strikingly modern.

Saunderson v. Rowles (1771) offers a similar but much shorter example.[40] As usual, Burrow's report begins with a short summation of the facts and the central question, followed by about two pages of the arguments of counsel. Burrow then presents Mansfield's judgment, which carefully recapitulates the facts in detail:

[37] *Carter*, 3 Burr. at 1909. [38] *Carter*, 3 Burr. at 1919. [39] *Carter*, 3 Burr. at 1911.
[40] *Saunderson v. Rowles*, (1771) 4 Burr. 2064.

> He stated very particularly and minutely, from his own Notes taken down at the Trial, (which He read to the Audience *verbatim*), the exact State of the Facts, as they came out upon the Evidence: Which he chose to do, that the Bar and the Students might be fully and exactly apprized of the true Circumstances whereupon the Court grounded their Opinion; and might not misapprehend Them to have determined *generally*, "That Victuallers could not in *any* Case be considered as Traders within the acts relating to bankrupts."[41]

The report continues, "The Facts, according to his Notes, He said, were *these*," and the remainder of the paragraph sets out a carefully detailed account that not only covers the essential factual points but also identifies the central legal question and its possible results. The plaintiff was the creditor of one Shrowder, "a Publican, that is, an Alehouse-keeper or Victualler." The question was whether a victualler who sells liquor "*in small Retail Quantities* by the Pot or Mug" should be regarded as a trader at large, which would make him "an Object of the Bankrupt Laws." "If He is, the Verdict is to be for the Defendant: If he is not, the Verdict is to be for the Plaintiff, with 31*l. Damages*."[42] Mansfield then turns immediately to the jurisprudence, showing that by analogy with innkeepers, who do not "get [their] Living by buying and selling, as a Trader does," a victualler similarly could "not be considered as a Trader at large," and therefore was not liable to a commission of bankruptcy.[43]

The judgment rehearses several of Mansfield's signature traits in a brief space. He rapidly dispenses with an apparently contradictory precedent by calling it a dictum, observing that when the case was decided, in 1697, the reporter (Lord Raymond) "was . . . a young Man," and adding that any reporter would find it "impossible . . . to take down in a perfect and correct Manner, *every obiter* Saying that may happen to fall from a Judge, in a long and complicated Delivery of his Opinion."[44] Mansfield also notes the great "Inconvenience" and "mischievous" results that would attend a contrary result, if a bankruptcy might arise "in every Case where a Victualler should be unable to pay his Debts."[45] In the space of about two pages, Mansfield states the facts and the main issue, reviews the jurisprudence and reaches a conclusion by analogy with innkeepers, repeats his views about the need

[41] *Saunderson*, 4 Burr. at 2067. The use of the third person may seem odd to modern readers, who are used to reading legal decisions in which judges write in the first person. This practice varied during the era of nominate reporting, and English decisions would not regularly use the first-person form until the Incorporated Council of Law Reporting became the official producer of law reports in 1865.

[42] *Saunderson*, 4 Burr. at 2067.

[43] *Saunderson*, 4 Burr. at 2068.

[44] *Saunderson*, 4 Burr. at 2068.

[45] *Saunderson*, 4 Burr. at 2069.

for accurate law reports and the dangers of hasty and misleading reports, and concludes by noting the policy rationale that supports the result. In its general structure and mode of analysis, the decision looks dramatically different from those of many of Mansfield's contemporaries (both on the King's Bench and in the other common-law courts), instead looking forward to those of the nineteenth century.

Others recognized that these habits distinguished Mansfield's writing. One commentator wrote that "his minute and accurate investigations, and his *perspicuous* and rational expositions, would alone be sufficient to establish his judicial celebrity."[46] Another praised his "profound discriminating and excursive mind," adding that "[h]is arrangement of a legal argument was equally luminous; his language was pure, copious, and perspicuous. ... For a space of nearly 30 years ... he was ... solicitous to simplify [the law's] proceedings and render its process intelligible."[47] Yet another commended him for his "*accurate, concise, and close manner of reasoning*, by which the most intricate and complicated train of facts, which would otherwise confound and embarrass the understanding of the most sensible jury, are reduced to *one single, plain, clear point.*"[48] In praising his conciseness and his ability to simplify, these commentators emphasized his judgments' clarity and his care in fashioning a rationale that could be transposed to later cases.

The repetition of the term "perspicuous" in these (and many other) encomia highlights a feature that contemporaries regarded as especially valuable in legal exposition. William Blackstone's *Commentaries*, first published in the 1760s, were widely praised on this ground, but his judicial decisions and oratory were not.[49] His brother-in-law James Clitherow wrote that Blackstone was "not ... happy in a graceful delivery or a flow of Elocution."[50] When Clitherow published a two-volume collection of Blackstone's reports, a reviewer remarked that readers of the *Commentaries* would be "totally disappointed" if, "seduced by the name Blackstone, [they] should expect to see any luminous characteristics of his

46 William David Evans, *A General View of the Decisions of Lord Mansfield, in Civil Causes* (London: Butterworth, 1803), 8.

47 Review of *A System of the Law of Marine Insurances, British Critic* 10 (1798): 185–87, at 185.

48 John Impey, *The Modern Pleader* (London: Butterworth, 1794), 40.

49 See Simon Stern, introduction to William Blackstone, *Commentaries on the Laws of England*, ed. Wilfrid Prest, bk. 2, *The Rights of Things*, ed. Simon Stern (1766; Oxford: Oxford University Press, 2016), vi–xxvi, at xxiii–xxiv.

50 James Clitherow, "Preface" to William Blackstone, *Reports of Cases Determined in the Several Courts of Westminster Hall* (London: Strahan, 1781), 1:vii–xxiv, at vii. See also Wilfrid Prest, *William Blackstone: Law and Letters in the Eighteenth Century* (Oxford: Oxford University Press, 2008), 72.

pen in these Reports; or ... hope to find the asperities of the law made smooth, and the jargon of technical language rendered accessible to unpracticed understandings."[51] These criticisms underscore the significance of Mansfield's achievement in presenting both the facts and the law in such an accessible manner.

Burrow and the Royal Society

In seeking to present judicial decisions in a more deliberately serviceable fashion, Mansfield and Burrow were not simply inventing new ways of structuring arguments, sequencing their steps, and emphasizing key features, but were also borrowing techniques developed in previous decades by members of the Royal Society. Burrow was made a Fellow of the Royal Society in 1737, and served as vice president for some thirty years (from 1752 until his death in 1782). He served twice, briefly, as president, in 1768 and 1772, and published eight articles and letters in the *Transactions of the Royal Society* between 1750 and 1769.[52] Through his ongoing association with many of the leading scientists and mathematicians of the day, Burrow observed the development of new ways of communicating ideas and information, published in the *Transactions*. The contents included mathematical proofs, reports of scientific experiments, and descriptions of natural phenomena.

Burrow, as a reporter, and Mansfield, as a judge, took a distinctive approach to their work by treating the judicial opinion more deliberately as an informational genre, in the sense that John Guillory develops in his article "The Memo and Modernity."[53] As Guillory writes, "Information demands to be transmitted because it has a shelf life, a momentary value that drives the development of our information technologies in their quest to speed up, economize, and maximize the effectiveness of transmission." He adds that information "constitutes the chief generic determinant ... in modes of writing such as the form, the memo, or the report."[54] Guillory does not discuss law reports in particular, and there are good reasons for

[51] [John Touchet], review of *Reports*, by William Blackstone, *Monthly Review* 67 (1782): 1–11, at 10. The attribution to Touchet comes from Benjamin Christie Nangle, *The Monthly Review, First Series, 1749–1789: Indexes of Contributors and Articles* (Oxford: Clarendon Press, 1934), 64. Touchet had reviewed the *Commentaries* in the same pages with great enthusiasm.

[52] Charles Richard Weld, *A History of the Royal Society, with Memoirs of the Presidents*, 2 vols. (London: Parker, 1848), 2:45–46, 58; *Oxford Dictionary of National Biography*, s.v. "Burrow, Sir James" (Oxford: Oxford University Press, 1907), 7:448.

[53] John Guillory, "The Memo and Modernity," *Critical Inquiry* 31 (Autumn 2004): 108–32.

[54] Guillory, "Memo and Modernity," 110, 112.

distinguishing them from other types of reports, but the very use of the term "report" hints at an affinity that both Mansfield's and Burrow's efforts reflect.

Guillory does, however, observe that legal language came to permeate informational genres in the course of the nineteenth century. He observes that this era witnessed "the development of legal or jurisprudential discourse as the favored technical language of ecclesiastical and state administration," and suggests that the vectors of influence may travel in both directions, proposing "an inquiry into how legal and other discourses have themselves changed as a result of assimilating the generic conventions of the commercial document."[55] One implication is that the rhetorical and formal features of the law report cannot be understood in isolation but must be examined in the context of contemporaneous developments in other informational genres.

Historians of related genres, particularly the medical case report, have similarly observed a shift, between the eighteenth and nineteenth centuries, involving greater specification of factual details at the outset and more carefully segmented sections dedicated to particular functions. These changes generally preceded those in law reports, offering another example in which scientists' methods provided a model that lawyers emulated. For instance, Brian Hurwitz describes a transition, during this period, from a practice of "featur[ing] dialogue and . . . a great deal of the patient's voice," with "dramatic techniques to *delay* the moment of diagnosis or the outcome of a case," to reports that are "divi[ded] . . . into distinct sections," with "a structure of successive staging – history of the present complaint, past medical problems, clinical examination, investigations and treatment effects – a formula that donates a particular shape and tone to the prose of the modern case report."[56] Janis McLarren Caldwell similarly notes that eighteenth-century medical reports tend to "mix . . . the patient's experience with medical observation" so that "[m]edical knowledge co-exists . . . with the story of human pain and courage," whereas their nineteenth-century counterparts adopt "the bipartite 'history and physical' which is the standard of medical reporting today."[57]

[55] Guillory, "Memo and Modernity," 117.

[56] Brian Hurwitz, "Clinical Cases and Case Reports: Boundaries and Porosities," in *The Case and the Canon: Anomalies, Discontinuities, Metaphors between Science and Literature*, ed. Alessanda Calanchi et al. (Göttingen: Vandenhoeck and Ruprecht, 2011), 45–57, at 45, 46–47.

[57] Janis McLarren Caldwell, *Literature and Medicine in Nineteenth-Century Britain: From Mary Shelley to George Eliot* (Cambridge: Cambridge University Press, 2004), 144, 146.

In a detailed analysis of articles published in the *Transactions of the Royal Society*, Charles Bazerman explains that by the end of the 1730s, reports appearing there had begun to exhibit a significant degree of organizational segmentation, "start[ing] with a statement of the phenomenon in dispute and then a discussion of the opponent's work or position," which was followed by "the author's own position with consequent experimental method and supporting results ... with perhaps some general conclusions."[58] By the century's end, the format becomes even more clearly segmented: "articles using experiments to prove general claims often begin with philosophic statements about general knowledge"; next they set out a problem; "[t]hen a series of claims resolve the problem, followed by supporting experiments"; and the article may end with a conclusion "discuss[ing] consequences of these claims." Overall, Bazerman explains, "the larger structure of the article is based on the logical order of the claims to be proved."[59]

Dwight Atkinson, building on this work, describes a series of developments that reflect changing epistemological views among doctors and scientists – and as the preceding discussion makes clear, the changing format of the legal case report participated in the same process. Atkinson notes that between 1700 and 1760, reports in the *Transactions of the Royal Society* became "more detailed and precise as the article form evolved."[60] Burrow, having served an important role in the Royal Society since 1737, could hardly have failed to perceive these changes. He was immersed in an organization whose activities centered on publishing informational reports, and his alterations to the form of the legal report reflect that experience. Given that he began reporting Mansfield's cases in 1756 and published his first two volumes in 1766, the timing could hardly be more fortuitous.

Atkinson points out that the reports in the *Transactions* became increasingly compartmentalized over time. By 1800, "many articles were sequentially organized as: *theory* ➔ *specific hypothesis* ➔ *experimental trial-as-final-proof*, with conclusions occasionally appended at report's end."[61] Another format for articles in the *Transactions*, also gaining popularity at this time, featured "a two- or three-part division of content – into a case

58 Charles Bazerman, "Reporting the Experiment: The Changing Account of Scientific Doings in the *Philosophical Transactions of the Royal Society, 1665–1800*," in *Shaping Written Knowledge: The Genre and Activity of the Experimental Article in Science* (Madison: University of Wisconsin Press, 1988), 59–79, at 76.

59 Bazerman, "Reporting the Experiment," 77.

60 Dwight Atkinson, "The Evolution of Medical Research Writing from 1735 to 1985: The Case of the *Edinburgh Medical Journal*," *Applied Linguistics* 13 (1992): 337–74, at 340.

61 Atkinson, "Evolution of Medical Research Writing," 340.

narrative plus either an autopsy account or a series of general remarks on the case, or both."[62] By the century's end, "explicit theory" had begun to assume "a more central position in scientific thought," and accordingly "research writing became increasingly objectivized, impersonal, and organizationally modular."[63]

If, as Atkinson contends, these highly segmented forms correspond to changing styles of reasoning and analysis, the work of Mansfield and Burrow may similarly be understood not only as aids for improving the findability and portability of a judgment's holding, but also as promoting a distinctive conception of the law. In a report that separates the facts of the case at hand, the governing principles, a review of the precedents, and the application of doctrine to the present case, the series of methodical sequences communicates a view of the law as embodying an orderly and systematic logic. The pattern also imposes a degree of objectivity on the analysis and anticipates various modern techniques that seek to convey the law's objectivity, such as the three-part test as a generic judicial device, and the use of model jury instructions with a flow chart to guide the jury's decision-making. Closer to Mansfield's era, historians have pointed out that the elimination of character evidence from the criminal trial, and the disaggregation of criminal offenses into "elements," similarly served to promote a sense of the law's objectivity. More broadly, the development of various objective standards, and a reconceptualization of tort and contract doctrines in objective terms, has been seen as one of the signal achievements of nineteenth-century lawyers and jurists.

The methodical approach that Burrow and Mansfield modeled played no small role in these developments. To insist on setting out the facts in order to clarify the breadth or narrowness of a judgment's holding, to isolate the essential issues and to make a show of focusing only on addressing them, and to mark and reject previous statements as dicta, loose notes of sayings, and general assertions – all these are ways are ways of advancing a view of the law as an orderly system that concerns itself with principles and that strives for consistency rather than making results turn on a particular judge's perspective. This is not to say that Mansfield purged the law of subjectivity, any more than the judges who followed him did, but only that he found a particularly effective way to communicate this attitude – and that Burrow's assistance provided an ideal means of reinforcing that message.

62 Atkinson, "Evolution of Medical Research Writing," 349.
63 Atkinson, "Evolution of Medical Research Writing," 342.

CHAPTER 7

Novel Subjects
Naturalization in Richardson and Edgeworth

Stephanie DeGooyer

Until the first half of the nineteenth century, England had minimal immigration laws in place. There were no established statutes or procedures for regulating the movement of citizens and foreigners. Passports were scarce and were primarily utilized by diplomats and merchants as letters of introduction or for ensuring secure travel during wartime. Such documents did not specify an individual's nationality, as they do today. An English subject's status was not yet legally defined.[1]

Before the Napoleonic period, moreover, the term "citizen" was not commonly used in England. That idea was more prevalent in contexts where people discussed citizenship in overseas colonies or in relation to broader British interests, or described a member of a city. Citizenship as we understand it today, with its associated rights and responsibilities, did not fully emerge in England until later in the nineteenth century when it became more closely associated with the growth of democracy and political reforms. Before this period, the question of who could be considered a subject of the king or queen was a far more important question.

The first common-law definition of the natural-born English subject – which would also become Britain's first theory of nationality – was established in 1608 with the ruling of *Calvin's Case* by the Court of Exchequer Chamber. The case directly addressed the issue of whether a three-year-old child born in Scotland after the union of the English and Scottish crowns could inherit property in London as a natural-born English subject. But beyond settling a toddler's inheritance, *Calvin's Case*

[1] See Mervyn C. Jones, *British Nationality Law and Practice* (Oxford: Clarendon Press, 1947), 39; John Hope Simpson, *The Refugee Problem: Report of a Survey* (London: Oxford University Press, 1939), 265; and W. E. Wilkinson, "Some Changes in the Laws of Naturalisation," *Law Magazine and Review: A Quarterly Review of Jurisprudence* 40, no. 2 (February 1915): 187–95.

also set down the rules to determine the definition of the natural-born subject that would ever after inform nationality law. As reported by Sir Edward Coke, later Chief Justice of the King's Bench, the judges concluded that Scots born after the union (the *postnati*) were subjects of the English crown because they were born under its protection. In their opinion, everyone born within the dominions of the King of England, whether in England or in the colonies, was under the protection of the king. According to the common law, they therefore owed allegiance to the king and were subject to all the duties and entitled to all the rights and liberties of Englishmen.[2] This opinion would have a significant influence on the legal architecture of the British Empire and the development of birthright citizenship in the United States.[3]

Calvin's Case, however, left many questions unanswered. In an era characterized by increased mobility, expanding trade, imperial ambitions, and concerns about migration to the New World, the case raised further inquiries. Could a foreigner ever become an English subject? Was it possible to alter or transfer a person's natural allegiance and religion? These questions emerged primarily in relation to the status of Scots born prior to the accession of James I (the *antenati*). Coke asserted that an individual's allegiance to the crown began at birth and persisted for life. In his opinion, the king lacked the authority to confer inheritable status upon anyone who was not inheritable according to common law. Yet Coke also contended that Parliament had the power to transform aliens such as the *antenati* into subjects, as he later stated in his *Institutes of the Lawes of England* (1628–44): "There is another kinde [of subject], and that is an Alien naturalized, and that must be by Act of Parliament."[4] Although *Calvin's Case* specifically addressed the status of Scots born after the Union

[2] See *Calvin's Case*, (1608) 77 Eng. Rep. 377; Herbert Broom, *Constitutional Law Viewed in Relation to Common Law*, 2nd ed. (London: W. Maxwell and Son, 1885), 31.

[3] See Barbara A. Black, "The Constitution of Empire: The Case for the Colonists," *University of Pennsylvania Law Review* 124 (1976): 1157–211; Mary Sarah Bilder, *The Transatlantic Constitution: Colonial Legal Culture and the Empire* (Cambridge, MA: Harvard University Press, 2004), 35–40; Paul D. Halliday, *Habeas Corpus: From England to Empire* (Cambridge, MA: Harvard University Press, 2010), 201–08; Christopher L. Tomlins, *Freedom Bound: Law, Labor, and Civic Identity in Colonizing English America*, 1580–1865 (New York: Cambridge University Press, 2010), 82–92; Craig Yirush, *Settlers, Liberty, and Empire: The Roots of Early American Political Theory, 1675–1775* (New York: Cambridge University Press, 2011), 34–40; Robert A. Williams, *The American Indian in Western Legal Thought: The Discourses of Conquest* (New York: Oxford University Press, 1990), 199–218; and Gavin Loughton, "Calvin's Case and the Origins of the Rule Governing 'Conquest' in English Law," *Australian Journal of Legal History* 8, no. 2 (2004): 143–80.

[4] Edward Coke, *The First Part of the Institutes of the Lawes of England: or A Commentary upon Littleton*, 4th ed. (London: M.F., I.H., and R.Y., 1639), 129.

of the Crowns, it also, and perhaps more significantly, raised questions about Parliament's ability to create new English subjects through naturalization.

Calvin's Case generated two conflicting concepts regarding nationality. The first defined nationality as an unalterable allegiance of the natural-born subject to their crown based on the "natural" link between birth and allegiance as articulated by Coke. The second concept, a direct challenge to the king's sovereign authority, introduced the notion that nationality could be formed or manipulated through parliamentary legislation. At the time, these two concepts were not typically considered contradictory. Neither Coke nor Parliament seemed concerned about whether laws concerning naturalization, whether enacted by Parliament or the king, ran counter to established principles of divine or natural law. Francis Bacon, the king's Solicitor General who represented the boy Calvin in the case, influentially argued that "by the Law of Nature, all men in the world are naturalized one towards another . . . . It was *Civill and National Lawes*, that brought in these words, and differences, of *Civis* and *Exterus*, *Alien & Native*."[5] Bacon represented naturalization as the ultimate natural process – as a return to the state of nature that men occupied before the development of civil law and national differences. But over time the idea of naturalization began to be appraised by many commentators as a radical new form of subject creation that challenged the idea of allegiance as entirely derived from natural law. This view of naturalization, most famously articulated by John Locke, held that nationality could be created or engineered, *ex nihilo*, by parliamentary statute. Individuals had the natural right to travel across national boundaries without the burden of being forever defined by the allegiance into which they were born. "A Child is born a subject of no Country, or Government," Locke explained in his *Second Treatise of Government* (1690).[6] Allegiance and nationality were part of the social contract; they were legal arrangements rather than a natural and indelible relationship between sovereign and subject. For Locke, nationality was volitional, and naturalization was the process of engineering nationality outside the rite of natural birth.

In this chapter I argue that naturalization, the process of transforming aliens into subjects through law, played a pivotal role in English society in

[5] Francis Bacon, *Three Speeches of The Right Honorable, Sir Francis Bacon Knight, Then His Majesties Sollicitor Generall . . . concerning the Post-Nati, Naturalization of the Scotch in England, Union of the Lawes of the Kingdomes of England and Scotland* (London: Richard Badger, 1641), 35–36.

[6] John Locke, *Second Treatise of Government*, in *Two Treatises of Government*, ed. Peter Laslett (1690; Cambridge: Cambridge University Press, 2005), 347.

the long eighteenth century. It is not possible, I contend, to understand the history of English subjecthood without also knowing that naturalization, understood as a process of turning aliens into subjects, was a crucial fictional process in this period. As a fictional process, naturalization was not limited to law. At a time when legal naturalization faced strong opposition in the legal and political spheres, the novel was emerging as a prominent literary form. The novel played a vital role in conveying the new ideas introduced by legal naturalization to readers. More significantly, it became a form of naturalization of its own, aimed at rectifying the setbacks and unfulfilled promises of legislative efforts to naturalize foreigners. Even though the concept of general naturalization was repeatedly rejected in the legal and political spheres, upsetting the aspiration of a "general naturalization bill" to admit all individuals regardless of religion or ethnicity, many novelists in the eighteenth and early nineteenth centuries, including Daniel Defoe, Tobias Smollett, Samuel Richardson, Laurence Sterne, Frances Burney, Maria Edgeworth, and Mary Shelley, took up questions concerning naturalization.[7] This chapter presents two case studies of novelists who exemplify different approaches to legal naturalization in the period. Samuel Richardson and Maria Edgeworth adapted the emerging genre of prose fiction to reimagine how foreigners might be received, assimilated, and legally protected in England. Both writers were particularly interested in questions about Jewish naturalization, and each offers a rich, though ultimately different, meditation on questions that interested jurists, philosophers, and novelists about naturalization more broadly in the period. In *The History of Sir Charles Grandison* (1753–54), his final novel, Richardson attempts to hold up the older view of Coke and Bacon, who considered naturalization to be part of a return to an original common human nature expressed in natural law. In *Harrington* (1817), by contrast, Edgeworth subscribes to the newer, Lockean, contractual and voluntarist approach: the idea that naturalization can be achieved through a Parliamentary statute without the necessity of natural law. Richardson's novel, in its refusal to incorporate both Jewish and Italian characters, ultimately betrays the promise of the older idea of naturalization premised in natural law, while Edgeworth's gimmicky ending, which exposes a Jewish character as also Christian, highlights the fears of a Parliamentary idea of naturalization that can convert strangers into subjects on the basis of will alone. At the same time, however, Edgeworth's novel reveals the

[7] For a discussion of these engagements, see Stephanie DeGooyer, *Before Borders: A Legal and Literary History of Naturalization* (Baltimore: Johns Hopkins University Press, 2022).

radical potential of the newer theory of naturalization and the creative power of fiction as a form of subject creation.

In its examination of naturalization and immigration in the work of these two British writers, this chapter contributes to the "transnational" turn in eighteenth-century studies and law and literature more broadly. Many literary historians today are trying to dismantle what are perceived as provincial, Anglocentric, and nationalist disciplinary agendas in the name of "global" or transnational literature. Yet often these scholars seek to introduce new methodological focus points for the study of eighteenth-century literature without an historical and legal understanding of how nationality was understood and how it was being worked out in this period. At the same time, legal theorists often too quickly reach for legal rulings to support modern immigration practices, ignoring the literary creativity involved in historical arguments about naturalization. The case studies that follow show how questions about how nationalities migrate and commingle in the fictional process of naturalization were central to both the project of the novel and the law in the eighteenth and early nineteenth centuries.

Naturalization and Natural Law in Samuel Richardson

In the later seventeenth century and the eighteenth century, various radical legislative efforts were made to naturalize foreigners. In 1664, a bill proposing "universal naturalization" for individuals of all nations and religions, including "Protestants, Papists, Jews, Mohametans, Turks, Moors, [and] Pagans," was presented to Parliament but swiftly rejected, as would be the fate of a similar bill in 1667.[8] Critics of naturalization argued that granting foreigners the privileges of English subjects would jeopardize England's trade and expose the nation to potential espionage.[9] Even more targeted efforts at naturalization faced intense criticism. In 1709, the Foreign Protestants Naturalization Act was passed to attract distressed Protestant Huguenot refugees from France to England, but it was revoked two years later by a new Tory-dominant Parliament. In 1753, a bill to naturalize Jews living in England barely passed the House of Commons before public outrage over anti-Semitism led to its repeal.

[8] See Caroline Robbins, "A Note on General Naturalization under the Later Stuarts and a Speech in the House of Commons on the Subject in 1664," *Journal of Modern History* 34, no. 2 (1962): 168–77; *Sundry Considerations Touching Naturalization of Aliens: Whereby the Alleged Advantages Thereby Are Confuted, and the Contrary Mischiefs Thereof Are Detected and Discovered* (London, [1695]), 3.

[9] See *Sundry Considerations.*

By mid-century, the idea of naturalization appeared to be at a legal and political crossroads.

The Jewish naturalization bill presented to Parliament in the spring of 1753 was not intended to mark a significant innovation in naturalization law. Although it ostensibly aimed to grant eligibility to all Jewish individuals who had resided in England for a minimum of three years, the bill primarily had a specific group of financiers, known for their loyalty to the government, in its sights. However, when the bill was passed on May 22, 1753, it triggered a passionate debate on matters of allegiance and religious tolerance in England at large. In the words of a commentator who signed himself "Britannicus" in the *London Evening Post*, the bill allowed for "an open sale . . . of the christian religion."[10] Critics such as this one contended that Jewish naturalization permitted Parliament to assume divine power and invite adversaries into the nation.

Supporters of the bill invoked a tract entitled *Reasons for Naturalizing the Jews in Great Britain and Ireland* (1714), authored by the Irish philosopher John Toland several years after the repeal of the 1709 Naturalization Act. Effectively, Toland argued that naturalization should not be premised on religious expression. Owning land and property should be enough to confer upon Jewish people the same rights as it did upon other English subjects. He saw naturalization as a means to acknowledge and encourage their economic impact on English society. More interestingly, he pointed out that Jews' lack of a specific homeland meant they did not have a prior allegiance that could compromise their commitment to English interests. They "have no common or peculiar inclination distinguishing [them] from others; but visibly partake of the Nature of those nations among which they live, and where they were bred."[11]

As opinions about the Jewish naturalization bill proliferated in the spring of 1753, Samuel Richardson was engrossed in revising the final draft of *The History of Sir Charles Grandison*. By the time the bill gained approval in May, Richardson had already printed the sheets for the first volume of the novel and was reviewing early proofs for the second. Amid this flurry of work, Richardson found himself drawn into the debate. In a letter to his friend and fellow writer Elizabeth Carter, written on June 12, he expressed initial approval for the law and even enclosed a "little Paper

10 Britannicus, *London Evening Post*, June 28, 1753, in *A Collection of the Best Pieces in Prose and Verse, against the Naturalization of the Jews* (London: M. Cooper, 1753), 30–33, at 32.

11 [John Toland], *Reasons for Naturalizing the Jews in Great Britain and Ireland, on the Same Foot with All Other Nations, Containing Also, a Defense of the Jews against All Vulgar Prejudices in All Countries* (London: J. Roberts, 1714), 19.

relating to that Affair" with his letter.[12] However, within a few months, Richardson's enthusiasm for the law had waned. On August 14, he wrote to Carter, stating, "[A]s the Jews get no great Matter by this Act, methinks I would wish them to declare, that seeing it is likely to excite popular Prejudices against them . . . they will humbly petition the Legislature, in the next Session, to repeal it."[13] As Bonnie Latimer notes, Richardson's rejection of the bill at this time aligned with the growing Whig consensus on the matter and reflected concerns that the bill had only exacerbated public intolerance against the Jews.[14]

Although *Grandison* was well underway during the public debate over Jewish naturalization and Richardson appeared to side with party politics on the matter, the controversy left a lasting imprint on his novel. As Latimer and other scholars have convincingly demonstrated, Richardson likely introduced his only Jewish character, the libertine Solomon Merceda, into *Grandison* in response to the ongoing debates about Jewish naturalization. While Merceda is a minor character who appears briefly, he possesses an outsized presence characterized by corruption and licentiousness. He serves as a stark contrast to Sir Charles's pious and gentlemanly demeanor. Moreover, Merceda provides Sir Charles with an opportunity to showcase his urbane tolerance, aligning with the prevailing Whig opinion on naturalization, while simultaneously underscoring the perceived inferiority associated with Judaism.

Latimer reveals how Sir Charles initially includes Merceda, as a Jew, within the ambit of Christian law in his speeches. When he gives a speech against dueling, he includes Merceda, and Judaism, within his definition of Christianity: "[I]t is dreadful to reflect, that the man who would endeavour to support his arguments against this infamous practice of duelling, by the Laws of Christianity, tho' the most excellent of all Laws (Excuse me, Mr. Merceda, your own are *included* in them), would subject himself to the ridicule of persons who call themselves Christians."[15] However, this

12 Samuel Richardson to Elizabeth Carter, June 12, 1753, in *Correspondence Primarily on "Sir Charles Grandison" (1750–1754)*, ed. Betty A. Schellenberg, *The Cambridge Edition of the Correspondence of Samuel Richardson*, ed. Thomas Keymer and Peter Sabor, vol. 10 (Cambridge: Cambridge University Press, 2015), 85.

13 Samuel Richardson to Elizabeth Carter, August 17, 1753, in *Correspondence*, 134.

14 Bonnie Latimer, "Samuel Richardson and the 'Jew Bill' of 1753: A New Political Context for *Sir Charles Grandison*," *Review of English Studies* 66, no. 275 (June 2015): 520–39, at 532.

15 Samuel Richardson, *The History of Sir Charles Grandison*, ed. E. Derek Taylor, Melvyn New, and Elizabeth Kraft, 4 vols. (1753–54; Cambridge: Cambridge University Press, 2022), 1:281. Hereafter cited parenthetically in the text by volume and page number.

inclusion is accompanied by a clear indication of the inferiority of Judaism and the subsequent need for Merceda's conversion – a conversion that Sir Charles eventually secures, though it is short-lived. Merceda continues down a path of corruption until he sustains severe injuries and makes a quick attempt at another conversion before dying. As Latimer aptly notes, by the conclusion of this ostensibly "tolerant" novel, Merceda has been relegated to his expected role as a cultural figure of fear, once again occupying his place in a quartet of other morally irredeemable personas, including the infidel, heretic, Turk, and Jew.[16]

I would suggest, however, that in order to gain a more complete understanding of the novel's relationship to naturalization and its debate in the eighteenth century, it is important to realize that Richardson's engagement with the debates extends beyond the topical political debate about Jewish naturalization. In Richardson's last novel, we see how a conception of naturalization emerged alongside an epistolary structure overriding national and religious difference through the paper conduits of letters. In his final novel, the exchange of letters via the epistolary form works to transcend national and religious differences. While the letters in *Pamela* (1740) are written almost entirely from the perspective of its titular character – a one-sidedness that did much to create a new sense of interiority in fiction – in *Grandison*, letters are written by many people and are enclosed, shared, and translated across a wider geographical distance. As is evident in a letter from Dr. Bartlett to Harriet Byron, the sharing of letters among a greater variety of people across national territories is an assumed practice in the social world of the novel: "The next morning, early, Mr. Grandison received the following Letter from his friend Signor Jeronymo. I translated it, my good Miss Byron, at the time I received it. I will send you the translation, only" (2:693). Here Dr. Bartlett explains and translates a letter from Grandison's Italian friend for Harriet in England, who is not the letter's primary recipient.

At the level of the plot, Richardson's final epistolary novel picks up the thread of a discourse about naturalization that first appeared in *Calvin's Case* and was developed in Toland's treatise. In his novel, Richardson appears to side with Bacon's view of naturalization. *Grandison* principally concerns the life of an Englishman, Sir Charles, who finds himself gripped by a "divided Love" with marriage prospects in both England and Italy (3:1216). Before meeting Harriet Byron, a young English orphan whose family estate has been entailed to a foreigner, Sir Charles had been living in

[16] Latimer, "Samuel Richardson and the 'Jew Bill' of 1753," 539.

Italy, where he had promised his hand to an Italian woman, Clementina della Porretta. The prospective marriage, however, is fraught with difficulties owing to their religious and national differences. Clementina's family and Clementina herself do not favor a marriage between a Roman Catholic Italian and a Protestant Englishman, and Sir Charles is reluctant to convert. In examining issues of transnational marriage, Richardson takes a wider social and political view than in his earlier novels, examining the national situation of his protagonists and the political events determining their lives as individuals.[17]

Much has been written about the tolerance Richardson extends toward Italian Catholics in *Grandison*, but in making a prospective marriage between individuals of two different religions and monarchical allegiances the novel's centerpiece, he also shows himself to be interested in the complications of religious tolerance for legal institutions such as marriage.[18] These concerns are particularly evident in the passage in which Grandison ruminates on how he might make compromises with Clementina and still conform to his Protestant faith. He says he is "Entirely satisfied" in his faith and loves his "native country" (2:635). He cannot sacrifice either of them. Grandison attempts to satisfy his Protestant faith and the faith of his future sons by compromising with Clementina on the country of his residence and the faith of their future daughters. To marry Clementina, he proposes alternating between living in England and Italy if he and his future sons can remain Protestant. Clementina, however, objects to these proposed articles, and to the marriage in general, as too heretical. Thus, in the end, Grandison's Protestant faith and English allegiance are not sullied, and in this sense, the novel might be thought to avoid the problems of naturalization entirely. Grandison abandons the idea of naturalization and marries an Englishwoman.

Yet the fact that Richardson broaches these compromising ideas in his novel, and makes them the focal point of its action, drew significant attention at the time. Even though the novel resolves with a felicitous

[17] Several articles have underlined the geographical and religious debates in the novel. See Lisa O'Connell, "Sir Charles Grandison, Natural Law and the Fictionalised English Gentleman," *Intellectual History Review* 23, no. 3 (2013): 349–63; Teri Doerksen, "*Sir Charles Grandison*: The Anglican Family and the Admirable Roman Catholic," *Eighteenth-Century Fiction* 15, no. 3–4 (April–July 2003): 539–58; Patricia Carr Bruckmann, "'Men, Women and Poles': Samuel Richardson and the Romance of a Stuart Princess," *Eighteenth-Century Life* 27, no. 3 (Fall 2003): 31–52; and Patrick Mello, "'Piety and Popishness': Tolerance and the Epistolary Reaction to Richardson's *Sir Charles Grandison*," *Eighteenth-Century Fiction* 25, no. 3 (Spring 2013): 511–31.

[18] For discussions of Richardson's sympathetic representation of Catholicism in *Grandison*, see S. K. Marks, *Sir Charles Grandison: The Compleat Conduct Book* (Lewisburg, PA: Bucknell University Press, 1986), 59; Margaret Anne Doody, *A Natural Passion: A Study of the Novels of Samuel Richardson* (Oxford: Clarendon, 1974); and Doerksen, "*Sir Charles Grandison.*"

marriage between two English subjects, Grandison's proposed marriage amendments to Clementina were the subject of major outcry. Richardson received several letters from readers who worried about the damage these articles might do to Grandison's Englishness and moral character. In a response to one reader, the Reverend Cox Macro, Richardson highlighted that it was important that Grandison not appear too punctilious with his faith. By acquiescing to the concerns of Clementina's Italian family, Grandison shows himself to be a moral person rather than a bigoted one. Clementina's family, Richardson maintained, faces a greater concession in agreeing to let their grandsons – the inheritors of property in England and Italy – be raised as Protestants. Richardson also argued that the effort at compromise conformed more readily to his readers' generic expectations of romance: Had Grandison not compromised on the purity of his national and religious allegiance, he maintained, readers would not believe the extent of his love for a lady of merit and fortune. In other words, it was more natural, in Richardson's opinion, for Grandison to negotiate his nationality and faith than to ruin his moral character.[19]

In an editorial "Concluding Note" to the novel, Richardson likewise makes clear that Grandison's actions, especially as they relate to his refusal to engage in a duel, are "imperfection[s]" that make him even more realistic (3:1695). Not only does Richardson suggest that Grandison's studied consideration for his faith and native home is natural, but he also links Grandison's behavior to "the Laws of all nations" (3:1696). Before the nineteenth century, "the laws of all nations" referred to the law of nature, as international, national, and domestic spheres were not yet analytically distinct.[20] Richardson thus responds to objections about Grandison's concessions by framing the protagonist as a subject of less tainted, more universal natural law, rather than of "silly modern custom" (3:1697). In *Grandison*, Richardson demonstrates an awareness of the legal and political barriers to transnational settlement, especially as they concern the transfer of property and religious practice across national territory. In this way he genuflects to the prior view of Coke and Bacon: All men are

[19] Samuel Richardson to the Reverend Cox Macro, March 22, 1754, in *Correspondence*, 195–99. This letter contained extracts from a response that Richardson had sent to another reader concerned about the same point.

[20] David Armitage, *Foundations of Modern International Thought* (Cambridge: Cambridge University Press, 2013), 70. See also Christopher Warren, *Literature and the Law of Nations, 1580–1680* (Oxford: Oxford University Press, 2015). As Warren argues, Christian readers of the early modern period would have understood the law of nations as referencing a fallen, less permanent state of relations between individuals for meanings of national law and law between nations (98).

naturalized to one another before they become natural members of a nation. Harriet encapsulates this view at length in a letter to Lucy:

> Sir Charles has seen more of the world, it may be said, than his sister has: He has travelled. But is not human nature the same in every country, allowing only for different customs? – Do not love, hatred, anger, malice, *all* the passions in short, good or bad, shew themselves by like effects in the faces, hearts, and actions, of the people of every country? And let men make ever such strong pretensions to knowledge, for their far-fetched and dear-bought experience, cannot a penetrating spirit learn as much from the passions of a Sir Hargrave Pollexfen in England, as it could from a man of the same or like ill qualities, in Spain, in France, or in Italy? And why is the Grecian Homer, to this day, so much admired, as he is in all these nations, and in every other nation where he has been read, and will be, to the world's end, but because he writes to nature? And is not the language of nature one language throughout the world, tho' there are different modes of speech to express it by? (1:197)

As Lisa O'Connell argues, Harriet's position here "is a vernacular statement of the fundamental presupposition of natural law theorists."[21] Before men are carved up into members of different national cultures, they are steeped in the same nature. Homer, whose birthplace was the subject of much speculation and contestation, is not a writer who proclaims the interests of a single nation; he writes from the state of nature itself. It is this original nature that makes it possible for individuals like Grandison to change or compromise the particulars of their allegiance or religion without sullying their character. We see a similar aesthetic maneuver in Richardson's first novel, *Pamela*, where the concept of naturalization as a technique empowering individual liberty over aristocratic hierarchy is shown to be substantially borne out in the creative and inherently fictional power of Pamela's account of her capture: the way the letters she writes progressively naturalize her as an authority against social and sexual conflict, and how, through that process, she acquires the authenticity of a subject speaking in her own right.

In many ways, the naturalization of religion in *Grandison* succeeds to a far lesser extent than the naturalization of class does in *Pamela*. At the conclusion of Richardson's final novel, the characters remain discriminated along national lines. Indeed, the marriage between two upper-class English subjects in *Grandison*, unlike the class-crossing marriage of Pamela and Mr. B., requires no naturalizing effort. As if to prepare for the impossibility

[21] O'Connell, "Sir Charles Grandison," 362.

of transnational marriage, in the novel's opening material, Richardson divides *Grandison*'s characters into three types – men, women, and Italians – a typology that, by turning nationality into a gender, or gender into nationality, signals the divided geographical sphere of the novel just as it indicates the formative importance of national origin for the recognition of marriage between men and women. The novel introduces a foreign, third term into the domestic institution of marriage that can never entirely be shaken off: Indeed, the marriage – the event that completes so much English fiction – is only the penultimate event of this novel. The final pages unfold with letters discussing the unsettled marital state of Clementina as she visits England and resides with Grandison and his new wife. Like Merceda, the novel can make no place for her. The novel then wraps up with Grandison escorting his former Italian love to France, extolling the future harmonization of their two countries: "Friendship, dearest creatures, will make at pleasure a safe bridge over the narrow seas; it will cut an easy passage thro' rocks and mountains, and make England and Italy one Country" (3:1685). While Grandison still fervently believes in the inherent ability of the individual to transcend religious and other divides, the plot of the novel suggests otherwise, leaving its Italian heroine in what might be called a paranational ambiguity, just as Merceda is scurrilously ejected from the novel after a hasty and unsatisfying bedside conversion. Neither of these positions can be made natural in Richardson's fiction.

It is striking how plaintively *Grandison* harks back to the possibility of naturalized allegiance in conformity with Bacon's view that "by the Law of Nature, all men in the world are naturalized one towards another."[22] Naturalization in this view does not create new national subjects through a civil process. Rather, it recalls the original naturalness of individuals under natural law, enabling the overlooking of national and religious difference for a deeper claim to resemblance and recognition through human nature. In contrast to Lockean writers and thinkers who regarded allegiance as radically contractual, in his final novel, Richardson suggests that naturalization cannot exist as a means of connection without the "more natural" agreement of human nature. Like Bacon and Toland, Richardson suggests that individuals can transcend national and religious differences on the basis of shared human nature. In this context, Richardson's work serves as a reflection on historical conditions where love and marriage between individuals could challenge the legal and social constraints of their time. Thus, in the immediate aftermath of one of the

[22] Bacon, *Three Speeches*, 35.

century's biggest challenges to a legal naturalization act – the Jewish naturalization statute – we find Richardson retreating not inward, but more broadly backward toward an ahistorical concept of natural relations, emphasizing shared human nature over legal distinctions.

Naturalization and Legal Fiction in Maria Edgeworth

In *Grandison,* Richardson tried to reclaim an older argument from natural law that individuals were naturally acquainted before they were defined as political and natural subjects. Yet, as the outsider position of Merceda and Clementina in the novel would suggest, Richardson's fiction remained in lockstep with the larger political world that swirled around him, one that, by the middle of the eighteenth century, was loudly denying room for Jewish and Catholic subjects in England. At the beginning of the nineteenth century, the Anglo-Irish author Maria Edgeworth would attempt to recognize this hypocrisy in her own fiction. In 1815 a Jewish American educator named Rachel Mordecai wrote a letter to Edgeworth that addressed some of the difficulties in the representation of naturalization in literature. In the letter, Mordecai questioned how Edgeworth could publicly write about the significance of early childhood education with justice and broadmindedness while at the same time delivering hostile and bigoted depictions of Jewish people in her fiction. In her response, Edgeworth acknowledged the justness of the educator's assessment. Her earlier writings were indeed riddled with anti-Semitic stereotypes, from the protagonist of her most famous novel, *Castle Rackrent* (1800), who refers to his wife as "my pretty Jessica," after the seduced daughter from Shakespeare's *Merchant of Venice*, to the short stories she had written for children, such as "The Prussian Vase" and "The Good Aunt," which feature tight-fisted and malicious Jewish characters, including Mr. Carat, a miserly Jewish jeweler who helps plot the robbery of a rich Christian woman. Struck by the accuracy of Mordecai's judgment, Edgeworth assured her American reader she would "make all the atonement and reparation in [her] power for the past."[23] In 1817, Edgeworth made good on her promise, publishing *Harrington*, an autobiographical novel about a young man who learns to overcome his childhood prejudice against Jews after falling in love with the daughter of a benevolent Spanish Jew.

[23] Maria Edgeworth to Rachel Mordecai, August 4, 1816, in *The Education of the Heart: The Correspondence of Rachel Mordecai Lazarus and Maria Edgeworth*, ed. Edgar E. MacDonald (Chapel Hill: University of North Carolina Press, 1977), 8.

As she prepared the draft of *Harrington*, Edgeworth read an array of materials related to the historical status of Jews in Britain and Europe, familiarizing herself especially with the legislative battles that Jews faced regarding naturalization. Edgeworth seems not only to have taken up Toland's argument in her novel but, like Richardson, to have crucially expanded on it to consider religious tolerance more generally: The novel is bookended by the furors surrounding the 1753 Jewish Naturalization Act and the 1780 Protestant Gordon Riots protesting the passage of the 1778 Catholic Relief Act, which sought to reduce official discrimination against British Catholics by granting them select liberties, such as the right to serve in the British navy and army.[24]

Like Richardson's late fiction, *Harrington* is closely aligned with the politics of legal naturalization. At the end of the novel, in a scene that is meant to be reminiscent of the Gordon Riots, an angry mob attacks the house of Mr. Montenero, a benevolent and wealthy Jewish American man who has recently moved to England, chanting, "No Jews, no wooden shoes!"[25] (Wooden shoes were associated with Catholic domination in France.) The mob seeks to oust not only Mr. Montenero and his Jewish family but also two wealthy women whom he has sheltered and who the mob believes are Catholics. In this reinterpretation of the riot, Edgeworth records the affinity in the public imagination between the legal and political disabilities suffered by Catholics and Jews in England and recommends a wider discussion of the prejudices linked to the dominant Protestant religion and Englishness that gripped naturalization politics in the eighteenth century. The scene of the Gordon Riots in the novel also registers a correspondence between Edgeworth's own biography and that of her Jewish characters. In 1798, during the United Irishmen's uprising against British rule, Edgeworth's father sought escape for his family from the Catholic rebels in the Protestant-protected town of Longford, where he was quickly suspected by Protestant leaders of being a French spy and nearly lynched.[26] Edgeworth reverses this outcome in her novel, having the Jewish and Catholic characters save the lives of the petulant and prejudiced Protestants. Through this reversal, and others, the novel probes not only the political and emotional dimensions of some of the most important

[24] On the Catholic Relief Act, see 18 Geo. III c. 60.

[25] Maria Edgeworth, *Harrington*, ed. Susan Manly (1817; Peterborough, ON: Broadview, 2004), 235. Hereafter cited parenthetically in the text.

[26] See Susan Manly, introduction to *Harrington*, ed. Susan Manly (Peterborough, ON: Broadview, 2004), 7–57, at 35.

controversies about naturalization in England but also how fiction works to rewrite these histories.

Edgeworth's account of the Gordon Riots raises a question about her effort to "make all the atonement and reparation in [her] power for the past": What is the unique value of the novel for reckoning with the recorded events and discriminations of legal and political history? Unlike Richardson, Edgeworth turns decisively to the novel as the genre that can best atone for the violent outcomes and prejudices attached to the Jewish Naturalization Act and the Catholic Relief Act; it is the genre, in the words of her father, that best functions as "an *amende honorable*" because the novel can allow Jews to appear, sympathetically, as fully realized human subjects.[27] This is to say that Edgeworth's father proposes the novel as a genre that can help make new subjects in the real political world by allowing readers to see characters represented in fiction as suffering individuals. The historian Lynn Hunt has likewise argued for the power of sentimental literature in the eighteenth and nineteenth centuries. The empathy fostered by the inner psychology of sentimental novels, Hunt argues, fostered the conditions of a "new social and political order."[28] For Hunt, empathy is a physiological process generated by literary texts. Yet as Edgeworth recognized, professions of sympathy for new subjects involve the positing of new literary representations against older literary protocols about who can be a subject. In practice, Edgeworth's attraction to the novel as "an *amende honorable*," which she submits to Mordecai as reparative and justice-oriented, is intently mindful of how narrative fictions are also openly responsible for generating one-dimensional representations of Jewish people and other foreigners.

For Edgeworth, the prejudicial treatment of Jews in English political life can be redressed only by considering how they have been represented in literature. From one angle, the history of literary representation is analogous to, and informative of, political discrimination against Jews: It is fictional writing that inculcates political prejudices in the first place. Indeed, Harrington's early phobia of Jews arises after his childhood nurse dresses some Christian beggars to look "like the traditionary representations and vulgar notions of a malicious, revengeful, ominous-looking Shylock" (79). Later, when Harrington begins reading, this dramatized association of Jews with maliciousness is reinforced by the representation

[27] Richard Lovell Edgeworth to Rachel Mordecai, August 4, 1816, in Lazarus and Edgeworth, *Education of the Heart*, 8.

[28] Lynn Hunt, *Inventing Human Rights: A History* (New York: W. W. Norton, 2007), 39.

of Jews he discovers in traditional and modern fiction. Harrington's alignment of the dramas and books of his youth with the psychological phobia he experiences of Jews articulates the linked ideas that characterized the public outcry against the Jewish Naturalization Act. As James Shapiro has shown, Shakespeare's portrayal of Shylock as a vengeful usurer in *The Merchant of Venice* was used as an authoritative portrait to successfully argue for the repeal of the act in 1753.[29]

Edgeworth mirrors the association between literary representation and politics in the novel when she has the fictional ideas that grip Harrington's early life find an outlet in his father's obnoxious anti-naturalization politics: "A subject apparently less likely to interest a child of my age than this Act of Parliament about the Naturalization of the Jews could hardly be imagined; but from my peculiar associations it did attract my attention" (85). Here, Harrington's subterranean fear of Jews, an antipathy he declares to be psychologically compulsive, reappears as politically logical. When asked by his father's confederates why the Jews should not be naturalized, Harrington attempts to string an irrational correlation into a political argument: "[B]ecause the Jews are naturally an unnatural pack of people," he says, "and you can't naturalize what's naturally unnatural" (87). Harrington, however, later exposes this logic as tautological. During a performance of *The Merchant of Venice*, Harrington comes to understand that the distinctions he has long held to be compulsively and inescapably natural are fictions. This realization first occurs in a moment of mediated sympathy when Harrington watches Mr. Montenero's daughter, Berenice, as she painfully observes the stereotypical portrayal of Jewish characters on stage: "My imagination formed such a strong conception of the pain the Jewess was feeling, and my inverted sympathy . . . so overpowered my direct and natural feelings, that at every fresh development of the Jew's villainy I shrunk as though I had myself been a Jew" (137). "Inverted sympathy" arises in this moment as another way of describing the work and effect of naturalization.[30] As Harrington observes Berenice's pained

[29] James Shapiro, *The Making of the National Poet: Shakespeare, Adaptation, Authorship, 1660–1769* (Oxford: Clarendon Press, 1992), 78.

[30] For a sustained reading of "inverted sympathy" in *Harrington* see Sarah Winter, "'Inverted Sympathy': Empathy and Mediation in Literary Transactions of Human Rights," in *The Routledge Companion to Literature and Human Rights*, ed. Sophia A. McClennen and Alexandra Schultheis Moore (New York: Routledge, 2015), 414–24. As Winter writes, "'Inverted sympathy' thus captures how empathy with another person's painful undergoing of stigmatization can take place in a rebounding and mediated way, producing psychologically robust effects, through a shared experience of a literary representation, performance, or work of art" (423). For further exploration of the mediation of sympathy in eighteenth-century sentimental novels vis-à-vis Adam Smith's

expressions as if they were his own, he reads and interprets her as a new text, one with a different set of associations and manifestations. Harrington once spoke of his terror at the sight of a Jew as involuntary and "invincible" (91), yet when observing Berenice watch *The Merchant of Venice*, he comes to see how literary representation mediates his desires and antipathies. It is through this recognition of the fictional basis of antipathy that Edgeworth seeks to rewrite the history of Jewish people in literature.

Thus, *Harrington* appears to challenge the traditional view of sympathy in the eighteenth-century novel, propagated most influentially by Hunt. Harrington's mediated experience of Jewish suffering gives him and Edgeworth's readers a fictionalized understanding of the interconnection between representation, politics, and sympathy. Mr. Montenero's explanation for the prejudice against Jews offers a more productive way to understand the intersection of literary texts and the symbolism and bureaucracy of politics. After the play's performance, Harrington discusses with Mr. Montenero the relationship of Shakespeare's work to depictions of Jews more widely, blaming the prejudices of Shakespeare's age for influencing his representation of Jews. Mr. Montenero counters with a surprising fact: Shakespeare reversed the source story for the play and transferred what had originally been a Christian's vengeful demand for a "pound of flesh" to a Jewish character. "[W]e Jews find it peculiarly hard," Mr. Montenero laments, "that the truth of the story on which the poet founded his plot should have been completely sacrificed to fiction, so that the characters were not only misrepresented but reversed" (144). In effect, by revealing this fictional reversal to Harrington, Mr. Montenero reveals the naturalness of a representation of Jews to be, in fact, "unnatural."

Yet this reversal of the reversal is ultimately undone by Edgeworth's final plot twist. It is a twist that Mordecai, in a follow-up letter to Edgeworth, described at first as especially shocking and egregious in light of the author's pledge to atone for past representational misdeeds. After Harrington asks for Berenice's hand in marriage, and Harrington's Christian parents move to accept a Jewess as their daughter-in-law, Mr. Montenero reveals Berenice to be the daughter of a Christian mother who was raised in the Protestant faith. Berenice's reward for acceptance into middle-class English society appears to be the discovery that she was always already a member of the society that rejected her as foreign, and Harrington's reward for upsetting the "natural" boundaries of Christian

theory of the impartial spectator, see Stephanie DeGooyer, "The Eyes of Other People: Adam Smith's Triangular Sympathy and the Sentimental Novel," *ELH* 85, no. 3 (Fall 2018): 669–90.

marriage by mixing his love and duty is what appears to be a rightful Christian marriage. Edgeworth believed that this *deus ex machina* would ultimately satisfy readers; indeed, she implied as much in a response to Mordecai's letter asking for a justification of the novel's romantic ending. "I really should be gratified," Edgeworth told Mordecai, "if I could have any testimony even were it ever so slight from those of your persuasion that they were pleased with my attempt to do them justice."[31] While Edgeworth defended what she saw as her reversal of expectations through a conventional ending, Mordecai's follow-up letter forced an alternative view of the novel's conclusion. While at first shocked by the ending, Mordecai now believed that by having Mr. Montenero keep Berenice's Christian birth a secret and bring up his daughter in the faiths of two religions, Edgeworth could also be said to demonstrate his "united liberality": his concern for "justice, benevolence, and morality" and religious tolerance.[32] Indeed, this interpretation is borne out by the final lines of the novel. Mr. Montenero suggests that it was Berenice's idea to disguise her origins in order to find a suitor who had a "spirit of toleration" (291). We have seen this line of thinking before, in the letter Richardson sent to the Reverend Cox Macro concerning Grandison's religious purity after Grandison briefly considers raising his unborn daughters in another faith.[33] (Edgeworth refers to this reading of *Grandison* in her novel, when Harrington's friend Lord Mowbray protests that, unlike Grandison, he would have "no religious scruples" in marrying a woman of another faith if he were in love with her [220].) In Mordecai's reading of the novel's ending, Edgeworth exposes Berenice as a Christian not to satisfy certain readers but to cast the heroine as both Jewish and Christian, neither naturally one nor naturally the other. At the end of the novel, Harrington's parents interpret Mr. Montenero's decision to provide a villainous servant with "asylum" in America as the action of a "good Christian" (295). Berenice, in the final lines of the novel, winkingly suggests, however, that this could be also the act of a "good Jew" (295). In this view, Edgeworth adapts a conventional story ending to make a comment about the importance of religious tolerance and to naturalize, in fiction if not in law, Jewish characters as also Christian. Mordecai's reading, in this way, upholds the Lockean view of naturalization as an

[31] Maria Edgeworth to Rachel Mordecai, June 21, 1821, in Lazarus and Edgeworth, *Education of the Heart*, 23.

[32] Rachel Mordecai to Maria Edgeworth, October 28, 1817, in Lazarus and Edgeworth, *Education of the Heart*, 16.

[33] Samuel Richardson to the Reverend Cox Macro, March 22, 1754, in *Correspondence*, 195–99.

artificial and fictional process that can turn a foreigner into a subject on the basis of an outward claim. A Jew can be a Christian, and vice versa, without the ability of an onlooker to discern the surface difference.

Edgeworth's undoing of the distinctions between Jewishness and unnaturalness is admittedly clunky. Early reviewers were less accommodating and creative in their interpretations of the novel than Mordecai, accusing Edgeworth of unrelenting didacticism at the expense of belief. More pointedly, Harrington's extreme phobia of Jews has struck more than a few readers as overly psychological and neglectful of the political issues surrounding the Jewish Question in England. For Catherine Gallagher, the novel "all too often makes the Jewish Question seem like a private obsession."[34] But the overt fictionality of naturalization, its calling attention to the way new subjects are created, challenges sacrosanct rules and traditions by showing how easily they can be mimicked. In the end, Edgeworth makes Berenice a subject, not with the eloquence of persuasion or logical insistence (as she herself would have believed), nor through sympathy from the reader (as Hunt would want), but through the cheap trick of a reversal. In this way, Edgeworth aligned her politics on naturalization with that of Locke and others who believed in the parliamentary power to fictionalize allegiance in law. In her novel, Edgeworth retrospectively naturalizes her Jewish heroine not by making her realize, conform to, or convert to Christian principles or by demonstrating her "humanity," as Richardson attempts to do with the Jewish and Catholic characters in *Grandison*, but by simply and indecorously announcing her to be Christian. In this way, Edgeworth's ending reflects the work of the new ideas of naturalization, which were considered scandalous for appearing to naturalize new subjects in England solely by the overtly political power of a parliamentary act.

Conclusion

Faced with the question of Jewish naturalization and integration, the authors under consideration in this chapter proceeded down different paths. Richardson chose to uphold the archaic arguments of Coke and Bacon, who had tried to make naturalization a matter of natural law rather than a legal fiction in their argument that all humans were originally in a natural state together. Richardson was observant enough in his private

[34] Catherine Gallagher, *Nobody's Story: The Vanishing Acts of Women Writers in the Marketplace, 1670–1820* (Berkeley: University of California Press, 1995), 311.

letters to his friend Elizabeth Carter to know that the idea of political naturalization was far from gaining acceptance by the English public. In *Grandison* he dealt with his only Jewish character as he had dealt with the question in real life: by sweeping the matter aside and hoping it would remain resolved. But by the early nineteenth century, Jewish naturalization – and naturalization politics more generally – had not subsided, especially in prose fiction. In attempting to atone for her ill-treatment of Jewish people in *Harrington*, Edgeworth considered the value of fiction for the politics of naturalization. The *deus ex machina* that restores the Jewish heroine to her Christian origins does not resemble the natural law argument about naturalization. This ending, which various commentators saw as unrealistic and contrived, dared readers to tell the difference between Berenice's and her father's Jewish and Christian qualities, suggesting that the characters could be seen as partaking of both. Edgeworth wished to rewrite literary history to change who could be a fully realized subject of literature; she sought, more than Richardson, to use the novel to directly change history itself. However, Edgeworth did so through a hackneyed plot twist that, while emphasizing the anxieties that many held about naturalization's secular and political procedures for over a century, resorts to a miraculous invention in order to advance her greater ambition of atoning for her own anti-Semitic past. Together, Richardson and Edgeworth show how novelists responded and contributed to naturalization's transformation from a supposedly natural process to an explicitly fictional process. In doing so, they shed light on questions concerning the nature of national and religious identity that remain with us to this day.

CHAPTER 8

Common Law and Cultural Difference in Scott's Ivanhoe *and* Chronicles of the Canongate

Anne Frey

Sir Walter Scott worked in the law throughout his writing career, training as a Writer Signet before assuming a position as the Sheriff of Selkirk for its more consistent remuneration. Although at the end of his life he complained that he found his writing and his legal tasks to be at odds, in novels such as *The Heart of Midlothian* (1818) and *Redgauntlet* (1824) he draws on legal cases.[1] More broadly his work endlessly relitigates what James Chandler (following Scott) calls "the specimen of all cases," the Jacobite rebellion and the criminal trials and property disputes it spawned.[2] Scott's novels address law in the context of Scotland's modernization, depicting changing philosophies of punishment and legal authority.[3] But Scott also sees law as a means of negotiating and marking Scotland's cultural identity. Even as he supported Scotland's political and economic integration into Britain under Hanoverian rule, Scott increasingly feared that this centralization would end Scotland's cultural distinctiveness.[4] In his nonfiction essays, Scott explicitly advocates for Scotland's common-law traditions as an important source of its identity. But Scott faced a challenge to Scotland's legal traditions not only from the centralizing pull of the British economy and government but also from the hybrid identities and mobile lives of Scots themselves, lives that carried them into other jurisdictions.

[1] As Scott attempted to write his way out of bankruptcy, he asked in an 1826 journal entry, "can the Sheriff Depute neglect his duty that the Author may mind *his*? – the thing cannot be; the people of Selkirk must have justice as well as the people of England books." Journal entry, August 3, 1826, in *The Journal of Walter Scott*, ed. W. E. K. Anderson (Oxford: Clarendon Press, 1972), 181.

[2] James Chandler, *England in 1819: The Politics of Literary Culture and the Case of Romantic Historicism* (Chicago: University of Chicago Press, 1998), 216.

[3] See Bruce Beiderwell, *Power and Punishment in Scott's Novels* (Athens: University of Georgia Press, 1992); Anne Frey, *British State Romanticism* (Palo Alto, CA: Stanford University Press, 2010), 88–115; and Nicole Mansfield Wright, *Defending Privilege: Rights, Status, and Legal Peril in the British Novel* (Baltimore: Johns Hopkins University Press, 2020), 83–107.

[4] Christopher Harvie, "Scott and the Image of Scotland," in *Patriotism: The Making and Unmaking of British National Identity*, ed. Raphael Samuel, vol. 2 (New York: Routledge, 1989), 173–92.

In his fiction and nonfiction, Scott argues for maintaining Scotland's common-law system but also worries that the very cultural and legal distinctiveness he demands for Scotland prevents Scots from navigating British customs and institutions to receive justice under British law. The problem was that when individuals moved to a new jurisdiction or when empire replaced local practices with imported procedures and authorities, individuals were judged by another culture's rules. If common law derives its legitimacy from connection to a particular location and history, Scott asks, can it be extended to a new jurisdiction? Can a new legal system speak for the history of a different people? And can common law legitimately rule a hybrid, mobile populace? Scott's novels from *Waverley* (1814) on frequently show the problems of Scots caught in British systems of justice. *Ivanhoe* (1819) and *Chronicles of the Canongate* (1827) more particularly highlight the difficulties of reconciling the role of custom in common law's legitimacy with a centralizing imperial state. In *Ivanhoe*, set four generations after the Norman conquest, the passage of time and a period of stability allow most English (Saxon and Norman alike) to forget that law does not always encode a region's customs. *Chronicles of the Canongate*, in contrast, shows Scottish subjects caught in legal systems they find foreign, including British military, English common-law, and Mughal courts. In *Chronicles of the Canongate*, Scott suggests that the victors' partiality means that history and historical fiction no longer suture past and present, and the law imposes tragedy as well as order.

Common Law and Cultural Identity in Scotland

The terms of the 1707 union of England and Scotland promised that Scotland could maintain many aspects of its continental-influenced legal system, and Scott worried that England was gradually reneging on this promise. In an 1808 essay in the *Edinburgh Annual Register*, "View of the Changes Proposed and Adopted in the Administration of Justice in Scotland," Scott criticized a series of proposed legal changes, such as employing English-style juries in civil cases.[5] Scott's worries escalated after the financial crisis of 1825 (in which Scott himself was financially ruined), when Britain threatened to outlaw the Scottish practice of issuing paper

[5] See [Sir Walter Scott], "View of the Changes Proposed and Adopted in the Administration of Justice in Scotland," *Edinburgh Annual Register* 1 (1808), 342–72. Hereafter cited parenthetically in the text.

banknotes. Scott's 1826 *Letters of Malachi Malagrowther* advocate retaining Scotland's home-grown financial system, and some historians credit this work with winning public sympathy and helping to preserve the Scottish banking system. More broadly, these essays defend the idea that not only banking but legal, juridical, and economic structures do not need to be the same in Scotland as in England, and that they should instead follow the practices that have accrued through custom over time.[6] In particular, Scott regretted that individuals could appeal the decisions of Scottish magistrates like himself to the House of Lords in London.[7]

Although legal scholars often describe Scotland's legal system as a civil-law system in distinction to the English and American common-law systems, Scott categorizes Scotland as using common-law logic and procedures, founded in and codifying regional customs that differ from those of England. In this, he follows Viscount Stair's *Institutions of the Law of Scotland* (1681), which also classifies Scottish law as a common-law system, albeit more influenced by continental jurisprudence than that of England. For many theorists, common law derives from the customs of the people it governs, encoding practices with, in William Blackstone's words, "higher antiquity than memory or history can reach."[8] In reality, historians note that common law often derived less from custom than from a central elite's desire to impose a shared legal system on the country, and that it always requires selection, interpretation, and arrangement.[9] For eighteenth-

6 See Sir Walter Scott, *Letters of Malachi Malagrowther on the Currency* (Edinburgh: Robert Cadell, 1844).

7 "The consequence," Scott wrote,

> will in time be that the Scottish Supreme court will be in effect situated in London. Then down fall – as national objects of respect and veneration – the Scottish bench – the Scottish Bar – the Scottish Law herself – And – And – there is an end of auld lang Sang. Were I as I have been I would fight knee deep in blood ere it comes to that – But it is a catastrophe which the great course of events brings daily nearer.

Journal entry, June 9, 1826, in *Journal of Walter Scott*, 156–57.

8 William Blackstone, *Commentaries on the Laws of England*, ed. Wilfrid Prest, bk. 1, *Of the Rights of Persons*, ed. David Lemmings (1765; Oxford: Oxford University Press, 2016), 51.

9 Sir John Baker traces the growth of a common law to administrative reforms by the Norman and Angevin kings, and to Henry II's desire to restore order after civil war. See *An Introduction to English Legal History*, 5th ed. (Oxford: Oxford University Press, 2019), 15–18. See also Amanda Perreau-Saussine and James Bernard Murphy, "The Character of Customary Law: An Introduction," in *The Nature of Customary Law: Legal, Historical and Philosophical Perspectives*, ed. Amanda Perreau-Saussine and James Bernard Murphy (Leiden: Cambridge University Press, 2007), 1–10. On the selection of the common law, see Frederick Schauer, "Pitfalls in the Interpretation of Customary Law," in Perreau-Saussine and Murphy, *Nature of Customary Law*, 13–34. On the importance of custom in common law, see also Gerald J. Postema, *Bentham and the Common Law Tradition*, 2nd ed. (New York: Oxford University Press, 2019); and Stephanie Elsky, *Custom, Common Law, and the Constitution of English Renaissance Literature* (Oxford: Oxford University Press, 2020). On the

century theorists, however, a judge's selections and incremental changes do not make law, but better reveal the law that always existed; in Chief Justice Lord Mansfield's words, the common law "works itself pure."[10] Blackstone also insists that it does not matter whether common law evolved in a community or was imposed by force, such as during the Norman conquest or the imposition of Danelaw. What matters, Blackstone argues, is that over time these customs became accepted and that through this long test of time they proved true or reasonable. Their acceptance, rather than their actual origin, determines that they are held in common. In theory, at least, common law reflects custom.[11]

Scott advocates for common law not only as the source and memory of Scotland's cultural distinctiveness but also as a way of retaining this distinctiveness while integrating into a modern polity and economy. In his *Life of Napoleon* (1827), which he researched and wrote while working on *Chronicles of the Canongate*, Scott argues that even if common-law systems are less logically coherent than statutory systems like the Code Napoléon, their ability to draw on centuries of varied cases as precedents allows the law to be more predictable and precise in assessing new situations.[12] Scots prided themselves on having fewer statutes and capital crimes than England and on allowing more discretion to judges, and Scott showcases that pride here.[13] In this view, the legal system in Scotland functioned as a purer form of common law than England's, which had been corrupted by Parliament's tendency to create new statutes.

Although common law allows for slow change in the region in which it arose, Scott argues that its ties to place and to customs mean that it cannot necessarily be applied to new locations. As he explains in his 1808 *Edinburgh Annual Register* essay, "in legislating for an ancient people, the question is not, what is the best possible system of law, but what is the best they can bear. Their habitudes and prejudices must always be respected; and, whenever it is practicable, those prejudices, instead of being destroyed, ought to be taken as the basis of new regulations" (353). When one considers whether to import laws from one region to another, therefore, "it is not enough that they have been found practically good in the country from which they are proposed to be transplanted" (353). Scott also insists

logic of precedent in nineteenth-century literature, see Ayelet Ben-Yishai, *Common Precedents: The Presentness of the Past in Victorian Law and Fiction* (New York: Oxford University Press, 2013).

[10] Quoted in Schauer, "Pitfalls," 31. [11] Blackstone, *Commentaries*, 1:49–51.

[12] Walter Scott, *Life of Napoleon* (New York: J. and J. Harper, 1827), 2:154–58.

[13] Regina Hewitt, *Symbolic Interactions: Social Problems and Literary Interventions in the Works of Baillie, Scott, and Landor* (Lewisburg, PA: Bucknell University Press, 2006), 50–53.

that common-law customs develop alongside practices that can mitigate drawbacks in the laws themselves. Scott describes this mutually implicated growth of law and cultural institutions through the organic metaphor of a tree: "it is only in its natural soil, where it has long been planted, that the tree can be expected to flourish: there only are to be found those peculiarities which have contributed to its beauty and vigour" (353).

Scott does not believe that all peoples are equally served by leaving their local traditions intact. He distinguishes between "civilized nations," which should keep their legal traditions, and colonies, which he believes lack a traditional governing structure and will need imported law. "A civilized nation, long in possession of a code of law, under which, with all its inconveniences, they have found means to flourish," Scott writes, "is not to be regarded as an infant colony, on which experiments in legislation may, without much charge of presumption, be hazarded" (345). The problem is that, though Scotland is an independent country joined with England as an equal partner in the Act of Union, England often treats Scotland as an "infant colony." Scott complains that England's proposed banking laws in particular were "calculated to make Scotland feel her own inferiority, and to give to her sister kingdom, united with her in a voluntary association, the insolent air of a conqueror, imposing his laws and customs on a colony which the fate of battles has laid at his feet" (359).

In Scott's day similar questions arose throughout the British Empire. Governors debated how to balance imported and local law, and locals negotiated the multiple systems for their own benefit. Among the British, liberals sought to give India British law and property rights, usually out of a sense of British law's superiority; they also used the supposed inferiority of local practices as an excuse for extending British rule into new regions. The nativists and paternalists, in contrast, advocated keeping local rule in place. Some officials argued for local rules out of practicality: It was not possible to extend British rule across the entire Indian territory, and leaving local traditions in place allowed judgments that the population could more clearly understand. John Malcolm, an East India Company official in the 1830s, insisted, "If we legislate in advance of the community, all will be doubt and confusion."[14] Other governors sought to keep local practices in place because they believed that India's supposed history of despotism authorized the British to rule despotically. What court carried jurisdiction depended on who was being tried (British and East India

[14] Minute of September 10, 1830, quoted in Nasser Hussain, *The Jurisprudence of Emergency: Colonialism and the Rule of Law* (Ann Arbor: University of Michigan Press, 2003), 59–60.

Company courts often retained the rights to try British citizens) and on the type of case (the company wished to control revenue), creating a confusing mix of procedures. In what Partha Chatterjee calls the "rule of colonial difference," even liberals who supported extending English law withheld full citizenship and bureaucratic power from non-British subjects.[15] Lauren Benton notes, however, that in the early nineteenth century non-British subjects also negotiated the multiple traditional and British legal systems and jurisdictions to seek legal agency and political and social position.[16] The debates over these practices were perhaps most visible in the trial of Warren Hastings, the first Governor General of Bengal, in which Edmund Burke accused Hastings of adopting local totalitarian rule to enrich himself and the East India Company.[17] But the debate continued until 1834, when Thomas Babington Macaulay led the attempt to replace the mix of British, local, and company legal practices with a systematic code based on English common law and British statutory law.[18]

Scott wrote his novels before Macaulay's legal reforms. The history of Scotland, however, shows the centralizing pressure of British authority on Scottish law, and therefore Scott foresees that Britain may likewise work to impose a more systematically British legal system in India. In *Chronicles of the Canongate*, Scott juxtaposes stories exploring the effects of internal and external colonialism and implies that India may lose its legal and cultural distinctiveness to Britain's centralizing authority, the centralizing authority he deplores in the Scotland of his day. In the *Chronicles*, Scottish characters meet tragic fates when they find themselves in British courts, and the greatest act of justice occurs in an unofficial Muslim court. But Scott portrays this justice at a moment when local Indian leaders are about to be defeated by Britain in the Mysore wars. Whereas Scott's nonfiction work advocates firmly for maintaining Scotland's independent legal traditions, his fiction explores both the necessity and the danger of custom's influence on the law. As Erin Sheley notes, literature that explores past legal

[15] Partha Chatterjee, *The Nation and Its Fragments: Colonial and Postcolonial Histories* (Princeton, NJ: Princeton University Press, 1993). See also Elizabeth Kolsky, "Codification and the Rule of Colonial Difference: Criminal Procedure in British India," *Law and History Review* 23, no. 3 (Fall 2005), 631–83.

[16] Lauren Benton, *Law and Colonial Culture: Legal Regimes in World History, 1400–1900* (New York: Cambridge University Press, 2004), 14, 127–31.

[17] See Sara Suleri, *The Rhetoric of English India* (Chicago: University of Chicago Press, 1992).

[18] Radhika Singha notes, though, that both before and after Macaulay's reforms the British governors "negotiated with existing normative codes to reorder them to law and civil authority, but also to establish circuits of communication with the ruled." *A Despotism of Law: Crime and Justice in Early Colonial India* (Delhi: Oxford University Press, 1998), vii–viii.

injustices both explains the evolution of legal norms and "create[s] space for minority truth even within the hegemonic structure of common law discourse."[19] Scott moves abroad and to India's recent past to find a moment of culturally distinctive Mughal justice, but he also foresees Mughal leaders falling to British power. In *Ivanhoe*, he reminds readers that England, too, was subject to conquest, with a population that suffered unfair judgments from foreign rulers. If custom-based law is superior to other forms of law, Scott suggests, then law entails tragedy, because as the British state extends its authority and individuals move across borders, fewer individuals are governed under their own customary practices.

Traveling Customs in *Ivanhoe*

Set in the twelfth century, when King Richard returns from the Crusades, *Ivanhoe* predates the formation of English common law. However, Scott explores the concepts underlying common law by questioning under what circumstances customs provide a fair framework for legal power, and specifically whether customary law can fairly govern a multi-ethnic society such as that uniting Saxons and Normans or, in unspoken comparison, the Scots and English. The novel portrays Ivanhoe, a Saxon who was disinherited by his father Cedric in part for swearing allegiance to the Norman King Richard. By the end of the novel, Richard convinces the Saxons that stability and prosperity require them to abandon their historical claims to the throne and acknowledge Norman overlords. But he gains their allegiance when, disguised as the "Sluggard Knight," he fights alongside Saxons to rescue Cedric and his daughter Rowena from Norman kidnappers. As Michael Ragussis suggests, Scott portrays Richard as continuing the mythic Saxon tradition of liberty, but also notes in his footnotes that this portrayal (for example, Richard's singing Saxon drinking ballads) could not be historically accurate.[20] Even though Scott portrays as foolhardy any attempt to restore Saxon rule, he portrays local, custom-based Saxon justice as fairer than corrupt Norman practices. He makes this argument most clearly by contrasting the practices of Locksley (Robin Hood) and his men with those of the Norman courts and Catholic monasteries. Locksley and his men are technically outlaws and operate

[19] Erin Sheley, *Criminality and the Common Law Imagination in the Eighteenth and Nineteenth Centuries* (Edinburgh: Edinburgh University Press, 2020), 5.

[20] Michael Ragussis, *Figures of Conversion: "The Jewish Question" and English National Identity* (Durham, NC: Duke University Press, 1995), 107.

by their own rules, but they treat visitors fairly and divide their spoils with each other. Operating from the forest, at the base of an oak tree, they naturalize the idea that English customs establish the most legitimate law and justice; the justice of the tree looks better than the Norman court, which allows favorites to accumulate wealth at the expense of native Saxons. And as Clare Simmons notes, as they divide their spoils in front of the Sluggard Knight who is actually King Richard, "Robin Hood and his men . . . model good law to the man who has failed to protect it at the national level."[21] In naturalizing common-law customs, Scott like Blackstone suggests that ancient popular customs prove closest to natural law.

Critics have read *Ivanhoe* as both advocating for common law and exploding its myths. Simmons suggests that *Ivanhoe* demonstrates the problem with multiple competing legal systems, and implies that "common law, both commonly applied and based on common sense" might preserve an English tradition of rights.[22] Cristina Constantini, in contrast, argues that Scott finds common law's claims to historical continuity of law belied by England's history of violent conquest.[23] Scott's narrator reminds us that the inhabitants of medieval England speak Saxon rather than Celtic because the Saxons in their turn conquered the Celts. Simmons and Constantini identify two contradictory impulses within Scott's work: Scott wants Scotland to assimilate sufficiently into Britain to benefit from the stability and prosperity of Hanoverian rule and participate in the British Empire, but wants Britain to respect Scotland's independent legal system and cultural traditions. He gestures toward this argument in *Ivanhoe*, which recognizes the value of common law but also shows that law becomes ineffective and unjust when it attempts to travel to new locations or to rule foreign people.

The problematic "laws" of chivalry provide one case in which Scott demonstrates the failure of foreign laws to fairly determine proper conduct in Britain. Although Ivanhoe praises chivalry as the "nurse of pure and high affection,"[24] the Norman nobleman Maurice De Bracy and Knight Templar Brian de Bois Guilbert attempt to use chivalric language to rape and conquer: De Bracy attempts to force the Saxon Rowena to marry him,

[21] Clare Simmons, *Popular Medievalism in Romantic-Era Britain* (New York: Palgrave, 2011), 176.

[22] Simmons, *Popular Medievalism*, 167. Simmons notes, however, that the ending still leaves open the question "of whether different codes of law can exist in the same place and time" (183).

[23] Cristina Constantini, "The Jews and the Common Law: A Question of Traditions and Jurisdictions: An Analysis through W. Scott's *Ivanhoe*," *Textus* 21 (2008): 467–86.

[24] Walter Scott, *Ivanhoe: A Romance*, ed. Graham Tulloch (1819; Edinburgh: Edinburgh University Press, 1998), 249. Hereafter cited parenthetically in the text.

and Guilbert seeks to make Rebecca his mistress.[25] Rowena critiques De Bracy's hypocrisy in using what she calls the French "jargon of a troubadour" to threaten and conquer (188). Scott's narrator notes the irony that aristocrats who serve an important constitutional function in enabling English liberty (like those who twenty-one years later would demand the Magna Carta from King John) could also act as agents of personal tyranny: "It is grievous to think that those valiant barons, to whose stand against the crown the liberties of England were indebted for their existence, should themselves have been such dreadful oppressors, and capable of excesses contrary not only to the laws of England, but to those of nature and humanity" (192). The problem is not only that the aristocrats apply different procedures to different people – after all, Scott approves when Locksley gives different amounts of spoils to different men – but that the Normans tyrannically impose a law that is not homegrown to lie about their motives. Claims for individual liberty, Scott implies, work only when articulated in a local community, whereas the Normans impose a language and systems of authority from afar.

The trial of the Jewish healer Rebecca more particularly demonstrates that customary prejudices may prevent the law and its interpreters from recognizing the validity of other knowledges and practices. Rebecca possesses medical and pharmaceutical knowledge handed down across generations, and she appeals to Jewish ethical codes in arguing that she should help the injured Ivanhoe, even if in aiding him she risks King John's wrath. Although Rebecca's medicine is effective, the Norman Templars accuse her of witchcraft. At her trial, the Grand Masters insist that she does the devil's work because her box of ointment "bear[s] some Hebrew characters on the lid," and they call as witnesses English doctors who "insinuated that, since the medicine was beyond their own knowledge, it must necessarily have been compounded from an unlawful and magical pharmacopeia" (325). Norman and church laws cannot recognize the validity of foreign customs and therefore judge them as criminal. Similarly, Scott implies, English common law cannot extend fairly to the Scots. As Scott

[25] Mark Schoenfield sees the continued interest in chivalry in Scott's day as showing the "diverse historical pressures that both signaled the desire of the law to function as a single integrated system and prevented such integration because it depended upon the historical differentiations it sought to eradicate." "Waging Battle: *Ashford v. Thornton, Ivanhoe* and Legal Violence," in *Medievalism and the Quest for the Real Middle Ages*, ed. Clare A. Simmons (Portland, OR: Frank Cass, 2001), 61–86, at 62. See also Gary R. Dyer, "*Ivanhoe*, Chivalry, and the Murder of Mary Ashford," *Criticism* 39, no. 3 (Summer 1997): 383–408; and Scott's anonymous essay "Chivalry," in *Supplement to the Fourth, Fifth, and Sixth Editions of the Encyclopedia Britannica* (Edinburgh: Archibald Constable, 1815–24), 116–44.

suggests in his 1808 essay, customs can be fair law only in the "natural soil" in which they arise, but the corollary is also true: A law based on custom incorrectly judges situations outside its ken.

In *Ivanhoe* as in Hanoverian Britain, Scott finds prosperity and stability the best arguments for accepting a new regime; a dynasty (whether Norman or Hanoverian) that rules for multiple generations becomes customary. However, the Jewish characters show the limits of this logic since they also have lived in England for generations but cannot be assimilated into the body politic. Marked as irredeemably other because of their different religious tradition, the Jews allow the Saxons and Normans to appear sufficiently similar to create a new English (and by extension British) culture and tradition, but, as Alison Lumsden argues, simultaneously show the costs and inevitable exclusions of all such national identities.[26] In praising Locksley's justice, and in making Richard even for a moment Locksley's subordinate, Scott continues to dream of local customary rule that can be traced to a time beyond the recent generation of invaders. Simultaneously, following Blackstone, he argues that conquest becomes custom at the moment when everyone defined as English (everyone except the Jewish characters) agrees on the changed order. In practice, he suggests, the Normans (and the Hanoverians) will rule, but they should do so in a way that respects local customs where possible and creates new national customs where that is not possible, rather than importing their own practices.

History and Justice in *Chronicles of the Canongate*

In *Ivanhoe*, Scott shows King Richard and the culture as a whole evolving to combine Norman and Saxon influences. In his own day, he fears that England is exporting its legal practices to Scotland without such evolutionary change. In *Chronicles of the Canongate*, Scott moves closer to his present day to ask more directly whether Britain can fairly export its legal procedures and whether it is possible to fairly judge individuals (like Rebecca) who move into foreign legal systems. He couples this legal issue with an aesthetic one. At the end of his second story, "The Two Drovers," Scott's narrator Chrystal Croftangry complains that he has run out of

[26] Alison Lumsden, "Inclusion and Exclusion in the British State," in *Literature and Union: Scottish Texts, British Contexts*, ed. Gerard Carruthers and Colin Kidd (Oxford: Oxford University Press), 147–64. On Rebecca's exclusion, see also Andrew Lincoln, *Walter Scott and Modernity* (Edinburgh: Edinburgh University Press, 2007), 77; and Ragussis, *Figures of Conversion*, 89–126.

material. The problem, he says, is that Scotland is growing more uniform and more similar to England. Scott had made this complaint in other novels, such as *The Heart of Midlothian.* But here he finds a new solution. Croftangry's friend the lawyer and agent Fairscribe counsels him to find new material in India: "I think you might do with your Muse of Fiction, as you call her, as many an honest man does with his own sons in flesh and blood . . . . Send her to India, to be sure. That is the true place for a Scot to thrive in." Croftangry is intrigued, but counters, "The only objection is, that I have never been there, and know nothing at all about them." Fairscribe reassures him, "You will tell us about them all the better that you know nothing of what you are saying."[27]

Fairscribe is a staunch Calvinist, and part of the joke is that he is too literal-minded and attached to rules – Scott calls him "a lawyer of the ordinary class of formalists" (22) – to be a good judge of imaginative works, but Croftangry takes his advice anyway. As Tara Ghoshal Wallace notes, Fairscribe's comment "anticipates (and invites) criticism of [Scott's] own authorial hubris."[28] Scott has in the past gone to great lengths (for example, in his footnotes) to show that he knows the history of which he writes; Fairscribe casts doubt on whether this knowledge has contributed to the interest of the novels. This hubris doubles as a critique of British imperial hubris more broadly. In assigning this appraisal of historical and adventure novels to a solicitor who represents Croftangry in property transactions, Scott draws parallels between the novel and the law. In this collection, he asks: When law knowingly accounts for a country's history, are its judgments more just than when it imposes British law? Or is historical knowledge of the kind that common law mythologizes simply another excuse for one nation to control another's territory and ignore the claims of its people? In common law and historical novels, history often does not prove accurate, useful, or just, especially when it is part of an expanding nation and empire's cultural and legal systems.

In *Chronicles of the Canongate*, Scott portrays two main problems with the logic of common law. First, laws that tie legitimacy to place belie the fact that people are hybrid and mobile. Second, knowing a person's or region's history does not impact judges' decisions if the judges are more interested in asserting power and order than in meting out justice to

[27] Walter Scott, *Chronicles of the Canongate*, ed. Claire Lamont (1827; London: Penguin, 2003), 155. Hereafter cited parenthetically in the text.

[28] Tara Ghoshal Wallace, *Imperial Characters: Home and Periphery in Eighteenth-Century Literature* (Lewisburg, PA: Bucknell University Press, 2010), 147.

individuals. Scott turns to criminal law to explore these problems. All three stories in *Chronicles of the Canongate* feature men who are executed after killing a friend because of mistaken notions of honor. The Scottish characters of "The Highland Widow" and "The Two Drovers" are sentenced to death for their crimes in military and English courts respectively; the mixed-heritage murderer in "The Surgeon's Daughter" is executed by the Mughal Sultan. Although other Scott novels portray characters (such as Fergus MacIvor in *Waverley*) who are sentenced to death in the English judicial system, *Chronicles of the Canongate* appears more pessimistic than Scott's earlier depictions because in the first two stories, the executed characters are the protagonists. Even as Scott worries that Scottish law and culture are assimilating too much into Britain to maintain their distinctiveness, he recognizes that too much cultural distinctiveness imperils Scottish lives in legal systems that do not respect their differences.

In "The Highland Widow," tragedy results when individuals resist change but also when British officials carry styles of punishment across regions. Hamish, the son of a Scottish clan leader who died fighting the British, remains loyal to the British government; he believes he would best embody his father's clan values of leadership and bravery by joining the British army that his father once opposed. His mother Elspat, however, wants her son to adopt his dead father's lifestyle of stealing cattle and resisting British rule. When Hamish returns home on leave after enlisting in the army, Elspat drugs him to make him oversleep and miss his muster. Hamish had never intended to desert. But afraid of the punishment he will receive, he (with his mother's encouragement) kills the Scottish officer who arrives at his house to arrest him on behalf of the British army. The military court then convicts and executes him for murder.

Scott blames Elspat for Hamish's plight, but he also blames British and Scottish officials who allow their fear of Highlanders to prevent them from negotiating policies with their Highland subjects. The British army's insistence on imposing English styles of punishment for deserters proves a secondary cause of Hamish's tragic desertion and act of murder. The British army punishes deserters with flogging, even though and perhaps because Scots find such punishment more degrading than death: For Hamish, flogging is "the punishment of dogs . . . for men worse than dogs, who know not how to keep their faith" (92). Scott suggests that British officers deliberately choose a degrading punishment to teach their Scottish recruits – who in clan armies were used to the "privilege of going and coming" after battles – the discipline of permanent service in an army (98). The British general in charge of Hamish's regiment, who was "regularly bred in the German wars," disregards local advice and insists there is "no better way of checking [desertions] than by causing an unusually severe example to be made of a deserter from an English corps" (99). Even if the general understands the reasons for Highlanders' difficulty with regular regimental discipline, he nonetheless employs punishments imported from foreign systems. The threatened flogging becomes not a deterrent to desertion but an incentive for murder. Carrying systems of punishment across regional lines promotes the most violent of crimes.

In novels such as *Ivanhoe* and *Redgauntlet*, Scott suggests that patriarchs and professionals can advocate for the downtrodden and that their benevolent actions will render radical social movements unnecessary.[29] In "The Highland Widow," however, the local minister who could have helped Hamish fails to do so. The minister meets Hamish on the road outside his house in a frantic state after realizing his mother has drugged him, but the minister's fear of Elspat prevents him from assisting her son. Instead of asking after Hamish's well-being, he reprimands him for not attending church. The minister later regrets his failure to help, since if he had known of Hamish's predicament he could have negotiated with the regiment. In "The Highland Widow," the patriarchs with the cultural knowledge and social position to explain Scottish culture to British authorities never do so. Knowing Scotland's cultural history does not encourage patriarchs to intervene in Hamish's fate.

In "The Two Drovers," likewise, the English judge is sympathetic to the Scottish defendant, Robin Oig McCombich, but ultimately does not allow his cultural knowledge to influence his judgment. The story recounts the experiences of two drovers, Robin and Englishman Harry Wakefield, who, in an allegory of the English–Scottish union, travel together amicably for mutual benefit. When Robin and Harry mistakenly contract for the same piece of pasture, however, their amity ceases. Robin suggests sharing the land or taking the case before an English magistrate. Harry, however, refuses, and, egged on by friends at a pub, starts a fistfight with Robin. For the English yeoman, friends who have a dispute must "have a turn-up" (136) before they reconcile, but Robin takes Harry's assault as a grave insult and feels ashamed of his inability to fight back. He sets off to fetch his dirk (a long dagger), which he had entrusted to a friend for safekeeping, returns to the pub, and kills Harry. Like the English general's use of

[29] See Dyer, "*Ivanhoe*," 392; and Wright, *Defending Privilege*, 84–95. As Dyer and Wright note, Scott recognizes the dangers of trusting patriarchs too completely.

foreign punishments in "The Highland Widow," Harry's use of English pub justice leads the Scottish protagonist to commit a murder.

In reflecting on the case, the English trial judge considers both whether a customary venue, like the pub, operates as a kind of law and whether Robin's identity as a Scottish Highlander should count in the evaluation of his crime. The "pugilistic code" of "Merry Old England" might be allowed as an alternate court, but, he says, only if "both parties are *in pari casu*, equally acquainted with, and equally willing to refer themselves to, that species of arbitrement" (144). He recognizes that Robin initially acted with great fairness and restraint and that his English companion displayed neither quality. The judge provides an anthropological context that extends some sympathy toward Robin's feelings of wounded honor and his eagerness for revenge, noting that in the Highlands, a "wild, untutored justice [developed]; for the fear of retaliation must withhold the hands of the oppressor where there is no regular law to check daring violence" (145). However, despite recognizing that the murder results from a Scottish moral code, the judge does not believe that this cultural history mitigates Robin's crime. He concludes that this history "of the Highlands in the days of the prisoner's fathers . . . cannot . . . alter the administration of the law" (145). Because Robin had time to consider his conduct and walked many miles to fetch his dirk, he should have remembered that in a "civilized" society only the law can administer justice. Robin is doubly ensnared, then, in two foreign systems of justice: first in English pub law, and then in the law court. Despite Scott's fears of legal and cultural uniformity in Britain, the very distinctiveness of Scottish culture from both English yeoman culture and English legal culture contributes to Harry's and Robin's tragic deaths.

The narrator reports that the people who observe the trial prove more sympathetic to Robin than the judge is: "[T]he generosity of the English audience was inclined to regard his crime as the wayward aberration of a false idea of honour rather than as flowing from a heart naturally savage, or perverted by habitual vice" (142). But the judge's outlook prevails with the jury. And at his execution, Englishmen taunt Robin for "attacking an unarmed man," misunderstanding his opinion of the insult he received and how it must be requited (146). In the last words of the story, Robin tells the English who taunt him, "I give a life for the life I took . . . and what can I do more?" (146). Robin can do no more in two senses, first because his life is the most he can give and second because he is caught in a legal system that does not give full credence to his understanding of the crime that was committed against him. His question also suggests that he is thinking in a traditional legal logic: In the Scottish clans he would die for committing a murder, and he expects to die in England as well. Bruce Beiderwell notes that Scott does not portray Robin's hanging, as if he distrusts his certainty that the law correctly employs the violence that it demands to keep for itself.[30] And Ian Duncan suggests that Robin's history "reveals the tragic production, rather than mystical persistence, of a 'primitive' residue of identity within the new, imperfectly unified – ethnically and culturally heterogeneous – eighteenth-century British state."[31] Scott is certainly aware that if the judge turns common law into a means for ensuring the reach of British rule, or "civilization," as he calls it, the judge gets to decide what is outside the realm of acceptable conduct (146). Although the judge opposes official to unofficial (pub) law, both are based in customs and equally foreign to a working-class Scot.

Regardless of the justice of the sentence, in having the judge detail a legal anthropology that he ultimately disregards, Scott suggests at least some sympathy with the idea that law should consider a people's history. The judge's decision, in contrast, decouples two elements of common law's claim to legitimacy: the law's ability to retell history and its appeal to justice. Common law suggests that individuals should be judged by practices accrued over time. For the judge in "The Two Drovers," recounting history provides what historical details give the historical novelist, what Duncan called an "authenticity effect," or what I might call for the law court a "legitimacy effect."[32] The judge's knowledge and his sympathy for the defendant allow him to appear to govern all equally, even as his judgment ignores the context he provides and furthers the cultural extinction he locates in the past. In "The Two Drovers," telling a people's history does not make the law more just to those people.[33]

[30] Beiderwell, *Power and Punishment*, 117.

[31] Ian Duncan, "Late Scott," in *The Edinburgh Companion to Sir Walter Scott*, ed. Fiona Robertson (Edinburgh: Edinburgh University Press, 2012), 130–42, at 133.

[32] Ian Duncan describes Scott's adoption of romance conventions such as found documents and fictional editors as an authenticity effect, following Fiona Robertson's phrase "fictions of authenticity." Duncan, *Scott's Shadow: The Novel in Romantic Edinburgh* (Princeton, NJ: Princeton University Press, 2007), 279; Robertson, *Legitimate Histories: Scott, Gothic, and the Authorities of Fiction* (New York: Oxford University Press, 1994).

[33] This argument provides a corollary to Wolfram Schmidgen's reading of the end of *Waverley*. Schmidgen argues that Scott adopts the logic of common-law critics Jeremy Bentham and Thomas Paine in arguing that the origins of law must be made visible, subject to the uniform authority of the nation-state. In *Chronicles*, I argue, Scott again claims that the nation-state should know prior traditions, but he shows the genuine cost to Scottish individuals when that knowing is decoupled from continuous experience. See Wolfram Schmidgen, *Eighteenth-Century Fiction and the Law of Property* (Cambridge: Cambridge University Press, 2002), 186–239.

Common Law and Cultural Hybridity in "The Surgeon's Daughter"

"The Two Drovers" leaves open the question of whether the judge should have allowed his knowledge of Scottish culture to change his recommended verdict. Scott does not want the justice system to abandon its common-law ties to custom but recognizes that the values of fairness and customary continuity are at times incompatible, and most so for the citizens from regions on the nation's periphery. The third story in *Chronicles of the Canongate* explores another problem with the logic of common-law custom: How does the law decide who – and therefore whose customs – belong to a place? Scott demonstrates that both our identifications with and our sentimental ties to places are often founded in lies. In the narrative that opens *Chronicles of the Canongate*, Croftangry explains how he ended up making the Canongate his home. Croftangry lost his family patrimony to debt. The family who bought the estate destroyed its magnificence by replacing "its old hereditary trees" with "exotics" unsuited to the climate, and the "tapestry, enamelled with daisies and with crowsfoot and cowslips" with "an impoverished lawn" of "sown grasses" that "failed with drought" (34). Some things – plants, for example – cannot successfully travel. Although his familial estate is now for sale, Croftangry decides not to buy it when he learns how much the local populace still resents his former profligate ways. Instead, he moves to the Canongate district of Edinburgh, where he had previously lived to escape his debts, and tells his housekeeper that the Edinburgh land belonged to his family in generations past. He even convinces the post office to rename "Littlecroft" "Little Croftangry." As Padma Rangarajan notes, the name Croft-an-righ denotes a proximity to the king that neither Croftangry nor his ancestors ever possessed, demonstrating "willed illusion on both a civil and familial scale."[34] Scott demonstrates here that place-based identities, even when officially sanctioned, may be lies, and may pretend to an antiquity that they do not possess. That "the men of letters belonging to the Post Office have sanctioned the change, and deliver letters so addressed" suggests that government is not sure of its own origin tales (50).

Croftangry's trick does no harm. In Scott's final story in the *Chronicles*, "The Surgeon's Daughter," however, characters who wish for a different origin are unwilling to accept the governing systems and social order, with

[34] Padma Rangarajan, "History's Rank Stew: Walter Scott, James Mill, and the Politics of Time," *Romanticism* 21, no. 1 (April 2015): 59–71, at 61.

tragic consequences. Hybrid, mobile characters cannot find a stable (even if false) place within local histories. Richard Middlemas is the son of an unmarried Englishman and a Portuguese Jewish woman who gives birth in the house of Doctor Gray when she needs medical attention. After Richard's birth, his parents are arrested for treason; his grandfather, a Portuguese Jew, refuses to recognize Richard and, leaving the baby in Gray's care, gives him as surname the Scottish town in which he was born. Richard abhors the simplicity and provinciality of his home and (encouraged by his nursemaid's stories) dreams of finding his parents and claiming the grand identity that he is sure awaits him. He falls in love and secretly proposes marriage to Gray's daughter Menie, but even this engagement cannot reconcile him to the community into which he was born. He tells his foster father that he is "a free-born Englishman" and therefore cannot work as hard as the Scots, who he says are "too moral, and too prudent, and too robust, for a poor pudding-eater to live amongst them" (182). As Richard's parentage is unknown during his youth, Gray does not consider him to be either Scottish or English even though Gray acknowledges that "the stranger child … had peculiar good right to such patronage and affection as he had to bestow" (189). Gray offers partnership in his medical practice instead to Adam Hartley, who although born in England, "came of kenned folk, and was very near as good as a born Scotsman" (189). As Anindyo Roy notes, for both Scott and Gray, Richard has the double faults of being half-Jewish and striving for a grander social position.[35] But if Gray equates identity with parentage, the lawyer Lawford believes in contrast that identity indicates neither birth nor parentage but how a person chooses to affiliate. He suggests that Richard's Jewish parentage can be fully compatible with British identity as long as he offers allegiance to the king: The Jews, he says "have no territorial property, because the law is against them," but "are well attached to government; they hate the Pope, the Devil, and the Pretender, as much as ony honest man among ourselves" (175). But even by this definition, Richard is suspect because he so easily discards English, Jewish, and rural Scottish identities, changing identity as necessary to strive for a higher-class position.[36] An identity that is too flexible does not impel loyalty to any authority. When Richard moves to India, he joins the Mughal Nawaub's army (alongside the equally hybrid cross-dressing Madam de Montreville), lures Menie to India to give

[35] Anindyo Roy, *Civility and Empire: Literature and Culture in British India, 1822–1922* (New York: Routledge, 2005), 38–50.

[36] On Scott's critique of Middlemas and Montreville, see Wallace, *Imperial Characters*, 157–60.

her to Tippoo Sultan, and possibly intends to give the Nawaub's fort back to the British. Hybridity of origin might be fine, Scott suggests, but only if Richard were willing to accept the stabilizing national, regional, and social class identities assigned to him at birth. Furthermore, as "The Highland Widow" and "The Two Drovers" demonstrate, hybrid identities place characters at the mercy of justice systems they do not understand. Richard is punished for his hybridity when Sultan Hyder Ali executes him for treason.

The one instance in the *Chronicles* in which characters successfully navigate foreign judicial systems is when Adam appeals to Hyder Ali (who is disguised as a fakir) to demand Menie's release. To plea before the sultan, Adam first requires access: He calls in a favor based on his prior assistance to one of the sultan's ministers. Second, Adam must employ the cultural norms of the extra-judicial court in which he makes his appeal. Through his work as a doctor, and in particular through serving the downtrodden regardless of their ability to pay, he has become fluent in multiple languages and social practices; he knows when to speak and when to remain silent, and explains his appeal with reference to a parable from the Koran. Ali admires Adam's reasoning, saying "Bismallah! Praised be God! He has spoken like a Moullah!" (159). For all that Adam talks "like a Moullah," though, he shows the difference between transcultural knowledge and hybridity. The precept that he quotes from the Koran, that "justice … must be imparted by him who holdeth power to all who require it at his hand" (275), expresses a moral that would be admired across cultures (and to which Scott would like to hold his patriarchs). Neither he nor his Muslim interlocutors in any way think that his facility in referencing the Koran means that he is Muslim or would take Ali's side in armed conflict. It is clear where Adam's allegiances lie. Adam in one sense serves as a stand-in for the novelist, as a middle-class character who learns through his profession the knowledge that enables him to appeal to the sultan. His knowledge, though, contrasts with the knowledge of both the author and the judge of "The Two Drovers" in that it is earned through years of experience. If Fairscribe suggests anyone can write about India, Adam's success suggests that the necessary knowledge to advocate in a foreign customary court is hard-won.

Ali provides another instance in which Scott portrays patriarchs with discretion as just and effective judges. Ali does not use English common law but does represent a customary authority that acts generously toward a foreigner, and a poor woman at that. Scott also portrays Ali following local custom and invoking his own despotic authority when he orders Richard's immediate execution by elephant. Scott calls this a "just punishment"

(285). In closing the *Chronicles* with such a moment of stereotypical exoticism – death by elephant – Scott argues for his fiction's ability to portray India's cultural distinctiveness. But he also portrays a customary justice system at the moment in which it is about to disappear. The kind of discretion that Ali possesses is increasingly impossible in a centralizing legal system. As in "The Highland Widow" and "The Two Drovers," imposing customary law on foreign individuals propels crime, and British authorities' cultural knowledge authorizes their severity rather than encouraging empathy. Legal officials see law and history through the lens of their own power, and confuse order with justice. And even though Adam's intercultural competence frees Menie, we would be hard-pressed to say that the story has a happy ending. His victory is for one case only. The narrator tells us that Adam "fell a victim to his professional courage" in treating a "contagious distemper"; the profession that gave him his ability to speak across cultures causes his death (285). Menie lives out her life as a spinster. And Ali will soon attack the British in revenge for their treachery, bringing war and devastation to Mysore; the war will end Ali's rule and obliterate such instances of intercultural understanding. This enmity is all the more tragic because Ali is the only patriarchal figure in the *Chronicles* who successfully saves a character and the only patriarch who acts based on a cross-cultural appeal.

To find a moment in which local patriarchs enact justice through customary authority, Scott sets "The Surgeon's Daughter" in both a prior moment and a distant location. Moving the collection's final story to India means not only finding and labeling what is distinctive about Indian culture but also imposing a plot arc that inevitably finds the power structures of Indian society falling (like Scottish Highland chiefs before them) to the inevitable push of British power and commerce. In "The Two Drovers," law looks like a historical novel because it appeals to historical knowledge as a badge of legitimacy, even as it creates a break between that history and present-day legitimate government. In writing not a novel but a series of short stories that traverse different locales, Scott emphasizes the continuity of the British imperial project as it moves from Scotland to India, a continuity that will pull local governments away from the customary systems they developed over time.

Scott follows eighteenth-century legal theorists in advocating for common law in part because it can accommodate slow change, and because, like the historical novel genre, it claims to preserve the particular historical culture of a region even as it acknowledges subsequent changes. He also recognizes, though, the costs of customary law. Scott's endings often demonstrate who must be ejected to create a unified British nation: The Scottish Highland chief Fergus is executed at the end of *Waverley*, even as Waverley memorializes him in a painting; Rebecca leaves England at the end of *Ivanhoe*. In *Chronicles of the Canongate*, however, Scott suggests that the issue is not simply who fits or does not fit into the nation, but how common law's claims to customary knowledge authorize the exclusion of alternative customs. The very cultural distinctiveness that the novelist and the common-law system preserve entangles characters – even Scots loyal to the British crown – in justice systems that do not understand them. And moving from local traditions to centralized law means that more individuals confront legal systems outside their knowledge and experience. As Scott nears the end of his career, he presents the imposition of British law as a series of tragedies.

CHAPTER 9

The Legal Character of Paupers in Early Nineteenth-Century England

Mark Schoenfield

Introduction: Landscaping Labor

The 1820 *Edinburgh Review*, reviewing four works addressing poverty and the poor laws in England, ridiculed the proliferation of such pamphlets, each containing "some little piece of favourite nonsense, by which . . . this enormous evil may be perfectly cured." One author "commends little gardens" and "the second cows; the third a village shop; the fourth a spade," the reviewer complained. The *Edinburgh* added to "this list of absurdities" several more elaborate plans, proposed or enacted, and in the *Edinburgh*'s view, failed, impossible, or incoherent. The reviewer, the anonymous Sydney Smith, noted how the plans emphasized character in establishing worthiness: "Merit is set up as the test of relief" by a "long examination of the life and character of each applicant."[1] The review reflects a fundamental and long-debated question: What role should or, perhaps more urgently, *could* the law take in the regulation of poverty and the alleviation of its distresses? Edward Copleston, by 1819 the Provost of Oriel College, Oxford, insisted that "the great merit and everlasting value" of Thomas Malthus was his demonstration – by examining "the actual constitution of things" – of the ineffectiveness of legal intervention to improve impoverished conditions, a finding that underscored reformers' "fundamental mistake" of confusing "moral duty with the task of

[1] [Sydney Smith], review of *Safe Method for Rendering Income Arising from Personal Property Available to the Poor-Laws*; *Summary Review of the Report and Evidence Relative to the Poor-Laws*, by S. W. Nicol; *Essay on the Practicability of Modifying the Poor-Laws*; and *Considerations on the Poor-Laws*, by John Davison, *Edinburgh Review* 33, no. 65 (January 1820): 91–92. This article responds as much to the works under consideration as to the Tory *Quarterly Review* and to pamphlets such as *Additional Remarks on an Article in "The Edinburgh Review," on the Causes and Cure of Pauperism* (Glasgow: Ogle, 1818), which accused the *Edinburgh* of arguing that the "pestilential atmosphere" that "Charitable Institutions . . . generate, [has] produced all the plagues of pauperism" (3).

legislation"; this error threatened to destroy "the very essence not only of benevolence, but of all virtue."[2]

Pauperism, as Lynn Lees details, was a legal configuration of poverty, with specific volitional steps needed to translate "destitute persons" into "paupers."[3] Yet a person could be constructed as a pauper either by birth or by virtue of being at risk of becoming one, indicating that pauperism was at once a material and a discursive social position. The legal regulations could exacerbate or mitigate the debilitations of poverty, which included restrictions on movement and labor (and pregnancy) and on the ability to form contracts. Justifying such regulation as the management of character, Patrick Colquhoun stated the problem on the title page of his 1806 *Treatise on Indigence* as how "To prevent Poverty from descending into Indigence." He declared crucial the "proper management of that branch of internal police" that applied to those whose "indigence exposes them to the miseries incident to the want of *shelter*, *food*, and *clothing*." He insisted that poverty, "the state of every one who must labour for subsistence," was an "indispensable ingredient in society" and the "source of *wealth*, since without poverty there would be *no labour*, and without *labour* there could be *no riches*, no *refinement*, no *comfort*, and no *benefit* to those who may be possessed of wealth."[4] Colquhoun's position reflects an attitude that poverty was, as Lees puts it, "expected, and by some even desired" as an engine of capitalist expansion.[5] This argument justified deploying legal pauperism to recruit poverty as a mechanism of regulatory control of a

[2] [Edward Copleston], *A Second Letter to the Right Hon. Robert Peel . . . on the Causes of the Increase of Pauperism, and on the Poor Laws* (Oxford: John Murray, 1819), 22, 17–18. Cosma Orsi situates Copleston and Malthus within an emerging debate on legislative effectiveness and its relation to character. Orsi notes that William Temple believed that laborers, governed "by hunger and lust," were "temperate and industrious" only if they were constantly laboring "to procure the common necessity of life," while Joseph Townsend believed that the poor were ignorant of "pride, honour, and ambition" and that hunger alone would "goad them on to labour." "The Political Economy of Inclusion: The Rise and Fall of the Workhouse System," *Journal of the History of Economic Thought* 39, no. 4 (December 2017): 453–81, at 457, quoting Temple, *Vindication of Commerce and the Arts* and Townsend, *Dissertation on the Poor Laws* (London, 1786). David Hitchcock argues that by deploying charity as a self-authorizing assessment of who was deserving, British society regulated the labor of the poor domestically and throughout the developing colonies. "'Punishment Is All the Charity That the Law Affordeth Them': Penal Transportation, Vagrancy, and the Charitable Impulse in the British Atlantic, c. 1600–1750," *New Global Studies* 12, no. 2 (2018): 1–20.

[3] Lynn Hollen Lees, *The Solidarities of Strangers: The English Poor Laws and the People, 1700–1948* (Cambridge: Cambridge University Press, 1998), 30.

[4] Patrick Colquhoun, *A Treatise on Indigence; Exhibiting a General View of the National Resources for Productive Labour, with Propositions for Ameliorating the Condition of the Poor* (London: Hatchard, 1806), 5, 7–8.

[5] Lees, *Solidarities of Strangers*, 21.

workforce and increasingly mobile population. As Sal Nicolazzo demonstrates, "Vagrancy offered a legal and tropological model for police as a mode of governance," one counterbalanced by eighteenth-century authors "using the uneasy aporia between vagrancy and legal subjectivity to dramatize troubling failures of juridical recognition."[6]

Samuel Taylor Coleridge, recognizing such "troubling failures," annotated several pages of Colquhoun's treatise, and contested the foundational claim of the necessity of subsistence labor by arguing that its apparent truth depended on the dubious assumption that the "present state of general Intellect and morals [was] supposed a fair average of the capabilities of society" rather than a function of the system that produced poverty as the optimal level of wealth for securing compliant workers. Coleridge insists the "Definition of Poverty is insidious" because it demands "such unceasing <bodily> Labor ... as precludes all improvement of mind," and then justifies subsistence wages by pointing to such unimproved minds. This self-sustaining poverty, which is treated by Colquhoun as symptomatic of human nature, is understood by Coleridge as robbery by the poor man's "unnatural Guardians" of "the very house-loom of his *human nature*," a theft that sustains the "useless & debasing luxuries for those who are privileged to live in Idleness."[7] Coleridge's choice of "house-loom" evokes its then nearly archaic meaning of "heirloom," in keeping with how wage-labor disrupts what Coleridge views as the natural inheritance due to all human beings, while also reinforcing the idea of self-reliant, sustainable labor that maintains household and community.

The disagreement between Colquhoun and Coleridge aligns with the tension identified by Michael Dean between Adam Smith's acknowledgment that, because labor is the basis of wealth, whatever "encourages the progress of population and improvement, encourages that of real wealth and greatness," and the problem of the governance of the poor as underlings. "Governance" here refers to the myriad power structures that transform and signify the human body as the instrument of labor, including the pronounced law, the institutions that enforce it (or wield it as an overhanging threat), and the print culture that disseminates both the law and the

[6] Sal Nicolazzo, *Vagrant Figures: Law, Literature, and the Origins of the Police* (New Haven, CT: Yale University Press, 2021), 3, 236.

[7] Richard Herne Shepherd, "Coleridge's Notes on Colquhoun," *Philobiblion* 1, no. 3 (February 1862): 65--66. Original annotations are reproduced at the University of Toronto's online supplement to *Marginalia*, vol. 12 of *Collected Works of Samuel Taylor Coleridge* (Princeton, NJ: Princeton University Press, 1969–2001).

narratives that give it substance.[8] The genealogy of governance that Dean charts reinforces Karl Polanyi's argument for the "great transformation" in which human life is reconceptualized as labor, a fictitious commodity made to impersonate the qualities of real commodities, those interchangeable items produced for sale.[9] The pauper is a precondition for the transformation of life into labor, serving as the reservoir of work-power that the laborer cannot store, and the sign of the artificiality of that transformation.

In this chapter, I examine depictions of paupers in late eighteenth- and early nineteenth-century British print culture, highlighting the ways in which writers both affirmed and contested the law's treatment of poverty. Paupers in this period comprised an amalgam of beggars and the underemployed or seasonably employed, and included people who survived on parish dole and those who worked for impoverishment-level wages. Some were soldiers discharged in peacetime and tenant farmers displaced by crop failures; others were abandoned spouses or children. Some paupers were aged or mentally distressed, and were often characterized by vagrancy. Any given individuals might shift among these categories as work availability and wages fluctuated or subsist in them simultaneously by both begging and working. These diverse individuals were consolidated into an unstable but discursively identifiable lowest class by regulatory laws and public perceptions forged by print culture. Paupers could, under the right conditions, find viable employment, though it was often disrupted by the settlement laws that allowed a pauper employed for a year in a particular parish to claim parish benefits; the laws motivated employers who paid taxes for such benefits to prevent yearlong continuous employment. As Polanyi explains in his account of the developing labor market under the Speenhamland system of outdoor relief beginning in the 1790s, the "figure of the pauper . . . dominated a discussion the imprint of which was as powerful as that of the most spectacular events in history."[10] In the next section, I explore entanglements of paupers with the law to show how the public imaginary, as instanced in the discourse of the periodical press and the wider, interconnected print culture of biography, poetry, and legal reporting, mediated the pauper as a conceptual category and as a figure

[8] Adam Smith, *An Inquiry into the Nature and Causes of the Wealth of Nations*, 2 vols., ed. R. H. Campbell and A. S. Skinner (Oxford, 1976), 2:566, quoted in Mitchel Dean, "A Genealogy of the Government of Poverty," *Economy and Society* 21, no. 3 (1992): 215–51, at 221.

[9] Karl Polanyi, *The Great Transformation: The Political and Economic Origins of Our Time* (1944; Boston: Beacon Press, 2001), chap. 6.

[10] Polanyi, *Great Transformation*, 87.

answerable to legal mechanisms which were themselves balanced between the categorical declarations of legal judgment and their representations, satirical, sentimental, and critical, in the public discourse. I then turn, in the final section, to the particular conundrum of the beggar as a persistent literary subject whose criminalized position entailed a theatricality marked by both tattered clothing and a panoptical state surveillance internalized in day-to-day encounters that ensured a legal susceptibility; yet I show how both imagined and actual beggars mobilized the very theatricality of which they stood perpetually accused to contest and evade this vulnerability.

Paupers amid the Law

Paupers appeared before the law in relation to settlement and criminal matters, as well as in the more Kafkaesque sense of coming into existence as a category under the gaze of the law. But they were entwined in other ways, shaping legal thought and using it, and serving as a mediating subject between the law and its public representations. These different appearances are evident in a wide range of texts in the era's print culture.

In its summary of "Interesting Decisions" that were "Selected for Popular Information," the 1808 *Literary Panorama* described several cases that underscored how the pauper was produced as a character who lacked agency. In the case of *Rex v. Inhabitants of Stowmarket*, the pauper John King was ordered to be removed from South Lopham to his birthplace in Stowmarket, which would be his settlement unless, by working elsewhere for a year, he could establish a new one. At age fourteen, he had been, in a typical practice, "allotted" from South Lopham to "Mr. Reynolds" of Stowmarket, who then sent him to Mr. J. Fox of Coddenham about seven miles away, and the "pauper made no objection to go conceiving that he had no discretion on the subject"; Mr. Fox "told him that he would give him clothes, and that he was to stay with him a year."[11] King was variously farmed out over the next several years, never having a formal agreement, as he "conceived himself obliged to accept these services, as being under the controul and jurisdiction of the house of industry." Lord Ellenborough, Chief Justice of the Court of Common Pleas, remarked that "All the parties seemed to have acted under the idea that *the boy was a parish slave.*" Even though he had labored for a sufficient time to gain a settlement and had been compensated for the work, no implied contract existed, because

[11] "Interesting Decisions in the Courts of Law and Equity," *Literary Panorama* 4 (September 1808): 1341–54, at 1349–50.

"the adoption of a contract must be the act of a free agent"; "can a person who is considered as a slave, and conceives himself to be such, be considered as having [voluntarily] adopted the acts of his masters?" he asked.[12] Ellenborough begins by deploying a metaphor – King has been treated like a slave – and then projects that into King's own state of mind over the several years of working, despite King having willfully married (a point not addressed in the summary). Further, the passive voice ("is considered as a slave") generalizes his employers' viewpoint into an attitude projected by the court. That a pauper could become enslaved by acquiescence to the law as he understood it is not remedied, but instead becomes the basis for sustaining his inability to create a new settlement and returning him to his birthplace. The narrative here turns on inferring consent from actions: King "made no objection to go," rather than "agreed to go," emphasizing the court's interpretive supremacy and the pauper's subservience both to those who would treat him as a slave and to those who would impute to him the independent choice of labor and his failure to make it.

The law also stripped paupers of other rights. Paupers could testify in only limited conditions and could not serve on juries because, as a writer for the *Literary Panorama* explained, while property is an imperfect proxy for "understanding or probity," it is the "only *ostensible* criterion" for "the respectability of an individual"; while a "pauper may be honest, shrewd, and firm," were he "dishonest, wilful, and corrupt, who can punish him for his folly or arrogance?"[13] The argument was that, because the pauper was immune to punishment, his condition must be one of always already punished. Of course, paupers were punished by courts, stripped to be beaten where they could not be stripped of property, and so this argument reduces the "*ostensible*" criterion of respectability to a device to produce that respectability by the exclusion of paupers. This consideration echoes the distinction with which the *Literary Panorama* article begins: "The distinguishing talent of Man above the brutes is, that intellectual faculty of discernment which qualifies him for social life."[14] This discernment, equally "qualifying" for social life and for service on juries, depends on property as its sign. As ownership implies attachment to community, its lack suggests a willingness to abandon social ties. Thus this logic reframes vagrancy as an attitude held by paupers instead of a condition imposed upon them.

[12] "Interesting Decisions," 1350.
[13] "Jury Court in Scotland," *Literary Panorama*, n.s. 5 (October 1816): 1–17, at 8.
[14] "Jury Court," 1.

Appearing anonymously in the *Athenaeum*, Thomas Hood's 1832 "Reply to a Pastoral Poet" highlights the pauper's alienated relationship to work as both a condition and an extension of his construction as a pauper.[15] Using anaphora to contrast rhetoric ("Tell") and evidence ("Show"), the first stanza divides between negating the dehistoricizing escapism of pastoral vision (lines 1–4) and emphasizing the precarity of the present (lines 5–8):

> TELL us not of by-gone days!
> Tell us not of forward times!
> What's the future – what the past –
> Save to fashion rhymes?
> Show us that the corn doth thrive!
> Show us there's no winter weather!
> Show us we may laugh and live, –
> (Those who love, – together).
>
> (lines 1–8)

The final line underscores both that paupers possess human emotions and that economics and law disrupt the ability to transform them into the stabilizing households of certified marriages, an ironic comment in the context of a pastoral tradition in which myriad forms of love escape scrutiny and regula(riza)tion. The second stanza, with the same rhyme pattern (ababcdcd), divides halfway between classical tropes of the sensual pastoral – sweet blossoms, passions blazing, "Hearts that may be won" – and the realities of wage labor that "doth forever press us" and the "famine" that "grins upon our board" (lines 12–14). The final two stanzas, contrasting rich and poor as well as desire and reality, detail how the tropes of pastoral are at once yearned for by the speaker and his class and yet foreclosed by the conditions of underpaid, relentless labor: "But if we stay to gaze or sigh, / We starve" (lines 23–24). Their human potential is transformed by their working conditions into the "pauper's fare" of "perpetual toil"; labor that should produce the ability to eat becomes the pauper's diet until life, in the ninth, and thus excessive, line of the final stanza is reduced to "only toil – and die!" (lines 19–20, 33). The speaker signs off as "Pauper." Hood emphasizes that the condition of pauperism is produced by the norms of privilege that elide labor in order to devalue it and then use the pauper's own anti-poeticism to justify the devaluation. Where the pauper represents the condition of pauperism as an alienated

[15] [Thomas Hood], "Reply to a Pastoral Poet," *Athenaeum*, no. 222 (January 28, 1832): 66. Hereafter cited parenthetically in the text.

awareness of lack – "The very winds which fragrance blow / But blanch *us* to the bone" (lines 27–28) – the pastoral poet colludes with the regulatory regime to which he pretends indifference; the effect of the wind is caused not by the wind alone but by the conditions of labor.

A response to "Reply to a Pastoral Poet" appeared the next month.[16] As if to confirm its interest in the pauper's legal and social condition rather than his poetic potential, the response, entitled "Answer to Pauper," comes not from a pastoral poet but from "Overseer," the legal authority in the parish paid to manage paupers. Its author, however, is also Thomas Hood. Written in the same stanzaic form and to the same length as the previous poem (excepting the ninth line of the final stanza), it unpacks the legal dynamics of Pauper's lament. Pretending to offer a point-by-point refutation of Pauper, the poem instead, in its callous overstatement, becomes a sarcastic defense of Pauper's argument. It announces that the "Cuckoo-song, or pensive dreams" referenced in Pauper's poem are "not your Parish," and therefore are off limits by settlement law for the restricted pauper (lines 7–8). Turning to the subject of passions, Overseer writes:

> – amorous fancies?
> While your betters' flames miscarry –
> If *you* love your Dolls and Nancys,
> Don't we *make* you marry?
> (lines 13–16)

These lines contrast the upper-class ability to produce (and perhaps abort) bastards with minimal consequences with the pressures that the settlement system could put on paupers to marry. Scoffing at the "Fragrant winds, that blanch your bones," Overseer sneers, the "poor can always keep" warm by "breaking stones," alluding to the hard labor of criminal punishment while also glancing at the appalling working conditions often inflicted upon poorhouse inhabitants (lines 18–20). Declaring that the pauper, bereft of ownership, has no concern with whether "corn doth thrive," Overseer announces, "You / Don't farm – but you are farm'd," triumphing in the dehumanized commodification that Pauper suffers (lines 26–28). Overseer concludes by invoking the illusion of choice – that paupers are lazy and their condition is a consequence of their character and decisions – and fuses overseers' practice of driving paupers to other parishes with death from malnutrition, overwork, and violence: "If such as

[16] [Thomas Hood], "Answer to Pauper," *Athenaeum* no. 225 (February 18, 1832): 114. Hereafter cited parenthetically in the text.

you don't like this world – / We'll pass you to the next" (lines 31–32). The faux-debate staged through these two poems argues for collusion between the legal status of the poor and pastoral poetry that abstracts the relationship of human beings to nature by displacing labor, resituating hunger as sexual or aesthetic desire, and, finally, representing human interventions as the expression of natural law. The class-signifying doggerel of the Pauper's lament, bitter but nonviolent, and of the Overseer's brutal (and Swiftian) response, staged as a cross-examination of the pauper's charges, becomes a sympathetic voicing of the perils of poverty as a denial of rights.

As these two disputing poems suggest, the pauper was conceived at once as the antithesis of the laborer and as characteristic of one; both have a presumed distaste for work and its associated pain, and both endure under the suspicion of disguise. The contradictory status of the pauper, ingenious and indigent, was reinforced by the unsettled status of being settled. As Steven King explains, belonging to either place or community was "multilayered" by "legal status," "custom," and "participation in local institutions." King notes that belonging was "fragile or contested" in the "instance when labour market crises led parishes to fall back on settlement law as the ultimate determination of belonging," thus choosing to expel even long-standing members of a community.[17] In a characteristic case, *Rex v. the Inhabitants of Clayhydon* (1790), the Court of King's Bench dealt with an appeal in which the pauper William Taylor had first been removed by two justices from Clayhydon (Clayhidon) to Ufculm (Uffculme); the Sessions court quashed that order, finding that Taylor had established a settlement, and the King's Bench was now asked to reverse that finding.[18] This is the agreed narrative: Taylor had bargained to work for W. Hodges for a year and did so until nine days before its expiration, at which point, on a Sunday morning, he went in search of employment for the next year. When he asked Hodges what work he should undertake upon returning on Tuesday morning, Hodges "told him he might go and serve the master he had worked for the day before [i.e., Monday]," and a short time later "paid him his wages up to that time only."[19] The question on which the appeal turned was whether the "*constructive service*, pursuant to a hiring for a year" would "confer a settlement." Lord Kenyon, although thinking that "attending strictly to the words of the Act of Parliament" might have

[17] Steven King, "Friendship, Kinship and Belonging in the Letters of Urban Paupers 1800–1840," *Historical Social Research* 33, no. 3 (2008): 249–77, at 249.

[18] "Adjudged Cases in the Court of King's Bench, Michaelmas Term, 31 Geo. III," *Lawyer's and Magistrate's Magazine . . . with the Decisions of the Judges in Their Own Words* 2 (1792): 366–68.

[19] "Adjudged Cases," 366.

produced "a greater certainty on this subject," recognized that *stare decisis* demanded the "construction which has so frequently been put upon it." A prior case, *Rex v. Islip*, found that "though the servant were not in the actual discharge of his duty in his master's house," he remained "liable to be called into" that service "during the remainder of the year." In this case, by contrast, Kenyon insisted that, even though the servant wished to continue in service and had not contracted elsewhere for the remaining days of the year, his acceptance of the money "put an end to the contract"; after that time, "the servant was no longer subject to the controul of the master."[20] With the concurrence of the other two judges, the court reversed the Sessions ruling. This case demonstrates the translation of traditional modes of labor into contractual relationships in which the exchange of money speaks beyond the intentions of the pauper receiving it. The pauper's effort to belong to the community – the very element that prompted him to lose his position, as he sought employment for the subsequent year – foreclosed his ability to do so.

Discussion of poverty, whether in literature or law, was (and is) a consideration of character. A doggerel, "Bad Habits," originally published sometime before 1825, connects the habitual practices of the laborer and the ruined clothing that marks the pauper, while highlighting the cruelty of the legally authorized overseer. The overseer chastises a pauper appealing for alms at the vestry, declaring, "mend your habits, nor dare this place haunt." The pauper, pointedly named Lazarus, responds punningly, "Amendment . . . both of us want; / But as to my *habits* . . . / they are mere shreds and tatters, and not worth the mending."[21] Shifting from the overseer's criminalizing gaze to the pauper's humanizing perspective, the poem contests the legibility of the pauper's criminal status by underscoring the slipperiness of condemning language. Colquhoun had insisted that "Idleness is a never-failing inroad to criminality," and in his categories of "the criminal and unfortunate individuals" that "infest the great metropolis," he indicates the interrelated material and psychological conditions that determine this inevitability.[22] The association of paupers with criminality was commonplace not because paupers disproportionately committed major crimes but rather for two main reasons. First, paupers' being – where and how they lived – was criminalized and analogized to such crimes. The unpleasantness of encountering a beggar became a crime

20 "Adjudged Cases," 367.
21 "Bad Habits," in John Bull, *The Laughing Philosopher* (London: Sherwood, 1825), 576.
22 Patrick Colquhoun, *A Treatise on the Police of the Metropolis* (London: Dilly, 1796), 87.

chargeable to that beggar. "Perception of vagrants as proto-criminals," Andrew McLeod explains, "shaped the terms of these statutes [regarding the poor] and their enforcement."[23] Second, paupers were presumed to be frauds, to be impersonating their own indigence. In "the contacts between pauper and administrator" (that is, the overseer for a parish), the official "formed an opinion" about "the character of the destitute person thrust before him" and in that scene, both participants "gave a performance for the benefit of the other," as well as for the community and, when reviewed by Parliamentary committees and public writers, the nation.[24]

The Ragged Case of Tattered Beggars

Representations of pauperism in early nineteenth-century print culture not only exposed contradictions in the law's treatment of paupers but also underscored the theatrical nature of the mendicant, which cast beggary as a professional mode characterized by inventiveness and effort, the very qualities that were presumed to evade poverty. As Dean details, the early modern concern with "'sumptuary' problems of the blurring of distinctions between estates" evolved as a "social policy" constituting "the Poor as an object of observation, comparison, and information collection."[25] Their dress, exemplified by the double-undress of being near nakedness and wearing tatters or rags, the residue of clothing rather than clothing itself, constitutes the pauper as immediately recognizable, a devolution of the liveried worker. For the pauper, both the temporality and the space of labor combine to regulate the body, and in turn, this regulation is inscribed on – and resisted through parodic means of – the body and its tatters that represent, while no longer being, clothing. Thus, in the 1817 popular illustrated *Vagabondiana*, the king of the Parisian beggars, who holds an annual "council of his offices and subjects" and is paid "the legal and accustomed tribute money," must, to be recognized *as* king, sport "a limb in all appearance shockingly diseased, but curable in a day's time," and be dressed in "royal habits . . . composed of a thousand bits of rag, of various colours."[26]

Before turning to the urban beggar in tatters as widely represented in print culture, I want to look at a presentation of an earlier form of pauper

[23] Andrew McLeod, "On the Origins of Consorting Laws," *Melbourne University Law Review* 37, no. 1 (2013): 103–42, at 105.

[24] Lees, *Solidarities of Strangers*, 33.

[25] Dean, "Genealogy," 224, 227.

[26] Francis Douce and John Thomas Smith, *Vagabondiana, or Anecdotes of Mendicant Wanderers through the Streets of London*, new ed. (1817; London: Chatto and Windus, 1874), 8.

against which this figure resonated, William Wordsworth's "The Old Cumberland Beggar," to suggest how the impending extinction of this beggar, which Wordsworth highlights in the poem's headnote, serves as the ground for the emergence of the modern beggar.[27] Adam Potkay demonstrates the importance of Wordsworth's face-to-face encounters with the poor,[28] but the encounter is askance in "The Old Cumberland Beggar." The narrator watches from a distance – "I saw an aged Beggar in my walk; / And he was seated, by the highway side," the poem opens – that allows the narrator to view the rounds of the beggar and their community-knitting effect – "Wher'er the aged Beggar takes his rounds, / The mild necessity of use compels / The acts of love"; this analytic perspective resonates with the legislating Stateman despite the narrator's critique: "restless in your wisdom, ye / Who have a broom still ready in your hand."[29] Wordsworth's interaction with the beggar as a face-to-face exchange is deflected onto the brief poem "Old Man Travelling," which Wordsworth, in the notes, described as an "overflowing" from "The Old Cumberland Beggar." The Old Man encounters the poet as he takes to the national roads, overflowing the proscribed rounds of the Old Cumberland Beggar and, as Toby Benis points out, becoming potentially subject to vagrancy laws.[30] The narrator's inquiry – "whither he was bound" – echoes an overseer's legal query, and the Old Man's response provides an inadvertent defense.[31] The simultaneity of the Old Cumberland Beggar and the Old Man Travelling points to a transition in the conceptualization of beggars as members of the local community and as displaced, urbanized professionals. Where the poem "Old Cumberland Beggar" performs, as Gary Harrison observes, the typical "act of historical displacement" that Jerome McGann identifies as characteristic of Romantic ideology, namely, replacing "an image and landscape of contradiction [and one might add

[27] David Green adumbrates this discursive transformation, explaining that "images of the poor" shifted from "sympathetic representations of the congeniality and fraternity of beggars toward a more discipline-minded moralism in which criminality and deception were key motifs." *Pauper Capital: London and the Poor Law, 1790–1870* (Burlington, VT: Ashgate, 2010), 48–49.

[28] Adam Potkay, *Wordsworth's Ethics* (Baltimore: Johns Hopkins University Press, 2012), 31.

[29] William Wordsworth, "The Old Cumberland Beggar, a Description," in *Lyrical Ballads with Other Poems*, 2nd ed., 2 vols. (London: Longman, 1800), vol. 2, lines 1–2, 68–69, 98–100. Hereafter cited parenthetically in the text.

[30] Toby Benis, *Romanticism on the Road: The Marginal Gains of Wordsworth's Homelessness* (London: Palgrave, 2000), 114–15.

[31] William Wordsworth, "Old Man Travelling; Animal Tranquility and Decay, a Sketch," in *Lyrical Ballads with A Few Other Poems* (London: Arch, 1798), line 15. Hereafter cited parenthetically in the text.

conflict] with one dominated by 'the power / Of harmony,'"[32] the poem "Old Man Travelling" reverses this pattern: It begins with an image of "settled quiet" (lines 7–8), yet ends with the Old Man's describing his son, a mariner, "dying in a hospital" (line 20), a historical invocation undermining the "peace so perfect" (line 13) that the speaker has projected onto him. His long journey from Cumberland to Falmouth enacts the labor of the modern vagrant who displaces the soon-to-be extinct class of such beggars as the Old Cumberland Beggar, despite emerging from him via the economic displacements caused by war and its consequent domestic shifts.[33]

Unlike the Old Cumberland Beggar, whose status is an emblem of common law, a figure from time out of mind about whom the narrator declares "from my childhood have I known; and then / He was so old, he seems not older now" (lines 22–23), Charles Lamb's contemporary beggar, in "Complaint of the Decay of Beggars in the Metropolis," is more typical of periodical representations. As both the representative of a class and an individual, he is inserted into the operations of statute law, answerable immediately to overseers, appealable to a local justice of the peace and then the Quarter Sessions, and ultimately litigable before the King's Bench.[34] This legal trail at once merged and stratified the local and national systems, scaling from overseers with usually no legal training but appointed for local knowledge to lawyers and judges of legal renown – and this complexity was reflected in how periodicals represented the pervasiveness of the poor. The barrister Gregory Lewin prefaced his 1827 treatise *A Summary of the Law of Settlement* by lamenting the "legal ingenuity" in the King's Bench that constructed a system "so diffuse, and irreconcilable with ordinary sense," and by proposing to distill this body of law for the "most zealous and patriotic of our country justices."[35]

That beggars possessed a certain claim of a quasi-legal nature by virtue of the moral imperative of charity was a common theme both produced

[32] Gary Harrison, *Wordsworth's Vagrant Muse: Poetry, Poverty and Power* (Detroit, MI: Wayne State University Press, 1994), 169, quoting Jerome McGann, *The Romantic Ideology: A Critical Investigation* (Chicago: University of Chicago Press, 1983), 86, quoting "Tintern Abbey" (lines 48–49).

[33] When the poem was republished as "Animal Tranquility and Decay, a Sketch," Wordsworth altered the dialogue to indirect report; in the 1815 version, he omits the encounter, aligning the revision with dynamics that, as in "Old Cumberland Beggar" "set aside . . . questions of poor relief" in favor of Romantic harmonization. Harrison, *Wordsworth's Vagrant Muse*, 170.

[34] Elia [Charles Lamb], "A Complaint of the Decay of Beggars in the Metropolis," *London Magazine* 5, no. 30 (June 1822): 532–36. Hereafter cited parenthetically in the text.

[35] Gregory Lewin, *A Summary of the Law of Settlement* (London: S. Sweet, 1827), vi–vii.

and undermined in short anecdotes that peppered the period's periodicals. "The Beggar's Dog," which appeared in the *Amulet*, begins with a poor man declaring repeatedly to "my poor Rover" that they must part, and then the narrative backtracks to the events that leads to this pathetic moment: The man was once convicted under the now-modified laws against poaching, a crime "punishe[d] with peculiar severity," although one that cannot be "considered of a very heinous nature" as it is discordant with the moral intuition of the "sturdy Englishman" who considers "the game that passed over his own fields, as his own property."[36] Having served his fourteen years of transportation, he returns to find his wife dead and his four children scattered. He would be eligible for parish relief now, except that "by a late regulation, no pauper was suffered to keep a dog." He tries unsuccessfully to negotiate, and, as "big tears fell upon his tattered garments," once again a sign of the beggar's authenticity, he attempts to explain to the dog why he must leave him. In a sentimental conclusion, one of his sons suddenly returns and allows his father and the faithful "Rover" to settle with him. In another story, "The Beggar," published in *The Mirror of Literature*, the narrator declares, "Get thee gone" to a beggar whose "dress was forlorn and tattered" because he has "been too often deceived," but as they stare at each other, interrogating one another with their looks, the narrator relents and in exchange for a shilling is rewarded with "the tear of gratitude, warm and fresh from the heart" that falls on his "extended hand" at the moment of exchange.[37] A squib, "Punishments," that follows this anecdote contrasts England with "Italy and parts of Germany," where "*felons*" must "clean the streets," while in "our beloved country," this "degrading occupation" goes to "those unfortunate persons, whose only crime is that of being poor."[38] Such ripostes, reiterated as filler in periodicals, intimate a social contract between beggars and the more fortunate that echoes Colquhoun's and Attwood's claims of the economic necessity of paupers in the regulation of the cost of labor.

"The Beggar of Algiers" makes this undergirding an explicitly legal claim. The tale was reprinted in *The Mirror of Literature* in 1824 from the 1787 *New Ladies Magazine*, but stripped of an introduction that presented it as an illustration of the differences in the customs of obligation in different nations, and thereby given a contemporary currency. In the tale, a Greek merchant becomes the executor of a will that includes a legacy

36 "The Beggar's Dog. A Sketch," *Amulet*, no. 23 (January 1826): 18–20.

37 "The Beggar," *Mirror of Literature* 1, no. 4 (November 23, 1822): 63.

38 "Punishments," *Mirror of Literature* 1, no. 4 (November 23, 1822): 63.

of "a certain sum of money to be disposed of among the indigent and distressed," and he finds a Moor, "lame, and almost blind" to whom he gives alms.[39] The Moor is so touched by the merchant's generosity that he follows him on crutches and exults "how exceedingly bountiful that Christian had been" and "the populace joined the cripple in his applause."[40] The beggar then situates himself near the merchant's home and receives daily alms for several months, until one day he learns that the merchant has left for Egypt. When he returns six months later, the beggar greets him joyfully and asks him "to pay him all his arrears at once," that is, the 180 rials of benevolence missed by his absence. When the merchant refuses, the beggar "laid his complaint before the Dey, and the merchant was sent for to make his defence"; the beggar argues that the public charity had "greatly augmented" the merchant's customers and that the beggar, acting in reliance on the steady alms, had been "induced" to quit "his business of making thread laces."[41] The merchant admits the factual elements of the Moor's claims but "insisted that, alms being a voluntary action, its continuance depended wholly on the donor." The verdict, however, goes against the merchant, who is "condemned to pay" the 180 rials plus "a piaster extraordinary as a recompense for his reproaches."[42] The beggar turns out to be an astute businessman and persuasive pleader.

Margaret Russett has attuned scholars of Romanticism to the body's role in imposture, a role highlighted in the performance of poverty. As Russett has demonstrated, forgeries and impersonations are tightly interwoven. The masqueraded self, the costumed body, and the self-authenticating text all project a performance of identity. The Caraboo hoax, like several of Russett's literary examples, demonstrates that such impersonations could model detachment from the economic world: Mary Baker, despite her poverty, in performing the Princess Caraboo, "never used her assumed name in a financial transaction."[43] In seeking a loan and faced with the problem of demonstrating his self-identity, Thomas De Quincey recognizes, as Russett frames it, that "the assumed priority of the natural over the represented person is itself a species of legal fiction."[44] For the poor, this quandary meant that papers validating their right to travel, rather than their own self-determination, characterized their status as vagrants. Their own persuasive narratives before overseers determined the status of

[39] "The Beggar of Algiers," *Mirror of Literature* 3, no. 88 (June 1824): 399–400, at 399.

[40] "Beggar of Algiers," 400. [41] "Beggar of Algiers," 400. [42] "Beggar of Algiers," 400.

[43] Margaret Russett, *Fictions and Fakes: Forging Romantic Authenticity, 1760–1845* (Cambridge: Cambridge University Press, 2006), 134.

[44] Russett, *Fictions and Fakes*, 5.

settlement, especially if supplemented by textual evidence. To be there was not to belong there, absent validating strategies.

In his persona Elia, Charles Lamb produces a theatricalized, modernized, and stationary variant of the Old Cumberland Beggar.[45] Where Wordsworth cautioned the "Statesmen" who "have a broom still ready in your hands / To rid the world of nuisances" ("Old Cumberland Beggar," lines 67–69), in "Complaint of the Decay of Beggars in the Metropolis," Elia attacks the "all-sweeping besom [i.e., broom] of societarian reform" that wishes to clean the city of the "whole mendicant fraternity," not least because its members are liable for impersonation (532).[46] Unlike Wordsworth's beggar, whose pauperism is undoubtable and whose rounds among rural poor are under surveillance which stabilizes his identity along with theirs, Elia's metropolitan beggars are anonymous and territorial. While noting their functions as "emblems, momentos," and so on, he links beggars to the theater, a connection undergirded by poor laws that criminalized the travel of both beggars and unlicensed actors. Elia's beggar's metropolitan circumstances moot questions of his unverifiable poverty by asserting his value as a street performer, whether he is a pauper imitating himself or an impostor playing the role. Elia affirms the irony that his reader will "pay . . . money to see a comedian feign these things, which, concerning these poor people, thou canst not certainly tell whether they are feigned"; that is, the pauper's is a stronger, more compelling performance (536). Further, the pauper becomes for all those living within a tentative economy – the only kind Elia acknowledges – a character available for imitation by those who may become impoverished. The beggar depends on a costuming he cannot avoid: "Rags, which are the reproach of poverty, are the Beggar's robes . . . the suit in which he is expected to show himself in public" (533). Like his clothing, the beggar's body is part of his theatrical accoutrement. Elia describes at length the "half-limbed giant," who is "a grand fragment, as good as an Elgin marble" and was "the man-part of a Centaur" who for forty-two years has "driven this out of door trade" of begging (535). Magnified by the context of the *London Magazine*, Elia's portraits of pauperism engage the political dispute as to the management of the impoverished and those who impersonated impoverishment. If pauperism is marked on the body, enduring in the

[45] Simon Hull, *Charles Lamb, Elia, and the London Magazine* (London: Pickering and Chatto, 2010), 138–47.

[46] On the intrinsic uncertainty in representations of the poor deployed across various genres, see James Harriman-Smith, "Representing the Poor: Charles Lamb and the *Vagabondiana*," *Studies in Romanticism* 54, no. 4 (Winter 2015): 551–68.

trace of Wordsworth's Old Cumberland Beggar's palsied hands, such a body can be counterfeited, its own form of social coinage.

The 1815 House of Commons committee report on urban "Mendicity and Vagrancy" is embedded in the discourse that transformed archetypal beggars such as the Old Cumberland Beggar into entrepreneurial, urban beggars. The report itself balanced statistical estimates and biographical anecdote. In its preface, the committee catalogues the disproportionate populations of beggars in the capital and their pernicious effect, but then comments: "It must be confessed that, serious as the subject is, no one could refrain from a smile on perusing some of the evidence."[47] A watchhouse-keeper, Samuel Roberts, recognized that the narratives offered the sentimental basis through which the statistics gained force. He declares: "My opinion is that a great number of the beggars who go about, are not in distress, that they are impostors: I have knowledge of one man in particular, [John Collins, the Soap Eater,] that . . . pretends to be in fits in the street; he chews soap" to produce the dramatic foaming at the mouth.[48] George Smeeton's 1822 *Biographia Curiosa* repeats this testimony and presents a "Beggar's Opera," an illustration of successful mendicants feasting, including John the Soap Eater and Toby, discussed below (Figure 9.1).[49] Other testimony includes set-pieces in which beggars appear as both competent and competitive, internally well-regulated and chaotic: Children are loaned out so that one "woman" begs with "twins who never grew older," and another with a "blind child hired to excite charity."[50] The rector of St. Clement Danes maintains that the beggars live "very well: especially if they are pretty well *maimed*, *blind*, or if they have *children*."[51] Such narratives come equipped with estimates of incomes from begging that exceed working-class wages, and so by the logic of the report, a successful beggar is, per se, a fraudulent one, necessarily capable of work – since begging is itself urban work.

The putatively wealthy beggar Bampfylde Moore Carew persisted as a deep legend about the urban pauper that reinforces the "Mendicity and

47 *Minutes of the Evidence Taken before the Committee Appointed by the House of Commons to Inquire into the State of Mendicity and Vagrancy in the Metropolis and Its Neighbourhood* (London: Sherwood, 1816), v.

48 *Minutes of the Evidence*, 180.

49 Naming the scene of feasting a "Beggar's Opera" extends the joke that opens John Gay's popular play, when the narrating Beggar comments, "I make one of their Weekly festivals at St. Giles [the location of the Rose and Crown, later nicknamed or renamed the Beggar's Opera after the play] . . . and am welcome to a dinner there whenever I please." John Gay, *The Beggar's Opera. As It Is Acted at the Theatre-Royal in Lincolns-Inn-Fields*, 2nd ed. (London: John Watts, 1728), [iii].

50 *Minutes of the Evidence*, 210.

51 *Minutes of the Evidence*, 212.

Figure 9.1 George Cruikshank, "A Scene at the Beggar's Opera in St. Giles's Sketched on the Spot," an idealized display of successful mendicants feasting, with John Collins the Soap Eater (no. 3) and Toby (no. 4) at the table. From George Smeeton, *Biographia Curiosa; or Memoirs of Remarkable Characters of the Reign of George the Third. With Their Portraits* (London: J. Robins, 1822).
Courtesy of the Yale University Library.

Vagrancy" narratives. An 1812 revised edition of a 1745 biography declares in its preface, "Mr. Carew can never be viewed in any other point than as an active *solicitor*, and in this respect he outstripped the most eminent lawyers, for he was always thankful for what he received."[52] Henry Wilson opens the first volume of his *Wonderful Characters* (1821–22) by resurrecting Carew. As Wilson explains, Carew was born into a well-established family and became infatuated with begging. The account traces his theatrical successes including a bet by a Mr. Pleydell that he would recognize Carew the next time they met. Carew disguises himself

[52] *Surprising Adventures of Bampfylde Moore Carew ... Containing a Dictionary of the Cant Language*, 2nd ed. (1812; London: Newman, 1813), a reworking of Robert Goadby, *Apology for the Life of Mr. Bampfylde-Moore Carew, Commonly Call'd the King of the Beggars; ... [Including] a Particular Account of the Original, Government, Language, Laws and Customs of the Gypsies*, 7th ed. (1745; London: Goadby and Owen, 1763). The comparison of beggar and lawyer mimics the textual record in which, as David Hitchcock describes it, "Running alongside this thin archival stream of lived experience," a "rich seam of cultural interpretation and representation, a body of knowledge, or discourse, about vagrancy ... replaces the silences of legal records with inventive, engaging tales of roguish duplicity, ingenuity, danger, and undeservingness." *Vagrancy in English Culture and Society, 1650–1750* (New York: Bloomsbury, 2016), 3. Hitchcock views Carew's unreliable biography as exemplary (4).

as an old woman and "borrow[s] a little hump-backed child of a tinker, and two others of a beggar," and troops off to Pleydell's.[53] Impersonating the "unfortunate grandmother of these poor helpless infants" (1:11), he wins both the bet and the "highly delighted" company's applause (1:12). Because he "so easily entered into every character, and moulded himself into so many different forms," he eventually is elected the new King of the Beggars. This achieved, he is "under no obligation to go on any cruise," but continues to do so anyway, his profession being imbricated in his identity and success as an impersonator (1:15).

Wonderful Characters displays malleable bodies as a performance of the bizarreness of human personalities, many turning their eccentricity to profits. A number of beggars feature, as in the story of "Toby, A Begging Imposture," who "lived upon the credulity of the too charitable metropolis"; in telling his tale, Wilson borrows liberally from the vagrancy report, and dissolves Toby's particular personality into the corporate identity of the London Beggar, despite his origins as "a negro" who, while on a journey from Bermuda, "lost all his toes," an "accident of great service" to his "daily perambulations" of begging (3:408). The language that Wilson uses to describe Toby's tasks casts him as a laborer, and pauperism as labor: he would "preach" and sing and "appeared almost bent double" until his "day's business" was done, when he would "walk upright" (3:408–09). Another story, an account of John Smith, focuses on Lewkner's-lane, where "the disciples of Bampfylde Moore Carew were to be found in crowds, and where *beggars* of all descriptions resorted to regale themselves upon the *good things of this life*, laughing at the credulity of the public" (3:214), a snicker that Wilson might have shared about any of his purchasers who read too believingly. But even for the cynical, these biographies sketched out a view of beggars as woven into the fabric of London life.

In 1818, Thomas Attwood distinguished productive laborers such as agricultural and manufacturing workers from non-productive laborers such as coachmen and footmen. He argued that from the perspective of capital, beggars are only a species of unproductive labor, providing channels through which capital can flow. From the perspective of laborers, therefore, they are competitors for "the food and clothing that would otherwise be consumed by labourers."[54] If the sociologic and political model hoped

[53] Henry Wilson, *Wonderful Characters: Comprising Memoirs and Anecdotes of the Most Remarkable Persons of Every Age and Nation*, 3 vols. (London: J. Robins, 1821–22), 1:11. Hereafter cited parenthetically in the text.

[54] Thomas Attwood, *Observations on Currency, Population, and Pauperism* (Birmingham: Wrightson, 1818), 33.

to distinguish poverty – the dip in fortunes to which anyone might be liable – from pauperism, a particularly recalcitrant performance of identity, the biographical figure of the impoverished underscored the arbitrariness of that distinction, as it swayed with the movement of capital. Whether as street performance or subsistence employment, the figure of the beggar produced the paradoxical consequence of the alignment between the capitalist's reliance on credit and the beggar's reliance on credulity.

In Wordsworth's *The Prelude* (1850), such beggars haunt the massive city where its inhabitants live "amid the same perpetual whirl / Of trivial objects, melted and reduced / To one identity, by differences / That have no law, no meaning, and no end –."[55] Wordsworth's metaphor is of financial circulation, in which the abstraction of money "melted and reduced" produces identities that are contingent and inconsistent. For the poor, a rapid increase in population and shifts in demographic organization occasioned "significant differences in poor law practices" in proximate parishes, resulting in both "overseers keen to shift the burden of support elsewhere" and "paupers willing to try their luck" across multiple parishes.[56] This internal instability is magnified by the conditions of labor, in which casual laborers do not know "when they rise in the morning, by what chance jobs in the streets or the markets they are to get food."[57] Such uncertainty situated many at the boundary between working and begging, with one activity potentially necessary to supplement the other. Wordsworth's examples of differences melded into sameness include a catalogue of beggars and peddlers; the poem presents a "travelling cripple" (7.203), a "begging scavenger, with hat in hand" (7.213), a "Jew" (7.217), and a "stately and slow-moving Turk" (7.217). Ultimately, an encounter with another beggar adjusts the poet's thinking and compels differentiation. He is "smitten" (7.637) by a "blind Beggar" (7.639)

> propped against a wall, upon his chest
> Wearing a written paper, to explain
> His story, whence he came, and who he was.
> . . . an apt type
> This label seemed of the utmost we can know,
> Both of ourselves and of the universe;

[55] William Wordsworth, *The Prelude* (1850), in *The Prelude: 1799, 1805, 1850*, ed. Jonathan Wordsworth, M. H. Abrams, and Stephen Gill (New York: W. W. Norton, 1979), bk. 7, lines 725–28. Hereafter cited parenthetically in the text by book and line number.

[56] Green, *Pauper Capital*, 51.

[57] Joseph Fletcher, "The Metropolis: Its Boundaries, Extent and Divisions for Local Government," *Journal of the Statistical Society*, 1844, quoted in Green, *Pauper Capital*, 54.

And, on the shape of that unmoving man,
His steadfast face and sightless eyes, I gazed,
As if admonished from another world.
(7.640–49)

As Russett notes, Wordsworth's imagery attaches the beggar to textuality and the limits of the legibility of identity and to the theatrical trope that underscores book 7's representation of London.[58] But it also raises the reflective question, for both writer and reader, about our own precarity, hidden beneath the very clothes that, necessarily, ultimately become tattered.

Another narrative, represented as biographical, echoes Wordsworth's dilemma of limits, but places it at the heart of the judicial system. In his retrospective *Sketches of the Irish Bar* (1854), Richard Sheil describes a moment of his initiation into legal culture around 1815. Walking to the "subterranean chamber" where the lawyers' apparel is kept, while meditating on "the dignity and importance" of his new position, he pauses before a "remarkable specimen of wretchedness"; like the wig and robes that distinguish the lawyer's significance, the "raiment [of the unfortunate man] served to set his destitution off."[59] Sheil describes the man's clothing and body in close detail. His "shirt of tattered yellow, which from a time beyond memory had adhered to his withered body" provides an immemorial status signifying his status as a pauper; his "hideous mouth" possessed "an habitual gape for food" (1:186–87). To "release" himself from this "painful image," the young lawyer explains, he "proceeded to invest [him]self in [his] professional trappings" and looks in a mirror to see "the judicial organ in a certain prominence upon [his] brow" (1:187) so that, like the wretched man, Sheil's clothing and body consistently express his profession, but with a physiognomy seemingly congenitally distinct from the pauper's. To emphasize this self-ironizing narration, young Sheil heads to court determined to try "an experiment in nodding" to appear intelligently engaged (1:188). In court, he observes the procession of the established lawyers, each with a distinct tell. Comforted by this parade, Sheil is shocked when a barrister "upsetting all opposition" advances to be heard – the pauper whom he had earlier eschewed, now Counsellor M'Mahon. To Sheil's astonishment, when M'Mahon addresses the court, the chancellor and Bar assume "an aspect of profound attention." Asked for which cause he appears, he replies, "In my own," and explains that

58 Russett, *Fictions and Fakes*, 40.

59 Richard Lalor Sheil, *Sketches of the Irish Bar . . . with Memoir and Notes by R. Shelton Mackenzie*, 2 vols. (New York: Redfield, 1854), 1:186. Hereafter cited parenthetically in the text.

despite therefore having "a madman for his client," he has "no money to fee [his] brethren," and "if [he is] mad, it is poverty, and persecution, and the Jesuits, that have made [him] so" (1:191–92). After this scene of shock and admonishment, Sheil admits, "I divested myself of my professional trappings ... with very different feelings" (1:192–93); he recognizes that the differences between the tatters of the pauper and the trappings of the barrister are more permeable than he had imagined. Sheil's misrecognition of the beggar is embedded in assumptions about the poor and their relation to labor and social value. His own admonishment, like the blind beggar's for Wordsworth, underscores that, as the law sought to regulate pauperism, paupers – both real and imagined – contributed to the public imagination on which the legal system depended for its wealth, recognition, and purpose.

CHAPTER 10

Liberty in "Parenthesis"

The Case of The Slave, Grace *(1827) and Antislavery Satire in* The History of Mary Prince *(1831)*

Sarah Winter

In 1822, an enslaved domestic servant named Grace James traveled from Antigua to England with Mrs. Ann Allan, who was, by the laws of the era, her owner. They returned to Antigua in 1823. James's legal status came into question two years later when she was subjected to flogging on Mrs. Allan's orders for alleged disobedience and told that she was still a slave. In response to this mistreatment, James presented herself to an Antigua customs officer on August 8, 1825, claiming that she was a servant and "free woman of colour" illegally imported to the island and detained in slavery by Mr. and Mrs. Allan in violation of the British slave trade abolition acts.[1] In a final judgment on James's status on appeal from the Vice-Admiralty Court in Antigua, published in the law reports as *The Slave, Grace* (1827), William Scott, Lord Stowell, Chief Justice of the English High Court of Admiralty, ruled that though James had been free during her residence in England, her enslavement revived upon her return to Antigua. Therefore, she remained the Allans' property.[2]

British abolitionists objected to Stowell's ruling because it enforced a narrow interpretation of an earlier decision in *Somerset v. Stewart* (1772). In that case, William Murray, Lord Mansfield, Chief Justice of the King's Bench, issued a writ of habeas corpus for James Somerset, a fugitive from slavery who had been recaptured in London for deportation and resale in

[1] James reports her flogging and refers to herself as a "free woman of colour" in the petition she submitted to the Colonial Secretary, Lord Bathurst, on August 31, 1825. See "Slaves in the Colonies; Information respecting the Case of a Person Residing in the Island of Antigua, Named Grace James," in *Parliamentary Papers*, vol. 26, *Papers and Correspondence Relating to New South Wales Magistrates; the West Indies; Liberated Africans; Colonial and Slave Populations; Slaves; the Slave Trade* (London: HMSO, 1826), 12, https://babel.hathitrust.org/cgi/pt?id=hvd.32044106490287&seq=433. Hereafter cited as *PP*. The statutes in question are 47 Geo. III c. 36 (1807), 59 Geo. III c. 97 (1819), and both 5 Geo. IV c. 17 and 5 Geo. IV c. 113 (1824). See "British Legislation on Africa and Slavery," *The Statutes Project*, https://statutes.org.uk/site/slavery-law/british-legislation-on-africa-slavery/.

[2] *The Slave, Grace*, (1827) 166 Eng. Rep. 179. Hereafter cited parenthetically in the text as *Grace* by page number in this report.

Jamaica. In response to the claim that Somerset was the property of Charles Stewart (or Steuart), a Scottish-born American merchant, Mansfield reasoned that English law did not allow slavery, so the relationship between Stewart and Somerset must be that of master and servant. Mansfield determined that because a master may not detain his servant and remove him from England, the cause claimed by Stewart was illegal, and therefore, "the black must be discharged." Mansfield's opinion that the state of slavery is "so odious, that nothing can be suffered to support it, but positive law," had a significant influence on later cases concerning enslaved people who traveled or fled into states or territories where slavery lacked a statutory (positive law) basis or had been abolished, particularly in the United States.[3] In his decision in Grace James's case, Lord Stowell acknowledged Mansfield's ruling in *Somerset* that English law did not recognize slavery. But he determined that James's freedom "had totally expired when [her] residence [in England] ceased" (*Grace*, 181). He asserted that enslaved people brought to England "go back with a perfect knowledge of the state which they are to re-enter," implying their consent to re-enslavement (185). The legal action before the court was self-disqualifying because no free subject would ever pursue such a "degrading remedy" by treating herself as an illegally imported commodity (181). By resorting to such a claim, Stowell implied, James had conceded her enslaved status. James's liberty, he observed, could persist only within the territorial "parenthesis" of English law (192).[4]

In a series of cases leading up to and including *Somerset*, antislavery activist Granville Sharp had innovated the use of the writ of habeas corpus to contest the legality of property in slaves on the basis that enslavement amounted to the unlawful, perpetual detention of an English subject.[5]

[3] *Somerset v. Stewart*, (1772) 98 Eng. Rep. 499, 510. This report reprints Capel Lofft's transcription of Chief Justice Mansfield's decision. For the later influence of *Somerset*, see William M. Wiecek, "*Somerset*: Lord Mansfield and the Legitimacy of Slavery in the Anglo-American World," *University of Chicago Law Review* 42 (1974–75): 86–146; and James Oldham, "New Light on Mansfield and Slavery," *Journal of British Studies* 27, no. 1 (January 1988): 45–68.

[4] Studying citations of *The Slave, Grace* in antebellum American cases contesting the recapture of fugitives from Southern slavery, Patricia Hagler Minter details how Stowell's decision became "a definitive rationale for pro-slavery constitutionalism and the portability/nationalization of American slavery." "'The State of Slavery': *Somerset, The Slave, Grace*, and the Rise of Pro-Slavery and Anti-Slavery Constitutionalism in the Nineteenth-Century Atlantic World," *Slavery and Abolition* 36, no. 4 (June 2015): 603–17, at 611.

[5] See Sarah Winter, "From Procedural Law to the 'Rights of Humanity': Habeas Corpus, *Ex parte Somerset* (1771–72), and the Movement toward Collective Representation in Early British Antislavery Cases," in *Empire and Legal Thought: Ideas and Institutions from Antiquity to Modernity*, ed. Edward Cavanagh (Leiden: Brill, 2020), 388–424.

These cases provided a model for later suits brought on novel premises by abolitionist lawyers and enslaved people such as Grace James. But the remedy James sought still considered her as chattel goods, while the Admiralty Courts overseeing customs cases disregarded her natural rights. Situating the case of *The Slave, Grace* within the history of such antislavery legal activism, this chapter foregrounds the ironies and contradictions in the law's conception of English liberty – revealed by James's recourse to legal remedies that were themselves marked by contradictions. The first part of the chapter examines the case records, including both published and unpublished legal opinions, press reports, and correspondence between Antigua authorities and the Colonial Office in London, to explain how James's assertion of her freedom was contested in the Antigua courts and supported by abolitionist lawyers in London. Of particular interest is the notion of "vested rights" that lawyers put forward to prove that James's freedom, once obtained in England, could not be alienated from her person. Also included in papers transmitted to the Colonial Office was James's testimony concerning Mrs. Allan's promise that James would remain free after their return to Antigua. Though it formed the basis of James's claim to freedom, this statement was not cited in the decisions of the Antigua or London Admiralty Courts.

When reported in London newspapers, Stowell's ruling in turn provoked mockery in editorials favoring abolition, as F. O. Shyllon has demonstrated.[6] The second section of the chapter analyzes how these critical editorials construed Stowell's opinion as an invitation to satirical treatment and, in effect, as itself an inadvertent satire on the nonsensical English law of freedom and slavery.[7] While Stowell ridiculed the remedy that James had sought to end her enslavement, these editorials in turn invited readers' skepticism toward the legitimacy of slavery itself. These commentaries made publicly manifest that the imperial law of slavery could summarily transform Grace James from a thing to a person, and then again to a thing, in any temporal order or duration convenient to the court's interpretation of the boundaries of English freedom.

As in the editorial rejoinders to Stowell's decision, satire and irony became key rhetorical strategies in antislavery pamphlets attacking

[6] See F. O. Shyllon, *Black Slaves in Britain* (London: Oxford University Press, 1974), 210–29. Shyllon refers to "Grace Jones," but most primary sources call her "Grace James."

[7] On legal satire by lawyers as "a more or less inexplicit dimension of the legal tradition," see Peter Goodrich, "Satirical Legal Studies: From the Legists to the *Lizard*," *Michigan Law Review* 103, no. 3 (2004), 397–517, at 405. Goodrich argues that "the satirical refers to a genre, a mode of making statements, and not to the intention of the author" (409).

slaveholders' justifications of chattel slavery. To rectify the omission of Grace James's testimony in the court record and reveal the stakes for enslaved people of the legal processes that obscured their agency, the final section of the chapter turns to literary analysis of the narrative of Mary Prince, an enslaved woman originally from Bermuda who was effectively trapped in London by Stowell's ruling after traveling there from Antigua with her purported owners in 1828. *The History of Mary Prince* (1831), dictated by Prince to an amanuensis and edited by the Scottish poet and secretary of the British Anti-Slavery Society, Thomas Pringle, is the only known published account by a woman enslaved in the British West Indies. Prince's oral narrative was reshaped by her editors so that her voice and its effect of authenticity have been described as "artefacts" of the narrative's deployment as abolitionist propaganda.[8] Likewise, Grace James's oral testimony was reshaped by an Antigua lawyer when reported to the Colonial Secretary. Both James's buried testimony and Prince's *History* should nevertheless count as evidence of enslaved people's own efforts to obtain their freedom by testing the inconsistencies of the law of slavery and freedom in the British Empire. In light of the wider satirical responses in the press to Stowell's decision, Prince's vehement criticisms of the slaveholders she knew intimately can also be read as knowingly ironic, and potentially satirical. The flogging of female and elderly slaves, which became synecdochical in antislavery writings for slaveholders' criminality, features prominently in both James's obscure and Prince's published narratives.[9] Prince's accounts of slave floggings present self-consciously stylized features that could be interpreted by metropolitan readers both as antislavery invective and as a subtly satirical response to the conventions of abolitionist publications. Prince's harsh criticisms of the married couple who had transported her from Antigua to London and then expelled her from their household without pay provoked a libel suit against Pringle; Prince's testimony at the trial unveiled her sexual history, which had been suppressed in the published narrative.[10] Despite the editorial intrusions on her narrative and the negative publicity she incurred, when conceived as

[8] See Kerry Sinanan, "The Slave as Cultural 'Artefact': The Case of Mary Prince," *Studies in Eighteenth-Century Culture* 49 (2020): 69–87.

[9] See Henrice Altink, *Representations of Slave Women in Discourses on Slavery and Abolition, 1780–1838* (London: Routledge, 2007), 130.

[10] See Kathryn Temple, *Scandal Nation: Law and Authorship in Britain, 1750–1832* (Ithaca, NY: Cornell University Press, 2003), chap. 4; and Sue Thomas, "*Pringle v. Cadell* and *Wood v. Pringle*: The Libel Cases over *The History of Mary Prince*," *Journal of Commonwealth Literature* 40 (2005): 113–35. Selections from Prince's testimony in the suit are reprinted in Mary Prince, *The History of Mary Prince: A West Indian Slave*, ed. Sara Salih (1831; London: Penguin, 2000), app. 3, 100–03.

legal testimony against slaveholders' criminality and as antislavery satire, Prince's *History* challenges Stowell's insistence that, by returning to their friends and family in the colonies after their temporary emancipation in England, Grace James and others in her circumstances had consented to their re-enslavement.

The Case of Grace James

The formal complaint issued by the Antigua customs office concerning Grace James stated that Mrs. Ann Allan had violated the provisions of England's 1819 and 1824 statutes, amending the original 1807 law abolishing the slave trade. Her alleged violation was to import James into England in 1822 and then back to Antigua in 1823 without providing the required paperwork to customs. In submitting herself for confiscation and forfeiture to the crown, James followed a strategy adopted by several other black Antiguans who had been re-enslaved on their return to Antigua after visiting England or other British territories where slavery was not legal, as documented in correspondence remitted by both the Solicitor General and the Acting Governor of Antigua to the Colonial Secretary, the Tory peer Lord Bathurst.[11] In reaction, the Acting Governor, Samuel Athill, at the direction of his Privy Council, ordered the Vice-Admiralty Court of Antigua to suspend all further action in relation to such cases. According to the minutes of a meeting between Athill and his Privy Council on August 15, 1825, they took this extraordinary step to prevent "a recurrence of such measures so likely to endanger if not totally ... to alienate the inheritance of all of His Majesty's subjects possessing slaves," until they received instructions from Bathurst.[12]

Richard Musgrave, the Antigua Solicitor General, incurred the censure of Athill and his Privy Council when he objected to their interference in his duties, for which, he insisted, he was answerable only to His Majesty's government.[13] Further, these officials allegedly threatened Musgrave with

[11] Others who presented themselves to customs officers included Robert Daniel, William Robday, John Smith, Jack Martin and his sister Rachel, and Ellen Christian and her child Sam; all are mentioned in the Antigua officials' correspondence with the Colonial Office (see *PP*, 26:1–41) or in newspaper reports. For an overview of the case records and litigation, see Stephen Waddams, "The Case of Grace James (1827)," *Texas Wesleyan Law Review* 13, no. 2 (March 2007): 783–94.

[12] *PP*, 26:30–31.

[13] Waddams argues that Musgrave and the customs officers seem to have acted on strong antislavery sentiments. See "Case of Grace James," 787–88. Musgrave was also an indebted plantation owner. He describes his precarious finances and the displeasure of Antigua officials in his August 31, 1826 letter to Lord Bathurst. See *PP*, 26:38.

arrest and obligated him to resign his seat in the Antigua House of Assembly. In a letter to Lord Bathurst on August 31, 1825, Musgrave recounted these reprisals and also complained that the Antigua judges, as interested members of the planter class, were biased and "unrestrained by principles of law, of which they are altogether ignorant."[14] Musgrave defended his own and the customs officers' actions on the basis that the Consolidated Slave Trade Act of 1824 had repealed all previous statutes concerning the slave trade and retroactively authorized prosecution of importations that had occurred before its passage. Thus this statute applied to James's return to Antigua in 1823, despite protests by the aggrieved slaveowners that it could not apply retroactively.[15] In respect to James and another Antiguan, Robert Daniel, who had also been confiscated, Musgrave argued that "the effect of that *virtual* release from the yoke of slavery" taking place on their arrival in England was such that "their right to freedom immediately became so completely vested by operation of law, as to put afterwards out of the power of the former owners ... in any manner to retract, or annex to it, any condition or qualification whatsoever."[16] Although he may be referring to the revival of their natural rights, Musgrave arguably seeks instead a positive legal basis for their freedom by suggesting an analogy with a vested right to property through a bequest, a right which is immediately secured and entitles the legatee to possession for the future. Unlike inherited property, however, vested personal rights to liberty would be permanent, since they are not a thing that can be alienated, and such rights would also negate the slaveholders' prior title.[17]

As a binding precedent for these cases, Musgrave refers to Lord Mansfield's decision in *Somerset*.[18] In addition, Musgrave explains that the confiscations by the customs officers were necessary because, although a writ of habeas corpus would normally issue according to statute in such cases from the Antigua Court of Common Pleas, such a remedy could not

[14] Richard Musgrave to Lord Bathurst, August 31, 1825, in *PP*, 26:15.

[15] Musgrave to Bathurst, August 31, 1825, in *PP*, 26:17. In a petition included in the dispatches to Lord Bathurst, William Bunthorn claims that his slave Robert Daniel should not have been confiscated because his importation to Antigua predated the passage of the 1824 Consolidated Slave Trade Act. See *PP*, 26:33.

[16] *PP*, 26:19.

[17] By putting forward the notion of "vested rights," Musgrave may have intended to avoid asserting a natural rights basis for James's and Daniel's claims to freedom, since their inherent human rights to life and liberty were negated by colonial slave laws and he believed that the Antigua courts were biased toward such laws. William Blackstone briefly discusses such vested rights to a bequest in the second volume of *Commentaries on the Laws of England*. See *Commentaries on the Laws of England*, ed. Wilfrid Prest, bk. 2, *Of the Rights of Things*, ed. Simon Stern (1766; Oxford: Oxford University Press, 2016), 346–47.

[18] *PP*, 26:21.

have been obtained for James and Daniel, since three of the judges served on the Antigua Privy Council that had already advised Athill to suspend further legal action in the cases.[19] Slaveholders' complaints concerning their loss of property, Musgrove avers, should also be disqualified since, in taking enslaved servants to England, they "by their *own voluntary act* induced these consequences which they now seek to avert."[20] While these official consultations were taking place, James and Daniel were held in the custody of the Antigua Collector of Customs.[21]

Responding to these communications on January 21, 1826, Lord Bathurst directed Governor Athill to allow the judicial proceedings in the Vice-Admiralty Court of Antigua to proceed. He insisted that Athill "ought to have recollected that in staying these proceedings [he was] suspending by [his] own authority the course of justice as by law directed to be administered." Since "the liberty of [his] fellow creatures eventually depended" on the outcome, it "was in truth a decision of right . . . for the law to decide." Bathurst anticipated that the decision of the Antigua Vice-Admiralty Court would be duly appealed to the High Court of Admiralty in London, where Lord Stowell, "the most distinguished judge" ever to preside there, would make a final determination in the case.[22]

A copy of the decision of the Antigua Vice-Admiralty Court indicates that the Collector of Customs had registered five counts in relation to James's confiscation, the first four applying to violations under the statutes abolishing the slave trade.[23] The fifth and most important count alleged that James was a free British subject, unlawfully held in slavery in Antigua.[24] In his judgment, dated August 5, 1826, Judge Nicholas Nugent noted the case's importance and acknowledged that *Somerset* authorized James's freedom in England.[25] He presumed that since Grace James had been free during her stay in England, she must have returned to Antigua voluntarily.[26] He determined that the extension of time of forfeiture of an unlawfully imported slave to five years under the Consolidated Slave Trade Act of 1824 applied to future cases, and not retroactively.[27] Warning that a decision on the "very novel, peculiar and . . . anomalous" claim to obtain a

[19] *PP*, 26:25. [20] *PP*, 26:24. [21] *PP*, 26:40. [22] *PP*, 26:40–41.

[23] The National Archives, Kew, United Kingdom, HCA 17/145/1802, 1. This copy of the Antigua Vice-Admiralty Court decision, dated March 23, 1827, was probably the one forwarded to London during the appeal before Chief Justice Stowell. It has not been discussed in the previous scholarship cited here.

[24] Shyllon, *Black Slaves*, 210–11. [25] The National Archives, HCA 17/145/1802, 18.

[26] The National Archives, HCA 17/145/180, 18.

[27] The National Archives, HCA 17/145/180, 23–26. Nugent determined that under the previous Slave Trade Act of 1819, the statute of limitations was two years, meaning that James's confiscation in August 1825 had come too late, since her return to Antigua took place in early 1823.

subject's freedom by means of forfeiture to customs as a "commodity" would test the court's jurisdiction, Judge Nugent stated that without a formal manumission, "there is nothing in the Law of Great Britain or the general law which declares [James] shall be absolved from these civil obligations which by her original condition attached to her in Antigua and which obligations have their root in the inherent social compact under which the colony exists."[28] Allowing that James "could not certainly be compelled to leave Great Britain against her will," Nugent noted,

> It seems to be placing a very slight restriction on an individual emerging from a state of Slavery to Freedom, that it should be only on one small spot of a few miles extent on the whole Earth where he shall be deemed and taken to be a Slave. The rest of the wide world is open before him to roam in without restraint or molestation.[29]

He observed, however, that if the Allans had induced her to return to Antigua "under solemn promises of Freedom," and then violated that implied contract, such an act of "manifest injustice and turpitude" would, if proven, nullify their claim to retain James.[30] Consigning James to her owners with costs and damages, Justice Nugent left the question of the legality of the novel customs case for the High Court of Admiralty to decide.[31]

With the copy of the Vice-Admiralty Court's decision was an affidavit dated July 13, 1826 from John Allan claiming James as his property and stipulating that she had "voluntarily" returned to Antigua with Mrs. Allan.[32] The packet sent by Musgrave to Lord Bathurst, however, included a petition from Grace James signed with her mark and dated August 31, 1825, most likely composed on her evidence by Musgrave.[33] According to her statement,

> when her mistress was about to return to [Antigua], she [James] was induced to accompany her as a servant, considering that by her residence in England she had acquired a right to freedom which had been vested in her, and relying upon the positive promise of her mistress that she should ever after be considered as free . . . . she remained with her mistress as a free

[28] The National Archives, HCA 17/145/180, 26–29.
[29] The National Archives, HCA 17/145/180, 29–30.
[30] The National Archives, HCA 17/145/180, 32.
[31] The National Archives, HCA 17/145/180, 36.
[32] The National Archives, HCA 17/145/180, 12–13.
[33] Waddams suggests that James's petition must have been written by Musgrave, since it bears the same date as Musgrave's letter to Bathurst and repeats his arguments about her vested rights. "Case of Grace James," 787.

> person until a short time since, when having the misfortune to offend her for a trifling cause, she was publicly flogged by her mistress's order on the estate, and told that she was still a slave . . . .[34]

Here James contradicts Justice Nugent's assumption that she had returned to slavery in Antigua voluntarily, and gives a statement that the Allans had broken their promise of freedom to her, implying a breach of contract that might have been actionable in her case. However, her petition seems to have been excluded from the trial record of the Vice-Admiralty Court, most likely because Antigua law and custom did not permit enslaved people to testify in court or by affidavit against white people.[35]

James's testimony that she had been flogged must have alarmed Lord Bathurst, because in May 1823 he had given orders that all flogging of enslaved women cease in Demerara and Berbice, and he had strongly recommended that self-governing West Indian colonies with legislatures enact similar laws or else they would receive a direct order from the king's Privy Council to this effect. Bathurst had issued these orders following a parliamentary resolution in May 1823, proposed by Foreign Minister George Canning, that laws providing for the amelioration of slavery should be passed by colonial legislatures.[36] This action represented the Tory government's support in principle for the gradual abolition of slavery in response to British abolitionists' contention that colonial assemblies would take no significant actions to ameliorate their harsh treatment of enslaved people.[37] After the Colonial Office transmitted in May 1826 a similar set of ameliorative measures couched in the form of heads of bills to be introduced in all West Indian legislatures, the Antigua House of Assembly still took no action.[38] Such West Indian intransigence toward imperial oversight, based on the dual argument that Parliament did not have the authority to legislate internal regulations for self-governing colonies and that such interference would only encourage slave rebellions, forms the political backdrop to the enslaved Antiguans' recourse to the customs office in their quest for a legal remedy for their re-enslavement and mistreatment.

34 *PP*, 26:12.

35 See Natalie Zacek, "Voices and Silences: The Problem of Slave Testimony in the English West Indian Law Court," *Slavery and Abolition* 24, no. 3 (2003): 24–39, at 25. See also Nicole Aljoe, "'Going to Law': Legal Discourse and Testimony in Early West Indian Slave Narratives," *Early American Literature* 46, no. 2 (2011): 351–81.

36 Robert L. Schuyler, *Parliament and the British Empire: Some Constitutional Controversies concerning Imperial Legislative Jurisdiction* (New York: Columbia University Press, 1929), 152–55.

37 Schuyler, *Parliament*, 162–67.

38 Schuyler, *Parliament*, 168–69.

In the second hearing on the appeal before the Admiralty Court in London on June 19, 1827, the King's Advocate, Sir Christopher Robinson, arguing for Grace James, referred to her testimony to dispute the idea that she had consented to return to Antigua:

> It had been said, the return in this case [to Antigua] was voluntary. He was not in a condition to deny this assertion, but he disbelieved it; and he thought the Judge in the court below, who had admitted that had the return been involuntary, the case would be changed, ought to have probed this point deeper. He [Robinson] would not believe that the act was voluntary; and as a point in the history of the case, he was entitled to state that the woman had denied to the Governor that she had willingly returned.[39]

In her petition, which was forwarded to the Colonial Office, James did not mention being forced to return to Antigua. Counsel for the Allans objected to Robinson's statement, possibly because this testimony had not been included in the trial record, and Lord Stowell declared that he would not take it into consideration.[40] Stowell noted that he had read the relevant correspondence with the Colonial Secretary and the records of the lower court decision (*Grace*, 179). However, despite Robinson's suggestion that James had been kidnapped, the Antigua Vice-Admiralty Court's silence concerning James's petition to Bathurst likely contributed to the omission of her sworn testimony in the later arguments by counsel before Lord Stowell and in his final judgment.[41] Robinson's questioning of the lower court's assumptions concerning James's voluntary return was nevertheless conveyed to the reading public through the press reports on the trial.[42] His protest underscores the gap in evidence concerning James's role in asserting her freedom.

In the subsequent hearing on June 26, 1827, Dr. Stephen Lushington, who served as counsel for the British Anti-Slavery Society, argued on behalf of the crown and for the appellants (Grace James and Robert Daniel) that Lord Mansfield's judgment in *Somerset* that slavery could not exist except when established by positive law should be upheld in this case. No municipal or statutory law in either England or Antigua required

[39] "Court of Common Pleas, Westminster, June 19," *Times* (London), June 20, 1827.

[40] "Court of Common Pleas, Westminster, June 19." Robinson's allegation excited protests and commentary in the press, however. See Edlie L. Wong, *Neither Fugitive nor Free: Atlantic Slavery, Freedom Suits, and the Legal Culture of Travel* (New York: New York University Press, 2009), 45.

[41] Perhaps James's petition to Lord Bathurst was never submitted to the court, or perhaps the court received but ignored it.

[42] On the press response to Robinson's allegations, see Wong, *Neither Fugitive nor Free*, 45.

that a person should "relapse into slavery" upon return to the colony where they were enslaved. Lushington asserted that the treatment of James and others as slaves upon return from England to Antigua, even if defended as customary law, was a bad custom that, according to a common-law maxim, must be abolished (*malus usus abolendus est*). Such a relapse into slavery would also violate equity and conscience. Responding to Justice Nugent's comments that James could have resided anywhere else and remained free, Lushington objected:

> [W]as she forever to be excluded from her place of birth? . . . Was it agreeable to conscience, that, if she returned to her native soil to see a sick parent, she became a slave? It was well to say, all is free save one little spot; but that little spot contained all that was dear; the world beside might be a desert.[43]

The lower court's determination that the time limit for action under the slave trade abolition acts prior to 1824 stood at two years did not apply in this case, he concluded, because a fundamental right to personal freedom was at stake.[44]

Lushington referred several times to Chief Justice Mansfield's jurisprudence as "the polar star in all these questions." In the *Somerset* decision, Lushington paraphrased, Mansfield had stated, "I cannot admit slavery without admitting all the consequences of slavery." On this basis, Lushington added, "the converse of this . . . was equally true. The admission of freedom was attended with all the consequences of freedom. No man could come to this country [England] without freedom attaching to him, . . . never to be taken away."[45] Here Lushington echoes Musgrave's notion of James's "vested right" to freedom.[46] Although this concept may have implied a natural law basis as an inherent right to freedom revived by residence in England, by construing James's acquired freedom as analogous to a property right, this concept of a "vested right" would counter both the legal title to property in a slave and the colonial law of chattel slavery as an inherited status from birth, which was itself an inversion of the English legal and political concept of birthright subjecthood or citizenship.[47]

43 "Court of Common Pleas, Westminster, June 26," *Times*, June 27, 1827.
44 "Court of Common Pleas, Westminster, June 26."
45 "Court of Common Pleas, Westminster, June 26."
46 American lawyers defending fugitives from Southern slavery would also point to their "vested right" to freedom in antebellum cases. See Minter, "State of Slavery," 612, 615n15, 617n32.
47 The terms "subject" and "citizen" are not fully interchangeable and speak to a specific historical development. On the history of birthright citizenship, see Polly J. Price, "Natural Law and Birthright Citizenship in *Calvin's Case* (1608)," *Yale Journal of Law and the Humanities* 9, no. 1 (Winter 1997): 73–146.

Replying to Robinson and Lushington in the final hearing on July 24, Dr. Jenner, defending the lower court's decision, argued that English common law did not apply in the case, since slavery had been recognized and permitted when the colony of Antigua was founded, even if it had never been formally enacted by statute. Lord Stowell added that English courts had upheld property in slaves in the colonies, and slaves had always been treated as chattels or things. Jenner insisted that the Allans' title had been established by Grace James's birth into slavery in Antigua. Making a paternalistic claim that would have been precluded if James's testimony concerning the Allans' broken promise of freedom had appeared in the lower court record, Jenner declared that "the Court was called upon for the first time to determine that a slave, not attempting to vindicate her freedom, was to be deprived of all aid and support from a family upon whom she now depended for maintenance." He warned that if the Admiralty Court reversed the lower court's decision, offspring of enslaved women who had returned from England would be emancipated, threatening the West Indian system of chattel slavery as a heritable status.[48] Since Robinson's statement concerning James's claim to freedom had been suppressed, Jenner's assertion that she was dependent on the Allans could not be refuted.

Chief Justice Stowell issued his ruling on November 6, 1827. With considerable scorn for the appellants' case, he upheld the lower court's decision. He ridiculed the customs agents' confiscations of James, Daniels, and other petitioners as contraband forfeited to the king, suggesting that such a remedy was, in effect, begging the question of their freedom, and "humiliating to a freeman": "It is a process very fit for the emancipation of a slave, but surely could never be recommended to a person already in possession of a state of liberty freely and fairly acquired" (*Grace*, 181). The remedy "betrays its imbecility" because the normal treatment in the case of contraband slaves, who are, after confiscation, generally "bound to some trade or enlisted in the army," is "only a transit from one species of slavery to another" (182). In this way, Stowell exposed a further contradiction in the legal remedy sought by the enslaved Antiguans: Far from liberating captives, the slave trade abolition laws only bound them over into another sort of obligatory service. Instead of resorting to such a nonsensical remedy, Stowell declared, "a free person" would "bring his action against the defamer of his rights . . . and who can doubt but that he would recover most overwhelming damages against the person who had assaulted his

[48] "Court of King's Bench, Tuesday, July 24," *Times*, July 25, 1827.

freedom, and compelled him to submit to a process that is only applicable to a slave" (181–82). Referencing *Somerset*, Stowell expressed his astonishment that, if it had applied to cases of enslaved people returning to the colonies, no one had ever taken advantage of it before this case (185). Moreover, slavery could not be a *malus usus* (a bad custom) since it was upheld by the king's Privy Council and the High Court of Chancery "every day … in all considerations of property" (190). Unlike inalienable natural rights, which were ignored in any case by the court, "vested rights" in liberty seemed to evaporate when weighed in the balance with the more substantial commercial jurisprudence of empire and private property.

While upholding Parliament's authority as the "general sovereign" (192) of its subject colonies and denying West Indian claims to self-governance, Stowell reserves his greatest contempt for those advocates of abolition who, by pursuing this cause, would seek to overturn slavery through "a very cheap measure here [in England] by throwing the whole expense on the colony," when in fact slavery is "in a peculiar manner the crime of this country," and if abolished by Parliament, it should be "only at the expense of both countries" (191). Stowell implies that statutes ameliorating slavery in the colonies amounted to a kind of national hypocrisy. France, he concludes, had at least been more consistent by discouraging the importation of enslaved people into the mother country from the colonies and declaring by edict that slaves brought to France are still bound to service there (192).[49] In contrast, by failing to clarify this question Britain has "put [slaves'] liberty, as it were, into a sort of parenthesis" (192).

In affirming the lower court's ruling, the judgment should have returned James to the Allans with costs for the litigation, although Stowell refused to address this issue explicitly.[50] *The Times* reported on March 13, 1828 that the Admiralty Court, under its new Chief Justice, Sir

[49] Stowell refers to the edict of October 1716, which enabled travelers from French colonies to retain their ownership of enslaved domestic servants brought to France, but also gave these servants a statutory basis to sue for their freedom in French courts if their purported owners failed to comply with other regulations under the edict. See Sue Peabody, *"There Are No Slaves in France": The Political Culture of Race and Slavery in the Ancien Régime* (Oxford: Oxford University Press, 1997), 15–18.

[50] Waddams, "Case of Grace James," 790. Robert Daniel's re-enslavement was decided at the same time. The companion Antigua customs case for John Smith and his sister Rachel, who had returned from Gibraltar to Antigua via Barbados in 1818, was decided separately. Here the King's Advocate found evidence that the Smiths' return to Antigua had been based on a written promise of emancipation. However, Lord Stowell determined that the promise was not signed by the owner of the two slaves, so the manumission was invalid. "Court of Common Pleas, Westminster, Dec. 8," *Times*, December 10, 1827. Minter discusses an additional plaintiff, Jack Martin. See "State of Slavery," 614nn5–6.

Christopher Robinson, the former King's Advocate in James's case, had determined that "the restitution should be the value . . . and not the person of the slave."[51] This final verdict likely secured James's liberty, but perhaps only in exile from Antigua, within the legal "parenthesis" of Britain's borders.[52]

The agency of enslaved people and the ambiguous legal personhood assigned to them in the British Empire came in and out of focus in Stowell's opinion, according to his tactics in proving a particular point. By asserting James's "perfect knowledge" (*Grace*, 185) of the enslavement she would return to, the judgment subverted her legal claim to a "vested right" of freedom because she had "voluntarily" voided this right by returning to Antigua. Stowell showed that such acquired rights, even if they existed, could be "divested" by a change in residence. As Edlie L. Wong has argued, by insisting on Grace's "voluntary" return, Stowell's decision also "paradoxically impos[ed] a model of contract on slaves, who became legal persons only as a matter of form."[53] To sequester James's freedom and *Somerset*'s sway within Britain's borders, Stowell silently determined that she was entitled only to choose whether to stay in England or return, but that once she acted upon this choice, her freedom "expired" and she "relapsed" into her status as a chattel or thing upon return to Antigua. This was the legal implication, for Stowell, of James's resort to a disqualifying confiscation as a "commodity." Manifestly, however, it was only the law that changed James from thing to person and then again to thing, even though James herself was self-evidently the same individual, capable of the same capacity for "perfect knowledge" and volition. Because her decision to approach the Antigua customs officers as well as her story of Mrs. Allan's broken promise were never acknowledged by the court, this continuity of James's personality and volition could be assumed by the court and, at the same time, ignored.

Press Responses to Stowell's Inadvertent Legal Satire

By supplying pointed "ridicule of folly and vices that have a social significance and ill effect," satirical writing was a key tactic of early

51 "In the Matter of the Slave Grace," *Times*, March 13, 1828.

52 An analogous ruling to *Somerset* in Scotland was *Knight v. Wedderburn* (1778), discussed in John W. Cairns, "After *Somerset:* The Scottish Experience," *Journal of Legal History* 33, no. 3 (December 2012): 291–312. James was thus free only within Britain's borders. Waddams surmises that James's vulnerability to punishment by the Allans made the crown prosecutors and Lushington anxious to secure her freedom. See "Case of Grace James," 793. It is unclear whether James had traveled to England during the appeal and was obliged to remain there or whether her freedom was purchased in Antigua.

53 Wong, *Neither Fugitive nor Free*, 39.

nineteenth-century legal and political reformers.[54] Earnest Christian abolitionists typically relied more on appeals to sentiment than on satire. But the legal transformations of Grace James from person to thing opened up Stowell's judgment to satirical treatments in the press, and even to its interpretation as itself a satire of the English law of freedom and slavery, in its implications if not its intent. Multiple newspapers in London and in the West Indies published Stowell's decision in full, while others abbreviated it, making it widely available.[55] While various editorials disagreed about the justice of the ruling, opinions on both sides mocked the idea that freedom once gained by a British subject could be lost by their departure from England.[56] According to an editorial in *The Sunday Times* sympathetic to the abolition of slavery, the decision "strikes us as manifestly absurd":

> Let us define what we mean by freedom. To what kind of constitutional freedom is the slave who touches the English shores intitled? Is it Austrian, French, Turkish freedom? Is it some Lunarian or Laputan freedom of which nobody ever heard or read except in a romance? Is it some qualified or conditional freedom, intangible by common reasoning, expiring, like a Lord Mayor's title, at the end of a certain period; or, like Cinderella's triumph, when the clock strikes twelve? Certainly not. He is intitled to English freedom, which is permanent and unalienable, integral, and perfectly defined.[57]

According to the writer, Stowell's judgment transforms the "judicial dogma" that an enslaved person's chains fall away once they arrive on English shores to its absurd opposite, by restoring their chains. In fact this result "is what the logicians term a solecism, or contradiction in terms – the proposition destroying itself."[58] With its comparisons to Jonathan Swift's famous satire of British rule over Ireland in *Gulliver's Travels* (1726), as well as to fairy tales, the editorial implies that Stowell's decision itself should be read, in the words of another editorial, as a "*reductio ad absurdum*," an unintentional caricature of the vaunted superiority of English freedom itself.[59] An editorial in *The New Times* similarly wondered "if the retrograding process, which the doctrine of Lord Stowell lays down, really takes place, it would be a curious question to discover its degrees. The flame of freedom, we suppose, begins to decay in brilliance as the weather grows warm, droops in the socket as the latitude

54 Goodrich, "Satirical Legal Studies," 399.
55 Shyllon, *Black Slaves*, 225n5.
56 Shyllon, *Black Slaves*, 212–20.
57 *The Sunday Times*, November 11, 1827, quoted in Shyllon, *Black Slaves*, 214.
58 *The Sunday Times*, November 11, 1827, quoted in Shyllon, *Black Slaves*, 216.
59 *John Bull*, November 18, 1827, quoted in Shyllon, *Black Slaves*, 217.

diminishes, and expires when the ship crosses the Tropic!"[60] Reducing the illustrious light of English freedom to an expiring candle, the spoof highlights its territorial and temporary nature by implying that rights expire with the passage of time, or according to climate and degrees of latitude, all of which limitations stood in for imperial jurisdictions and distinctions of race and status. A letter from "Matius," published in *John Bull* and sympathetic to the West Indian planters, correspondingly mocked the slave's acquisition of freedom by traveling to England: "[C]onsistently with that law as at present understood, may not one ... ask, at what precise stages of his voyage from Jamaica to Great Britain, [he] progressively sloughs off all his habits and dependencies as a slave, and becomes, precisely as he advances to the northward, more and more liberated and enlightened?"[61] For those on both sides of the abolition question, the law of freedom and slavery as it stood after Stowell's ruling seemed to parody itself.

By refusing to vest James's possession of freedom permanently and beyond British shores, Stowell had unveiled the legal and territorial restrictions that could be placed on English rights more generally. These critical press responses indicate that, in the years leading up to the 1833 Slavery Abolition Act, white metropolitan readers, when they were not sympathetic to West Indian interests, were increasingly offended by legal decisions concerning slavery that dented the reputation of the English liberty enjoyed by free British citizens.

Antislavery Satire in Mary Prince's *History*

Reading Prince's *History* can help us better understand both the legal questions and the contradictions at the heart of Grace James's case. Even as Stowell's decision revealed the futility of successive parliamentary efforts to curb West Indian slaveholders' customary violence, it also removed any question of criminal liability for slaveholders like the Allans for their abuses of enslaved people by depicting the institution of slavery as a "national crime."[62]

60 *The New Times*, November 9, 1827, quoted in Shyllon, *Black Slaves*, 217.

61 *John Bull*, November 18, 1827, quoted in Shyllon, *Black Slaves*, 218.

62 In a January 1828 letter to American judge Joseph Story asking his opinion of the decision in *The Slave, Grace*, Stowell called himself a "rather stern Abolitionist" in regard to the slave trade. Stowell's suggestion that slavery abolition should involve financial compensation to slaveowners discredits strategies for slavery abolition through the courts, but does not indicate whether he supported parliamentary abolition. Story replied to approve Stowell's reasoning. See Waddams, "Case of Grace James," 791–93.

By contrast, Prince's account of her life named living slaveholders, thus holding them publicly accountable and indirectly indicting the courts, officials, and laws that supported their legal impunity. Her words, though hedged by the text's editorial apparatus, make Prince "a representative of that vast mass of enslaved people in the British West Indies who had no opportunity to tell their stories to the British public," and, more specifically, offer insight into Grace James's motivations for her suit.[63]

The History of Mary Prince was a work of joint authorship that was initiated by Prince herself. She dictated her narrative of her life to Susanna Strickland, an author and friend of the Pringle family, who employed Prince as a domestic servant in their London home.[64] Prince met Thomas Pringle when she visited the office of the British Anti-Slavery Society in Aldermanbury looking for assistance and work in August 1828. She had been forced to leave the service of the Wood family, who had brought her with them from Antigua to London earlier that year as a nursemaid to one of their children, but who had instead demanded that she work without pay as a laundrywoman, despite her severe rheumatic symptoms.[65] In his editorial preface, Pringle notes that "the narrative was taken down from Mary's own lips" and "written out fully, with all the narrator's repetitions and prolixities." For publication, the transcript was "afterwards pruned into its present shape; retaining, as far as was practicable, Mary's exact expressions and peculiar phraseology," though Pringle admits that grammar was regularized "to render it clearly intelligible."[66] Pringle published the *History* at his own expense, rather than under the auspices of the Anti-Slavery Society, so that the profits could be dedicated to Prince's support. The text was commercially successful, going into three editions within the first year.[67] While its recasting by Pringle and Strickland has caused many critics to doubt its authenticity, Prince's narrative, given her ability to read, likely represents her words more reliably than did Musgrave's lawyerly redaction of Grace James's petition.[68] The two women shared common

[63] Clare Midgley, *Women against Slavery: The British Campaigns, 1780–1870* (London: Routledge, 1992), 89.

[64] On Prince's initiative to contribute her story to the cause of slavery abolition, see Thomas Pringle, "Preface," in Prince, *History*, ed. Salih, 3–5, at 3.

[65] Prince's rheumatism may have been due to her arduous work over ten years in the salt ponds on Turk's Island (present-day Turks and Caicos Islands). See Prince, *History*, ed. Salih, 18–23, 31–36.

[66] Pringle, "Preface," 3.

[67] Ryan Hanley, *Beyond Slavery and Abolition: Black British Writing c. 1770–1830* (Cambridge: Cambridge University Press, 2019), 88–89.

[68] For an overview of scholarship questioning the authenticity of Prince's voice, see Sinanan, "Slave as Cultural 'Artefact.'" Prince recounts how she was taught to read by Moravian missionaries in Antigua after she joined their church, explaining that "I got on very fast." See *History*, ed. Salih, 29.

circumstances: The ruling in *The Slave, Grace* (1827), which Prince almost certainly must have learned of from the Pringles, also prevented her from returning to her husband in Antigua, Daniel James, a free man of color.[69] When approached by politician members of the Anti-Slavery Committee, including Dr. Lushington, the Woods refused to allow them to purchase Prince's freedom so that she could return home, and they also became alarmed by the prospect that a petition for Prince's freedom would be presented in the House of Commons.[70] Though James's place of residence after her court case ended is unknown, Prince was suffering the gradual failure of her eyesight at the time of publication of her *History*, so she most likely remained in paid service with the Pringles in London, though she may have returned to Antigua after the Slavery Abolition Act took effect in 1834.[71]

Prince frequently treats the injustice of her enslavement with irony, demonstrating her critical consciousness and sharpening her accusations concerning the cruelty and violence of slave owners.[72] In recounting her childhood, she exposes the warped domestic life of the slaveholding family through an ironic treatment of the idea of "home." Born on a farm in Brackish-Pond, Bermuda, Prince grew up with her mother and siblings in the household of Captain and Mrs. Williams, who was a kind mistress. But after Mrs. Williams died, the captain decided to sell some of his slaves in order to cover the cost of his remarriage. Shocked and grief-stricken at the prospect of being separated from her family, Prince describes her terror on being sold at the age of twelve with two of her sisters at a public auction. She recounts her mother's final instructions to her daughters, who were to be separated from each other: "When the sale was over, my mother hugged and kissed us, and mourned over us, begging of us to keep up a good heart, and do our duty to our new masters. It was a sad parting; one went one way, one another, and our poor mammy went home with nothing."[73] Prince's telling juxtaposition of "mother" and "home," both icons of domestic value, ironizes them by their equivalence with "nothing," implying not only the

69 For analysis of the two women's parallel circumstances, see Wong, *Neither Fugitive nor Free*, 48–54. On the legal complexity of enslaved West Indian women's marriages, see Katherine Paugh, "The Curious Case of Mary Hylas: Wives, Slaves, and the Limitations of British Abolitionism," *Slavery and Abolition* 35, no. 4 (2014): 629–51.

70 "Supplement to the History of Mary Prince, by the Editor [Thomas Pringle]," in Prince, *History*, ed. Salih, 39–63, at 40–41. The petition to the Commons for Prince's freedom produced no result. See Salih, introduction to *History*, ed. Salih, vii–xxxiv, at xi.

71 Pringle, "Postscript – Second Edition," in Prince, *History*, ed. Salih, 4–5, at 4.

72 On enslaved people's critical consciousness and resistance, see Saidiya V. Hartman, *Scenes of Subjection: Terror, Slavery, and Self-Making in Nineteenth-Century America* (New York: Oxford University Press, 1997).

73 Prince, *History*, ed. Salih, 12.

heartbreak and deprivation of the enslaved family, but also the absence of human compassion from the white slaveholders, who routinely inflicted such suffering to fund their household expenses.

Like Grace James, Prince underwent routine floggings and witnessed the brutal beatings of other enslaved men, women, and children, in some cases, to death. Moira Ferguson points out that such scenes were "standard features" of slave narratives and argues that Prince's accounts of floggings resemble "the format of cases reported in the *Anti-Slavery Reporter*, the press organ of the Anti-Slavery Society," suggesting Pringle's editorial influence.[74] A letter written by Mrs. Pringle testifying to her inspection of Prince's scarred back was read to an audience of women members at a meeting of the Anti-Slavery Society in April 1831, and included in the *History* as an appendix.[75] Such intrusive authentication of Prince's story contrasts with the critical and objective edge that her narrative of her flogging brought to this formula intended to recruit women to the cause of abolition.[76] She focalizes the scene through her own eyes, presenting a view of her abuser that taxonomizes the white "master" as a common species displaying variations on a customary behavior:

> Though we worked from morning till night, there was no satisfying Mr D—. I hoped, when I left Capt. I—, that I should have been better off, but I found it was but going from one butcher to another. There was this difference between them: my former master used to beat me while raging and foaming with passion; Mr D— was usually quite calm. He would stand by and give orders for a slave to be cruelly whipped, and assist in the punishment, without moving a muscle of his face; walking about and taking snuff with the greatest composure. Nothing could touch his hard heart – neither sighs, nor tears, nor prayers, nor streaming blood; he was deaf to our cries, and careless of our sufferings. – Mr D— has often stripped me naked, hung me up by the wrists, and beat me with the cow-skin, with his own hand, till my body was raw with gashes. Yet there was nothing very remarkable in this; for it might serve as a sample of the common usage of the slaves on that horrible [Turk's Island].[77]

This depiction, both precisely anatomical and appealing to the reader's horror and sympathy through invocations of the sufferers' sighs, prayers, and blood, presents the reader with a case study of the brutal and sadistic

[74] Moira Ferguson, introduction to *The History of Mary Prince: A West Indian Slave, Related by Herself*, ed. Moira Ferguson, rev. ed. (Ann Arbor: University of Michigan Press, 1997), 1–51, at 24.

[75] See Prince, *History*, ed. Salih, 64, 87n1.

[76] On women's role in abolitionism and as the target audience for Prince's narrative, see Midgley, *Women against Slavery*; and Hanley, *Beyond Slavery and Abolition*, 90–91.

[77] Prince, *History*, ed. Salih, 20.

abuser, who unknowingly reveals himself to his victim as a unique individual in his furious affect or lack thereof while inflicting pain, but whom Prince classifies as a common type.[78] By subtly revising the abolitionist formula which would cast her as the victim, Prince's narrative also deflects the reader's voyeurism and takes narrative control of the scene, depicting herself as an active observer and not simply a stripped and beaten female body exploited in abolitionist propaganda to arouse indignation and support for antislavery campaigns. Though it is unlikely that Prince was familiar with political satire, this scene presents a quasi-caricature of slaveowners that could have reminded readers of the lawyers and politicians caricatured by radical satirists like William Hone.[79] Pringle may have reshaped Prince's account to emphasize its typification of the criminal slaveholder. But a sympathetic reader's interpretation of the scene as a subtle satire of abolitionist propaganda could have been supported by its larger context in the antislavery press and pamphlet debates. Prince's accounts of floggings also provide testimony with a legal bearing, holding up for condemnation the criminal torture of enslaved fellow humans that Lord Stowell declined even to stigmatize as a *malus usus* because of his determination that imperial commerce, administration, and jurisprudence all sanctioned slavery in the colonies. Prince's flogging scene thus supplements Grace James's missing testimony and helps us understand why James voluntarily turned herself over as contraband to vindicate her status as a "free woman of colour" and escape such assaults.

Similarly emphasizing her determination and critical consciousness, Prince reveals how she decided to leave the Woods' service in London, after Mrs. Wood repeatedly threatened to expel her because she was unable to manage the backbreaking work of laundering clothes for the entire household:

> She said, she supposed I thought myself a free woman, but I was not; and if I did not do it directly I should be instantly turned out of doors. I stood a long time before I could answer, for I did not know well what to do. I knew that I was free in England, but I did not know where to go, or how to get my living; ... But Mr Wood said he would send for a constable to thrust me out; and at last I took course and resolved that I would not be longer thus treated, but would go and trust to Providence.[80]

[78] On satire blended with sentimentalism, see Lynn Festa, "Satire to Sentiment: Mixing Modes in the Later Eighteenth-Century British Novel," in *The Oxford Handbook of Eighteenth-Century Satire*, ed. Paddy Bullard (Oxford: Oxford University Press, 2019), 645–60.

[79] See Marcus Wood, *Radical Satire and Print Culture, 1790–1822* (Oxford: Clarendon Press, 1994).

[80] Prince, *History*, ed. Salih, 33.

Mrs. Wood's claim that Prince was not free matches James's account of Mrs. Allan's reassertion of ownership in Antigua after flogging her. Prince's recollection of her resentment at the injustice of this treatment, "after I had lived with them for thirteen years, and worked for them like a horse, to be driven out in this way, like a beggar,"[81] exposes the structural irony of the Antigua Vice-Admiralty Court's determination that Grace James had been free to "roam . . . without restraint or molestation" in England, a place where she too would have lacked work, home, and family. Though the Woods intended to trap Prince in an impossible choice either to accept continued duress or to starve in the streets, she "resolved" instead to exercise her limited mobility and right to seek paid work as a "free woman of colour" in London and lend her support to abolishing slavery.

Conclusion

By criticizing the affront to the legal status of the free person caused by Grace James's treatment as contraband for the purposes of liberating her from slavery, Lord Stowell inadvertently exposed the weak jurisdiction of the English High Courts over imperial governance in the colonies to a British public increasingly skeptical about the legitimacy of slavery, and to a West Indian planter class defiant against parliamentary efforts to reform their legal license to abuse enslaved people. Prince's depiction of the white slaveholders she knew as a criminal class of petulant, frenzied, and relentless "butchers," though less influential in her own time, appears today as much more prescient of future political struggles, and thus more consequential, than Lord Stowell's now obscure judgment in *The Slave, Grace*. Through caustic humor and somber irony, newspaper editorials and Prince's narrative illustrated the unjust consequences of the decision's legal "*reductio ad absurdum*," read by critics as an unintentional satire of an English freedom deemed compatible with legalized slavery. Responding to Stowell's judgment within the wider abolition debates, Pringle's publication of Prince's *History* mobilized her accusations against individual slaveowners and her hopes in exile to secure her liberty and right to travel.

By combining methods of legal history and literary analysis, this chapter has attempted to restore the testimonies of enslaved people like Grace James whose voices were silenced and whose agency was overlooked in official legal processes. Prince's choice to publish her life story demonstrates how enslaved people could implement abolitionist legal strategies

[81] Prince, *History*, ed. Salih, 33.

and politics, and use print culture, to contest the ambiguous freedom they could only secure in Britain without paying their enslavers. Even as the vaunted English liberty could be undone by its containment within the "parentheses" of legal decisions and territorial borders, it could also be demanded as a right through oral testimony and the printed word by resolute witnesses to the crimes of slavery such as James and Prince.

CHAPTER 11

Yearning for Restriction in the Romantic Novel

Propagating Conservative Legal Norms in Right-Wing Literary Podcasts and Religion-Centered Editions of Works by Jane Austen and Mary Shelley

Nicole Mansfield Wright

"The real battle for America's soul is not waged in legislative halls but in lecture halls. Congratulations to the courageous souls at Ignatius Press for firing off what is nothing less than a direct hit in the culture war," Christopher Check, the Executive Vice President of the Rockford Institute, a conservative think tank, declares in his endorsement of the Ignatius Critical Editions, a right-wing Catholic series featuring some of the most renowned classics of English literature. He elaborates: "For too long, the Western Canon has been co-opted by those who, in fact, hate the West and the three things for which she stands: the good, the beautiful, and the true. These magnificent editions, edited by a scholar who loves all three, belong on the shelves of every campus bookstore, every high-school classroom, and every home school."[1] In implying that students and instructors wield more power than Congress does to shape the nation's "soul," Check expresses a view long propounded by some of the most influential conservative donors, including the Koch, Olin, and Scaife families.[2] Donors anticipate a substantial return on their investments in educational ventures: a rising cohort of young adults who will carry conservative perspectives into sites that shape America's laws, ranging from

[1] See Christopher Check, quoted in "Editorial Reviews," Ignatius Press, https://ignatius.com/frankenstein-7fp/. The reviews in this section appear to refer to the Ignatius Critical Editions as a series, rather than to particular editions.

[2] See Jane Mayer, *Dark Money: The Hidden History of the Billionaires behind the Rise of the Radical Right* (New York: Penguin Random House, 2017); Nancy MacLean, *Democracy in Chains: The Deep History of the Radical Right's Stealth Plan for America* (New York: Viking, 2017); Jack Crosbie, "Charles Koch Fellowship Institute Funds Journalists," *Columbia Journalism Review*, December 6, 2018, www.cjr.org/watchdog/charles-koch-institute-fellowship-journalism.php; Jack Lubbock, "How Charles Koch Funds a Roster of Young Right Wingers at Young Voices UK," *Left Foot Forward*, January 12, 2022; Jennifer De Forest, "The Rise of Conservatism on Campus: The Role of the John M. Olin Foundation," *Change: The Magazine of Higher Learning* 38, no. 2 (2006): 32–37; and Erin Cady, "The John M. Olin Fellowships and the Advancement of Conservatism in Legal Academia," *Harvard Journal of Law and Public Policy* 39 (2016): 917–62.

voting booths to jury benches, academia, law firms, and judges' chambers. In 2007, the legal scholar Benjamin Wittes warned of "the dark side of a strange youth culture in the conservative legal establishment, one that offers extraordinary opportunities to people at bizarrely young ages."[3] He lamented that from the early 2000s, powerful conservatives were cultivating law graduates and "jumping [them] over hundreds of better-qualified lawyers" to eminent positions in federal agencies and the judiciary. Recently, this trend has accelerated.[4] Other initiatives, such as the *National Review*'s "Great Books" podcast, strive to amplify the voices of scholars from conservative institutions beyond lecture halls, piping them into the AirPods of educated professionals who are not the core demographic of "shock jock" talk radio and partisan news channels.

How do conservative donors and publishers seek to shape students' legal worldviews? They have adopted a long-term approach that complements short-term tactics such as campaign advertisements and viral social media content. Producing conservative textbooks and editions of canonical literature has been central to their endeavor. This chapter considers deliberations over personal autonomy in renditions of British Romantic-era novels by two ventures that target conservative audiences: the Ignatius Press's Ignatius Critical Editions and the "Great Books" podcast of the long-standing conservative magazine *National Review*. The chapter focuses on three novels featured by both ventures: Jane Austen's *Pride and Prejudice* (1813) and *Mansfield Park* (1814), and Mary Shelley's *Frankenstein; or, The Modern Prometheus* (1818). Both ventures reflect conservatives' long-term campaign to reshape popular and academic discourse on legal norms and ideas of justice, but not by submitting their work to mainstream academic publications: Instead, conservatives are developing a "walled-garden" alternative to conventional academic venues.[5] The Ignatius Critical Editions are aimed at high school and college students, whom conservative tastemakers deem an

[3] Benjamin Wittes, "The Conservative Legal Establishment's Strange Youth Culture," *Brookings*, May 28, 2007, www.brookings.edu/opinions/the-conservative-legal-establishments-strange-youth-culture/.

[4] See, for example, Amanda Hollis-Brusky and Celia Parry, "'In the Mold of Justice Scalia': The Contours and Consequences of the Trump Judiciary," *The Forum* 19, no. 1 (Berlin: De Gruyter, 2021): 117–42; and Jennifer Rubin, "A Counterintuitive Insight about Really Young Judges," *Washington Post*, March 6, 2019, www.washingtonpost.com/opinions/2019/03/06/counterintuitive-insight-about-really-young-judges/.

[5] As Salil K. Mehra explains, "[T]he term 'walled garden' has become an epithet to epitomize a proprietary (and likely sterile) community." "Paradise Is a Walled Garden? Trust, Antitrust, and User Dynamism," *George Mason Law Review* 18, no. 4 (Summer 2011): 889–952, at 889.

especially impressionable yet elusive demographic.[6] The "Great Books" podcast seeks to expand the reach of conservative scholars beyond their home institutions.

Conservatives have long asserted that teachers and professors motivated by a progressive political agenda are introducing students to harmful ideas that run counter to conservative tenets. Donors frame the programs they fund as a means of countering that influence. Indeed, advertisements during the "Great Books" podcast warn that "leftist teachers and administrators are indoctrinating the next generation [of students]"; the advertisements encourage listeners to apply for free membership packs for "the conservative student in your life."[7] Questions of personal autonomy are particularly salient in conservative content attempting to influence students, voters, and other target audiences, with legal ramifications ranging from civil rights to criminal justice, protected speech, and reproductive rights.

Conservatives tend to regard pre-1900 canonical British literature as a treasure to be safeguarded for at least two reasons. First, this literature is deemed a manifestation of the exceptional cultural achievements of the West.[8] Second, it is seen as a bulwark against societal change. Responding to a popular magazine's proposal to dethrone some classic novels and replace them with newer works by less canonical, female, and minority authors, one conservative journalist asserted in 2018: "The brave new world that the cultural left wishes to establish cannot come about as long as 'folklore' (which includes art, literature, history, and other sources of national identity) remains rooted in the ideas and values of the Judeo-Christian West."[9]

Conservative scholars feel sidelined by discourse in the humanities and social sciences, and non-specialist conservative audiences are puzzled or

[6] See, for example, Isaac Schorr, "A Wake-Up Call for Conservatives," *National Review*, April 14, 2021, www.nationalreview.com/2021/04/a-wake-up-call-for-conservatives/.

[7] John J. Miller, "Episode 232: *William Tell* by Friedrich Schiller," *National Review*, "Great Books" podcast, June 14, 2022, at 17:57, www.nationalreview.com/podcasts/the-great-books/episode-232-william-tell-by-friedrich-schiller/.

[8] See, for example, Joseph Epstein, "Don't Fire the Western Canon," *National Review*, December 27, 2021, 31–33. In qualifying his celebration of the "superiority of the Western canon" by acknowledging, "I do not know enough about Chinese or Indian or Islamic culture to argue that they pale beside the Western canon" (31), Epstein echoes some earlier critics including Harold Bloom, who, while suggesting that canonical Western authors were superior to all others, acknowledged their own limited knowledge of non-Western traditions. See Bloom, *The Western Canon: The Books and School of the Ages* (New York: Harcourt Brace, 1994), 20, 25, 531.

[9] Thomas D. Williams, "GQ Magazine Deems the Holy Bible One of the Most 'Overrated' Books of All Time," *Breitbart*, April 20, 2018, www.breitbart.com/entertainment/2018/04/20/williams-gq-proposes-remolding-culture-updating-classic-literature/.

angered by it.[10] In some cases, their concerns reflect reality: In recent years, leading eighteenth-century-studies journals have tended to reflect today's conservative political values less frequently relative to progressive perspectives. Scholars across the political spectrum share the view that eighteenth-century thought and literature were vital to the origins of modern institutions. Yet in comparison to the surge of interest in "decolonizing" eighteenth-century studies, as well as the continued decades-long pattern of attention to matters of race and gender – a corrective to previous generations' disregard – the perspectives of conservative-minded critics have received less attention.

Indeed, scholars have neglected the renditions of literary classics produced by Ignatius Press and *National Review*. The Ignatius Critical Editions have received little scholarly notice, apart from Jillian Snyder's examination of conservative press editions of Shakespeare. Likewise, conservative literary podcasts have not been subject to scrutiny.[11] There has been modest attention to conservative versions of eighteenth-century classics, whether pertaining to leisure reading, as in Juliette Wells's study of Austen-inspired Christian romances, or to educational use, as in Margaret Eustace France's study revealing that, for years, the only edition of Daniel Defoe's *The Farther Adventures of Robinson Crusoe* (1719) still in print was published by the right-wing religious nonprofit Focus on the Family.[12] Yet beyond this small cohort of leading-edge interventions, there has been minimal interest in efforts of conservative presses and media outlets to issue their own literary editions and programming. This neglect is puzzling, given the ongoing furor over campaigns to ban books. Conservative renditions of the classics deliberately fly under the radar, tucked behind paywalls (the "Great Books" podcast) or advertised on Christian websites unfamiliar to the secular public (Ignatius Press). Rather than seeking a broad-based following, developers aim to cultivate an audience within or adjacent to conservative communities.

Relegated to the margins of academia, conservative scholars in turn exclude liberal and progressive perspectives from materials they produce.

[10] See Eric Kaufmann, "Academic Freedom in Crisis: Punishment, Political Discrimination, and Self-Censorship," *Center for the Study of Partisanship and Ideology Report* 2 (2021): 1–195.

[11] Jillian Snyder, "Counterpublic Shakespeares in the American Education Marketplace," in *Shakespeare Survey 74: Shakespeare and Education*, ed. Emma Smith (Cambridge: Cambridge University Press, 2021), 195–207.

[12] Margaret Eustace France, "Robinson Crusoe, Home-School Hero," *Digital Defoe: Studies in Defoe and His Contemporaries* 3, no. 1 (Fall 2011), 5–28, https://cedar.wwu.edu/digitaldefoe/vol3/iss1/2/; and Juliette Wells, "True Love Waits: Austen and the Christian Romance in the Contemporary U.S.," *Persuasions* 28, no. 2 (Spring 2008), https://jasna.org/persuasions/on-line/vol28no2/wells.htm.

This chapter contends that these initiatives deserve more attention, for they enlist literary classics in the battle to advance conservative legal principles. In the wake of the 2022 US Supreme Court decision in *Carson v. Makin* allowing expanded state funding of parochial schools, conservative-oriented series including the Ignatius Critical Editions are poised to become more widely adopted as course textbooks. Similarly, as the pivot from paperbound media to online content continues, the audience for conservative-oriented cultural analyses such as the "Great Books" podcast will continue to grow. The time is ripe for dissolving the silos between liberal academia and conservative discourse.

My analysis of Ignatius Press's and *National Review*'s treatments of *Pride and Prejudice*, *Mansfield Park*, and *Frankenstein* shows recurrent efforts to reconceptualize freedom and personal autonomy in a manner congruent with the political priorities of the Christian right – including traditionalist Catholic think tanks and business magnates. These materials also echo conservative theological writings that, taking up centuries-old debates, posit a distinction between "fundamental rights" (foremost those pertaining to property) and the "political and social concoctions of men" (including reproductive rights).[13] Abiding by restrictions on choice – especially for members of subordinate groups – is extolled, paradoxically, as conducive to contentment and true freedom. These interpretations are intended to influence readers' understanding of and investment in legal norms and the world they will shape.

I assemble a variety of sources to contextualize the background of the Ignatius Critical Editions and the "Great Books" podcast, and then turn to each venture's treatments of eighteenth-century literary classics, focusing on passages from the conservative scholars' commentary that foreground questions of personal autonomy. This chapter takes a holistic approach, discerning patterns across the series' critical apparatus. It then examines the implications of these efforts to transmit conservative legal norms across generations.

Ignatius Critical Editions: Challenging Opinions of Personal Autonomy

The case built by the Ignatius Critical Editions (also known as ICE) for restricting personal autonomy is manifest, first, in the scope of its coverage.

[13] See, for example, David Gough, "The Right to Relinquish Rights," sermon for Maryland Temple Church, Temple Hills, MD, May 21, 2017, www.thbchurch.org/sermons/sermon/2017-05-21/the-right-to-relinquish-rights; and John Cobin, "What 'Rights' Do Christians Have?," *Times Literary Examiner*, July 20, 2005, republished at https://libertarianchristians.com/2011/07/07/what-rights-do-christians-have/.

Ignatius Critical Editions are presented as "a tradition-oriented alternative to popular textbook series such as the Norton Critical Editions or Oxford World['s] Classics."[14] The latter series are widely available and frequently assigned in college courses. The arrangement of the Ignatius Critical Editions' apparatus resembles that of the Norton editions: Each volume consists of a scholar's introduction, a note on the text, the main text with footnotes, and several analytical essays. In contrast to other conservative editions of the classics (such as the Focus on the Family series), Ignatius Critical Editions texts are unexpurgated, as are the Norton editions. Unlike the Norton series, however, the Ignatius Critical Editions do not include contemporary reviews or contextual materials from the era of publication, and the footnotes only clarify vocabulary. Moreover, whereas the Norton Critical Editions aim to include "a wide range of interpretations – from contemporary perspectives to the most current critical theory" – the Ignatius Critical Editions take an exclusionary approach: "While many modern critical editions have succumbed to the fads of modernism and postmodernism," the press announces on its website, "this series will concentrate on tradition-oriented criticism of these great works."[15] Thus, while the Ignatius Press claims that its editions "represent a genuine extension of consumer choice, enabling educators, students, and lovers of good literature to buy editions of classic literary works without having to 'buy into' the ideologies of secular fundamentalism," their approach reduces another dimension of choice, restricting the array of critical perspectives available to readers. Because the books are marketed to educators and parents, rather than to students who will be the primary readers, this presentation of reduced options as an "extension of … choice" is emblematic of the reframing, within the critical essays of the Ignatius Critical Editions, of restrictions on personal autonomy as beneficial. As will be shown, those essays advocate for restrictions on three types of autonomy: socially subordinate groups' legal and political autonomy; women's sexual and bodily autonomy; and readers' interpretive autonomy. Although much of the criticism in the Ignatius Critical Editions offers plausible alternative interpretations to some radical leftist and feminist interpretations of literary classics, too often the critics drift from focusing on the source text into politicized tangents, or distort it in the service of supporting right-wing principles and legal values.

[14] "About Ignatius Critical Editions," Ignatius Press, https://loc.ignatius.com/ignatiuscriticaleditions/about.htm.

[15] "About the Series," on back cover of Jane Austen, *Mansfield Park*, ed. Claudia L. Johnson (1814; New York: W. W. Norton, 1998); "About Ignatius Critical Editions."

The series' advocacy of right-wing views reflects its background. While the Norton Critical Editions were established in 1961, during the ramping up of the Civil Rights movement, Ignatius Press arose in 1978, amid a resurgent conservative movement between the 1971 "Powell Manifesto" and the "Reagan Revolution" of the 1980s. It was an audacious incursion into a city regarded as hostile to conservative thought: San Francisco, characterized by the crowdsourced platform Conservapedia as a place of "moral degradation" and "very strong liberal tendencies" born of "the Hippie culture that flocked to this city in the 1950s and 1960s."[16] The founder, Joseph Fessio, a Jesuit priest, had unusual proximity to well-springs of conservative power: His doctoral dissertation advisor was Joseph Ratzinger, who later became Pope Benedict XVI.

The antipathy to autonomy in the Ignatius Critical Editions reflects the founder's conservative Catholic worldview and pushback against what he views as an inordinately permissive society. It is important to note that Catholicism is far from monolithic, and the traditionalist views detailed here are by no means representative of the Catholic faithful in general.[17] Fessio and Ratzinger were working in the wake of Vatican II, a landmark council that ushered the Catholic Church into the modern era. Among other changes, the Mass was overhauled to expand the role of religious sisters and female congregants. Both men questioned these modifications. Ratzinger introduced Fessio to the writings of the scholar who would become the focus of his dissertation: Hans Urs von Balthasar, a conservative theologian of whom one scholar averred: "It is difficult to overstate [his] significance for the Church's theology of sex since Vatican II."[18] Among the ideas supported by Balthasar was the belief that "woman is … the help, the security, the home man needs … the vessel of fulfillment

[16] "San Francisco Values," *Conservapedia*, last edited by "RobSmith" on January 11, 2025, www.conservapedia.com/San_Francisco_values.

[17] Ignatius Press and *National Review* take markedly conservative perspectives. The worldview of self-described "tradcaths" (younger churchgoers supporting reversion to pre-Vatican II practices) differs significantly from that of the majority of American Catholics, who largely support progressive positions on the legality of contraceptives and the ordination of women. See Michael Lipka, "Majority of U.S. Catholics' Opinions Run Counter to Church on Contraception, Homosexuality," Pew Research Center, September 19, 2013, www.pewresearch.org/short-reads/2013/09/19/majority-of-u-s-catholics-opinions-run-counter-to-church-on-contraception-homosexuality/; and Gregory A. Smith, "Like Americans Overall, Catholics Vary in Their Abortion Views, with Regular Mass Attenders Most Opposed," Pew Research Center, May 23, 2022, www.pewresearch.org/short-reads/2022/05/23/like-americans-overall-catholics-vary-in-their-abortion-views-with-regular-mass-attenders-most-opposed/.

[18] Tina Beattie, "Sex, Death and Melodrama: A Feminist Critique of Hans Urs von Balthasar," *The Way* 44, no. 4 (October 2005): 160–76, at 160.

expressly designed for him."[19] Such ideas have challenged some feminist Catholic scholars to attempt to reconcile the value they find in Balthasar's treatises, highly esteemed by church leaders, with the priority they place on expanding female agency within the church and society.[20]

Decades later, Fessio and Ratzinger (now Benedict) deplored this expansion of women's autonomy. In 1988, Fessio published an op-ed advocating the banning of female altar servers and Eucharistic ministers.[21] In a 2005 homily, Benedict decried "erroneous interpretations of freedom"; he termed abortion "freedom to kill."[22] In another 2005 homily criticizing "the dissolution of matrimony" by "trial marriages" and same-sex couplings, he lamented "an anarchic freedom that wrongly passes for true freedom of man."[23]

Putting his values into practice with a view to influencing the American judiciary, Fessio responded to landmark US Supreme Court opinions expanding gay rights and reproductive rights in the 1990s and 2000s by contacting Catholic media to decry the decisions. He chastised the Catholic Justice Anthony Kennedy, who voted with the majority, for betraying his faith, and proposed that clergy at the church Kennedy attended should remonstrate with him.[24] During the same period, Fessio became what one critic – Frank Cocozelli, an attorney and President of the Institute for Progressive Christianity – described as the "right-hand man" of Thomas Monaghan, the Domino's Pizza founder.[25] Monaghan devoted

[19] Hans Urs von Balthasar, *Theo-Drama: Theological Dramatic Theory*, vol. 3, *The Dramatis Personae: The Person in Christ*, trans. Graham Harrison (San Francisco: Ignatius Press, 1992), 286.

[20] See Michelle A. Gonzalez, "Hans Urs von Balthasar and Contemporary Feminist Theology," *Theological Studies* 65, no. 3 (September 2004): 566–95, esp. 568; and Beattie, "Sex, Death and Melodrama," 161.

[21] Joseph Fessio, "Admittance of Women to Service at the Altar as Acolytes and Lectors," *Fellowship of Catholic Scholars Newsletter* 11, no. 2 (March 1988): 14–16.

[22] Benedict XVI, homily, Mass of Possession of the Chair of the Bishop of Rome, Basilica of St. John Lateran, May 7, 2005, www.vatican.va/holy_father/benedict_xvi/homilies/2005/documents/hf_ben-xvi_hom_20050507_san-giovanni-laterano_en.html.

[23] Benedict XVI, Address of His Holiness Benedict XVI to the Participants in the Ecclesial Diocesan Convention of Rome, Basilica of St. John Lateran, June 6, 2005, www.vatican.va/content/benedict-xvi/en/speeches/2005/june/documents/hf_ben-xvi_spe_20050606_convegno-famiglia.html.

[24] Fessio criticized Justice Kennedy and the Supreme Court majority for their decision in *United States v. Windsor*, which struck down the Defense of Marriage Act (2013), and *Planned Parenthood v. Casey* (1992), which upheld abortion rights. Carl E. Wilson, "Fr. Joseph Fessio, SJ, Laments SCOTUS Rulings: 'We Are About to Sink Even Lower, God Help Us,'" *Catholic World Report*, June 26, 2013, www.catholicworldreport.com/2013/06/26/fr-joseph-fessio-sj-laments-scotus-rulings-we-are-about-to-sink-even-lower-god-help-us/.

[25] Frank Cocozelli, "The Pizza Man Delivers His Dream Town and Dream School," *Talk2Action*, October 9, 2006, www.talk2action.org/story/2006/10/9/162913/621/shadow_war/The_Pizza_man_Delivers_His_Dream_Town_and_Dream_School. See also Anne Hendershott, *Status Envy: The Politics of Catholic Higher Education* (2009; New York: Routledge, 2017), 206–08.

his $900 million dollar fortune to right-wing Catholic nonprofits: He founded the Thomas More Legal Institute as the "Christian response to the ACLU" to influence legislation, with a mandate "to restore time-honored moral and family values" and "protect the sanctity of human life."[26] He also established the Ave Maria School of Law (AMSL) in Naples, Florida, to expand the conservative ranks of right-wing Catholic legal scholars, attorneys, and judges.[27] Conservative Supreme Court justices and nominees were significantly involved in the school: Antonin Scalia contributed to the development of the curriculum, and Clarence Thomas and Robert Bork taught there. Such institutions were needed, Monaghan claimed, because existing Catholic law schools focused on social justice and were not sufficiently conservative. In his account of Monaghan's philanthropy, Cocozelli warned: "The Domino[']s Pizza King is using his vast wealth to try to transform the basis of American Jurisprudence from the principles of the Enlightenment to one based upon an ultra-Orthodox Catholic vision of natural law principles."[28] In 2003, shortly after AMSL was established, Monaghan appointed Fessio the Chancellor of Ave Maria University, the institution into which AMSL was supposed to be absorbed. Monaghan's influence extended to the Ignatius Critical Editions series editor, Joseph Pearce, who wrote the philanthropist's 280-page "overwhelmingly positive" authorized biography (published in 2016), with ample attention to Monaghan's support for conservative Catholic legal education.[29]

In light of this background, the recurrent emphasis in the Ignatius Critical Editions on upholding traditional views of the law, justice, and personal autonomy – in accordance with right-wing Catholic principles – and discounting the perspectives of liberal academia and movements including the Catholic "liberation theology" movement of the 1970s is

[26] Domenica Marchetti, "Delivering on His Word: Pizza-Empire Founder is Giving Away His Fortune to Catholic Causes," *Chronicle of Philanthropy*, October 7, 1999, web.archive.org/web/20070927220142/http://philanthropy.com/free/articles/v11/i24/24000101.htm; Thomas More Legal Institute, "About the Thomas More Law Center," www.thomasmore.org/about-the-thomas-more-law-center-1/; and "Welcome to the Thomas More Law Center," www.thomasmore.org.

[27] Amanda Hollis-Brusky and Joshua C. Wilson, *Separate but Faithful: The Christian Right's Radical Struggle to Transform Law and Legal Culture* (Oxford: Oxford University Press, 2020), 111; and Domenica Marchetti, "Philanthropist Puts His Faith in a New Law School – and Stirs Up Debate," October 7, 1999, *Chronicle of Philanthropy*, web.archive.org/web/20051220093132/http://philanthropy.com/free/articles/v11/i24/24001401.htm.

[28] Cocozelli, "Pizza Man."

[29] Kathy Schiffer, "Joseph Pearce Has Written the Definitive Biography on Tom Monaghan," *National Catholic Register*, March 6, 2017, www.ncregister.com/blog/joseph-pearce-has-written-the-definitive-bio-on-tom-monaghan; Joseph Pearce, *Monaghan: A Life* (Charlotte, NC: TAN Books, 2016).

cast into relief as a means of proselytization; the essays attempt to transmit those values to readers. There are repeated avowals that, for subordinate groups including women and the poor, restriction (by the self as well as by law and society) is more salutary than the exercise of personal autonomy. These views are manifest in endorsements of restrictions on women's legal, bodily, and sexual autonomy; the economic autonomy of subordinate groups in society; and readers' interpretive autonomy. To understand how legal and theological principles of the Christian right, specifically conservative Catholicism, are threaded through the critical apparatus of the Ignatius Critical Editions, it will help to examine specific instances of each type.

In his introduction to the 2008 Ignatius Critical Edition of *Pride and Prejudice* edited by Pearce, Christopher Blum sends up post-second-wave feminist interpretations of Austen's best-known heroine:

> To our jaded and unromantic world, that Elizabeth should find herself in her love for Mr. Darcy is old-fashioned and constricting. She must be reinterpreted, like every other heroine in Austen's novels, and become a strong-willed woman, an independently minded woman, a feminist. It is a sad distortion of the novelist's mind to reduce her conception of humanity to that of a struggle between the sexes. For while she may have agreed with Mary Wollstonecraft in finding Rousseau's depiction of womankind demeaning and inaccurate, her mind was more at one with Louis de Bonald's observation that marriage had "under the influence of Christianity, received all of its dignity and sweetness," and that "woman is the natural friend of man." It is the surpassing sweetness of this friendship that grows between Elizabeth and Mr. Darcy that makes *Pride and Prejudice* such a hopeful and beautiful story about human nature.[30]

Here Blum does not simply interpret the text, but also offers Elizabeth and Darcy's relationship as a model for misguided moderns: an ideal romantic union. In an interview, Pearce, the editor of the volume, stated that one of his purposes for developing the Ignatius Critical Editions was to present canonical literary works as moral guides: "The classics enable us to judge the present from the telescopic perspective of the past."[31] Channeling Bonald and Balthasar, Blum encourages readers to see women's proper role as supporters of men, rather than viewing them as independent

[30] Christopher Blum, introduction to Jane Austen, *Pride and Prejudice*, ed. Joseph Pearce, Ignatius Critical Editions (1813; San Francisco: Ignatius Press, 2008), ix–xxi, at xvii–xviii.

[31] Joseph Pearce, quoted in Paul Senz, "Ignatius Critical Editions Present Great Literary Works, Reject Fad and Fashion," *Catholic World Report*, December 26, 2019, www.catholicworldreport .com/2019/12/26/ignatius-critical-edition-present-great-literary-works-reject-fad-and-fashion/.

persons. Bonald, a French philosopher and devout Catholic, was a foundational conservative thinker who greatly influenced contemporary views on law and gender; yet he is a peculiar choice for defending a conservative view of marriage. Although he argued that the foremost duty of government institutions was to keep families intact, he emigrated with his two older sons from war-torn France, leaving his wife to cope with their other children, and lived apart from them for more than a decade while pursuing his career.[32] The quotation Blum chooses is one of Bonald's sunnier statements on marriage. Bonald elsewhere represented marriage as a joyless slog to be undertaken in order to raise children and bolster social order.[33] In his influential treatise *Du divorce, considéré au XIXe siècle* (1801), Bonald, noting that women initiated divorce at a higher rate than men, argued they were weaker ("plus faible") beings who should be prevented from usurping men's power.[34] France consequently banned divorce in the Bonald Act of 1816 to protect women from their own mercurial nature.[35] Balthasar – the focus of the dissertation of Fessio, the Ignatius Press founder – would, centuries later, describe men and women as "of equal rank" in the eyes of God, while claiming that women's duty is to be the helpmeet of men, replicating Eve's role in the Garden of Eden.[36] What the religious studies scholar Michelle A. Gonzalez has characterized as Balthasar's view of women as "separate but equal" (a phrase with grim resonance in both American and French legal history) has significant ramifications for the conceptualization of women as legal persons; paeans to woman as man's "friend" (Bonald) or "help" (Balthasar) are shadowed by the theorists' assertions that women are second-class citizens.[37] By invoking these conservative male theorists and declining to engage with the scholars he disparages, or even to cite them, Blum implies that

[32] David Klinck, *The French Counterrevolutionary Theorist Louis de Bonald (1754–1840)* (New York: Peter Lang, 1996), 45–46, 82, 134.

[33] Antony Copley, *Sexual Moralities in France, 1780–1980: New Ideas on the Family, Divorce, and Homosexuality: An Essay on Moral Change* (London: Routledge, 1989), 90–91.

[34] Louis de Bonald, *Du divorce, considéré au XIXe siècle*, 3rd ed. (1801; Paris: Le Clère, 1818), 81. According to the translation most often cited in traditionalist Catholic scholarship, women initiate divorce more often because they are "weaker or more impassioned, not because they are less happy." Louis de Bonald, *On Divorce*, trans. and ed. Nicholas Davidson (New Brunswick, NJ: Transaction Publishers, 1992), 106.

[35] Copley, *Sexual Moralities*, 90. For implications of conservative attempts to shape marriage law according to the work of Bonald and other Napoleonic-era conservatives, see Joanna Alexandra Norland, "When the Vow Breaks: Why the History of French Divorce Law Sounds a Warning about the Implications for Women of the Contemporary American Marriage Movement," *Wisconsin Women's Law Journal* 17, no. 2 (2002): 321–46, at 329–30.

[36] Balthasar, *Dramatis Personae*, 285.

[37] Gonzalez, "Hans Urs von Balthasar and Contemporary Feminist Theology," 570.

"independently minded" women (some of the most prominent Austen scholars, including Margaret Anne Doody, Claudia L. Johnson, and Devoney Looser, are female) should be deprived of amplification of their views, given that their criticism challenges traditionalist discursive investments in male primacy.

In supporting conventional gender power relations, the traditionalist scholars contributing to Ignatius Critical Editions of Austen's novels (with some refreshing exceptions in the series' edition of *Sense and Sensibility*) laud female characters who refrain from asserting themselves. Blum favorably compares Mrs. Gardiner to Mrs. Bennet: "The contrast with Mrs. Bennet could not be more complete . . . . Mrs. Bennet is effusive, indiscreet, awkward, and loud. She declares and declaims in public, in front of the servants."[38] He praises Mrs. Gardiner's quietness as wise: "Most importantly, her discretion and judgment lead her to restrain her speech at appropriate times."[39] On its own, a preference for reserve over boisterousness could be construed as uncontroversial common sense. Yet Blum also commends female fragility, casting the ideal woman as vulnerable in mind and body. Of Mrs. Gardiner, he writes approvingly: "That she is 'not a great walker' only adds to her delicacy. [In contrast], Mrs. Bennet, we may presume, shares her youngest daughter's height and 'high animal spirits.'"[40] In a similar vein, in his essay for the Ignatius Critical Edition of *Mansfield Park*, Paul J. Contino likens Fanny Price to "the suffering servant in Isaiah 53." After quoting Scripture – "He was oppressed, and he was afflicted, yet he opened not his mouth; like a lamb that is led to the slaughter, and like a sheep that before its shearers are silent, so he opened not his mouth" – Contino develops his analogy:

> Fanny is a person who "open[s] not [her] mouth" even when "oppressed" and "afflicted." Even when she is forced by Mrs. Norris to cut roses and walk twice across the park in the hot sun, Fanny feels sick but does not complain, even when rebuked by Mrs. Norris for sitting on the sofa. It takes Edmund, sympathetic to Fanny's silence and, throughout the early part of the novel, her spiritual brother, to inquire about and protest against the injustice.[41]

Contino's suggestion – that complaints are unacceptable from a woman but can be considered if a privileged man takes up the woman's

[38] Blum, introduction to *Pride and Prejudice*, xv.
[39] Blum, introduction to *Pride and Prejudice*, xv.
[40] Blum, introduction to *Pride and Prejudice*, xvi.
[41] Paul J. Contino, "*Mansfield Park* and Isaiah 53: Fanny Price's Redemptive Role," in Jane Austen, *Mansfield Park*, ed. Eleanor Bourg Donlon, Ignatius Critical Editions (1814; San Francisco: Ignatius Press, 2010), 500–10, at 502.

cause – aligns with the Christian right's view that the socially disadvantaged should not protest injustice inflicted by the powerful.[42]

In critical essays in the Ignatius Critical Editions, Austen and other authors are presented as devout Christians with a shared mission of advocating for obligation to community and family over personal autonomy. (One of the key differences between the Ignatius Critical Editions and the "Great Books" podcast involves the relative salience of Christianity. Whereas the Ignatius Critical Editions underscore the importance of Christian themes and identity to the eighteenth-century authors whom the series features, the podcast does not foreground Christianity so overtly.) At times, this casting entails minimizing inconvenient details or omitting information that would complicate the authorial portrait. In the Ignatius Critical Edition of *Gulliver's Travels*, Swift's notorious antipathy to Catholicism is reduced to a brief footnote, with the effect of deemphasizing major theological differences between Catholics and Protestants so that Swift is made to stand alongside other authors featured in the series as unified in an overarching Christian identity. Katy Carl, a contributor to the Ignatius Critical Edition of *Mansfield Park*, points to an oft-cited line from one of Austen's letters – "I am by no means convinced that we ought not all to be Evangelicals" – as evidence that Austen "advocates for a seamless integration of faith and daily life."[43] Carl writes: "[W]e are balked by Austen's own fervor of devotion. She never flaunted her faith but does not seem to have been shy about expressing either." Yet Carl makes no mention of Austen's earlier statement in an 1809 letter: "I do not like the Evangelicals."[44] That Austen made such different statements over the course of her correspondence shows that her religious worldview was not consistent throughout her life. Indeed, as Janine Barchas states: "Austen's personal views on evangelicals appear to have evolved over time . . . . [In her 1809 letter,] [f]aith was a personal matter and not, she implied, fit food for proselytizing via novel writing."[45] Moreover, as Juliette Wells notes, the evangelism of the

[42] David Barker, Kimberly Nalder, and Jessica Newham, "Clarifying the Ideological Asymmetry in Public Attitudes toward Political Protest," *American Politics Research* 49, no. 2 (March 2021): 157–70.

[43] Katy Carl, "'The Greatest of Nuisances'? Fanny Price as Work in Progress in *Mansfield Park*," in Austen, *Mansfield Park*, ed. Donlon, 487–99, at 492–93. For the quotation from the letter, see Jane Austen to Fanny Knight, November 18–20, 1814, in *Jane Austen's Letters*, ed. Deirdre Le Faye, 4th ed. (Oxford: Oxford University Press, 2011), 292.

[44] Jane Austen to Cassandra Austen, January 24, 1809, in *Jane Austen's Letters*, 177.

[45] Janine Barchas, *The Lost Books of Jane Austen* (Baltimore: Johns Hopkins University Press, 2019), 143.

Regency era and the evangelical power bloc of recent decades are distinct movements, although they share similarities.[46] Carl rationalizes the disconnect between what she construes as Austen's endorsement of evangelism, on the one hand, and the scarcity of episodes of prayer or expressions of faith in Austen's novels, on the other, as indicative of the author's understanding that some matters were too profound for novelistic treatment: "Portrayal of prayer in narrative, unless done with the utmost care and skill, can seem banal, trite, cheap, ludicrous."[47] Reframing paucity of evidence as substantiating her argument, Carl commends Austen for "avoiding too-explicit portrayal of religion's effect on character" and declares that "Austen's idea of virtue is inextricably connected with her idea of religious goodness, of holiness."[48]

Would contemporary readers have understood Austen's novels as pervaded by her faith? Still another reason that conservative educational materials such as the Ignatius Critical Editions deserve more attention from scholars is that the popular reception of eighteenth-century and other literature by Christian audiences remains underexamined. As Barchas notes: "Although whole studies are devoted to the religious concerns of Jane Austen's plots" and "studies of Austen and the clergy focus on her Anglican upbringing and speculate about her private faith," the "religious contexts of Austen's reception have faded from view in our increasingly secular world – especially as the experiments that offered her up in the guises of church hymnals, temperance books, and Bibles are now scarce or unrecorded." To further complicate the picture, "Today's readers may associate a religious book with an earnest conservative outlook, but the circulation of Austen in liturgical dress was rarely po-faced."[49] Attention to the Ignatius Critical Editions sheds light on contrasting attempts to place Austen and her works within a Christian worldview.

Similar attempts to use Romantic-era fiction as support for twenty-first-century conservative views can be seen elsewhere in the Ignatius Critical Editions. Far from sharing the reserve attributed to Fanny in *Mansfield Park*, Mary Shelley is characterized in the 2008 Ignatius Critical Edition of her novel *Frankenstein; or, The Modern Prometheus* (1818) as a wayward child brought low by sexual excess. In his introduction, Pearce presents Shelley's novel as a veiled autobiography and "a lament for lost innocence." Pearce speculates: "The teenage author, as the victim of the 'freedoms' championed by her father and her lover (and, posthumously, a legion of

[46] See Wells, "True Love Waits." [47] Carl, "Greatest of Nuisances?," 492.
[48] Carl, "Greatest of Nuisances?," 493. [49] Barchas, *Lost Books of Jane Austen*, 127–28.

contemporary critics of her work), seems to be longing to escape into the peace and purity of traditional morality." He concludes:

> Isn't there more than a suggestion that the pursuit of the illicit, the eating of the forbidden fruit, leads to lost innocence and the self-loathing that accompanies despair? Has Mary Shelley discovered that the "freedoms" offered by Godwin and Percy Shelley, and by other tempters of humanity, are not only elusive, but illusory? Has she learned the hard way that such "freedoms" do not make men into gods, or women into goddesses, but that they turn men into monsters and women into their willing victims? Isn't there more than a sneaking suspicion that *Frankenstein*, far from being a feminist work, is the vision of innocence screaming to be liberated from its "liberation" and longing to be free from its abuse by Promethean promiscuity?[50]

This passage bundles together unlike things – Godwin's endorsement of sexual equality, his unconventional political ideology of anarchy, and Percy Bysshe Shelley's libertine sexuality – and implicates all as the source of Mary Shelley's misery. For women, he suggests, "freedoms" are uniquely damaging. This passage is reminiscent of Pope Benedict's assertion of a clear-cut distinction between true freedom (corresponding to valid law) and "anarchic freedom" (corresponding to destructive law). Pearce's introduction sheds little light on Mary Shelley's perspective. Instead, it castigates women's "liberation" – a term of mid-twentieth-century vintage – and strives to impress conservative values upon readers. It also collapses the difference between the sexual mores of Shelley's time and today. (Here is a sample instance in which the series' dearth of contextual materials, in contrast to the abundant selections in the Norton Critical Editions, is particularly disadvantageous to readers' understanding.) Readers' reviews of other Ignatius Critical Editions attest that other texts beyond their Romantic-era offerings are similarly marred by intrusive proselytization.[51] "When an introduction . . . has a statement as stupid and ignorant as the following, one has to question the scholarly merit of the work," one reviewer complained.[52] Another dismissed that same introduction as "religious rambling" and "political trash."[53]

[50] Joseph Pearce, introduction to Mary Shelley, *Frankenstein*, ed. Joseph Pearce, Ignatius Critical Editions (1818; San Francisco: Ignatius Press, 2008), ix–xxvi, at xxv–xxvi.

[51] Amazon.com merges reviews for various presses' editions of the Austen and Shelley novels; no space is dedicated exclusively to reviews of the Ignatius Critical Editions.

[52] "StatusNomadicus," "Religious rambling in intro . . . nope! 30November2018 (Ignatius Version)," review of the Ignatius Critical Edition of Boethius, *The Consolation of Philosophy*, December 1, 2018, www.amazon.com/gp/customer-reviews/RFD1FPQPDMUSP/ref=cm_cr_arp_d_rvw_ttl?ie=UTF8&ASIN=1586174371.

[53] "Cleveland Thornton," "Ok Translation by Mediocre Professors," review of the Ignatius Critical Edition of Boethius, *The Consolation of Philosophy*, May 11, 2021, www.amazon.com/gp/customer-reviews/R7L23WQUZ0T4G/ref=cm_cr_arp_d_rvw_ttl?ie=UTF8&ASIN=1586174371.

Pearce's introduction and other essays in the Ignatius Critical Editions tend to characterize women's sexual autonomy as involving behavior that is chosen and avoidable, without attending to the possibility that financial precarity and other systemic factors may influence such actions. According to the Catholic conservative worldview, the legal guardrails of yore should be reinstated to protect women from sin. In contrast, other social realities are characterized as impervious to the efforts of human beings and institutions. In "The Grace of Inequality," an essay in the Ignatius Critical Edition of *Pride and Prejudice*, Anthony Esolen argues that law must not address social and economic disparities:

> I will not apologize for Jane Austen's England, wherein rank was a plain fact of life, and no one assumed that the man who shod the master's horses should advise him on national policy. That world needs no apology, because it is our world, too. Whatever may be the mysteries of God's grace, which can fashion a true but unnoticed greatness in the stableboy, filling him with good things while sending the rich away empty, it is still obvious to us that God has *not* made us equal in intelligence, natural character, physical prowess, and fortune. And it is well that he has not, says the great tradition of Christian thinking on the matter, since inequality is one of the beauties of a society bound not by legal uniformity but by love.[54]

Rank as a "plain fact of life," natural and unchangeable as the weather, and "fortune" and "intelligence" as qualities directly endowed by God, rather than fashioned at least in part by luck and social conditions: This line of argument conforms to present-day Christian conservatives' worldview and enlists Austen to vouch for it. (The pervasiveness of guns in society is cast similarly in the 2010 Ignatius Critical Edition of *Gulliver's Travels* as defying human rectification.[55]) Yet the notion that inequality is presented in Austen's novels as unchangeable and salutary is questionable in light of lengthy episodes in which characters are depicted in the act of knowingly choosing to perpetuate it – as when, in *Sense and Sensibility*, Fanny Dashwood, contravening the wishes of her father-in-law, persuades her husband to minimize financial assistance to his stepsisters. Austen also exposes the damage inflicted on the helpless by the powerful, as when

[54] Anthony Esolen, "The Grace of Inequality," in Austen, *Pride and Prejudice*, ed. Pearce, 381–94, at 382–83.

[55] Dutton Kearney explains, "Swift understands that we can never go back to a time without gunpowder; the solution to the threat of modern annihilation must be worked out in a way that diminishes its negative impact." "Virtue, Politics, and *Gulliver's Travels*," in Jonathan Swift, *Gulliver's Travels*, ed. Dutton Kearney, Ignatius Critical Editions (1726; San Francisco: Ignatius Press, 2010), 387.

wealthy, beautiful Emma humiliates the impecunious, homely Miss Bates during an outing for all to see. Then there is the passage in *Mansfield Park* in which Sir Thomas's judgment comes into question when he enlists the meddlesome Mrs. Norris in his efforts to inculcate his daughters with a sense of superiority over their poor relation Fanny:

> "There will be some difficulty in our way, Mrs. Norris," observed Sir Thomas, "as to the distinction proper to be made between the girls as they grow up: how to preserve in the minds of my *daughters* the consciousness of what they are, without making them think too lowly of their cousin; and how, without depressing her spirits too far, to make her remember that she is not a *Miss Bertram*. I should wish to see them very good friends, and would, on no account, authorise in my girls the smallest degree of arrogance towards their relation; but still they cannot be equals. Their rank, fortune, rights, and expectations will always be different. It is a point of great delicacy, and you must assist us in our endeavours to choose exactly the right line of conduct."[56]

To be sure, Austen is no advocate for the eradication of social and economic distinctions, and her novels favorably portray the leadership of benevolent landowners such as Darcy over the servants of their estate. Yet her writings demonstrate that a society governed by rank is, at least to an extent, bound by fear – those in subordinate positions are constantly reminded of the risks of falling into poverty, of losing a good reputation – and that the selfishness that exacerbates inequality could not be more unlike love.

The conservative ideology with which the critical apparatus of Ignatius Critical Editions is freighted would come across as less rigid if alternative perspectives were seriously engaged. Instead, the series restricts its readers' interpretive autonomy. In his introduction to the Ignatius Critical Edition of *Gulliver's Travels*, Dutton Kearney initially seems to buck the trend by challenging the notion that "literature is a philosophical delivery system, a thinly disguised treatise whose teachings are to be extracted and put into practice"; he instead considers it "a distinct mode of knowledge, an imaginative cosmos within which readers learn practical wisdom through characters' choices and the consequences of those choices."[57] Other contributors to the series, though, are openly amenable to literature serving as propaganda: The editor of the Ignatius Critical Edition of *Mansfield Park*, Eleanor Bourg Donlon, wrote a newspaper opinion article urging

[56] Jane Austen, *Mansfield Park*, ed. James Kinsley (1814; Oxford: Oxford University Press, 2008), 9.
[57] Dutton Kearney, introduction to Swift, *Gulliver's Travels*, ed. Kearney, ix–xvii, at x.

conservative authors to turn progressives' "literary-critical fascination" with "suppressed narratives of the ... marginalized" to their advantage by writing "abortion stories" to advocate for "the unborn child": "For the writer, therefore, there is a moral duty to speak for those who cannot."[58]

Yet later in Kearney's introduction to *Gulliver's Travels* and throughout the Ignatius Critical Editions of eighteenth-century fiction, it is telling which critical perspectives are characterized as distorting literature into a vehicle for ideology. While acknowledging that "feminist critics often dismiss Swift as a misogynist," Kearney contends, "[R]educing his work by reading it through a lens of race, class, and gender often tells us less about Swift than it does about an individual literary critic."[59] This perspective resembles the originalism that the Roberts-era Supreme Court has used in cases such as *Dobbs v. Jackson* (2022) to reject arguments for rights that are not "deeply rooted in the Nation's history and traditions"[60] – thus dismissing feminist legal interpretations, given that reproductive and numerous other legal rights for women were not widely recognized or codified during the eighteenth century. Yet to argue that certain interpretations are illegitimate because they were marginal, unrecognized, or even unimaginable during the eighteenth century is to compound historical injustice, discrediting perspectives that center the marginalized because they were unfairly disregarded in the past. It also deprives readers – and, particularly, the impressionable students who constitute the target audience of the Ignatius Critical Editions – of an opportunity to learn to entertain a panoply of contrasting views and to exercise their critical reasoning to discern among them. Certainly, it is possible for precocious students to "read against the grain," but they are likely to be exceptions. Pearce's assertion in an interview about Ignatius Critical Editions that "reading the classics liberates us from narrow-mindedness" is belied by his dismissal, in the same interview, of other critical approaches. In the series, he asserts, "there is no nonsense: no feminist criticism, no Marxist criticism, no deconstructionism, no queer theory."[61] Indeed, the series website offers its edition of *Frankenstein* as "an antidote to the poison that

[58] Eleanor Bourg Donlon, "The Abortion Story," *National Catholic Register*, February 24, 2009, www.ncregister.com/commentaries/the-abortion-story.

[59] Kearney, introduction to Swift, *Gulliver's Travels*, ed. Kearney, xvi.

[60] *Dobbs v. Jackson Women's Health Organization*, no. 19-1392, slip. op. at 5 (S.Ct. June 24, 2022), quoting *Washington v. Glucksberg*, 521 US 702, 721 (1997), www.law.cornell.edu/supremecourt/text/19-1392.

[61] Paul Senz, "Ignatius Critical Editions Present Great Literary Works, Reject Fad and Fashion," *The Catholic World Report*, December 26, 2019, www.catholicworldreport.com/2019/12/26/ignatius-critical-edition-present-great-literary-works-reject-fad-and-fashion/.

has contaminated the critical understanding" in literary theory over the past several decades.[62] The historical record of eighteenth- and nineteenth-century antecedents of critical theory – the radical views on gender of Mary Wollstonecraft, Shelley's mother, being one ready example – contradicts Pearce's claim that the series' interpretive worldview is self-evidently correct. Pearce and the other contributors strive to cultivate a blindered, rigid mode of textual interpretation that will advance the juridical objectives of the Christian right, preparing impressionable students to be receptive to the disingenuous and selective originalism seen in references to the eighteenth century by the conservative Christian justices on the Rehnquist and, subsequently, the Roberts Supreme Court.

The *National Review*'s "Great Books" Podcast: Relitigating Personal Autonomy on a New Media Platform

Alarmed that conservative university students were being "converted to a *Nation-New Republic* type of 'liberalism,'" William G. Buckley founded the *National Review* in 1955 as a "magazine of conservative opinion" that would offer an alternative perspective.[63] From its early essays such as Buckley's "Why the South Must Prevail" (1957), published during the Civil Rights movement, the magazine has been a high-profile platform for weighing in on proposed legislation and other matters of law; it is a venue for trying out innovative legal theories.[64] The current editors' mission is to "change the terms of debate over our country's . . . future for the better."[65] Academia remains a motivating scourge. In 1960, Buckley supported the formation of Young Americans for Freedom, which aimed to gather students into the conservative fold. As audiences have shifted online, the publication's efforts to contest liberal academia have continued with its "Great Books" podcast.

Despite its consistent attempts to influence public discourse, the magazine has largely flown under the radar of scholarly analysis. Observing the magazine's impact – "it initiated a strategic framing of conservatism that

62 Description of *Frankenstein*, Ignatius Critical Editions, https://loc.ignatius.com/ignatiuscriticaleditions/shelley-frankenstein.htm.

63 MacLean, *Democracy in Chains*, 86; "About Us," *National Review*, www.nationalreview.com/about/?utm_source=menu&utm_medium=desktop&utm_campaign=about&utm_term=second&utm_content=about-NR.

64 William Hogeland, "William Buckley's Legacy in the Politics of Denial and the Denial of Politics," *American Political Thought* 6, no. 4 (2017): 657–64.

65 "About Us."

could effectively launch a movement and ... aligned that belief system with the needs of a previously unmobilized audience" – the media scholar Susan Currie Sivek wondered in 2008 why "little research has been done on [the] magazine's role in aiding this process of definition for social movements."[66] Although the "Great Books" podcast is but one facet of the magazine's initiatives, it exemplifies conservatives' strategy of cultivating support for their opinions not only explicitly, through political commentary on the controversies of the day, but also over the long term via subtler cultural means.

Launched in 2017, the "Great Books" podcast is well positioned to undertake this supplementary education. It is designed as an entry-level introduction to the classics. Host John J. Miller described his venture as "weekly, 30-minute conversations with scholars and experts about the books they love," designed for those who "believe that politics is downstream of culture."[67] Notably, the announcement implies that "experts" are worth a listen – a notion that contrasts with what one commentator has called "the death of expertise," that is, the decline, particularly in conservative communities, of trust in doctorate-bearing specialists.[68] The expert guests on the "Great Books" podcast are exempted from suspicion because most hail from conservative religious institutions. Miller and several of his guests are professors at Hillsdale College – a conservative Christian institution that has provided a career springboard for right-wing pundits, hosted speeches by Republican politicians such as Sarah Palin, and garnered ample funding from fundamentalist donors. Some guests, such as Susannah Fullerton, an independent scholar and expert on Austen, present their outsider vantage point as an asset; Fullerton's website states, "Unlike other research books, Susannah's works are just right for a popular readership ... Susannah's writing style is easy and enjoyable to read."[69] The dearth of scholars affiliated with Ivy League or flagship state universities is not coincidental. Rather than ushering listeners into a "marketplace of ideas," the podcast herds them into a partisan domain that consistently reinforces a traditionalist worldview.

Miller does not frame his approach as a polemical intervention. Instead, he sidles up to the legal and political import of the literature he discusses.

[66] Susan Currie Sivek, "Editing Conservatism: How *National Review* Magazine Framed and Mobilized a Political Movement," *Mass Communication and Society* 11, no. 3 (2008): 248–74, at 249.

[67] John J. Miller, "Great Books" podcast, *National Review*, September 23, 2017, www.nationalreview.com/corner/great-books-podcast/.

[68] See Tom Nichols, *The Death of Expertise* (Oxford: Oxford University Press, 2017).

[69] Susannah Fullerton, "Books & Spoken Word CDs," https://susannahfullerton.com.au.

His conversations are sufficiently accessible that listeners who have not read the literature can follow along. During the first half of each segment, he summarizes the plot of the selected work, then gradually pivots to underscoring conservative values. As in the Ignatius Critical Editions, many of the podcast discussions of eighteenth-century literature contrast true freedom, which is said to involve obeisance to tradition, with illusory freedom, which entails prioritizing personal autonomy. In the *Pride and Prejudice* episode, Miller and his guest Lorraine Murphy, a Hillsdale literature professor, laud the restrictions of the past while presenting today's sexual autonomy as chaotic:

MILLER: [Austen's characters] live in such a rules-bound world. I look at it and I think, Gosh, I'm glad I live when we do now, when we don't have so many rules. On the other hand, I wonder: Have we lost something? Do they have advantages we don't have, and wish we had back?

MURPHY: I think we have a certain nostalgia for the world she portrays, which is a very ordered, regulated, in some ways a very narrow world. We live in a society where there are so few limitations, so few boundaries. And yet I think young people would especially feel this, young people who are trying to negotiate relationships: How do I find who to marry? How do I find my soulmate, so to speak? They're awash in a sea of information – and they look at Jane Austen's world. These challenges are framed and contextualized. In a context where they're guided, they're limited, they're taught to make good judgments; they negotiate these problems. And I think that there's something refreshing about the order of Austen's world.

MILLER: It's like the opposite of hook-up culture. Human nature never changes . . . but the rules of courtship have changed. They're different now. And you look at it and think: As restricting as it can seem, it has some value. For men and for women.[70]

The podcast discussion is far less strident than the treatments of sexual autonomy in the Ignatius Critical Editions; the speakers acknowledge the complexity of these matters rather than issuing moral pronunciations. Whereas the passage from Pearce's essay on *Frankenstein* barrages readers with leading questions, the questions posed here indicate that the conservative approach has both advantages and disadvantages. Even so, they likewise idealize restrictions on personal autonomy.

Unlike the Ignatius Critical Editions, the "Great Books" conversations do not explicitly attribute the social ills they describe to literary theory.

[70] John J. Miller, "Episode 2: *Pride and Prejudice* by Jane Austen," *National Review*, "Great Books" podcast, September 14, 2017, at 18:06, www.nationalreview.com/podcasts/the-great-books/great-books-pride-and-prejudice/.

Yet they sometimes criticize legal and political ideas that anticipated today's progressive political thought. In the *Frankenstein* episode, Amy Sturgis casts Mary Shelley's personal turmoil as proof of the deficiency of the legal-political ideology of Shelley's father:

> She's run off with Percy Bysshe Shelley ... she's still a teenager, running with the rock stars of her era .... Her lover, her to-be-husband, is one of the great Romantic poets .... They're crashing with Lord Byron, who's a great Romantic poet and author: "mad, bad, and dangerous to know." And they're living in a world that is sort of set apart from anything like consequence. And she sees, already, in a way, the repercussions of this. I mean, her father was dedicated to the principle of sexual equality and a degree of free love .... She saw over and over again the fact that Shelley and Byron were doing all kinds of things: having illegitimate children ... doing things without any thought of the repercussions for other people. And that's how, in fact, she lost a couple of her own babies, because they were constantly moving in bad conditions, in areas where disease were, trying to flee Percy's creditors. She was, in a sense, the only adult in the room, even though she's a teenager, and the other people are adults.[71]

Sturgis does not draw a distinction between Godwin's deficiencies as a father and the credibility of his theories pertaining to women's rights. The emphasis on "consequences" for sex out of wedlock is a longtime right-wing talking point: [I]n a clip publicized by the Heritage Foundation's 2023 viral post advocating for "ending recreational sex," the writer Mary Harrington advised a "movement against the [birth control] pill ... returning the danger to sex ... and really, the consequentiality to sex."[72] By characterizing Mary Shelley as a misled daughter and teenage bride who placed her children at risk of death but subsequently questioned her wanton ways, Sturgis fits her into a cultural script of repentance favored by the Christian right – as with the case of Norma McCorvey, the plaintiff in *Roe v. Wade* (1973), who eventually converted to Evangelical Christianity and then to Catholicism and joined the anti-abortion movement.[73] In Miller's words, "libertinism ... she was surrounded by it in her personal life; she participated in it, even. But then maybe had some second

[71] Amy Sturgis, in John J. Miller, "Episode 84: *Frankenstein* by Mary Shelley," *National Review*, "Great Books" podcast, May 21, 2019, at 28:30, www.nationalreview.com/podcasts/the-great-books/episode-84-frankenstein-by-mary-shelley/.

[72] Heritage Foundation [@Heritage], "It seems to me ...," X (formerly Twitter), May 27, 2023, 1:00 pm MDT, https://x.com/Heritage/status/1662534135762624520.

[73] For McCorvey's shifting stance, see Joshua Prager, *The Family Roe: An American Story* (New York: W. W. Norton, 2021).

thoughts about all of it."[74] Thus Miller casts Shelley's sexually autonomous past as a cautionary tale with a redemption arc.

The Right-Wing Endgame

Today's conservative strategy of developing educational materials for a niche market – a self-perceived embattled minority of homeschoolers and devout Christians who spurn public schools – is a departure from an approach taken during an earlier stage of the culture wars by proponents of the canon. In the 1980s, when campuses were riled by battles over preserving "Western Civ" core classes, the educator and literary critic E. D. Hirsch, Jr. introduced the concept of "cultural literacy." He argued that students were ill-served by contemporary language arts curricula, which in some cases had replaced literary classics with texts representing ethnic minorities' perspectives.[75] Idealizing a time when Americans shared a pool of cultural references, he presented a list of literary and other works that every student should know in order to participate in civic life. By the late 1990s, conservative educators were increasingly giving up on this approach. Instead, they collaborated with religious organizations and conservative presses to develop a parallel realm of literary discourse geared specifically for conservative-minded students. Rather than designing curricula and materials for the general student population, they developed materials specifically for the target audience of Christian students in parochial and homeschool environments.

The Ignatius Critical Editions and the "Great Books" podcast are part of an extensive network of conservative efforts to shape students' and voters' views of legal and political norms. The conservative influence network encompasses brick-and-mortar institutions such as Liberty University, online ventures such as the Prager University Foundation (more popularly known as PragerU), academic institutions such as the Koch Center at George Mason University and the Bruce D. Benson Center for the Study of Western Civilization at the University of Colorado, student organizations (both grassroots and "AstroTurf") such as Learning Liberty, YouTube tutorials and websites developed by the likes of the Institute for Economic Education, and scholarship competitions offered by the Ayn Rand Institute and other groups. Amid these developments, new editions

[74] Miller, "Episode 84: *Frankenstein* by Mary Shelley," at 27:05

[75] E. D. Hirsch, Jr., *Cultural Literacy: What Every American Needs to Know* (Boston: Houghton Mifflin, 1987).

of eighteenth-century and Romantic-era classics by Austen, Shelley, and others – and podcasts featuring these works – have been developed as conduits for conservative perspectives.

Although some conservative literary discourse reduces literary classics to didactic vehicles, its commentary can also be viewed as sharing with much progressive scholarship the conviction that literature matters – that it is not merely a leisure pursuit or status item of cultural capital, but rather a battleground on which fundamental values are contested. Eighteenth-century-studies specialists can no longer afford to ignore conservative discourse. We must widen the scope of analysis to include conservative editions, commentary, and perspectives – so as to engage, more robustly, with right-wing views regarding justice, freedom, and rights.

Select Bibliography

Primary Sources

Legal Cases

Calvin's Case, (1608) 77 Eng. Rep. 377.
Hamilton v. Mendes, (1761) 2 Burr. 1198.
Johnson v. Smith, (1760) 2 Burr. 950.
King v. Lake, (1671) 86 Eng. Rep. 289.
King v. Lake, (1671) 89 Eng. Rep. 12.
Raynard v. Chace, (1756) 1 Burr. 2.
R. v. Browne, (1706) 90 Eng. Rep. 1134.
R. v. Brown [sic], (1706) 88 Eng. Rep. 911.
R. v. Clerk [sic], (1728/29) 94 Eng. Rep. 207.
R. v. Peters, (1758) 1 Burr. 568.
The Slave, Grace, (1827) 166 Eng. Rep. 179.
Somerset v. Stewart, (1772) 98 Eng. Rep. 499.
Zouch v. Parsons, (1765) 3 Burr. 1794.

Other Primary Sources

"An Act for the Better Preventing of Clandestine Marriages," 26 Geo. II c. 33, in *The Statutes at Large*, ed. Danby Pickering, vol. 21 (Cambridge: Joseph Bentham, 1766), 124–30.

"Adjudged Cases in the Court of King's Bench, Michaelmas Term, 31 Geo. III," *Lawyer's and Magistrate's Magazine … with the Decisions of the Judges in Their Own Words* 2 (1792): 366–68.

Aristotle, *The Art of Rhetoric*, trans. Robin Waterfield (Oxford: Oxford University Press, 2018).

The Nicomachean Ethics, trans. David Ross, ed. Lesley Brown (Oxford: Oxford University Press, 2009).

Austen, Jane, *Mansfield Park*, ed. Eleanor Bourg Donlon, Ignatius Critical Editions (1814; San Francisco: Ignatius Press, 2010).

Mansfield Park, ed. James Kinsley (1814; Oxford: Oxford University Press, 2008).

Pride and Prejudice, ed. Joseph Pearce, Ignatius Critical Editions (1813; San Francisco: Ignatius Press, 2008).

Bacon, Francis, *Three Speeches of The Right Honorable, Sir Francis Bacon Knight, Then His Majesties Sollicitor Generall, ... concerning the Post-Nati, Naturalization of the Scotch in England, Union of the Lawes of the Kingdomes of England and Scotland* (London: Richard Badger, 1641).

Blackstone, William, *Commentaries on the Laws of England*, ed. Wilfrid Prest, bk. 1, *Of the Rights of Persons*, ed. David Lemmings (1765; Oxford: Oxford University Press, 2016).

Commentaries on the Laws of England, ed. Wilfrid Prest, bk. 2, *Of the Rights of Things*, ed. Simon Stern (1766; Oxford: Oxford University Press, 2016).

Commentaries on the Laws of England, ed. Wilfrid Prest, bk. 3, *Of Private Wrongs*, ed. Thomas P. Gallanis (1768; Oxford: Oxford University Press, 2016).

Bonald, Louis de, *Du divorce, considéré au xixe siècle*, 3rd ed. (Paris: Le Clère, 1818).

"British Legislation on Africa and Slavery," *The Statutes Project*, https://statutes.org.uk/site/slavery-law/british-legislation-on-africa-slavery/.

[Browne, Joseph?], *The Country Parson's Honest Advice to the Judicious Lawyer, and Worthy Minister of State, My Lord Keeper* (London, 1706), reprinted in *Poems on Affairs of State: Augustan Satirical Verse, 1660–1714*, vol. 7, *1704*–1714, ed. Frank H. Ellis (New Haven, CT: Yale University Press, 1975), 156–59.

Coke, Edward, *The First Part of the Institutes of the Lawes of England: or A Commentary upon Littleton*, 4th ed. (London: M.F., I.H., and R.Y., 1639).

Colquhoun, Patrick, *A Treatise on Indigence; Exhibiting a General View of the National Resources for Productive Labour, with Propositions for Ameliorating the Condition of the Poor* (London: Hatchard, 1806).

Defoe, Daniel, *A Journal of the Plague Year*, ed. Paula R. Backscheider (1722; New York: W. W. Norton, 1992).

Douce, Francis, and John Thomas Smith, *Vagabondiana, or Anecdotes of Mendicant Wanderers through the Streets of London*, new ed. (1817; London: Chatto and Windus, 1874).

Dryden, John, *Discourse concerning the Original and Progress of Satire*, in *The Works of John Dryden*, vol. 4, *Poems 1693–1696*, ed. A. B. Chambers, William Frost, and Vinton A. Dearing (Berkeley: University of California Press, 1956–90).

Edgeworth, Maria, *Harrington*, ed. Susan Manly (1817; Peterborough, ON: Broadview, 2004).

Fielding, Henry, *Tom Jones*, ed. John Bender and Simon Stern (1749; Oxford: Oxford University Press, 1996).

Francis, Richard, *Maxims of Equity, Collected from, and Proved by Cases, Out of the Books of the Best Authority, in the High Court of Chancery* (London: E. and R. Nutt, and R. Gosling, 1727).

Hawkins, William, *A Treatise of the Pleas of the Crown*, 2 vols. (London, 1716).

Impey, John, *The Modern Pleader* (London: Butterworth, 1794).

"Interesting Decisions in the Courts of Law and Equity," *Literary Panorama* 4 (September 1808): 1341–54.
"Jury Court in Scotland," *Literary Panorama*, n.s. 5 (October 1816): 1–17.
Lazarus, Rachel Mordecai, and Maria Edgeworth, *The Education of the Heart: The Correspondence of Rachel Mordecai Lazarus and Maria Edgeworth*, ed. Edgar E. MacDonald (Chapel Hill: University of North Carolina Press, 1977).
Lewin, Gregory, *A Summary of the Law of Settlement* (London: S. Sweet, 1827).
Locke, John, *Second Treatise of Government*, in *Two Treatises of Government*, ed. Peter Laslett (1690; Cambridge: Cambridge University Press, 2005).
[Mackworth, Sir Humphrey?], *Affidavits, Certificates, and Presentments; Proving the Facts Mentioned in the Case of Sir Humphry Mackworth, and the Mine-Adventurers* (London, 1705).
The Case of Sir Humphry Mackworth, and of the Mine-Adventurers (London, 1705).
Minutes of the Evidence Taken before the Committee Appointed by the House of Commons to Inquire into the State of Mendicity and Vagrancy in the Metropolis and Its Neighbourhood (London: Sherwood, 1816).
Mist's Weekly Journal, no. 175 (August 24, 1728).
Prince, Mary, *The History of Mary Prince: A West Indian Slave*, ed. Sara Salih (1831; London: Penguin, 2000).
Richardson, Samuel, *Correspondence Primarily on "Sir Charles Grandison" (1750–1754)*, ed. Betty A. Schellenberg, *The Cambridge Edition of the Correspondence of Samuel Richardson*, ed. Thomas Keymer and Peter Sabor, vol. 10 (Cambridge: Cambridge University Press, 2015).
The History of Sir Charles Grandison, ed. E. Derek Taylor, Melvyn New, and Elizabeth Kraft, 4 vols. (1753–54; Cambridge: Cambridge University Press, 2022).
Scott, Sir Walter, *Chronicles of the Canongate*, ed. Claire Lamont (1827; London: Penguin, 2003).
Ivanhoe: A Romance, ed. Graham Tulloch (1819; Edinburgh: Edinburgh University Press, 1998).
[Scott, Sir Walter], "View of the Changes Proposed and Adopted in the Administration of Justice in Scotland," *Edinburgh Annual Register* 1 (1808), 342–72.
Selden, John, *Table-Talk: Being the Discourses of John Selden Esq.* (London: E. Smith, 1689).
Sheil, Richard Lalor, *Sketches of the Irish Bar . . . with Memoir and Notes by R. Shelton Mackenzie*, 2 vols. (New York: Redfield, 1854).
Shelley, Mary, *Frankenstein*, ed. Joseph Pearce, Ignatius Critical Editions (1818; San Francisco: Ignatius Press, 2008).
"Slaves in the Colonies; Information respecting the Case of a Person Residing in the Island of Antigua, Named Grace James," in *Parliamentary Papers*, vol. 26, *Papers and Correspondence Relating to New South Wales Magistrates; the West Indies; Liberated Africans; Colonial and Slave Populations; Slaves; the Slave Trade* (London: HMSO, 1826), 1–41.
Smith, Adam, *The Theory of Moral Sentiments*, ed. Knud Haakonssen (1759; Cambridge: Cambridge University Press, 2004).

The Wealth of Nations, ed. Edwin Cannan (1776; New York: Modern Library, 2000).
State Law: Or, the Doctrine of Libels, Discussed and Examined, 2nd ed. ([London], [1730]).
Sundry Considerations Touching Naturalization of Aliens: Whereby the Alleged Advantages Thereby Are Confuted, and the Contrary Mischiefs Thereof Are Detected and Discovered (London, [1695]).
Swift, Jonathan, *Gulliver's Travels*, ed. Dutton Kearney, Ignatius Critical Editions (1726; San Francisco: Ignatius Press, 2010).
[Toland, John], *Reasons for Naturalizing the Jews in Great Britain and Ireland, on the Same Foot with All Other Nations, Containing Also, a Defense of the Jews against All Vulgar Prejudices in All Countries* (London: J. Roberts, 1714).
Wilson, Henry, *Wonderful Characters: Comprising Memoirs and Anecdotes of the Most Remarkable Persons of Every Age and Nation*, 3 vols. (London: J. Robins, 1821–22).
Wordsworth, William, *Lyrical Ballads with Other Poems*, 2nd ed., 2 vols. (London: Longman, 1800).
The Prelude: 1799, 1805, 1850, ed. Jonathan Wordsworth, M. H. Abrams, and Stephen Gill (New York: W. W. Norton, 1979).

Secondary Sources

Abramowicz, Sarah, "English Child Custody Law, 1660–1839: The Origins of Judicial Intervention in Parental Custody," *Columbia Law Review* 99, no. 5 (June 1999): 1344–91.
Aljoe, Nicole N., *Creole Testimonies: Slave Narratives from the British West Indies, 1709–1838* (New York: Palgrave Macmillan, 2012).
Anker, Elizabeth S., and Bernadette Meyler, eds., *New Directions in Law and Literature* (New York: Oxford University Press, 2017).
Astbury, Raymond, "The Renewal of the Licensing Act in 1693 and Its Lapse in 1695," *The Library*, 5th ser. 33, no. 4 (1978): 296–322.
Bailey, Merridee L., and Kimberley-Joy Knight, "Writing Histories of Law and Emotion," *Journal of Legal History* 38, no. 2 (2017): 117–29.
Baker, Sir John, *An Introduction to English Legal History*, 5th ed. (Oxford: Oxford University Press, 2019).
Balkin, Jack M., and Sanford Levinson, "Law and the Humanities: An Uneasy Relationship," *Yale Journal of Law and the Humanities* 18, no. 2 (Summer 2006): 155–87.
Bandes, Susan, ed., *The Passions of Law* (New York: New York University Press, 1999).
Bandes, Susan, Jody L. Madeira, and Kathryn D. Temple, eds., *Research Handbook on Law and Emotion* (Northampton, MA: Edward Elgar, 2021).
Baron, Jane B., "Law, Literature, and the Problems of Interdisciplinarity," *Yale Law Journal* 108, no. 5 (March 1999): 1059–85.

Beattie, J. M., *Crime and the Courts in England, 1660–1800* (Princeton, NJ: Princeton University Press, 1986).

Beiderwell, Bruce, *Power and Punishment in Scott's Novels* (Athens: University of Georgia Press, 1992).

Bender, John, *Imagining the Penitentiary: Fiction and the Architecture of Mind in Eighteenth-Century England* (Chicago: University of Chicago Press, 1987).

Benton, Lauren, *Law and Colonial Culture: Legal Regimes in World History, 1400–1900* (New York: Cambridge University Press, 2004).

Bertelsen, Lance, *Henry Fielding at Work: Magistrate, Businessman, Writer* (New York: Palgrave, 2000).

Binder, Guyora, and Robert Weisberg, *Literary Criticisms of Law* (Princeton, NJ: Princeton University Press, 2000).

Blum, Christopher, introduction to Jane Austen, *Pride and Prejudice*, ed. Joseph Pearce, Ignatius Critical Editions (1813; San Francisco: Ignatius Press, 2008), ix–xxi.

Bricker, Andrew Benjamin, "Is Narrative Essential to the Law? Precedent, Case Law and Judicial Emplotment," *Law, Culture and the Humanities* 15 (2019): 319–31.

Libel and Lampoon: Satire in the Courts, 1670–1792 (Oxford: Oxford University Press, 2022).

Brooks, Peter, and Paul Gewirtz, eds., *Law's Stories: Narrative and Rhetoric in the Law* (New Haven, CT: Yale University Press, 1996).

Contino, Paul J., "*Mansfield Park* and Isaiah 53: Fanny Price's Redemptive Role," in Jane Austen, *Mansfield Park*, ed. Eleanor Bourg Donlon, Ignatius Critical Editions (1814; San Francisco: Ignatius Press, 2010), 500–10.

Corfield, Penelope, *Power and the Professions in Britain 1700–1850* (London: Routledge, 1995).

Cover, Robert, "Nomos and Narrative," in *Narrative, Violence, and the Law: The Essays of Robert Cover*, ed. Martha Minow, Michael Ryan, and Austin Sarat (Ann Arbor: University of Michigan Press, 1995), 95–172.

DeGooyer, Stephanie, *Before Borders: A Legal and Literary History of Naturalization* (Baltimore: Johns Hopkins University Press, 2022).

Delgado, Richard, "Storytelling for Oppositionists and Others: A Plea for Narrative," *Michigan Law Review* 87, no. 8 (August 1989): 2411–41.

Delson, B. Rudolph, "Typography in the U.S. Reports and Supreme Court Voting Protocols," *New York University Law Review* 76 (2001): 1203–32.

Dolin, Kieran, *A Critical Introduction to Law and Literature* (Cambridge: Cambridge University Press, 2007).

ed., *Law and Literature* (Cambridge: Cambridge University Press, 2018).

Drew, Erin, *The Usufructuary Ethos: Power, Politics, and Environment in the Long Eighteenth Century* (Charlottesville: University of Virginia Press, 2021).

Duxbury, Neil, *The Nature and Authority of Precedent* (Cambridge: Cambridge University Press, 2008).

Easterling, Keller, *Extrastatecraft: The Power of Infrastructure Space* (New York: Verso, 2016).

Epstein, Joseph, "Don't Fire the Western Canon," *National Review*, December 27, 2021.
Fortier, Mark, *The Culture of Equity in Restoration and Eighteenth-Century Britain and America* (Farnham: Ashgate, 2015).
France, Margaret Eustace, "Robinson Crusoe, Home-School Hero," *Digital Defoe: Studies in Defoe and His Contemporaries* 3, no. 1 (Fall 2011), 5–28, https://cedar.wwu.edu/digitaldefoe/vol3/iss1/2/.
Frey, Anne, *British State Romanticism: Authorship, Agency, and Bureaucratic Nationalism* (Palo Alto, CA: Stanford University Press, 2010).
Ganz, Melissa J., *Public Vows: Fictions of Marriage in the English Enlightenment* (Charlottesville: University of Virginia Press, 2019).
Gladfelder, Hal, *Criminality and Narrative in Eighteenth-Century England: Beyond the Law* (Baltimore: Johns Hopkins University Press, 2001).
Goodrich, Peter, "Satirical Legal Studies: From the Legists to the *Lizard*," *Michigan Law Review* 103, no. 3 (2004): 397–517.
Gordon, Robert W., "Professionalisms Old and New, Good and Bad," *Legal Ethics* 8, no. 1 (2005): 23–34.
Gregg, Melissa, and Gregory J. Seigworth, eds., *The Affect Theory Reader* (Durham, NC: Duke University Press, 2010).
Guillory, John, "The Memo and Modernity," *Critical Inquiry* 31 (Autumn 2004): 108–32.
Hamburger, Philip, "The Development of the Law of Seditious Libel and the Control of the Press," *Stanford Law Review* 37, no. 3 (February 1985): 661–765.
Hanley, Ryan, *Beyond Slavery and Abolition: Black British Writing c. 1770–1830* (Cambridge: Cambridge University Press, 2019).
Hitchcock, David, *Vagrancy in English Culture and Society, 1650–1750* (New York: Bloomsbury, 2016).
Holdsworth, W. S., *A History of English Law*, 6th ed., 12 vols. (London: Methuen, 1938).
Hollis-Brusky, Amanda, and Joshua C. Wilson, *Separate but Faithful: The Christian Right's Radical Struggle to Transform Law and Legal Culture* (Oxford: Oxford University Press, 2020).
Hone, Joseph, "Legal Constraints, Libellous Evasions," in *The Oxford Handbook of Eighteenth-Century Satire*, ed. Paddy Bullard (Oxford: Oxford University Press), 525–41.
Hunt, Lynn, *Inventing Human Rights: A History* (New York: W. W. Norton, 2007).
Hussain, Nasser, *The Jurisprudence of Emergency: Colonialism and the Rule of Law* (Ann Arbor: University of Michigan Press, 2003).
Ibbetson, David, "*The Earl of Oxford's Case* (1615)," in *Landmark Cases in Equity*, ed. Charles Mitchell (Oxford: Hart, 2012), 1–32.
Innes, Joanna, "Prisons for the Poor: English Bridewells, 1555–1800," in *Labour, Law, and Crime: An Historical Perspective*, ed. Francis Snyder and Douglas Hay (London: Tavistock Publications, 1987), 42–122.

Johnson, Nancy E., ed., *Impassioned Jurisprudence: Law, Literature, and Emotion, 1760–1848* (Lewisburg, PA: Bucknell University Press, 2015).
Jones, Mervyn C., *British Nationality Law and Practice* (Oxford: Clarendon Press, 1947).
Kennedy, Duncan, "The Structure of Blackstone's Commentaries," *Buffalo Law Review* 28, no. 2 (1979): 205–382.
Keymer, Thomas, *Poetics of the Pillory: English Literature and Seditious Libel, 1660–1820* (Oxford: Oxford University Press, 2019).
King, Peter, *Crime and Law in England, 1750–1840: Remaking Justice from the Margins* (Cambridge: Cambridge University Press, 2006).
Crime, Justice, and Discretion in England, 1740–1820 (Oxford: Oxford University Press, 2000).
Klinck, Dennis R., *Conscience, Equity and the Court of Chancery in Early Modern England* (Farnham: Ashgate, 2010).
Landau, Norma, *The Justices of the Peace, 1679–1760* (Berkeley: University of California Press, 1984).
Larkin, Brian, "The Politics and Poetics of Infrastructure," *Annual Review of Anthropology* 42 (October 2013): 327–43.
Lees, Lynn Hollen, *The Solidarities of Strangers: The English Poor Laws and the People, 1700–1948* (Cambridge: Cambridge University Press, 1998).
Lemmings, David, *Gentlemen and Barristers: The Inns of Court and the English Bar, 1680–1730* (Oxford: Clarendon Press, 1990).
Professors of the Law: Barristers and English Legal Culture in the Eighteenth Century (Oxford: Oxford University Press, 2000).
ed., *Crime, Courtrooms and the Public Sphere in Britain, 1700–1850* (Farnham: Ashgate, 2012).
Levine, Caroline, "Infrastructuralism, or the Tempo of Institutions," in *On Periodization: Selected Essays from the English Institute*, ed. Virginia Jackson (English Institute, 2010), www.fulcrum.org/epubs/ws859g78b?locale=en#/6/20[div1_c02]!/4/2[div1_c02]/2/2/1:0.
Levinson, Sanford, and Stephen Mailloux, eds., *Interpreting Law and Literature: A Hermeneutic Reader* (Evanston, IL: Northwestern University Press, 1988).
Lieberman, David, *The Province of Legislation Determined: Legal Theory in Eighteenth-Century Britain* (Cambridge: Cambridge University Press, 1989).
MacLean, Nancy, *Democracy in Chains: The Deep History of the Radical Right's Stealth Plan for America* (New York: Viking, 2017).
Macpherson, Sandra, *Harm's Way: Tragic Responsibility and the Novel Form* (Baltimore: Johns Hopkins University Press, 2010).
Massey, Doreen, *For Space* (London: Sage Publications, 2005).
Mezey, Naomi, "Law as Culture," in *Cultural Analysis, Cultural Studies, and the Law: Moving beyond Legal Realism*, ed. Austin Sarat and Jonathan Simon (Durham, NC: Duke University Press, 2003), 37–72.
Miller, John J., "Episode 2: *Pride and Prejudice* by Jane Austen," *National Review*, "Great Books" podcast, September 14, 2017, www.nationalreview.com/podcasts/the-great-books/great-books-pride-and-prejudice/.

"Episode 84: *Frankenstein* by Mary Shelley," *National Review*, "Great Books" podcast, May 21, 2019, www.nationalreview.com/podcasts/the-great-books/episode-84-frankenstein-by-mary-shelley/.

Minda, Gary, *Postmodern Legal Movements: Law and Jurisprudence at Century's End* (New York: New York University Press, 1995).

Minter, Patricia Hagler, "'The State of Slavery': *Somerset, The Slave, Grace*, and the Rise of Pro-Slavery and Anti-Slavery Constitutionalism in the Nineteenth-Century Atlantic World," *Slavery and Abolition* 36, no. 4 (June 2015): 603–17.

Moran, Mayo, *Rethinking the Reasonable Person: An Egalitarian Reconstruction of the Objective Standard* (Oxford: Oxford University Press, 2003).

Nicholson, Donald, and Julian Webb, *Professional Legal Ethics: Critical Interrogations* (Oxford: Oxford University Press, 1999).

Nicolazzo, Sal, *Vagrant Figures: Law, Literature, and the Origins of the Police* (New Haven, CT: Yale University Press, 2021).

Nixon, Cheryl, "Gender, Law, and the Birth of Bourgeois Civil Society," in *Law and Literature*, ed. Kieran Dolin (Cambridge: Cambridge University Press, 2018), 124–41.

Nussbaum, Martha C., "Equity and Mercy," *Philosophy and Public Affairs* 22, no. 2 (Spring 1993): 83–125.

Poetic Justice: The Literary Imagination and Public Life (Boston: Beacon Press, 1995).

O'Connell, Lisa, *The Origins of the English Marriage Plot: Literature, Politics and Religion in the Eighteenth Century* (Cambridge: Cambridge University Press, 2019).

Oldham, James, C., *English Common Law in the Age of Mansfield* (Chapel Hill: University of North Carolina Press, 2004).

The Mansfield Manuscripts and the Growth of English Law in the Eighteenth Century, 2 vols. (Chapel Hill: University of North Carolina Press, 1992).

Olson, Greta, *From Law and Literature to Legality and Affect* (Oxford: Oxford University Press, 2022).

Orsi, Cosma, "The Political Economy of Inclusion: The Rise and Fall of the Workhouse System," *Journal of the History of Economic Thought* 39, no. 4 (December 2017): 453–81.

Outhwaite, R. B., *Clandestine Marriage in England, 1500–1850* (London: Hambledon Press, 1995).

Pearce, Joseph, introduction to Mary Shelley, *Frankenstein*, ed. Joseph Pearce, Ignatius Critical Editions (1818; San Francisco: Ignatius Press, 2008), ix–xxvi.

Perreau-Saussine, Amanda, and James Bernard Murphy, eds., *The Nature of Customary Law: Legal, Historical and Philosophical Perspectives* (Leiden: Cambridge University Press, 2007).

Peters, Julie Stone, "Law, Literature, and the Vanishing Real: On the Future of an Interdisciplinary Illusion," *PMLA* 120, no. 2 (March 2005): 442–53.

Polanyi, Karl, *The Great Transformation: The Political and Economic Origins of Our Time* (1944; Boston: Beacon Press, 2001).

Postema, Gerald J., *Bentham and the Common Law Tradition*, 2nd ed. (New York: Oxford University Press, 2019).

Punter, David, "Fictional Representation of the Law in the Eighteenth Century," *Eighteenth-Century Studies* 16, no. 1 (Fall 1982): 47–74.

Reid, Christopher, *Imprison'd Wranglers: The Rhetorical Culture of the House of Commons, 1760–1800* (Oxford: Oxford University Press, 2012).

Ross, Trevor, *Writing in Public: Literature and the Liberty of the Press in Eighteenth-Century Britain* (Baltimore: Johns Hopkins University Press, 2018).

Sarat, Austin, ed., *Rhetorical Processes and Legal Judgments: How Language and Arguments Shape Struggles for Rights and Power* (Cambridge: Cambridge University Press, 2016).

Sarat, Austin, Matthew Anderson, and Cathrine O. Frank, eds., *Law and the Humanities: An Introduction* (Cambridge: Cambridge University Press, 2010).

Sarat, Austin, Cathrine O. Frank, and Matthew Anderson, eds., *Teaching Law and Literature* (New York: Modern Language Association of America, 2011).

Schmidgen, Wolfram, *Eighteenth-Century Fiction and the Law of Property* (Cambridge: Cambridge University Press, 2002).

Schuyler, Robert L., *Parliament and the British Empire: Some Constitutional Controversies concerning Imperial Legislative Jurisdiction* (New York: Columbia University Press, 1929).

Seaton Siebert, Fredrick, *Freedom of the Press in England, 1476–1776: The Rise and Decline of Government Control* (Urbana: University of Illinois Press, 1965).

Shaw, Julia J. A., *Law and the Passions: Why Emotion Matters for Justice* (Abingdon, Oxon: Routledge, 2020).

Shyllon, F. O., *Black Slaves in Britain* (London: Oxford University Press, 1974).

Sinanan, Kerry, "The Slave as Cultural 'Artefact': The Case of Mary Prince," *Studies in Eighteenth-Century Culture* 49 (2020): 69–87.

Staves, Susan, *Married Women's Separate Property in England, 1660–1833* (Cambridge, MA: Harvard University Press, 1990).

Stern, Simon, "Literary Analysis of Law: Reorienting the Connections between Law and Literature," *Critical Analysis of Law* 5, no. 2 (2018): 1–8.

Stern, Simon, Maksymilian Del Mar, and Bernadette Meyler, eds., *The Oxford Handbook of Law and Humanities* (New York: Oxford University Press, 2020).

Temple, Kathryn D., *Loving Justice: Legal Emotions in William Blackstone's England* (New York: New York University Press, 2019).

Scandal Nation: Law and Authorship in Britain, 1750–1832 (Ithaca, NY: Cornell University Press, 2003).

Valverde, Marian, *Infrastructure: New Trajectories in Law* (Abingdon, Oxon: Routledge, 2022).

Waddams, Stephen, "The Case of Grace James (1827)," *Texas Wesleyan Law Review* 13, no. 2 (March 2007): 783–94.

Wallace, John W., *The Reporters*, 4th ed. (Boston: Soule and Bugbee, 1882).

Weisberg, Richard, "What Remains 'Real' about the Law and Literature Movement?," *Journal of Legal Education* 66, no. 1 (Autumn 2016): 37–43.

Weisberg, Robert, "The Law-Literature Enterprise," *Yale Journal of Law and the Humanities* 1, no. 1 (December 1988): 1–67.

Wells, Juliette, "True Love Waits: Austen and the Christian Romance in the Contemporary U.S.," *Persuasions* 28, no. 2 (Spring 2008), https://jasna.org/persuasions/on-line/vol28no2/wells.htm.

Wessel, Jane, *Owning Performance / Performing Ownership: Literary Property and the Eighteenth-Century British Stage* (Ann Arbor: University of Michigan Press, 2022).

West, Robin, *Narrative, Authority, and Law* (Ann Arbor: University of Michigan Press, 1993).

White, James Boyd, "Law and Literature: 'No Manifesto,'" *Mercer Law Review* 39 (Spring 1987): 739–51.

The Legal Imagination: Studies in the Nature of Legal Thought and Expression, 45th anniversary ed. (1973; New York: Wolters Kluwer, 2018).

Williams, Ian, "Early Modern Judges and the Practice of Precedent," in *Judges and Judging in the History of the Common Law and Civil Law: From Antiquity to Modern Times*, ed. Paul Brand and Joshua Getzler (Cambridge: Cambridge University Press, 2012), 51–66.

Winter, Sarah, "From Procedural Law to the 'Rights of Humanity': Habeas Corpus, *Ex parte Somerset* (1771–72), and the Movement toward Collective Representation in Early British Antislavery Cases," in *Empire and Legal Thought: Ideas and Institutions from Antiquity to Modernity*, ed. Edward Cavanagh (Leiden: Brill, 2020), 388–424.

Wong, Edlie L., *Neither Fugitive nor Free: Atlantic Slavery, Freedom Suits, and the Legal Culture of Travel* (New York: New York University Press, 2009).

Wright, Nicole Mansfield, *Defending Privilege: Rights, Status, and Legal Peril in the British Novel* (Baltimore: Johns Hopkins University Press, 2020).

Zacek, Natalie, "Voices and Silences: The Problem of Slave Testimony in the English West Indian Law Court," *Slavery and Abolition* 24, no. 3 (2003): 24–39.

Zomchick, John P., *Family and the Law in Eighteenth-Century Fiction: The Public Conscience in the Private Sphere* (Cambridge: Cambridge University Press, 1993).

Index

Page numbers in italics refer to illustrations.

For EU product safety concerns, contact us at Calle de José Abascal, 56–1°, 28003 Madrid, Spain or eugpsr@cambridge.org.

www.ingramcontent.com/pod-product-compliance
Ingram Content Group UK Ltd.
Pitfield, Milton Keynes, MK11 3LW, UK
UKHW020619051025
463523UK00028B/114

* 9 7 8 1 0 0 9 2 2 4 1 3 0 *